# Culture
# and
# International
# Relations

# Culture
# and
# International
# Relations

Edited by
## Jongsuk Chay

PRAEGER

New York
Westport, Connecticut
London

**Library of Congress Cataloging–in–Publication Data**

Culture and international relations / edited by Jongsuk Chay.
    p.    cm.
   Includes bibliographical references.
   ISBN 0–275–93018–1 (alk. paper)
    1. International relations and culture.  I. Chay, Jongsuk.
JX1255.C83  1990
   327.1'01—dc20      89–16191

Library of Congress Catalog Card Number: 89–16191
ISBN: 0–275–93018–1

First published in 1990

Praeger Publishers, One Madison Avenue, New York, NY 10010
A division of Greenwood Press, Inc.

Printed in the United States of America

The paper used in this book complies with the
Permanent Paper Standard issued by the National
Information Standards Organization (Z39.48-1984).

10  9  8  7  6  5  4  3  2  1

Dedicated to my wife, Jungpil

# Contents

# *Preface*

The cultural dimension of international relations is one of the most neglected topics in the field. It is perceived as too broad and its boundaries as too vague, with the result that one's energies can easily be wasted in this uncertain territory. Because of my background and special interest in both international relations and the humanities, I felt that I should attempt to do something about this situation. Consequently, I turned to Richard Falk for advice, and he, as usual, responded thoughtfully, suggesting that I undertake this volume.

Because of the breadth of the subject and the size of the ensuing project, I discovered that I needed the collaboration of specialists in international relations and the various fields of the humanities. Many of those I approached responded positively to my challenge, and about two dozen active scholars in a variety of subject areas set to work during the fall of 1986. In the meantime, three overall objectives were established for the project: to survey the work that had been completed to date in the area where international relations and the key disciplines of the humanities— anthropology, history, philosophy, literature, music, and the arts— intersect; to determine the impact of cultural differences upon the foreign policy-making process and international interactions; and to push forward as much as possible the frontiers of knowledge in the field.

Some of my colleagues were very thoughtful as well as candid in pointing out that they thought the project was too vast and that the work would be unmanageable. My response was to underscore the importance of the task, insisting that someone had to undertake it and that the only thing needed was enough courage to address the vastness of the job. Eight authors completed their work by the spring of 1987, and their papers were presented to enthusiastic audiences at two lively panels at the annual convention of the International Studies Association in that year.

This 18-chapter book is organized in five parts. The Introduction and Overview (Part I) provides a theoretical survey, together with a definition of the field. The next five chapters (Part II) examine the state of scholarship in the area where international relations and the key fields of the humanities—anthropology, history, literature, music, and philosophy—intersect. Two parts are devoted to the roles played by cultural differences in shaping foreign policy and in influencing international relations. In Part III, U.S. international political culture receives special attention from four major scholars, while in Part IV, four chapters examine closely other cultures of the world—Africa, Asia, Latin America, and the Middle East. Completing the volume are the last four chapters (Part V), which cover some of the major issues in the field.

The editor of the volume is most thankful to those who participated in the project. Without their willing and active cooperation, successful completion would have been impossible. The encouragement and assistance of Professor Falk was essential to establishing high standards for the book. Many of my colleagues at Pembroke State University—Robert W. Brown, Thomas J. Leach, Raymond J. Rundus, and David K. Eliades—generously consented to read chapters. Shirley Deese gave me tireless and dedicated assistance by typing many parts of the book. Shirley Rogers' assistance in the preparation of the manuscript is also appreciated. Sincere thanks go to Dan Eades, the editor at Praeger, who has been graceful and patient throughout the process of readying the manuscript for publication. As usual, my wife, June, has been most helpful in giving me constant encouragement and support for the project.

# Part I

---

# Introduction and Overview

# 1

# *The Concept of Culture in the Theory of International Relations*

## R. B. J. Walker

Culture and international relations easily appear to be mutually contradictory terms. To speak of "culture" is to invoke the creative capacities of human beings, to point, for example, to the constitutive role of values and visions, to the power of language and aesthetic expression, to communities great and small engaged in reconstructing normative aspirations and reshaping the possibilities for a decent way of life. To speak of "international relations," by contrast, is to draw upon an altogether bleaker account of the human condition, to refer to missiles and bombs, trade figures and debts, statesmanship and diplomacy, intrigue and force. It is to echo assertions about naked power and the sacrifice of cultural creativity and normative aspiration to the supposedly more enduring determinations of survival or supremacy. From the dark depths of international relations, the term culture takes on an aura of frivolity. It appears to refer to the idealistic and utopian, to the veneer of civilized decency that is always stripped away by the harsh realities of power politics and international conflict.

Read rather differently, however, culture and international relations seem to converge on common ground. Not least, both terms make grand gestures. Both may be used to refer to the broadest dimensions of human existence.

When opposed to *nature*, for example, or used by certain schools of social theory and anthropology, culture almost becomes synonymous with human activity as such. Similarly, international relations reminds us that no matter how parochial we may be laboring in our own oasis, we are all caught up in processes that affect people living in all parts of the world. The modern states-system has specifiable origins in the transition from feudalism to capitalism and the emergence of the state as the primary locus of political identity in Europe some five centuries ago. Since then, the states-system, like capitalism, has become an all-pervasive condition of human life almost everywhere.

As grand gestures, culture and international relations now point us in the direction of some of the most powerful and universalizing structures in the modern world. Both terms can be read as evocations of the global, or the planetary, or humanity as such. They remind us of the profound changes in social and political life associated with new military and communications technologies, global monetary transactions, transformations in the international division of labor, and an increasing awareness of our collective vulnerability to ecological decay and nuclear extermination. But even while gesturing toward emerging patterns of universality, both terms also offer more than a hint of just how difficult it is to think and act coherently on the basis of claims about global processes, planetary imperatives or cosmopolitan humanity. It is here that the convergence of culture and international relations is especially significant.

The most obvious difficulties arise from the way both culture and international relations not only make grand gestures toward universality, but also remind us of the highly specific, localized, chauvinistic and deeply fragmented character of human experience. When culture becomes cultures, references to the creative capacities of human beings in general turn into either the celebration of, or consternation about, the sheer diversity of human communities. Similarly, the primary lesson learned by most of those who study peoples and states, the seemingly inevitable tendency for cooperation to collapse in the face of interstate competition and rivalry. Far from celebrating the virtues of cultural diversity, the analysis of international conflict points to the distinct possibility that contemporary patterns of political fragmentation will bring about our collective demise. The promises of culture once again shrivel in the bleak landscape of international relations.

## ON THE CONCEPT OF CULTURE

These brief observations give some indication of why quotation marks are important. Terms like "culture" and "international relations" refer to enormously complex accumulations of theoretical speculation about human affairs. They embody assumptions and contradictions arising from specific historical contexts. As such, they evade precise definition and invite critical scrutiny of how and why they have come to take on their present meanings.

In the case of culture, as Raymond Williams has emphasized, history has bequeathed to us "one of the two or three most complicated words in the English language."[1] This is not just because culture can refer to so many different phenomena, although the breadth of reference is clearly enormous. Rather, in the course of its historical emergence it has been the site of serious philosophical and political dispute. As one of the most essentially contested concepts both in European social and political thought in general and in the institutionalization of specialized academic disciplines in this century, it has taken on quite distinct and often incompatible meanings in a variety of intellectual and disciplinary traditions. Two very broad themes have been especially important for the way the concept of culture enters into contemporary Western debates about social and political processes, in general, and informs the analysis of international relations, in particular.

First, culture has usually been articulated on the basis of philosophical claims and analytical methods that presume a fundamental ontological difference between idea and matter, language and world. To this day, references to culture stimulate suspicions of idealism, memories of Platonist, Cartesian, or other claims about the autonomy of ideas and values from more mundane material forces. Conversely, those who object to the presumptions of idealism seek to explain culture as epiphenomenal to something else, and thus to reduce it to "nature" or "economy" or "the barrel of the gun." In this sense, the concept of culture presents many of the same problems as the concept of ideology, although there is usually less concern with the way cultural forms may be judged according to epistemological criteria of truth or falsity.

As with the concept of ideology, both idealist and reductionist accounts of the relationship between consciousness and matter have become increasingly suspect. Hardly a major philosophical movement in this century has failed to offer a critique of the fallacies of dualism and to struggle toward alternative accounts of language, consciousness, and so on. That there is little consensus about which alternative accounts are more acceptable does not detract from the overwhelming consensus on the need for an alternative.

Thus those working with the concepts of both culture and ideology are now likely to draw on notions of hegemony derived from Antonio Gramsci, or "discourse" in the senses generated by philosophers of language and poststructuralist social theorists and literary critics. Indeed, those who have worked with the concept of ideology in its more critical senses now tend to abandon it in favor of terms like hegemony and discourse precisely because these terms are used to suggest a more complex and mutually constitutive interplay of phenomena that were once so easily lined up on either side of the great Cartesian divide.[2] They stress the way seemingly abstract ideas and seemingly concrete processes converge in texts and institutions, song lyrics, advertisements, images of the desirably masculine/feminine and the politician's gleaming smile. Similarly, those now working with culture are now likely to refer to "cultural practices" or "cultural production" or "signifying practices" that are embodied in all forms of social activity, again while resisting the ingrained habits of either reductionist determinism or voluntarist idealism.[3]

The second broad theme that has shaped the contemporary meaning of culture is perhaps even more complex and involves the conflicting claims of universalism and pluralism as these were articulated in the eighteenth century. The specific twist given to the term by Herder is perhaps the most familiar landmark in this part of the story. Against the universalizing histories of the Enlightenment, against the universalizing connotations given to the term "civilization," Herder's insistence on the plurality of cultures soon became a central motif of Romanticism, and played an important role in the articulation of nationalist sentiments in the nineteenth century. It is in this form that the concept of culture remains associated with the insistence on diversity, fragmentation, and relativism, on the celebration of traditions arising from particular communities against the claims of a universalizing humanity—claims that, as Herder himself noted, have tended to arise from particular, though dominant communities.[4]

Two resolutions of the competing claims of universality and particularity have been especially influential in shaping the way we think about cultural life now. One is the subsumption of cultural diversity into the claims of state: cultural difference becomes a matter of national identity. Diversity is tolerated, but only within the sharply circumscribed limits permitted by the states that can co-exist in the states-system. Although even this degree of diversity entails a risk of belligerent fragmentation and war, the states-system itself promises at least a degree of cohesion, a community of nations through which separate cultures may remain somehow autonomous and different while participating in a common "conversation of humankind."

The other resolution involves the emergence of institutionalized disciplines through which other cultures may be studied, analyzed, and compared. Here the rise of anthropology is especially important, bringing with it varying degrees of sensitivity to the problems of ethnocentricism. This resolution has tended to depend on the presumption of certain claims about the Self as the representative of universality against which the differences of the Other may be distinguished.[5] Thus we have become familiar with the "primitive," the "barbarian," the "noble savage," the "undeveloped," the "Oriental," or the "enemy." We have also become familiar with the charges of relativism leveled against those who have questioned the arrogance of such categories.

In the modern world, the limits of both of these historically specific resolutions are becoming increasingly obvious. The diversity and passion of contemporary cultural energies are more difficult than ever to capture as variations on a theme of nationalism, even in the states in which various forms of federation have been constructed to accommodate ethnic and religious cleavages. And while the arrogance of ethnocentricism and even racism are by no means invisible, it is increasingly difficult to objectify the different as absolute Other in a way that passes for sound scholarship, let alone as a basis for more just and peaceful forms of human community. Again, the concept of culture can be understood as an expression of deep and troubling questions, questions about who we think we are, and where we think we might be going.

## ON THE NEGLECT OF CULTURE IN
## THEORIES OF INTERNATIONAL RELATIONS

Given that the concept of culture has been so deeply infused with assumptions and contradictions about idealism/materialism and universalism/pluralism, it is little wonder that it continues to play a contested role in contemporary social and political theory. No doubt those who like their concepts to be precisely and operationally defined may find culture to be frustratingly vague and tendentious. They are likely to be perplexed by the variety of meanings given to it by anthropologists, sociologists, art historians, students of mass media, and so on. For others, it is precisely its character as a site of vigorous contention that makes it interesting. Yet in one field—the analysis of international relations—the concept of culture evokes neither careful empirical analysis nor complex theoretical discussion. Where, for example, sociological and political theory are characterized by a general embarrassment at the difficulty and yet urgency of reconceptualizing processes that have conventionally been separated into matter and consciousness, theorists of international relations continue to celebrate the supposedly age-old schism between realists and idealists or utopians as constitutive of the special character of their subject. And where the reification of the relation between universality and pluralism into the anthropological categories of Self and Other has occasioned deep passion on the grounds of ethnocentrism and even racism, parrallel reifications in the field of international relations pass almost unnoticed. Consequently, the concept of culture plays a rather different role, in this context, one that would be expected by those trained within traditions of sociological, political, or anthropological theory.

This is not to deny that there have been significant attempts to treat culture as a serious aspect of international relations. Writers like F.S.C. Northrop[6] or Adda Bozeman,[7] for example, have developed perspectives grounded almost entirely in a sensitivity to cultural difference. Among those who have understood that the international system forms a kind of political community—albeit one that is radically different from the conventional model of a national community based on a common identity within territorial borders—considerable attention has been paid to the norms and unwritten rules, the conventions of statesmanship and legal procedure, the diplomatic and commercial cultures that are taken for granted by all those who act within the international system.[8] Among those concerned with the normative analysis of possible future worlds, questions about cultural creativity have been treated very seriously indeed.[9] And there are obviously analyses of many substantive themes—international communications, human rights, influences on foreign policy formulation—in which the concept of culture, in all its diverse meanings, plays a prominent role. If one added up all the literature that could somehow be said to refer to culture in an international context, especially where the analysis of international relations converges with comparative politics and sociology, it would be possible to construct an extensive list of citations.

Even so, no one can credibly claim that the analysis of culture and international relations has been treated as a subject of great significance or urgency. The term performs a largely catch-all function, its multiple meanings providing a convenient label by which to identify a variety of themes left over after all the primary explanatory variables—military and economic power, national interest, bureaucratic rivalries, structural insecurities generated in a system of fragmentation, patterns of domination arising from the hegemony of great powers or from the global patterns of production, distribution and exchange—have been dealt with.

It is especially instructive to examine the way the term ideology is still so often used merely as a synonym for doctrine, or even, echoing the presumptions of the Cold War and the "end of ideology" debates of the 1950s, as a view to be ascribed to some Other. Even when used in a more critical sense, it is usually taken to imply little more than the manipulation of illusions by identifiable interests, the claims of justice and enlightenment made by the self-satisfied powers, for example, or the rhetoric and propaganda with which statesmen disguise their more dubious deeds.

More complex, and arguably much more helpful approaches to the problems identified by the term ideology in international relations are now beginning to emerge among those who draw on wider currents of contemporary social and political theory to understand the assumptions and plays of power at work in the dominant forms of international relations theory.[10] Some analysts have begun to examine the "intertextual" character of international practices, such as the crossover of assumptions and images between competitive sport and military strategy.[11] Similarly, there has been a growing interest in the cultural and discursive character of contemporary patterns of militarization, especially with the way conceptions of "nuclear deterrence," "war and peace" and "friend and enemy" have been constituted in the practices of national defense, and with the metaphorical and linguistic forms through which such practices have been legitimized.[12] But again, this kind of literature, drawing equally upon concepts of culture, ideology, discourse, hememony, and language, has emerged largely on the margins of international relations as an institutionalized discipline. It remains obscure, even alien to those whose training has been primarily within the positivistic, realist, or policy-oriented mainstreams.

It is in the context of these mainstreams especially that it is again important to emphasize the range of possible connotations. The primary categories of international relations theory have been constituted historically in ways that are at least as complicated as those through which the concept of culture has developed. As products of a specifically European experience, they tend to pose many of the same contradictions and difficulties as the concept of culture. In fact, if one seeks to explain the relative neglect of culture in international relations, and to understand why the term occasions so little theoretical controversy in this context, we quickly become caught up in precisely the same philosophical questions that have constituted the concept of culture itself. In the context of international relations theory, however, the highly problematic nature of the conventional answers to these questions remains obscured by the way the conventional answers provide some of the most powerful presuppositions on which theories of international relations are predicated. Three themes are especially important here: One concerns the continuing distinction between ideas and matter in this context. A second involves the way any questioning of the usefulness of this distinction is deflected into debates structured around historically specific resolutions of the relation between universalism and pluralism. And the third involves the way in which this specific resolution is articulated and legitimized on the ground of the sovereign claims of state and national identity. In short, questions about culture are translated into questions about "values," and questions about values come to an abrupt halt with the assertion of state sovereignty as the ultimate source of value, and thus the ultimate agent in the conflict between different value communities.

Various forms of idea/matter dualism continue to exercise an exceptionally strong influence on theorists of international relations. Whether as a Hobbesian materialist metaphysics; or as a utilitarian reduction of human action to the pursuit of material self-interest; or as a cynical power politics; or, conversely, as the conviction that it is possible to change the world simply by conjuring up visions of a better future, the analysis of international relations has been deeply indebted to forms of reductionism and idealism that are arguably incapable of sustaining a serious analysis of cultural life in any context.

Yet this problem, while clearly significant, has often been dealt with in a more interesting and sophisticated way. Instead of broad references to culture we find a concern with the problem of values or ethics. This may involve a straightfoward complaint about the absence of moral standards in the conduct of international affairs. But in a more significant line of argument, values and ethics are associated specifically with a particular understanding of political community as possible only within states. This argument rests ultimately on claims about authority, obligation, legitimacy, and so on, familiar from traditions of *political* theory in which universalist ethical standards are reconciled with the particularist claims of states. That is to say, claims of universality come to be articulated in terms of the claims of citizenship and state sovereignty rather than the claims of human beings as such. The implication is that while ethical conduct and values may be appropriate within a sovereign community, they are more difficult to justify in relations of power between states. Thus in international affairs, order takes on a higher priority than justice, order being understood as a consequence of pragmatic intrigue and the necessary use of force. Values and, by extension culture are thus not only excluded from the amoral realm of realpolitik, except as ideology or propaganda, but are likely to be indicted as hindrances to the special responsibilities of statesmen struggling to maintain order in a realm tragically devoid of ethical standards.[13]

It is in this context that it is necessary to understand the special force of the conventional debate between realists and idealists or utopians in the theory of international relations. The primary argument is not so much about the place of values, visions, or utopian aspirations, as such, as about the dangers of transposing values appropriate for sovereign political communities into a realm supposedly characterized not by sovereign community but by competition between sovereign communities. It is in this context also that one can understand the constant slippage from "idealism" in the sense in which it is opposed to materialism to "idealism" in the sense opposed to political realism.

Perhaps the most interesting and important rendering of this theme can be traced to the so-called crisis of historicism associated with German philosophy and socio-political theory in the early decades of this century. The connection is provided by the influence, both direct and indirect, of Max Weber's response to that crisis on the way the discipline of international relations became institutionalized in the United States in the postwar era.[14] For Weber, writing in the shadow of Nietzsche rather than of Hegel, the increasing rationalization of the world brings with it, paradoxically, the eclipse of meaning, the "iron cage" of a meaninglessly efficient modernity in which values can find no firm grounding in reason itself. In the face of a looming relativism of value choice, Weber calls for a new kind of individual, one capable of something resembling a stoic fortitude, an "ethic of responsibility" in a disenchanted world. And for Weber, this ethic of responsibility is tied ultimately to the necessities of state, a connection that can be understood in the context of his own nationalist commitments, as well as his understanding of the possibilities of constitutional reform and charismatic leadership. For all of Weber's own considerable contributions to a comparative sociology of culture, it is this statist resolution of the problem of ethics in a rationalizing modernity that has had the greatest impact on theorists of international relations like Hans Morgenthau and Raymond Aron. Again, the implication is fairly blunt: community, values, and even *virtu* within, power and force without. Culture dissolves into cultures: cultures translates into values; values bring on the problem of relativism; and relativism reduces everything to an irreducible clash of power politics.

This leads directly to the third aspect of the relative neglect of cultural processes in the analysis of international relations. For if culture can ultimately be resolved into the categories of political community, into statist nationalism and exclusionist distinctions between ''them'' and ''us,'' then culture becomes nothing more than an affirmation of the most fundamental assumptions of the theory of international relations as these have emerged since the early modern period. If questions about culture turn out to be little more than questions about sovereignty and national identity, then there are only two interesting avenues worth exploring. One is the way in which ''culture,'' understood as anthropological difference, constitutes the central problem to be overcome, a corroboration of the deeply fractured character of human communities. The other is the way such divisions have in fact been overcome by the fragile accommodations of statesmanship. Such accommodations, of course, are generally assumed to have been worked out pragmatically and instrumentally, in ways that require little concern with values or visions.

Thus on the one hand, culture is so all pervasive that it involves only the affirmation of difference, of relativism and the seemingly permanent reality of conflict between cultural communities. On the other, culture is insignificant precisely because we have in fact managed to find ways of living together in a states-system. We have managed to cope with cultural difference by learning to respond politically, or economically, or technologically so as to cooperate within a modernity that, while having parochial European or Western or capitalist roots, has become the dominant way of life—the culture of modernity—everywhere.

## FROM CULTURE TO PRACTICE

The concept of culture, I have suggested, is most usefully understood historically. It cannot be dissociated from the intellectual categories that we now associate with modernity. Categories articulated around sharp distinctions between ideas and matter and between universality and particularity have been especially important. They are also especially problematic.

Obviously much more is also involved, not least the institutionalization of specialized academic disciplines, with their own research agendas and methodologies. Different scholars define and use the term in different ways depending on the discipline in which they work. Yet beyond all these disciplinary differences, the deeper philosophical debates through which the concept of culture has been shaped over the past three or four

centuries, and shaped within a specifically European or Western environment, continue to pose awkward and far-reaching questions.

If we refuse to fall back into the great Cartesian divide, how do we make
sense of language, or the production of aesthetic expression, or the relations between technology and the reconfiguration of political community? What exactly is going on when scenarios and game plans turn into
batteries of missiles stalking beneath the sea? And if we refuse to reduce
cultural difference to the mapping of state boundaries, how do we make
sense of the dynamics of contemporary religious politics; or the eruptions
of ethnic violence; or the sense of identity established between women
coming from different parts of the world, or aboriginal peoples coming
together to share experiences they hold in common; or the effects of
satellite communications systems; or the tendency for societies
everywhere to experience sharper and sharper rifts between those who
have managed to find an appropriate niche within the global division of
labor and those who are effectively being cast aside, displaced to the
margins as the new Other outside a world economy that is increasingly
interconnected?

Questions like these suggest that in order to use a term like culture in
the contemporary world, it is necessary both to be critically aware of, and
to develop a conscious amnesia toward those assumptions and contradictions through which the term has been shaped historically. The
conventional categories of international relations theory seem particularly inappropriate in a world in which the claims of sovereignty co-exist
with both complex interpenetrations of cultural identity and plausible
scenarios about ''interdependence'' or an emerging ''global civilization.''
Resolutions of the relationship between universality and particularity at
the level of the state alone cannot provide a serious analysis of the patterns of contemporary political community, or claims to authority and
legitimacy, or emerging conceptions of human identity or the configura-
tions of economic and military power in the modern world.

To understand the concept of culture as the product of specific historical
transformations is thus to understand that to attempt to come to terms
with culture now is to engage with questions of political practice. And
where conventional accounts of political practice have been tied almost
entirely to the claims of states to distinguish friend and enemy, community
and anarchy, inside and outside, contemporary transformations have put
these claims increasingly into question. Thus the significance of the concept of culture in the analysis of contemporary international relations is
not that it offers a convenient category of socio-scientific explanation, or
a convincing account of human nature, or a helpful classification of the
different kinds of human practices there have been. Rather it hints at all
the uncertainties of modernity, and at a multitude of struggles—on the
grounds of tradition or postmodernity, of gender, race, religion and

ethnicity, or socialism or capitalism, of the Other, of the future, of the local community, of the state and of the planet—to reconstitute the conditions of human existence in the face of tremendous structural transformations.[15] The categories of international relations theory systematically define these uncertainies and struggles as marginal. As categories, they betray their own historical and cultural specificity.

## NOTES

1. Raymond Williams, *Keywords*, rev. ed. (London: Fontana, 1983), p. 87. See also, Williams, *Marxism and Literature* (Oxford: Oxford University Press, 1977); and *Culture* (London: Fontana, 1981). For less historically sensitive and thus, in my view, much less helpful attempts to classify the different sense in which the concept of culture has been used, especially in relation to anthropological analysis, see, e.g., Milton Singer, "The Concept of Culture," *International Encyclopedia of the Social Sciences*, ed. David L. Sills (New York: Crowell-Collier, Macmillan, 1968), pp. 527–543 and Alfred L. Kroeber and Clyde Kluckhohn, *Culture: A Critical Review of Concepts of Definitions* (New York: Vintage Books. 1963).

2. See, as typical expressions of the rethinking occurring around the concept of ideology over the past decade, Chantal Mouffe, ed., *Gramsci and Marxist Theory* (London: Routledge and Kegan Paul, 1979); Sakari Hanninen and Leena Paldan, eds., *Rethinking Ideology* (New York: International General, 1983); Michael Shapiro, ed., *Language and Politics* (Oxford: Basil Blackwell, 1984): John B. Thompson, *Studies in the Theory of Ideology* (Oxford: Polity Press, 1984); Jorge Larrain, *Marxism and Ideology* (London: Macmillan, 1983); Ernesto Laclau and Chantal Mouffe, *Hegemony and Socialist Strategy* (London: Verso, 1985); Nannerl P. Keohane, Michelle Z. Rosaldo and Barbara C. Gelpi, eds., *Feminist Theory: A Critique of Ideology* (Chicago: University of Chicago Press, 1981); Terry Eagleton, *Literary Theory: An Introduction* (Oxford: Basil Blackwell, 1983); Christopher Norris, *Deconstruction: Theory and Practice* (London: Methuen, 1982); Michael Ryan, *Marxism and Deconstruction: A Critical Articulation* (Baltimore: Johns Hopkins University Press, 1982); as well as the now burgeoning literatures informed by the seminal work of Gramsci, Michel Foucault, and Jacques Derrida.

3. See, e.g., Cary Nelson and Lawrence Grossberg, eds., *Marxism and the Interpretation of Culture* (Urbana: University of Illinois Press, 1988); David D. Laitin, *Hegemony and Culture: Politics and Religious Change Among the Yoruba* (Chicago: University of Chicago Press, 1986); and Benedict Anderson, *Imagined Communities: Reflections on the Origin and Spread of Nationalism* (London: Verso, 1983).

4. I have explored this theme further in "World Politics and Western Reason: Universalism, Pluralism, Hegemony," in R. B. J. Walker, ed., *Culture, Ideology, and World Order* (Boulder: Westview Press, 1984), pp. 182–216.

5. As should be clear from the argument below, this theme of the "politics of otherness," of the constitution of "difference" by negation of the identity of "the same" and the variety of struggles to refuse the categories through which mutually exclusive conceptions of self and other, friend and enemy, are legitimized, provides the crucial connection between the analysis of culture in general social and political theory and the historically specific ways in which culture has

been analyzed in the theory of international relations. Among a rapidly growing literature, see, e.g. Edward Said, *Orientalism* (New York: Random House, 1979); Lati Mani and Ruth Frankenberg, "The Challenge of *Orientation*," *Economy and Society* 14:2 (May 1985):174–192; Shiraz Dossa, "Political Philosophy and Orientalism: The Classical Origins of a Discourse," *Alternatives* 12:3 (July 1987):343–358; Albert Memmi, *The Colonizer and the Colonized* (London: Souvenir Press, 1974); Tzvetan Todorov, *The Conquest of America: The Question of the Other* (New York: Harper & Row, 1982); Michael Shapiro, "The Constitution of the Central American Other: The Case of Guatamala," in Shapiro, ed., *The Politics of Representation: Writing Practices in Biography, Photography and Policy Analysis* (Madison: University of Wisconsin Press, forthcoming 1988); Eric R. Wolf, *Europe and the People Without History* (Berkeley: University of California Press, 1982); Ashis Nandy, *The Intimate Enemy: Loss and Recovery of Self under Colonialism* (Delhi: Oxford University Press, 1983); Nandy, *Traditions, Tyranny and Utopias: Essays in the Politics of Awareness* (Delhi: Oxford University Press, 1987); Partha Catterjee, *Nationalist Thought and the Colonial World: A Derivative Discourse* (London: Zed Books, 1986): Anthony Smith, *The Geopolitics of Information: How Western Culture Dominates The World* (London: Faber and Faber, 1980); Johannes Fabian, *Time and the Other: How Anthropology Makes Its Object* (New York: Columbia University Press, 1983); George E. Marcus and Michael M. J. Fischer, *Anthropology as Cultural Critique* (Chicago: University of Chicago Press, 1986); David Cairns and Shaun Richards, *Writing Ireland: Colonialism, Nationalism and Culture* (Manchester University Press, 1988); Michael T. Ryan, "Assimilating New Worlds in the Sixteenth and Seventeenth Centuries," *Comparative Studies in Societies and History* 23:4 (October 1981):519–538; James Clifford, "On Ethnographic Surrealism," *Comparative Studies in Society and History* 23:4 (October 1981):539–564; Sergio Moravia, "The Enlightenment and the Sciences of Man," *History of Science*, 18, P. 4; 42 (December 1980):247–268; Lionel Gossman, "History as Decipherment: Romantic Historiography and the Discovery of the Other," *New Literary History* 18:1 (Autumn 1986):23–57; Jonathan Friedman, "Beyond Otherness or: The Specularization of Anthropology," *Telos 71 (Spring 1987):161–170; Louis Gates, Jr., ed., "Race," Writing and Difference* (Chicago: University of Chicago Press, 1986); and the special issue on "The Nature and Context of Minority Discourse," *Cultural Critique*, No. 6 (Spring 1987).

6. See e.g., F. S. C. Northrop, *Philosophical Anthropology and Practical Politics* (New York: Macmillan, 1960); Northrop, *The Meeting of East and West: An Inquiry Concerning World Understanding* (New York: Macmillan, 1952); and, with H. H. Livingston, (eds.), *Cross-Cultural Understanding: Epistemology in Anthropology* (New York: Harper & Row, 1964). Compare Walker, "World Politics and Western Reason," pp. 206–209.

7. Adda Bozeman, *Politics and Culture in International History* (Princeton: Princeton University Press, 1960) and *The Future of Law in a Multicultural World* (Princeton: Princeton University Press, 1971).

8. Hedley Bull, *The Anarchical Society* (London: Macmillan, 1977); Hedley Bull and Adam Watson, eds., *The Expansion of International Society* (Oxford: Clarendon Press, 1984); Michael Donelan, ed., *The Reason of States* (London: George, Allen & Unwin, 1978); James Mayall, ed., *The Community of States* (London: George, Allen & Unwin, 1982); R. J. Vincent, "Western Conceptions of a Universal

Moral Order," in Ralph Pettman, ed., *Moral Claims in World Affairs* (New York: St. Martins, 1977), pp. 52–77; Vincent, "The Factor of Culture in the Global International Order," *Yearbook of World Affairs*, 1980, pp. 252–262; Vincent, "Race in International Relations," in Walker, ed., *Culture, Ideology and World Order*, pp. 44–59; Vincent, *Human Rights and International Relations* (Cambridge: Cambridge University Press, 1986); and Friedrich Kratochwil, *Rules, Norms and Decisions* (Cambridge University Press, forthcoming).

9. Richard A. Falk, Samuel S. Kim, and Saul H. Mendlovitz, eds., *Towards a Just World Order* (Boulder: Westview Press, 1982); Richard Falk, *The Promise of World Order: Essays in Normative International Relations* Philadelphia: Temple University Press, 1987); Samual S. Kim, *The Quest for a Just World Order* (Boulder: Westview Press, 1984); Lynn H. Miller, *Global Order: Values and Power in International Relations* (Boulder: Westview Press, 1985); Mel Gurtov, *Global Politics and the Human Interest* (Boulder: Lynne Rienner Publishers, 1988). For helpful analysis of the problem of cultural and ethical diversity in the specific context of international law, see Edward McWhinney, *United Nations Lawmaking Cultural and Ideological Relativism and International Law Making for an Era of Transition* (New York: Holmes and Meier, 1984).

10. Richard K. Ashley, "The Geopolitics of Geopolitical Space: Towards a Critical Theory of International Politics," *Alternatives* 12:4 (October 1987):403–434; Ashley, "The Poverty of Neorealism," in Robert O. Keohane, ed., *Neorealism and Its Critics* (New York: Columbia University Press, 1986), pp. 255–300; Robert Cox, "Social Forces, States and World Orders: Beyond International Relations Theory" in Keohane, ed., *Neorealism and its Critics*, pp. 204–254; Cox, "Gramsci, Hegemony and International Relations: An essay in Method," *Millennium: Journal of International Studies* 12:2 (Summer 1983):162–175; John McLean, "Political Theory, International Theory and Problems of Ideology,"*Millennium: Journal of International Studies*, 10:2 (Summer 1981):102–125; R. B. J. Walker, "Realism, Change and International Political Theory," *International Studies Quarterly* 31:1 (March 1987):65–86; Walker, "The *Prince* and 'The Pauper': Tradition, Modernity and Practice in the Theory of International Relations," in James Der Derian and Michael J. Shapiro, eds., *International/Intertextual Relations: The Boundaries of Knowledge and Practice in World Politics* (Lexington: Lexington Books, forthcoming); David Campbell, "Recent Changes in Social Theory: Questions for International Relations," in R. Higgott, ed., *New Directions in International Relations: Australian Essays* (Canberra: Australia National University, forthcoming); and Jim George, "The Study of International Relations and a Positivist/Empiricist Theory of Knowledge: Implications for the Australian Discipline," in Higgott, ed., *New Directions in International Relations*.

11. Especially Der Derian and Shapiro, eds., *International/Intertextual Relations*, and Shapiro, *The Politics of Representation*.

12. Paul Chilton, ed., *Language and the Nuclear Arms Debate: Nukespeak Today* (London: Francis Pinter, 1985); Glenn D. Hook, "The Nuclearization of Language: Nuclear Allergy as Political Metaphor," *Journal of Peace Research* 21:3 (1984):259–275; Robin Luckham, "Armament Culture," *Alternatives* 10:1 (Summer 1984):1–44; Bradley S. Klein, *Strategic Discourse and Its Alternatives*, Center on Violence and Human Survival Occasional Paper No. 3 (New York: CUNY, John Jay College

of Criminal Justice, 1987); Klein, "Hegemony and Strategic Culture: American Power Projection and Alliance Defence Politics," *Review of International Studies* 14 (April 1988):131–146; Klein, "After Strategy: The Search for a Post-Modern Politics of Peace," *Alternatives* 13 (Forthcoming, July 1988): G. M. Dillon, "Defence, Discourse and Policy Making: Britain and the Falklands," San Diego: University of California Institute of Global Conflict and Co-operation Working Paper, No. 4 (1988); R. B. J. Walker, "The Concept of Security and International Relations Theory," San Diego: IGCC Working Paper No. 3 (1988); Walker, "Culture, Discourse, Insecurity," in Mendlovitz and Walker, eds., *Towards a Just World Peace*, pp. 171–190; and Walker "Contemporary Militarism and the Discourse of Dissent" in Walker, ed., *Culture, Ideology and World Order*, pp. 302–322.

13. The classic statement is in Martin Wight, "Why Is There No International Theory?" in H. Butterfield and M. Wight, eds., *Diplomatic Investigations* (London: George, Allen and Unwin, 1966), pp. 17–34. For historical context, see also Andrew Linklater, *Men and Citizens in the Theory of International Relations* (London: Macmillan, 1982). For critical commentary, see Ashley, "The Geopolitics of Geopolitical Space"; and Walker, "The *Prince* and 'The Pauper'."

14. See especially the two essays by Max Weber: "The National State and Economic Policy," trans. Ben Fowkes, *Economy and Society* 9:4 (November 1980):428–449 and "Politics as a Vocation," in *From Max Weber: Essay in Sociology*, trans. and ed. by H. H. Gerth and C. Wright Mills (New York: Oxford University Press, 1946), pp. 77–128. Also see, for example, Stephen P. Turner and Regis A. Factor, *Max Weber and the Dispute over Reason and Value* (London: Routledge and Kegan Paul, 1984); Wolfgang J. Mommsen, *Max Weber and German Politics* (Chicago: University of Chicago Press, 1984); Sam Whimster and Scott Lash, eds., *Max Weber, Rationality and Modernity* (London: George Allen and Unwin, 1987); Wolfgang J. Mommsen and Jurgen Osterhammel, eds., *Max Weber and His Contemporaries* (London: George Allen and Unwin, 1987); Raymond Aron, "Max Weber and Power-politics," in Otto Stammer, ed., *Max Weber and Sociology Today*, trans. K. Morris (Oxford: Basil Blackwell, 1971), pp. 83–100; Hans J. Morgenthau, "Fragment of an Intellectual Autobiography: 1904–1932," in Kenneth Thompson and Robert J. Myers, eds., *Truth and Tragedy: A Tribute to Hans J. Morgenthau* (Washington, DC: New Republic Book Co., 1977), pp. 1–17; and Michael Joseph Smith, *Realist Thought from Weber to Kissinger* (Baton Rouge: Louisiana State University Press, 1986).

15. These themes are pursued in R. B. J. Walker, *One World, Many Worlds: Struggles for a Just World Peace* (Boulder, CO: Lynne Rienner and London: Zed Books, 1988); Saul Mendlovitz and R. B. J. Walker, eds., *Towards a Just World Peace* (London: Butterworths, 1987); and Warren Magnusson and R. B. J. Walker, "Decentering the State: Political Theory and Canadian Political Economy," *Studies in Political Economy* (forthcoming 1988). See also, for example, Raymond Williams, *Towards 2000* (New York: Pantheon, 1983); Dan Smith and E. P. Thompson, eds., *Prospects for a Habitable Planet* (London: Penguin 1987); Ashis Nandy, "The Politics of Secularism and the Recovery of Religious Tolerance," *Alternatives* 13:2 (April

1988): 177–194; Lester Edwin J. Ruiz, "Theology, Politics, and the Discourses of Transformation," *Alternatives* 13:2 (April 1988): 155–176; Charles S. Maier, ed., *Changing Boundaries of the Political* (Cambridge: Cambridge University Press, 1987); and Roberta Hamilton and Michele Barrett, *The Politics of Diversity* (London: Verso, 1987).

# Part II

---

# The Humanities and International Relations

# 2

# *Is War a Cultural Universal? Anthropological Perspectives on the Causes of Warfare in Human Societies*

## James M. Wallace

War is one topic that is of interest both to anthropologists and international relations specialists. There are few people in the world today who would advocate war as a practical way to resolve political differences, yet it appears to be as common today as it has been over the last 10,000 years since the Neolithic Revolution.

A fundamental issue in the study of war is the role of warfare in human society, whether it is or is not inevitably part of the fabric of human nature and society. This basic question has been at the heart of much of the research done by anthropologists. The research data is derived primarily from studies of ancient primitive and complex societies as well as from contemporary foraging bands, horticultural and pastoral tribes, and chiefdoms all over the world. Anthropologists have not systematically studied warfare among contemporary nation-states to any significant degree. Nevertheless, their findings are of immediate concern to people of modern, industrialized societies because they give us a good idea of how important warfare is to the conduct of international relations. This chapter addresses four fundamental issues about war that anthropologists have studied intensively. It concludes with a discussion about why anthropologists only recently are becoming more heavily involved in the study of warfare in modern nation-states.

## ANTHROPOLOGICAL PERSPECTIVES IN THE STUDY OF WARFARE

The anthropological interest in warfare has not been specifically the province of any single specialty area within the discipline. It is not, for example, a primary or even secondary area of concern for most political anthropologists. Much of the study of warfare has revolved around basic issues dealing with the cultural role of warfare in human life, particularly as it has been observed in small-scale societies. The basic issues that have been at the core of this study have focused on four issues. These are: (1) whether war, aggression, and conflict are a normal, biological feature of human nature; (2) whether warfare is a cultural universal; (3) how warfare has contributed to the evolution or development of the modern nation-state; and (4) what the causes and functions of war might be. The first pertains to the broader "nature vs. nurture" debate. We shall see that, generally, anthropologists have rejected the hypothesis that warfare developed out of human instincts. The second question addresses the idea of natural selection for war as a cultural rather than an instinct-derived institution. More anthropologists are inclined toward this view, but many are not. However, most would agree that all state-level societies have developed war-related institutions, and this fact provokes the third question on the role of warfare in state formation, a question much discussed in anthropology. But many anthropologists are not persuaded by the theories of cultural evolution, state formation, or the nature vs. nurture debate, yet they are very interested in why warfare is, nevertheless, so common in human societies. This explains the presence of the fourth issue, which concerns, on a somewhat more general level, theories dealing with causes and functions of war.

There are, of course, many other aspects of conflict that interest anthropologists. Some of them are with internal conflict, feuding, conflict resolution, military strategy, political administration of warfare, and warfare and kinship structure. But central to all of this other research is the question of whether humans have a biological predisposition toward violence and warfare.

### Is There a Human Instinct for Armed Conflict?

Anthropologists have generally come down quite squarely on the nurture side of the nature-nurture debate, and so it is not surprising that anthropologists have been quick to criticize perspectives that apply genetic imprinting to aggressive tendencies in humans. Works by Konrad Lorenz,[1] Robert Ardrey,[2] and Lionel Tiger and Robin Fox,[3] for example, have been influential in espousing the instinctual theory of human aggression as an explanation for warfare. Their claims have been criticized heavily by M. F. Ashley Montagu,[4] Geoffrey Gorer,[5] and Samuel S. Lim,[6] among many others. Keith Otterbein[7] finds the Lorenz-Ardrey theories "simplistic to the point of being tautological." He also writes that all conflict is not warfare and that it does not explain why some groups are more prone to warfare than others. Victor Barnouw, a psychological anthropologist, takes a more measured stance when he makes the distinction between closed and open instincts. "Closed instincts are behavior patterns that are fixed in every detail, while open instincts are looser with strong general tendencies such as to get home or to seek water. More advanced animals are programmed in this more general fashion."[8] So, for humans, instinct does not function in a closed way, rather culture exists as an outgrowth and supplement to it. This means that culture is innate in humans, and that culture operates in a general way without specific programming. With respect to warfare, it is clearly a part of culture and only in a very distant way could one conclude that it is instinctual. To put it another way, warfare is primarily a cultural phenomenon that potentially can arise in all societies, but may not, given particular historico-societal and environmental conditions.

Ruling out instinct, however, does not rule out the possibility that warfare might instead be a human cultural necessity for survival and that all successful societies have developed the social institutions necessary for engaging in warfare. In other words, like the incest taboo, language, and religion, it might be a cultural universal, something necessary for human survival.

In sum, most anthropologists would hold human aggression is learned and is not an innate part of human nature.[9] There is so much cross-cultural variation in warfare that the causes must be determined by the particulars of human socio-cultural systems.[10]

### Is Warfare a Cultural Universal?

Anthropologists have also debated this question often, as well. It is premised upon the idea that warfare efficiently waged confers a survival advantage upon the society employing it. Therefore, cultures with customs or practices associated with successful warfare are more likely to survive intersocietal struggles. This is often labeled the "survival-value" theory. Nevertheless, some anthropologists believe that warfare is not a universal phenomenon. They conclude this after examining the data for a number of societies. David Fabbro,[11] for example, lists seven "peaceful societies" as having had no war: the Semai (Malaysia), Siriono (Bolivia), Mouti Pygmies (Zaire), !Kung San (Southern Africa), Copper Eskimo (Canada), Tristan Islanders (South Pacific), and the Hutterites (North America). Alexander Lesser mentions also the Andaman Islanders (Indian Ocean), the Semang (Malaysia), the Todas (India), and the Yahgan (Chile), and concludes, "Evidently, conquest warfare and its modern development of war to advance national interest is not an inherent, inevitable feature of human life—too many societies have existed in human history without it.[12] William A. Haviland[13] adds,

There is ample reason to suppose that war has become a serious problem only in the last 10,000 years, since the invention of food production techniques, the rise of the city and the invention of centralized states. Thus, war may not be so much an age old problem as a relatively recent one.

Martin Nettleship[14] states that war is a phenomenon of civilization, different from primitive fighting, and that although war is associated with civilized states, it did not "spring up full blown as a new tool of the emerging states."

As one studies warfare, one need not forget that all societies also have means of peaceful conflict resolution. The existence of peaceful conflict is apparently also a cultural universal.[15] Most cultural anthropologists have generally assumed that social stability is the normal state for humans. Warfare is often so destructive that it seems to stand out more than conflict resolution techniques. Conflict resolution probably is less studied by anthropologists than is warfare.[16] Most often, peaceful conflict resolution occurs through some form of community action. In small-scale societies, such as foraging bands and horticultural tribes, the kinship group is relatively autonomous, and it is this group that frequently serves as the mediator in disputes. When conflicts occur between kinship groups, mediation will be attempted by elders, special chiefs, or other community groupings. In larger societies a complex legal system may operate in addition to informal dispute-processing techniques to resolve conflicts peacefully. Furthermore, all societies have some technique for internalizing social control mechanisms.

In conclusion, anthropologists are divided on whether warfare is a cultural universal. However, all anthropologists agree that war is primarily a cultural rather than biological phenomenon and that conflict resolution techniques are found in all societies.

## Has Warfare Contributed to the Formation of the State?

There is a long history of anthropological work suggesting a relationship between warfare and sociopolitical complexity. Many of the theories associated with the topic suggest that there have been certain limiting factors that have caused societies to select for the state as the encompassing political institution. Warfare has been treated as one factor in a complex of limiting factors that have encouraged the development of the state. One of the chief recent proponents of this point of view is Robert Carneiro.[17] Categorized as "circumscription theory," his idea is, briefly, that as population density increases, the supply of cultivable land diminishes, which leads to competition for resources. The competition takes the form of warfare. The society with more successful methods of waging war, including superior military organization, imposes their will and their institutions on the vanquished. Tribe fights tribe, and chiefdoms emerge as an interim solution to the needs of organization. Chiefdoms eventually gives way to states.

Military circumscription is one type of integrative mechanism conducive to the formation of the state. Successively larger political units were formed to fight for more land, until eventually the early states (Incas, Egyptians, among others) emerged. This process continues with the emergence of empires, and presumably is still an ongoing phenomenon. Support for his theory comes from Otterbein's extensive cross-cultural comparison of 50 societies regarding political complexity and the evolution of warfare. He concludes "that as political communities evolve in terms of increasing centralization, the manner in which they wage war becomes more sophisticated."[18] He also finds that there is no evidence supporting the idea that a well developed military system will deter the attacks of enemies. This is particularly important as we consider the current nuclear build-up as a rationale for deterrence in the relationship between the East and the West. However, neither Carneiro nor Otterbein state that warfare is the principal cause of state formation; they, with Ronald Cohen,[19] believe that war is a necessary, but not sufficient cause. R. Brian Ferguson takes an even more cautious stance, "War is not, by itself, the cause of political evolution, although it is one cause, when combined with other necessary circumstances and trends."[20]

Regardless of which theory one uses to explain the development of the state, anthropologists generally hold that warfare has played an important role in contributing to state formation. Its role has to do at least with helping to satisfy requirements for greater control of and coordination of military power for both offensive and defensive purposes. Furthermore, the development of a military force, military strategy, and military equipment contributes to social differentiation and political complexity. Warfare may also play a role in the development of diplomats, peace negotiators, and others who have the capacity to settle disputes,[21] which is also a function of the need for coordination as one aspect of appropriate defensive strategies.

Cohen[22] makes the interesting suggestion that the evolution of larger and larger political entities has to have an end point, and that we may be reaching that now. Modern states are so big, and the potential for destruction so total, that we may find that peace has a greater chance and we may enter a period of smaller states emerging from the desire of national ethnic groups for their own state.

## What Are Some of the Principal Causes of Wars?

Although anthropologists have dismissed the innate aggression hypothesis of Lorenz, Ardrey, and others, as largely inapplicable to humans, there has been much discussion about other causes of war. These theories can be grouped into three broad categories: biological, psychological, and structural.

## Biological Perspectives

Anthropologists do not deny that conflict is endemic. They disagree on whether there is a human predisposition toward violence. The universality of dangerous sports and games leads Margaret M. Clark[23] to suggest that humans may have some predisposition to resort to violence as one means of conflict resolution. However, violence does not have to lead to war; it may be expressed in the form of intra-group conflict, raiding and/or feuding. Cara Richards[24] suggests that humans are competitive and that competition can be either predatory (disruptive and harmful) or emulative (beneficial and stimulating). Cooperation is interrelated with competition rather than being mutually exclusive.

Another type of biological theory concerning the human tendency toward violence and warfare arises from considerations of environmental and/or dietary preferences. A famous test case in anthropology concerns the Bolivian highland Aymara. The case centers on the development of nutritional stress. Modern Aymara are reported to be aggressive, anxious, and sullen. Archaeologists maintain that the Aymara were one of the most bellicose of all the people the Incas conquered. But Ralph Bolton[25] suggests that the Aymara suffer from hypoglycemia and that this biological condition results in the symptomatic behavior noted by previous anthropologists. Hypoglycemia is caused by protein poor, high carbohydrate diets. The biological effects have cultural consequences: rebelliousness and frequent warfare.

In sum, biological theories explaining warfare are still in the minority view within anthropology. Critics point out that motivation must be considered, even from a biological and evolutionary perspective. If warfare has contributed to human survival, then at any given moment societies engaging in warfare have explicit motives for war. In order to understand how warfare has evolved in humans we need to examine human psychology to determine what have been successful survival strategies.

## Psychological Perspectives

The key question in this category is: To what extent has the motivation for warfare and conflict been a conscious or unconscious element in humans? The factors that can cause stress may be unconscious or conscious.

One example of the role of unconscious factors is found in Ruth Benedict's national character study of the Japanese.[26] She finds a frustration cause that explains, in part, Japanese participation in World War II. She notes that Japanese are treated indulgently by their parents, but once reaching adulthood they are faced with rigid strictures of conformity and obligations as they seek a place of respect in the world. If they are unable to achieve this, they may behave passionately in an uncontrollable way.

Pre-World War II conditions affected Japanese greatly. Benedict implies that they were trying to find their rightful place on the world stage as a great nation, but saw themselves as being inpeded by the Allied powers. Frustrated with the impasse, they retaliated.

This case is also an example of the "frustration-aggression hypothesis." It is discussed at length by David Krakauer, "An intelligent species is also necessarily a conflicted species. Without instincts . . . man must be constantly making up his mind. The choices are many and difficult. . . . Overt aggression sometimes breaks out in epidemic proportions and is present always in endemic proportions. . . . "[27] Krakauer does not say that frustration causes war, but he does suggest that once war has come into existence as a cultural strategy, a society is more likely to go to war. He also implies that frustration adds fuel to the fires and makes wars more ferocious. Some anthropologists suggest that the frustrations of daily life can lead to external warfare. This may even have the positive consequence of reinforcing social solidarity within the group, as may have occurred in Japan between 1931 and 1945.

Frustration-aggression hypotheses typically are explanations of violence the cause of which is unknown to the participants. Nevertheless, there are many conscious motivations: "(1) maintenance and improvement of existing subsistence standards; (2) energetic efficiency, or more specifically, maintenance of labor requirements; (3) protection against life-threatening hazards, either environmental or human."[28] Also, there are always "prestige, revenge, and unfulfilled social obligations."[29] Thus, for any particular political community there will probably be several goals of war. That which predominates depends on the given circumstances at any particular moment.

An interesting case is that of the Aztecs. The Aztecs were a major civilization with advanced organizational and technological achievements with a large standing army in constant readiness for war. According to Frances H. Berdan[30] the Aztecs had two types of warfare: general warfare and ritual warfare. General warfare had several functions: intimidation of enemies and potential allies, revenge for persecution or victimization of Aztec merchants by other political communities, satisfaction of soldiers' needs for acquisition of honors, and conquest for increased economic control over land and production. Often, mistreatment of merchants was merely a pretext for conquering distant provinces. Political leaders achieved their status often based on their battlefield prowess; it was the highest honor to die in battle or to be sacrificed. Although religion was intimately entwined with all warfare, there was a special type of ritual warfare designed primarily to acquire sacrificial victims. This was the "war of flowers," which grew out of planned, mutual arrangements by the Aztecs and neighboring states. The sole purpose of the wars was to get enemies for sacrifice to the god, Huitzilopochtli. In one particularly "successful" war of this type, the Aztecs took approximately 20,000 prisoners who were eventually sacrificed on the alters of the pyramids dedicated to Huitzilopochtli.

> The practice of human sacrifice was of intense importance to the central Mexican peoples. . . . According to their beliefs, they had to ensure the continuation of the universe. The only way this could be successfully accomplished is with the continual offering of human blood.[31]

It can be seen from these examples that motivations for warfare are varied, but the range of variety is not great. In other words, the type of immediate cause for a specific war at a specific time could be one of only a few basic reasons, as summarized by Otterbein: "subjugation and tribute, land, plunder, trophies and honors, and revenge."[32]

## Structural Perspectives

Consistent with anthropology's functionalist and evolutionary theories, many researchers have been particularly interested in the role that warfare plays in the survival and maintenance of a society and culture. This is evident, for example in the concerns of Carneiro and others supporting the circumscription theory of state formation.

A perspective that has become quite popular in recent years is the ecological adaptation approach. The ecological perspective examines the social and biotic environment for hidden factors that explain the adoption of specific cultural traits as adaptive responses to environmental constraints. Usually, the members of the society are themselves unaware of these hidden factors.

Marvin Harris,[33] in an analysis of the case of the Yanomamo Indians of Venezuela, provides a theory to explain the complex relationships between warfare, environment, and population growth when he suggests that the competition over scarce animal protein in the diet can provoke fratricidal raiding. For many societies, resource deprivation leads to intra-societal warfare, which functions to keep the size of human group levels low enough to support a population in a given environment. This, in turn, ensures the survival of the society, even if it does not allow it to grow.

For example, among the Tsembaga Maring of New Guinea[34] we find that religious ritual has, in addition, a "regulating" function in so far as it pertains to environmental and economic factors. The Tsembaga Maring rituals associated with warfare occur periodically, every 12 to 20 years. During this period the pig population, decimated by the big *kaiko* ritual held just prior to the previous round of fighting, gradually recoups its former size. When it reaches an unmanageable level, males call for another *kaiko*, initiating a new round of feasting and fighting. The peacetime period also allows land captured during the previous fighting to fallow, because there is a taboo against occupying enemy territory until the appropriate ritual ("uprooting the *rumbim*") is performed, which occurs only prior to the next round of warfare.

These two examples illustrate the structural role warfare can have in human societies. But this is not the only type. Another one, called the fraternal interest group theory, is now a classic example of how the social structure itself may be a leading cause of warfare.

Fraternal interest group theory uses social structural explanations to explain why internal warfare is more frequent in some societies than in others. In societies where dissension is rife, there exist groups of kinship-linked males who rely on force whenever the interests of one of their group is threatened. Societies that practice patrilocal residence are particularly prone to internal warfare, whereas in societies with matrilocal residence, related males are dispersed over a large region and thus are unable to give support easily to each other. Otterbein[35] cites the Yanomamo, the Tausug of the Philippines, the highland New Guinea Jale, and the Higi of Nigeria as case studies.

Closely related to Otterbein's work is that of the classic work on the pastoral Nuer of the Sudan by E. E. Evans-Pritchard.[36] The Nuer have a kinship system that has come to be called a "segmentary lineage system." The opposition and conflict inherent in the grouping of fraternal interest groups leads the Nuer to expand geographically at the expense of neighboring tribes. When the Nuer are not fighting others they are fighting among themselves. Conflict is so endemic that there is a special chief, called the "Leopard Skin Chief" who comes from a specific lineage and whose sole duty is to arbitrate conflicts. Fraternal interest group conflict appears to be inherent to a patrilocal, unilineal social structure that has an uncentralized political system. Presumably, centralized political systems are able to control this conflict better.

Stratification itself, according to Morton Fried,[37] is a potential cause of war. Stratified societies are societies with differences in income and power levels. The economic and political interests of the different classes do not coincide. Sometimes, classes with more power pursue their own interests through warfare. The whole society may go to war to satisfy the interests of a particular social class. While he gives no example of what he means, World War I would probably serve as one.

Ferguson[38] makes an interesting counterpoint to Fried as he suggests that as one moves up the scale from the primitive societies to modern, industrial ones, the social institution of war becomes increasingly more autonomous. For him, war takes on a life of its own, barely constrained by the parameters of the societies that wage war. Furthermore, the environment is only one element in a variety of factors that can contribute to warfare. He argues that there is a qualitative difference between warfare in state societies and less centralized ones. One of the main factors for this difference is the "organizational complexity" of the military, which itself becomes more autonomous from other political interests within the society.

Cohen[39] adds that as military organizations become more complex, the frequency of warfare between the large nations decreases. While warfare becomes more efficient, it also becomes more costly, in terms of both the economy and human lives. At the same time, warfare is more likely between states with unequal military forces. Otterbein[40] has shown that societies with greater military sophistication are more successful in territorial expansion.

Currently, the world is divided into a few major alliance groups. Interstate wars may not be as frequent as they were in the past, but today many governments are contending with issues of ethnic autonomy. Perhaps, as Cohen suggests, there has been a limit reached on the use of war by the larger states, and "smallness and peace may be the result."[41]

## ANTHROPOLOGICAL POLITICS AND THE DISCIPLINE'S CONCERN WITH WAR

Many anthropologists think that warfare has not been studied intensively enough, and that peace studies have been almost completely overlooked.[42] The reasons for this lay grounded partly in historical factors in the development of the discipline and partly in the nature of the research enterprise. The founding fathers of anthropology focused on traditional societies they encountered either in America or in Africa and the Pacific, and participant observation, applicable mainly to small populations, became the dominant methodology. Many anthropologists did not put the society they were studying into a broader context, such as an international scenario, because they viewed the "traditional" community or village or society that they were studying as an autonomous, integrated whole. The society outside the village, that is, the nation-state in which they were located, was seen to be a source of traits that might change the natural order, so anthropologists often tried to separate the traditional cultural traits, from the modern elements. In the last two decades the number of anthropological studies have increased greatly.[43]

It was in the late 1960s and 1970s that the study of warfare by anthropologists began to intensify. A ground-breaking symposium on war was held as a plenary session at the 1967 annual convention of the American Anthropological Association. The ad hoc committee formed the previous year to bring it about insisted that anthropologists have a "moral and professional concern for the effects of war on the human species."[44] In the wake of the ever-widening Vietnam War, there was a widely held complaint among those attending the 1967 symposium that anthropologists had not studied the causes and consequences of warfare. This dearth began to be rectified shortly thereafter with the publication of two massive compendia on war [45] and a book on peasant wars by Eric Wolf.[46]

The theoretical interest anthropologists have with warfare continues into the 1980s. Christopher Boehm[47] has written a major piece on the anthropology of feuding, and Otterbein, long a principal figure in the anthropology of war, has revised his book on the evolution of war.[48] More importantly, two major anthologies of war and peace have been published recently. One treats several case studies from materialist and ecological perspectives of the anthropology of war[49] and the other deals with contemporary issues on both peace and war.[50]

For the most part anthropologists unfortunately have *not* focused their research efforts on aspects of global warfare and international relationships. Ferguson laments anthropological parochialism and states that anthropology has much to offer in the study of war in human society. He feels that, ''no academic discipline is better equipped to explain the social dynamics of popular uprisings or to document the human consequences of superpower aggression, wars between Third World states, and internal state policies of tribal, ethnic, or class oppression.''[51] The present contributions of anthropology to the study of war remain, nevertheless, important ones.

## NOTES

1. Konrad Lorenz, *On Aggression* (New York: Harcourt, Brace and World, 1966).

2. Robert Ardrey, *The Territorial Imperative* (New York: Atheneum, 1966).

3. Lionel Tiger and Robin Fox, *The Imperial Animal* (New York: Holt, Rinehart and Winston, 1971).

4. M. F. Ashley Montagu, *Learning and Non-Aggression: The Experience of Non-Literate Societies* (New York: Oxford University Press, 1978).

5. Geoffrey Gorer, ''Man Has No 'Killer' Instinct,'' In *Man and Aggression*, ed. A. F. Ashley Montagu (New York: Oxford University Press, 1968), pp. 74–82.

6. Samuel S. Lim, ''The Lorenzian Theory of Aggression and Peace Research: A Critique,'' *Journal of Peace Research* 13 (1980): 253–276.

7. Keith Otterbein, ''The Anthropology of War,'' in *Handbook of Social and Cultural Anthropology*, ed. John Honigmann (Chicago: Rand McNally College Publishing, 1973), p. 928.

8. Victor Barnouw, *Culture and Personality*, 4th ed. (New York: Random House, 1985), p. 221.

9. Recently, anthropologists have endorsed the Seville Statement on Violence drafted at a May 1986 meeting of world scientists held in Spain, sponsored by the Spanish National UNESCO Commission. The Seville Statement provides a concise summary of what a majority of anthropologists publicly believe with regard to human nature and warfare.

(1)It is scientifically incorrect to say that we have inherited a tendency to make war from our animal ancestors. (2) . . . That war or any other violent behavior is genetically programmed into our human nature. (3) . . . That in the course of human evolution there has been a selection for aggressive behavior more than for other kinds of behavior. (4) . . . That humans have a "violent brain." (5) . . . That war is caused by "instinct" or any other single motivation.

Memorandum from Edward J. Lehman, Executive Director of the American Anthropological Association to the members of the Association, September 15, 1987.

10. R. Brian Ferguson, "Introduction: Studying War," in *Warfare, Culture and Environment*, ed. R. Brian Ferguson (Orlando, FL: Academic Press, 1984), p. 14.

11. David Fabbro, "Peaceful Societies," in *The War System: An Interdisciplinary Approach*, eds. Richard Falk and Samuel S. Kim (Boulder, CO: Westview Press, 1980), pp. 180–203.

12. Alexander Lesser, "War and the State," in *War: The Anthropology of Armed Conflict and Aggression*, ed. Morton Fried, Marvin Harris, and Robert F. Murphy (Garden City, NY: Natural History Press, 1967), p. 95.

13. William A. Haviland, *Cultural Anthropology*, 5th. ed. (New York: Holt, Rinehart and Winston, 1987), p. 300.

14. Martin Nettleship, "Definitions," in *War: Its Causes and Correlates*, ed. Martin A. Nettleship, R. Dale Givens, and Anderson Nettleship (The Hague: Mouton, 1975), p. 86.

15. E. Adamson Hoebel, *The Law of Primitive Man* (New York: Atheneum, 1968), p. 4.

16. Laura Nader and Barbara Yngvesson, "On Studying the Ethnography of Law and Its Consequences," in *Handbook of Social and Cultural Anthropology*, ed. John Honigmann (Chicago: Rand McNally and Co., 1973), p. 883.

17. Robert Carneiro, "A Theory of the Origin of the State," *Science* 469 (1970): 733–738.

18. Keith Otterbein, *The Evolution of War; A Cross-Cultural Study*, (New Haven, CT: HRAF Press, 1970), p. 104.

19. Ronald Cohen, "Wars and State Formation: Wars Make States and States Make Wars," in *Warfare, Culture and Environment*, ed. R. Brian Ferguson (Orlando, FL: Academic Press, 1984), pp. 329–358.

20. Ferguson, "Introduction, Studying War," p. 56.

21. Cohen, "Wars and State Formation," p. 337.

22. Ibid., p. 353.

23. Margaret M. Clark, "The Cultural Patterning of Risk-Seeking Behavior: Implications for Armed Conflict," in *Peace and War; Cross-Cultural Perspectives*, ed. Mary L. Foster and Robert A. Rubinstein (New Brunswick, NJ: Transaction Books, 1986), p. 83.

24. Cara Richards, "The Concept and Forms of Competition," in *War: Its Causes and Correlates*, ed. Martin A. Nettleship, R. Dale Givens, and Anderson Nettleship (The Hague: Mouton, 1975), pp. 93–109.

25. Ralph Bolton, "The Hypoglycemia-Aggression Hypothesis: Debate Versus Research," *Current Anthropology* 25 (1984) pp. 1–53.

26. Ruth Benedict, *The Chrysanthemum and the Sword* (Boston: Houghton Mifflin, 1946).

27. Daniel Krakauer, "The Species Specific Framework of Man and Its Evolution," in *War: Its Causes and Correlates*, ed. Martin A. Nettleship, R. Givens, and Anderson Nettleship (The Hague: Mouton, 1975), p. 127.

28. Ferguson, "Introduction, Studying War," p.38.

29. Ibid., p. 41.

30. Frances F. Berdan, *The Aztecs of Central Mexico; An Imperial Society* (New York: Holt, Rinehart and Winston, 1982), pp. 105–118.

31. Ibid., p. 111.

32. Otterbein, *The Evolution of War*, p. 64.

33. Marvin Harris, "A Cultural Materialist Theory of Band and Village Warfare: The Yanomamo Test," in *Warfare, Culture and Environment*, ed., R. Brian Ferguson (Orlando, FL: Academic Press, 1984), pp. 111–140.

34. Roy Rappaport, *Pigs for the Ancestors: Ritual in the Ecology of a New Guinea People* (New Haven, CT: Yale University Press, 1968).

35. Otterbein, "The Anthropology of War," p. 938.

36. E. E. Evans-Pritchard, *The Nuer* (Oxford: Clarendon Press, 1940).

37. Morton Fried, *The Evolution of Political Society; An Essay in Political Anthropology* (New York: Random House, 1967), p. 215.

38. Ferguson, "Introduction, Studying War," p. 59.

39. Cohen, "Wars and State Formation," pp. 354–355.

40. Otterbein, *The Evolution of War*, pp. 1–7.

41. Cohen, "Wars and State Formation," p. 355.

42. Mary L. Foster and Robert A. Rubinstein, eds., *Peace and War; Cross-Cultural Perspectives* (New Brunswick, NJ: Transaction Books, 1986), p. xii.

43. See Ferguson, "Introduction, Studying War," pp. 61–81, for a thorough bibliography.

44. Morton Fried, Marvin Harris, and Robert F. Murphy, eds., *War: The Anthropology of Armed Aggression* (Garden City, NY: Natural History Press) p. x.

45. Martin A. Nettleship, R. Dale Givens, and Anderson Nettleship, eds., *War: Its Causes and Correlates* (The Hague: Mouton, 1975); and R. Dale Givens and Martin A. Nettleship, eds., *Discussions on War and Human Aggression* (The Hague: Mouton, 1976).

46. Eric Wolf, *Peasant Wars of the Twentieth Century* (New York: Harper & Row, 1969).

47. Christopher Boehm, *Blood Revenge: The Anthropology of Feuding in Montenegro and Other Tribal Societies* (Lawrence, KS: University Press of Kansas, 1984).

48. Keith Otterbein, *The Evolution of War; A Cross-Cultural Study*, 2d. ed. (New Haven, CT: HRAF Press, 1985).

49. R. Brian Ferguson, ed., *Warfare, Culture and Environment* (Orlando, FL: Academic Press, 1984).

50. Foster and Rubinstein, eds., *Peace and War.*

51. Ferguson, "Introduction, Studying War," p. 51.

# 3
# *Diplomatic History and International Relations*

## Jongsuk Chay

Diplomatic history, or the history of international relations, and international relations have a special relation, just as do economic history and economics, and social history and sociology. Because of the broad scope of its coverage—political, economic, social, as well as cultural: in short practically every aspect of human life—history has played a role in creating the trunk of the tree of civilization from the beginning of human learning in the ancient period. As the tree grew, branches began to spread out, and gradually the study of politics, economics, society, and culture all became distinctive and independent fields of learning. As a part of this process, the study of government and politics began; further branching brought into being the field of international relations. At the same time, the main stem produced some of its own branches—political, economic, social, and cultural histories—and from some of these branches came in turn smaller branches, namely diplomatic history, agricultural history, and art history, to name but a few.

Setting obvious differences between the two fields aside, this common genealogical background has given diplomatic history and international relations a special relationship. And this special relationship between the two fields seems to have some bearing upon their attitude toward each other. The elder cousin seems to view the younger, more progressive relative with a mixed feeling of suspicion and envy, while the younger cousin may look at his old-fashioned relative with some contempt and pity.

To explain the relationship between these two related fields, two major questions will be raised in this chapter: What is the role of diplomatic history in the study of international relations, and what contribution can the study of international relations make to diplomatic history? Even though the cases are rather scarce, a few bold researchers in the two fields have made courageous attempts at working together, and their achievements well deserve special attention. The most important concern is about the future: What will be the future of the two-field relationship? What should students of the two fields do about the probable future tendency of the relationship?

Modern science and its methodology has a great impact upon practically every branch of learning, the humanities as well as the social sciences. But, the degree of the impact varies depending upon the field; international relations is one of the fields that has greatly felt the impact of scientific methods, while diplomatic history has been little influenced by the new methods. To be raised then is the question: How much of a role has diplomatic history, a still largely traditional field, played in the study of international relations, a field active in adopting the scientific method?

One way to estimate the extent of this influence is to survey recent publications in international relations, especially books and articles published in major journals. A comprehensive examination of all books and articles published in the field is much beyond the scope of this essay; accordingly, the scope of the investigation was limited to checking book reviews included in the *Book Review Digest* during the ten-year period between 1974 and 1983. Of the 187 books listed under the heading of international relations, 25 used a historical approach or a chronological narrative style. Only 12 were either totally or partially quantitative. The remaining 150 works fell between these two extreme approaches, which may be called loosely analytical or normatively theoretical.[1] This cursory investigation indicates that the historical approach still plays a rather important role in the study of international relations. The number of books with a historical approach is much smaller than that of those with the analytical approach, but it is larger than those with the quantitative approach. The implication of this finding will be discussed shortly together with the findings from a survey of articles.

With regard to the articles, a simple survey of the three major journals in international relations (*World Politics, International Studies Quarterly,* and *The Journal of Conflict Resolution*) was carried out. When the 38 volumes of *World Politics,* the entire publication run from October 1948 to July 1986, were checked, it was found that 23 articles used a historical approach; 161 belonged to the quantitative mode; and the rest, 455 articles, were loosely analytical or theoretical in nature. An annual average of 1.5 articles with a historical approach, or about 11 percent, is not a large number. And the percentage became even smaller when the two other journals were examined. *The International Studies Quarterly,* the major organ of publication for the International Studies Association, published only nine articles with a strictly historical approach in the 25 volumes that appeared between March 1962 and December 1986, an average of one article every three years—indeed a small number. This ratio becomes even smaller in

*The Journal of Conflict Resolution,* the most quantitatively oriented of the three; in its entire history of publication, 30 volumes between January 1957 and December 1986, only eight articles with a historical approach were published—one every four years.

What meaning does this data have for the question of the role of history in international relations? First of all, a discrepancy between the book count and the article count should not surprise anyone. Like any other field and perhaps even more so in this field, there are different sectors in international relations; and the conservative sector might find the book a more congenial medium for publication, while the more liberal one would find the article form more suitable to the fast-moving frontiers of knowledge. However, the size of the gap should be explained. One plausible explanation suggests that the authors of the books include a large number of area studies people; in the case of the articles, the area specialists should have found publication outlets in their own area specialty journals, leaving the three journals to the more quantitatively oriented authors. Another reason accounting for the relatively small number of books with a quantitative approach may be that many of the findings in the sector are still fragmented and the conclusions too tentative for book form.[2]

These explanations and adjustments notwithstanding, this large discrepancy still has importance for the issue of the role of history in international relations. The fact that there are very few articles with a historical approach in the journals and there are more books in the field with a historical approach seems to signify a trend in past decades: The role of diplomatic history in international relations has been declining while the field has been becoming more quantitative. This trend continues presently and will surely continue in the coming years.

In sum, through a simple survey of the selected books and articles in international relations, it was found that: one, a goodly number of students of international relations are traditionalists, some of whom still use a historical approach; nevertheless, the trend is toward a more and more sophisticated quantitative approach. Many of the traditionalists in international relations will remain with that orientation for some time to come at least, and probably for a long time, not by choice in many cases but because of inevitability. The rest of the traditionalists, although probably not a large number, still see merit in a historical approach and will choose to remain with this approach in the future. Since the Renaissance period, science has become continuously and increasingly more attractive in the whole world—non-Western as well as Western; hence, the tendency for the progressive sector of international relations to become more quantitatively oriented is certainly understandable. Because the ultimate purpose of the whole orientation is a search for more accuracy and truth, the tendency is a definite benefit for the field.

When we turn to observe the role played by international relations in diplomatic history, we face a general attitude of "indifference."[3] Just as before, for pragmatic reasons, the review section of *The Journal of American History* was chosen as the basis for a survey of books in U. S. diplomatic history. For the same ten-year period, between 1974 and 1983, over 200 books belonging to the category of diplomatic history were reviewed in this journal; of this relatively large number of books, not a single one was found using quantitative techniques. Even books employing normative theories are quite rare. And only a few books used something close to a conceptual framework. John Lewis Gaddis' *Strategies of Containment: A Critical Appraisal of Postwar American National Security*, published in 1982, was organized around the idea of containment, as the title indicates. Almost a decade earlier, 1974, a work with a more genuinely conceptual framework, that of deterrence, *Deterrence in American Foreign Policy: Theory and Practice*, was published. Even though it won the 1975 Bancroft Prize, this fine book containing 15 historical cases along with some theoretical discussions, was written by a political scientist (Alexander L. George), who probably has a great interest in history. Akira Iriye and others have turned to image and culture, new dimensions rather than concepts, and have made a valuable contribution to the field.[4] For the articles, all 10 volumes of *Diplomatic History*, the official journal of The Society for Historians of American Foreign Relations, were checked. Almost all of the articles in the journal are either chronologically or topically organized, and there is not even one quantitatively or theoretically oriented article. Only a few (at least four can be identified) articles use a conceptual framework like "interdependence," "culture," and "ideology."[5]

It is rather interesting to see such a fashionable word in international relations as "interdependence," appear a decade ago in the very first issue of the *Diplomatic History*.[6] However, this is definitely an exception. Both in books and journal articles, historians of U. S. diplomacy seem to be content with their traditional approach and they appear unconcerned about what has been going on in closely related fields like international relations and U.S. foreign policy. If some of them have taken an interest in the new approaches and new methodologies of international relations, it does not show in their publication. Until one makes an extensive survey of diplomatic historians, one cannot find the real reason for this indifference. Only guesswork will be attempted here. The most important reason for the lack of interest seems to be that traditional historians have a firm conviction that their long-tested approach is still the best, probably the only valid approach, in many of their minds, to reach truth in historical studies; they correspondingly view the high-sounding theories and exotic techniques in international relations with great suspicion.[7] Another reason for the indifference may be the highly technical nature of quantitative approach. It is a fair assumption that in diplomatic history there are a good number of people—especially young scholars—with much interest in the new techniques and theories, but it is not easy to acquire knowledge of social science techniques. Acquisition of the new techniques is not an impossible task, but it is quite costly in terms of time and effort, and, as Melvin Small pointed out years ago, it is an enterprise with few professional payoffs.[8] There must be many other reasons, but these two are strong enough to deter diplomatic historians from trying to borrow new methods from the related fields.

After this brief discussion of the roles diplomatic history and international relations play in each other's field, we may now view the two fields from some distance. In a sense, the present status of the two disciplines' relationship is quite natural: most diplomatic historians simply disregard the works of specialists in international relations and concentrate on their historical studies; and most students in international relations do the same—advance the theoretical frontiers of the field leaving the diplomatic historians behind. But, like any case of chauvinism, the problem facing these two fields is that, because they shut each other out, they are not even aware of missed opportunities. One field is mainly concerned with facts, the other with theories and techniques. A grave danger in this is that the one has great difficulty in seeing the big picture systematically and clearly while the other departs more and more from reality. The point to be stressed here is that the work done in these two fields is complementary; either facts or data combined with theories supported with data from the real world will enhance the understanding of the subject studied. Historians need both intensive studies of the small picture and broad-based studies of the big picture; to accomplish this, they need theories and social science techniques. Thus, macro-history is needed, combined with microhistory. Specialists in international relations also need micro-studies as well as macro-studies, and to do this they need what historians can offer. Now, what can we do to solve this problem of mutual indifference between diplomatic historians and students in international relations? Before turning to this question, a brief examination of a few cases of cooperation between the two fields seems to be in order.

Melvin Small, Paul Gordon Lauren, and others who have given serious thought to the matter of the relationship between diplomatic history and international relations think that one way to solve the problem is by doing teamwork.[9] Some experimentation has been made by groups of scholars in the two fields, and the findings are significant and the experience is valuable for everyone with an interest in the subject. Without doubt there have been many small-scale projects of cooperation among historians and internationalists; and there are (one of them is still continuing) at least three large-scale projects of cooperation between the two fields. The first to begin was the Stanford Studies in International Conflict and Integration project, with Robert C. North as the leader and a number of political scientists as team members. In terms of materials they dealt with and the extensive use of historical writings for background understanding, the field of history was deeply involved and the venture can be called a joint project between the two fields; however, in terms of the personnel involved, this was not a true joint project. Historians may have rendered assistance as research assistants and consultants, but the key investigators were all political scientists. According to North, the original plan was to spend only a limited amount of time on the period leading to the outbreak of World War I in 1914 and then to move on to other historical cases of crises. But the project bogged down with the study of this important historical event, and important findings were made that were reported in a number of publications.[10] The important points to be noted concerning this experiment are: The project made an extensive preliminary study of historical writings; it made an effective use of content analysis, which seems to have considerable value for historical studies; it carefully selected the data in three categories—attribute data, cognitive data, and action data; the findings shed much light on the outbreak of World War I; and the team seems to have worked well together.[11]

Another cooperative project began at Cornell University about ten years after the Stanford project had started and was carried out by the people at Cornell and at the University of California at Berkeley. The project leader was Richard Rosenrance, a political scientist, and other major co-investigators were political scientists. This team used students of history as assistants or coders. The project undertook an intensive study of the relationship among the five major powers in Europe during the 11-year period between 1870 and 1881—Austria, Germany, Russia, England, and France. The main objective of the project was to study the relationship between power, status, and balance of power (explanatory or independent variable) and cooperation/conflict (explained or dependent variable). Data was selected by relying on the "expert knowledge of diplomatic historians" and by using a number of history books listed in the American Historical Association's *Guide to Historical Literature* (1961). The research procedures and the findings were reported in both the Sage International Studies Series and *The Journal of Conflict Resolution*. Later, the project drew the attention of historians, and their comments and investigators' responses brought out a number of controversial issues involved in the quantitative study of historical data.[12] The choice of the 109 variables, the mode of data analysis, the findings and the ensuing controversies and clarifications—are all important for our subject.

The most significant joint history and international relations project is the Michigan project, which began in 1963 and still continues. For our purpose, this project is significant for several reasons. Together with J. David Singer, a political scientist and the originator of the project, the historian Melvin Small has been involved from the earlier stages of the project as one of the two key investigators. If the background of the investigators is to be considered as the most important criterion for cooperative projects, then this is the only true one among the three discussed here. Second, the 165 years between 1816 and 1980, the better part of the last two centuries of history, is a long time span, and the choice of this period makes the project, along with the findings, a significant historical project. Intensive studies of important six-week periods (as was the case with the Stanford project) and studies of important 11-year periods (as was the case with the Cornell project) are certainly meaningful; but, a study of much longer duration, as long as nearly two centuries, is important for both political scientists and historians, especially for the latter. Thirdly, the project produced a large and important body of data and some preliminary analysis, both of which have been used in numerous analytical studies. Fourth, although there must have been some difficulties and painful moments involved in the cooperative project, the project seems to have maintained a high level of cooperation between the two groups of scholars—international relationists and diplomatic historians. All of these factors make this project a unique case of genuine and fruitful cooperation between the two fields.[13]

These three examples of collaboration have been discussed in order to give those with an interest in the possibilities of cooperation between these two fields confidence about the prospects for interdisciplinary efforts. Of course, we do not know how many attempts have failed because they rarely reach our ears. Metaphorically, if we look at the bottle of history–international relations cooperation, we see that only the bottom portion is filled while the upper part remains empty. In view of the great difficulties involved in two-field collaboration—difficulty in communication as well as different premises and purposes, not to mention other factors—we should rejoice at the filled part rather than mourning when we look at the empty portion of the bottle.[14] One can easily notice in cooperative works, including the Singer-Small project, an unevenness in both contribution and the end product—especially the latter. For satisfactory cooperation, both labor and the fruits of labor should be about equal between or among the parties involved.

What about suggestions for the future? If we begin with the possibilities of cooperative works in the future we can agree that despite the difficulties inherent in this kind of cooperation, the effort should continue because, however small the product, the effort itself is extremely valuable. Some, more political scientists than historians, are optimistic about the possibilities.[15] If each of the two sides tries to contribute according to its unique qualities and capabilities—historians with their rich, detailed understanding of historical events and international relationists with their theories and analytical tools—on a truly equal basis, the cooperation will not only be less difficult but also more fruitful.

An alternative to this collaborative approach is combining "the best of the two worlds" in one body. In essence, this is the approach adopted by both the Stanford and Cornell groups. Even if the two-group collaboration works out under ideal conditions, the project seems to end up with a multidisciplinary work rather than true interdisciplinary cross-fertilization. An integration of different disciplines in one person seems to be the best, probably the only, way to achieve a truly interdisciplinary effort. The obvious difficulty in this approach is learning the theories and techniques of another field, which is by no means easy. But, it is also not impossible. Social science methods may not be acquired instantly, but a full semester of additional work as a part of graduate training or a year of postdoctoral training will usually be sufficient to learn advanced-level social science methods. Acquisition of the historical research method is a much simpler task.

Whether the job of integrating the methods of history and international relations is accomplished by one person or by many persons, an important question concerns what should be done about the technical facilities and preparedness coming from the combined efforts of historians and internationalists? A first proposal calls for the building of a comprehensive data base on major issues in diplomatic history and international relations such as war and peace; massive teamwork is needed to push back the Michigan-type "data making" to at least 1500 A.D., and, one hopes, to the very beginning of human civilization, for both hard (numerical) data and soft (communication) data. The work sounds enormous, but, as we go back to early historical periods, the materials, both numerical and verbal, are less extensive and the task is therefore not an impossible one. Benefits to be gained from this kind of comprehensive data set will be great; political scientists can build theories on the bases of much firmer ground and historians will be able to make a systematic study of the whole of human history.

Once the data base is built, several methods of analysis can be used for both theory building and historical analysis. It may be "primitive," but the easiest and still a very useful method is the case study approach. Alexander L. George and others have made valuable comments on the "controlled comparative" case study method, and because this method can be applied to a process of practical policy making, it has drawn the attention of Earnest R. May and others.[16] As Melvin Small said, historians can make a significant contribution to this method with "rich case studies."[17] Another relatively easily adoptable method for the analysis of historical data is content analysis. This method has already been used effectively by the Stanford team and by other groups and individual researchers. With necessary care in the adoption of the unit of coding and the use of appropriate statistical methods, this method will be very useful for the analysis of historical data.

Two highly controversial but still very important categories for historical data analysis are the role of theory and the employment of statistical techniques. Most international relationists with an interest in historical data analysis would not have any problem here; convincing diplomatic historians still remains a difficult task. First of all, theories help historians see clearly the long-term trends and tendencies of historical events.[18] Theories are also useful for historians who seek to interpret historical events. Greater use of conceptual frameworks will also be useful; balance of power, alliance, deterrence, coercive diplomacy, and similar concepts have already been suggested.[19] The concept of "deterrence" will be especially important for a long time to come for both internationalists and diplomatic historians. The use of appropriate statistical methods for the analysis of certain data is still controversial even among internationalists; historians are much more difficult to convince about the use of any part of the statistical method. However, once numerical data is generated for a systematic study of historical events, statistical analyses are indeed necessary, almost inevitable. It is entirely appropriate for historians to go all the way to the "causal analysis" to trace the proper "path" of causal connections among variables, in addition to correlation, multiple regression, factor analysis, and other minor statistical techniques according to the nature of the data and the objectives of the particular analysis. Modern history is, alter all, a "causal history," and finding causal factors for historical events is a most important task for historians.[20]

Two more techniques should be added: one is simulation and the other the general systems approach. J. David Singer and others have already suggested the usefulness of simulation for historical data.[21] Running simulations with historical data, with either men or machines or a combination of the two to check for alternative possibilities for historical events, is a useful device to increase our understanding of past events and to explore future possibilities in policy making. The basic assumption in this approach is that what has happened in the past was only one of several possibilities and that the policy adopted was not the only possible policy. For both research and classroom instruction, this method will be helpful for historical data. Either consciously or unconsciously, many are using a limited-scale systems framework. Here, the proposal calls for the adoption of the "general systems" approach for the analysis of historical data. Even though diplomatic history deals with only a small and particular segment of history, researchers in the field now tend to investigate practically all aspects of a nation or a society, sometimes even the totality of the whole world; to look at the given subject under investigation as a whole seems to be not only desirable but also necessary.[22]

None of the methods of data analysis suggested here is new. A point to be made clear is that many useful social science methods are available for diplomatic historians as well as for internationalists; much more important, we need open-mindedness, versatility, and imaginativeness as well as technical skillfulness in dealing with the strategy of historical data analysis.

The last part of the proposal concerns the end product of the cooperative or one-man interdisciplinary enterprise. All of the products of the three cooperative projects reviewed earlier and similar products from minor projects are useful, and we should have more of them in the future. However, they are political science or international relations works using historical data; what we also need in the future are works of the other kind—historical studies using theories and techniques of international relations. It is desirable that a group of historians adopt theories and techniques of both social and natural sciences and that a mixed group of students in history, international relations, and social and natural sciences produce histories using social science theories and techniques. Further, we should move forward to produce well integrated works of history and international relations; here we want neither international relations work nor a historical one, not even a work combining international relations and history, but a truly integrated work which may be called "an international relations history." Then a new problem would arise: since the product is neither history nor international relations, it would not be accepted by most in either field. But it will be both a history and an international relations work at the same time, and it will be a valuable product in that sense. Works along this line already exist: Alexander L. George's book, mentioned earlier, *Deterrence in American Foreign Policy*, and Melvin Small's *Was War Necessary?* George's work truly is not a full integration of the two fields; rather, it is a work of international relations with history. Small's book contains more history than international relations.[23] But these pioneering works are wonderful examples of the kind we would like to see more in the future. After all, the two fields are complementary, each with its own strengths and its own uniqueness. Our hope is for new progress from this marriage.

It has been confirmed that history has still some role to play in works in international relations; that, in view of current trend, this role will surely diminish in the future; and that the theory and methods of international relations have a small role in diplomatic history. In this age of specialization, the situation cannot be otherwise. Because of this tendency for specialization, many of the works in the two fields have been achieved, and these accomplishments should be commended. However, while congratulations are due for the accomplishments of specialization in diplomatic history and international relations, future efforts are recommended for interdisciplinary cooperation and for the integration of the data, theories, and methods in the two fields. Of course, this suggestion goes against the general trend in the two fields, and much hesitation and resistance are expected. Despite the difficulties of resistance, hopes for new products from the cross-fertilization are also high. The standard works in the two fields will surely sustain the two in the future; but, only the kind of special efforts suggested here will bring new, even unusual results.

## NOTES

1. *The Book Review Digest*, published between 1964 and 1985.
2. The few monographs with a totally quantitative approach include: Nazli Choucri and Robert C. North, *Nations in Conflict: National Growth and International Violence* (San Francisco: Freeman, 1975); Manus I. Midlarsky, *On War; Political Influence in the International System* (New York: Free Press, 1975); Bueno de Mesquita, *The War Trap* (New Haven, CT: Yale University Press, 1981); Stephen M. Meyer, *The Dynamics of Nuclear Proliferation* (Chicago: The University of Chicago Press, 1984).
3. Paul Gordon Lauren, "Diplomacy: History, Theory, and Policies," in Lauren, ed., *Diplomacy: New Approaches in History, Theory, and Policy* (New York: Free Press, 1979), p. 6. For a similar view, see Melvin Small, "The Quantification of Diplomatic History," in ibid., p. 69; Thomas J. McCormick, "The State of American Diplomatic History," in Herbert A. Bass, *The State of American History* (Chicago: Quadrangle Books, 1970), p. 123; Paul W. Schroder, "Quantitative Studies in the Balance of Power," *Journal of Conflict Resolution* 21(1977):4; Alexander L. George and Richard Smoker, *Deterrence in American Foreign Policy: Theory and Practice* (New York: Columbia University Press, 1974). p. 45.
4. Akira Iriye, ed., *Mutual Image: Essays in American-Japanese Relations* (Cambridge, MA: Harvard University Press, 1975); Iriye, ed. *Power and Culture; The Japanese-American War, 1941-1945* (Cambridge, MA: Harvard University Press, 1981); Morrell Heald and Lawrence S. Kaplan, *Culture and Diplomacy: The American Experience* (Westport, CT: Greenwood, 1977); Frank A. Ninkovich, *The Diplomacy of Ideas: United States Foreign Policy and Cultural Relations, 1938-1950* (Cambridge, MA: Harvard University Press, 1981).
5. Thomas H. Etzold, "Interdependence 1976" *Diplomatic History* 1:35-45; Akira Iriye, "Culture and Power: International Relations as Intercultural Relations," *Diplomatic History* 3:115-128; Frank A. Ninkovich, "Ideology, the Open Door and Civilization as Ideology," *Diplomatic History* 10:221-245.
6. Etzoid, "Interdependence 1976" *Diplomatic History* 1(1977): 34-45.
7. Alexander L. George, "Case Studies and Theory Development: The Method of Structured, Focussed Comparison," in Lauren, ed., *Diplomacy*, p. 45.
8. Small, "Quantification of Diplomatic History," p. 87.
9. Small, "The Quantification of Diplomatic History, pp. 86-87; Lauren, "Diplomacy: History, Theory, and Policy," pp. 11-13; Schroder, "Quantitative Studies," pp. 19-20; Ole R. Holsti, "Historians, Social Scientists, and Crisis Management; An Alternative View," *Journal of Conflict Resolution* 24(1980):665.
10. Robert C. North, "The Stanford Studies in International Conflict and Integration," in Frances W. Hoole and Dina A. Zinnes, eds., *Quantitative International Politics: An Appraisal* (New York: Praeger, 1976), pp. 349-353; Ole R. Holsti, *Crisis Escalation War* (Montreal:McGill–Queen's University Press, 1972); Holsti, "The 1914 Crisis," *American Political Science Review* 59(1965):365-378; Holsti, Robert C. North, Richard Brody, "Perception and Action in the 1914

Crisis," in J. David Singer, ed., *Quantitative International Politics: Insights and Evidence* (New York: Free Press, 1968), pp. 123–158; Dina A. Zinnes, "The Expression and Perception of Hostility in Power Crisis," in *Quantitative International Politics*, 85–122.

11. See North, "The Stanford Studies," pp. 350–353; Holsti, *Crisis Escalation War*, pp. 2, 365.

12. Richard Rosencrance, et al., *Power, Balance of Power, and Status in Nineteenth Century International Relations*, International Studies Series, vol. 3 (Beverly Hills, CA:Sage, 1974); Brian Healy and Arthur Stein, "The Balance of Power in International History," *Journal of Conflict Resolution* 17(1973):33–61; Schroder, "Quantitative Studies," pp. 13–22; Healy and Stein, "A Final Rejoinder," *Journal of Conflict Resolutions*, pp. 57–74; Melvin Small, "Doing Diplomatic History by Numbers," *Journal of Conflict Resolutions*, pp. 23–24; Alan Alexandroff, Richard Rosencrance, and Arthur Stein, "History, Quantitative Analysis, and Balance of Power," *Journal of Conflict Resolution*, pp. 35–56.

13. Some of the procedures and findings of the project are reported in Melvin Small and J. David Singer, *Resort to Wars; International and Civil Wars, 1816–1980* (Beverly Hills, CA: Sage, 1982); Small and Singer, *The Wages of War, 1816–1965: The Statistical Handbook* (New York: Wiley, 1972); J. David Singer, ed., *The Correlates of War I; Research Origins and Rationale* (New York: Free Press, 1979); Singer, Stuart Bremes, and John Stuckey, "Capability Distribution and Major Power War, 1820–1965," in Bruce Russett, ed., *Peace, War, and Numbers* (Beverly Hills: Sage, 1972); Melvin Small and J. David Singer, "The Diplomatic Importance of States, 1816–1970: An Extension and Refinement of the Indicator," *World Politics* 25(1973):577–599; J. David Singer, "The Correlates of War Project: Continuity, Diversity, and Convergence," in Hoole and Zinnes, eds., *Quantitative International Politics: An Appraisal*, pp. 21–42.

14. Small, "Quantification in Diplomatic History," pp. 70, 72, 87. In his December 4, 1986, communication to the author, Melvin Small indicates that his experience of collaboration with the political scientists was satisfactory.

15. Holsti, "Historians," p. 665; George, "Case Studies," p. 45; Samuel F. Wells, "History and Policy," in Lauren, *Diplomacy*, p. 270.

16. For case studies, see George, "Case Studies," pp. 46–47; Singer, *Correlates*, p. 186; Wells, "History and Policy," p. 270. For the use of history for policymaking, see May, *Lessons of the Past; The Use and Misuse of History in Foreign Policy* (London: Oxford University Press, 1973); Richard E. Newstadt and Ernest R. May, *The Uses of History for Decision-Making* (New York: Free Press, 1986); Lauren, "Diplomacy: History, Theory, and Policy," p. 9; Wells, "History and Policy," p. 273; Lawrence Evans, "Dangers of Diplomatic History," in Bass, ed., *The State of American History*, p. 143.

17. Small, "The Quantification of Diplomatic History," p. 86.

18. Hubert M. Blalock, a major scholar in the field of social science methodology, has made interesting remarks on the subject in *Basic Dilemmas in the Social Sciences* (Beverly Hill, CA: 1984), pp. 86–99.

19. For an example of the use of the conceptual framework, see Paul Gordon Lauren, "Theories of Bargaining with Threats of Force: Deterrence and Coercive Diplomacy," in Lauren, *Diplomacy*, pp. 183–211, especially pp. 188–192, 192–196; Robert V. Dingman, "Theories of, and Approaches to, Alliance Politics," in

Lauren, *Diplomacy*, pp. 245–266, especially p. 248. For the advocacy of theories, see Robert Jervis, "Systems Theories and Diplomatic History," in Lauren, *Diplomacy*, p. 239; Lauren, "Theories of Bargaining," p. 202; Schroder, "Quantitative Studies," p. 19; Dingman, "Theories," pp. 251–254.

20. For causal analysis, see Herbert B. Asher, *Causal Modeling*, Sage University Papers Series: Quantitative Applications in the Social Sciences, No. 07–003 (Beverly Hills: Sage, 1976); Hubert M. Blalock, *Causal Inferences in Nonexperimental Research* (Chapel Hill: University of North Carolina Press, 1961); Blalock, ed., *Causal Models in the Social Sciences* (Chicago: Aldine, 1971). Singer's advocacy in clear language is useful: *Correlates*, pp. 178, 188. Also see, George, "Case Studies," p. 44.

21. Singer, "Correlates of War Project," pp. 191–194; McCormick, "The State of American Diplomatic History," p. 126.

22. Since 1972, The General Systems Society has published annual yearbooks and many articles in this publication, especially the ones in the early issues, are important for understanding this approach.

23. Small, *Was War Necessary? National Security and U.S. Entry into War*, Sage Library of Social Research vol. 105 (Beverly Hills, CA: Sage, 1980).

# 4

# *A Literary Perspective on World Peace*

## Thomas J. Leach

From Homer to Tolstoy, writers have been giving us a literary perspective on war and peace. For many, this has become simply an endless repetition of the basic human themes of greed, lust, power, guilt, courage, and honor. The stories remain essentially the same; only the names are changed and the places.

There is much truth in this view, but a closer look at the literary trends of the past century will enable us to see a brighter, more meaningful picture. The analysis will include four parts: Part one will examine American transcendentalism's assertion that spirit and nature are unified; part two will examine the split between these two occasioned in literary naturalism; part three will examine the inclination of writers since World War II to look to science for the solutions to the puzzles of nature, and to find the answers increasingly absurd; part four will argue that science fiction, utilizing insight from mythology and transpersonal psychology, is affirming a reunion of spirit and nature. This new vision of an age-old insight provides the basis for a renewed belief on the part of modern man to transcend the hopelessness and absurdity that increasingly characterize twentieth century technological society.

I

"The essence of transcendentalism is to be found in Emerson's repeated statement that nature is a symbol of spirit."[1] Thus, for Emerson, Thoreau, and Whitman the world was a symbol of higher truth. Harmony could be perceived in nature, even though such authors were well aware of the processes of conflict, competition, and death. There was a natural order, reflecting a larger whole, and man's place in that scheme of things is apprehended through a continuing contemplation of and immersion in nature.

Further, much of the deeper significance of that interaction is perceived by man through intuition. Such insights are not the result of rational assessment or logical deduction. Thus, the writer may not prove incontestably that the individual is part of the larger plan, nor can he through empirical methodology demonstrate that the plan justifies or exemplifies spiritual truths. Rather, he must rely on expressions of his own perceptions, examples of his own insights, and hope the reader will eventually arrive at similar conclusions by embarking on a parallel journey.

Increasingly, during the 1830–1860 period, these writers and others, including Cooper, Poe, Hawthorne, and Melville warned about the tendency to rely too heavily on science and technology rather than the wisdom of the heart. Although each of these writers moved on to explore his own beliefs concerning the conflicts between head and heart or pragmatism and idealism, and while each is not grouped strictly within the transcendental group of writers by many literary scholars, they shared the vision of transcendent values and insights gained from nature and intuition.

In his *Leatherstocking Tales*, James Fenimore Cooper repeatedly demonstrated in all five volumes the way in which Natty Bumppo develops and reflects high ethical values derived from nature, from the Indians, and from the restraints of civil law. The tensions between the freedom of the wilderness and the responsibilities of society, between pagan virtues and Christian ethics, between civil law and moral choice, are resolved in a series of balances between the opposites which illustrate the primary belief that wholeness and health may be realized through a life in harmony with the world.

Throughout the *Leatherstocking Tales*, Natty manages a precarious balance between the opposing forces surrounding him. He does not, however, as most of the other characters do, side with one "good" side and oppose the "bad" side. Rather, he recognizes the strengths in both sides, and borrows from each accordingly. Further, he acknowledges weaknesses, or at least shortcomings, in both and eschews these. Herein lies the strength and wisdom of his moral vision: to blend wisely with conflicting traditions, utilizing the best from each world: English, French, Indian, and nature.

## II

This unity of Spirit and nature is split toward the end of the nineteenth century by the movement called naturalism. As Charles C. Walcutt has argued so persuasively in his excellent *American Literary Naturalism: A Divided Stream*, "when this mainstream of transcendentalism divides, as it does toward the end of the nineteenth century, it produces two rivers of thought. One, the approach to Spirit through intuition, nourishes idealism, progressivism, and social radicalism. The other, the approach to nature through science, plunges into the dark canyon of mechanistic determinism."[2]

The major naturalistic writers from Crane to Steinbeck have shown the increasing tendency of society to rely on the mechanistic view. Our own century has provided significant breakthroughs in science and technology. We see remarkable examples in all areas of the progress of science, and with that progress has come both an increasing reliance on science for the answers to all our questions and a decreasing belief in the Truth of the Spirit. We tend, obligingly, to ignore or overlook the problems created as a result of progress, choosing to emphasize instead the "more is better" approach made possible by science.

In his masterpiece of naturalistic writing, *The Red Badge of Courage*, Stephen Crane showed how those forces outside the individual increasingly limited his choices and determined his fate. The idealistic Henry Fleming goes off to the glorious adventure of the war filled with unrealistic illusions of what he might accomplish. As he confronts the reality of armed conflict, with maimed and dying comrades fleeing in terror from the real and imagined destruction facing them, he learns to modify his image of himself—and humanity. He sees clearly that he and all his comrades are like cogs in a huge mindless mechanism; that those gigantic forces clash blindly till one or the other is destroyed or unable to go on fighting; he also tempers his youthful courage with compassion, seeing that his friends are as helpless as he in the maelstrom of the martial conflict.

He affirms the value of humanity in conflict, seeing that he is capable of courage. He sees that a larger purpose may be served by the individual, even though in some respect he may appear insignificant. He even learns something of wisdom and humility, when he learns that the daring and dangerous action he has helped succeed is merely a diversion in relation to the main emphasis of the battle. Finally, he comes, as so many other characters in naturalistic fiction do, to feel victimized, dominated, intimidated, and frustrated by a world too complex and powerful to be understood or controlled.

The majority of naturalistic writers in the twentieth century, from Crane to Hemingway and Mailer, have portrayed the conflicts of war as the result of deterministic forces beyond the comprehension of the individual. Each person is merely a pawn caught up in the whirlpool of economic and political conflicts that lead finally to war.

Hemingway's contribution to a vision of peace in literature comes through his idea of a code, which is explored by an apprentice just learning about the world, and by an exemplar who has experienced much of the pain and conflict and now is willing to pass his wisdom along to a younger generation. "The code does not ask that a hero be fearless or entertain illusions about refuge or escape. But it insists that he discipline and control his dread and, above all, that he behave with unobtrusive though unmistakable dignity."[3] Also, "the code asks of a man that he try to impose meaning where none seems possible, that he try in every gesture he makes to impress his will on the raw material of life."[4] There are, indeed, fine qualities and good lessons to be learned from the Hemingway hero. "He is an exemplar for modern man who feels many times powerless in "a world he never made." But unlike the equally lonely and isolated heroes of many novels of the twentieth century, Hemingway's hero rejects attitudes of ignominy and abasement. Parts of a world are salvageable. A man knows when he does his work well, and earns pleasure and dignity from the knowing and doing."[5] His heroes inhabit a world of war, violence, and killing very similar to the world we all inhabit in the twentieth century. Yet, through the vision the code provides, he is able to maintain courage, dignity, and a personal sense of honor. "The great wonder is that he still hungers for life and is capable on so many occasions of tenderness and humaneness, and of the nobility of spirit that animates his tragedy and informs his vision."[6] These qualities provide a useful basis for a vision of an individual at peace with himself in a world of ongoing conflict.

## III

The themes of initiation, command, psychology of combat, and technology have been thoroughly explored by Peter G. Jones in his excellent study *War and the Novelist: Appraising the American War Novel.* In the chapter on initiation he comments on the influence of Crane and Hemingway in shaping subsequent perceptions. He also mentions the relevance of Jessie Weston's *The Quest of the Holy Grail* in providing the theme of a rite. Weston comments: "I think we shall not go far astray if we conclude that the test preceding, and qualifying for, initiation into the secrets of physical life, consisted in being brought into contact with the horrors of physical death, and that the test was one which might well end disastrously for the aspirant."[7] This initiation idea connects Hemingway with the traditional literature of war.

Jones believes Hemingway's contribution to the idea of initiation to be significant. Hemingway used dramatic structure, exploited a biased and unreliable narrator, and created an atmosphere reeking of existential angst that established a model for later writers.[8] Hemingway and Mailer furnish illustrations of the way in which war novels demonstrate that "choosing rationally, man establishes and maintains an opposition with the world that continuously defines him as man."[9] Jones believes the war novel normally has an ethical base, that either vents outrage at war's senselessness or describes a search for meaning in its dilemmas.[10]

Many of the novels show the destructive side of military conflict. The meaning, however, is almost always negative, as well. Fear, cowardice, death, anxiety, and spiritual numbness provide a dramatic focus for a great many novels from 1900 to 1960, including John Dos Passos's *Three Soldiers*, Richard Matheson's *The Beardless Warriors*, Irwin Shaw's *The Young Lions*, Harry Brown's *A Walk in the Sun*, Anton Myrer's *The Big War*, Joseph Heller's *Catch-22*, Norman Mailer's *The Naked and the Dead*, James Jones's *The Thin Red Line*, Humphrey Cobb's *Paths of Glory*, William Faulkner's *A Fable*, James G. Cozzen's *Guard of Honor*, Anton Myrer's *Once an Eagle*, John Hersey's *The War Lover*, Glen Sire's *The Deathmakers*, Tom Chamales' *Never So Few*, David Halberstam's *One Very Hot Day*, and John Sack's *M*. As varied as they are, however, they do not significantly extend our understanding of war and its effects. As Jones explains, "novels of command are . . . devoted to the political and sociological repercussions of military affairs. The men who wield high command in wartime exude an attraction not dissimilar to that of the Aristotelian dramatic hero: the protagonists are powerful figures; their decisions exert direct, vital influence on the fates of myriad lesser men who labor under them on behalf of the state and of the civil populace that it represents. In this literature weak men do not achieve flag rank. Among those who do, the most menacing flaw is an indiscriminate lust for power beyond the well-defined limitations of military power in American society."[11]

The ethical "ought," as Jones indicates, is a major concern in many of these novels. "Seldom far from the foreground of any of the war novels is the predicament of the individual who attempts to conduct himself in accordance with any rationally coherent set of beliefs."[12] In this regard, two novels clearly stand out as examples of the finest and most influential novels since World War II: Joseph Heller's *Catch-22* and Kurt Vonnegut, Jr.'s, *Slaughterhouse-Five*.

"Heller's Yosarian reflects in its totality the absurdity of the world, accepting only his own judgment as a moral criterion. Through experience he gains an insight into the absurd, which covers all his experience."[13] The black humor of the novel provides "a safety valve for pressures that might otherwise unbalance reason."[14] The constant tension and conflict, not just from men in war, but from individuals facing the governmental bureaucracy surrounding war, provides a major focus of Heller's novel. He "stresses the total dehumanization of individuals by the imponderable processes of the technological bureaucracy that conducts the war effort."[15] As Jones concludes, "More than any of the novels previously discussed, *Catch-22* demonstrates the fact of alienation in the world. Not religious, sexual, or social guilt, but the fundamental alienation of people from both human reason and emotion."[16]

Kurt Vonnegut's eloquent novel *Slaughterhouse-Five* cries out against the dark despair of an increasing technological meaninglessness. The novel is about survival and man's relation to the growing body of scientific knowledge. In his study of Vonnegut, Richard Giannone comments: "Science in our time has become a source of moral imperatives addressed to our deepest spiritual needs . . . . As we can tell from the model of the Gospels that Trout revises, the rival of science for belief is Christianity."[17] The novel is the story of the Allied attack on Dresden, Germany, on February 13, 1945. As a German POW, Vonnegut lived through that experience, and his subsequent novel is, in a sense, a purging both of the nightmare experience and the guilt he feels for the action. Dresden was a cultural, not a strategic, center. Its destruction by the Allied incendiary bombs was both an outrage against humanity and a negation of any possible moral basis for such destruction.

The novel deals with the nature of the violence in man, and, as Giannone indicates, "Vonnegut plumbs the dark forces in the human spirit. Sentimentality, egotism, blind patriotism, materialism, these are the enemy; and for Vonnegut they are the signal qualities of American life. Against them stand conscience and feeling."[18] The novel presents a complex, multilevel view of existence, war, and time. Through this often confusing collage of fictional and real events, Vonnegut manages to convey his genuine affection for the German people, his outrage for their loss—both of life and irreplaceable art work—and his belief that both sides have lost something of value in this all-out conflict: human decency.

In his struggle to survive the nightmare of the battle and its aftermath, Vonnegut comes to an overwhelming indictment of war and a corresponding endorsement for human love. He confronts the annihilation of Dresden squarely, issues the challenge that it was meaningless, urges that it not happen again, and ends by affirming the present moment as a meaningful response to the horrors of the past through the redeeming acts of the spirit of love.

In a subsequent work, *Happy Birthday, Wanda June,* Vonnegut retells the famous homecoming of Odysseus in a modern setting. The protagonist, Harold Ryan, is a professional soldier, who returns at the age of 50 in disguise to test his wife's fidelity and to wreak destruction on her suitors. Unlike Homer, who saw these acts as necessary and heroic, Vonnegut "shows how its emphasis on violent destruction, carried into our crowded, contingent world, turns man into a killer and persons into worthless objects of heroic exploitation. What served Odysseus well now endangers all life. To survive now we need compassion and mercy. Dresden and Hiroshima and Vietnam are sins against life, not victories."[19]

Thus, we can see Vonnegut bringing the traditional concepts of war and the hero full circle to a reconsideration of Homeric values to demonstrate that a shift in values and perspective is needed for a modern world. We cannot proceed into a future of computers, lasers, and nuclear weapons with a set of values and ideals that has left such a legacy of death and destruction since the Stone Age.

## IV

The traditional naturalistic novel, as we have seen, has demonstrated over the past century that individuals and countries become increasingly motivated and directed by forces outside themselves. In addition, these novels have shown that when inner-directed values have been important, they have tended to illustrate the validity of the Darwinian "survival of the fittest" or the materialistic values of "more is better."

The most positive statement about these novels within the context of this chapter are that: (a) a personal code may enable the individual to endure; (b) a perspective on both the individual and national levels points to destructive, counterproductive, and even absurd results; (c) many still view the age-old function of war as an initiation rite as valid; but many others remain uncommitted to international conflict as an extension of national policy; (d) the ultimate threat of nuclear annihiliation adds the final deterrent to the idea of war as a means of resolving international conflict.

As Eric Homberger concludes in his essay on the United States in *The Second World War in Fiction*, "at a deeper level, Heller's humour is serious, indeed even political. It is firmly based upon the perception (so widely to be observed in American war novels) that the old clarity between enemy and friend, them and us, was no longer meaningful in the conditions of modern warfare. *Catch-22* submerges its bitterness and irony, but its meaning is not to be mistaken: the old claims of patriotism and loyalty have, for the *Catch-22* generation, lost their power, have indeed become an obscene charade."[20]

These conclusions point toward a future of pointless aggression, nuclear annihilation, or total domination by some superpower. The alternative is clear: If we are to have peace, we must change our ways of thinking about human violence and conflict. The patterns of the past lead us further into the dark wood of despair. We must discover a new path, or reaffirm an old one: the spiritual perspective of the transcendentalists, while gaining from the experience of the past century and the insights of the naturalistic writers. We need a vision for a more peaceful world that acknowledges the differences, proposes syntheses and new models for cooperation and coexistence. As many writers have indicated, we are in a no-win situation. If one side loses, we all lose.

The major aspects of the spiritual way of knowing, which, as we have discussed, have lost emphasis in modern fiction—and modern life—are gaining a new emphasis in some of the science fiction/fantasy writings of the past few decades. Although no informed person would wish to argue that this body of work is uniformly inclined in the directions suggested by transcendentalism, there are quite a few of the better writers in this area who do.

Writers such as Arthur C. Clarke, Ray Bradbury, Robert Heinlein, Isaac Asimov, Theodore Sturgeon, Philip K. Dick, Marge Piercy, and Ursula K. LeGuin are pushing the boundaries of contemporary fiction toward a vision of humanity's future, one that includes the possibility of a more peaceful world. According to these authors, more spiritual values will have to gain ascendency over our current emphasis on materialism. Conscience, in other words, will have a direct bearing on policies and decisions at every level. Intuition will play an increasingly important part, as people come to see that logic is not the sole basis for wise solutions and, finally, women will assume their rightful place as equals in a world fit for humanity, not just one shaped by a macho vision for male egos.

All of this presumes that the vision of war and peace provided by fiction can be something more than a mirror to clarify hindsight. If we can only use fiction to re-view our mistakes, we may be doomed to keep repeating them. Historians have often said, "If we cannot learn from the mistakes of the past, we may be doomed to repeat them." However, we have not yet been able to use those lessons to envision a more peaceful world. Something more is needed. Perhaps the writers of the new generation, utilizing the spiritual insights of transcendentalism, tempered by the perspectives of naturalism, and added to the experience of modernism, may finally generate insights capable of providing the necessary catalyst— or blueprint—for a more peaceful world.

## NOTES

1. Charles Child Walcutt, *American Literary Naturalism, A Divided Stream* (Westport, CT: Greenwood, 1956), p. 10.

2. Ibid., pp. vii and viii.

3. Arthur Waldhorn, *A Reader's Guide to Ernest Hemingway* (New York: Farrar, Straus and Giroux, 1972), p. 26.

4. Ibid., p. 27

5. Ibid., p. 28.

6. Ibid., p. 29.

7. Peter G. Jones, *War and the Novelist: Appraising the American War Novel* (Columbia: University of Missouri, 1976), p. 7.

8. Ibid., p. 8.

9. Ibid., p. 9.

10. Ibid., p. 11.

11. Ibid., p. 13.

12. Ibid., p. 15.

13. Ibid., p. 23.

14. Ibid., p. 48.

15. Ibid., p. 49.

16. Ibid., p. 52.

17. Richard Giannone, *Vonnegut: A Preface to His Novels* (Port Washington, NY: Kennikat, 1977), p. 85.

18. Ibid., p. 87.

19. Ibid., p. 99.

20. Eric Homberger, "United States," *The Second World War In Fiction* (London: Macmillan, 1984), p. 205.

# 5
# *Music and International Relations*

## Estelle R. Jorgensen

My purpose in this chapter is twofold. First, I shall outline several social processes illustrative of the important role music plays in international relations and cite examples of each drawn from the literature in the history and sociology of music. Second, I shall sketch a theoretical framework in which the interface of music and international relations can be analyzed and suggest considerations for melding aspects of music and international relations in the future.

The list of social processes developed by the sociologist Henry Zentner[1] provides a useful perspective from which to view music and international relations. In particular, seven processes are of interest, namely, image preservation, loyalty maintenance, personification, socialization, information exchange, cooperation and competition. While there is no claim for exhaustiveness in this list, it does illustrate the variety of ways in which music contributes to, and is affected by, international relations.

### SOCIAL PROCESSES

*Image preservation* refers to the way in which a country as a collectivity is either seen, or imagines itself to be seen, by others. Presumably, a state does not wish to convey the impression that it is faltering or in decline, but rather, strives to project a collective consciousness—an image—that is envisaged by others to be stable or progressive. Image maintenance norms control, among other things, the means or the procedures by which this process is to be carried on.

Music provides an important means whereby heads of state may impress others with their personal political power and wealth and that of the state they represent. Combining as it may both sound and spectacle, it is a potent force for conveying the state's image. The history of Western music is replete with numerous examples,[2] witnessed by such musical patrons as James I, Louis XIV, Frederick the Great, and Pope Leo X.

Historically, music has been used in the context of image preservation on two types of occasions: first, at the celebration of dynastic marriages that were both familial and political events. The tradition of music as an integral element of marriage celebrations exemplified in those contracted between various European houses in the fifteenth and sixteenth centuries, for example in the Gonzaga dynasty of Mantua,[3] continues in the musical pomp and circumstance surrounding weddings in the contemporary European royal families, most recently those in the House of Windsor.

Second, music has long played an important role in political events. The arrivals of visiting ambassadors and heads of state have traditionally been marked with musical ceremonial and entertainment provided in their honor, as, for example, by Henry VIII's King's Musicke, an ensemble of singers and instrumentalists who travelled with the king to supply musical entertainment, and the elaborate displays of music and dancing arranged by his daughter, Elizabeth I.[4] Louis XIV's act of marking his military successes with an opera[5] illustrates a similar musical celebration to that of the Jewish women who greeted King Saul and David and their returning victorious armies with song and dancing: "Saul has slain his thousands, and David his ten thousands."[6] Moreover, music has been a central part of ceremonials associated with the coronation of heads of state, notably in the English royal houses where a long monarchical tradition persists.

A link between political ambition and the lavishness of ceremonial, suggesting that the greater the head of state's political ambition the more pretentious the musical display, is evident in the literature. Guglielmo Gonzaga of Mantua, for example, seized the political advantage of being seen to be "a model Christian prince" of the Counter-Reformation, and devoted himself to the erection of the ducal basilica of Santa Barbara at Mantua—a "dynastic temple" and a "theatre for Gonzaga politico-religious ceremonies."[7] Others, such as Karl Eugen of Württemberg,[8] impoverished their states to finance the excesses of their courts, especially the mounting of operatic spectacles. In recent times, international events such as the opening ceremonies of the Olympic games have included music as part of the proceedings to impress spectators with the political might of the host country.

*Loyalty maintenance* refers to the need to ensure that the members of the state remain loyal and patriotic, and their morale is sustained. The underlying assumption is that individuals have more or less choice to voluntarily leave (or escape in the case of countries whose borders are closed to emigration) if they are dissatisfied with what their country has to give them. The notion that, over the long run, some reward must be given to the citizenry so that they will desire to remain in a state, underlies this process which is governed by morale norms that specify the ways in which this is to be accomplished and the principles that are to govern its operation.

Examples of the role of music as a means whereby patriotism and a people's morale is enhanced may also be cited. It played an important part in the spectacle staged by Philip the Good as part of his strategy of rallying Burgundian nobles around his banner to fight another crusade,[9] constituted an agent whereby patriotic and revolutionary feelings were stirred in the French revolution,[10] and exemplified as well as contributed to the rising tide of European nationalism in the nineteenth century.[11] In Italy, for example, Giuseppe Verdi's operas, notable *Giovanna d'Arco*, *Attila* and *La Battaglia di Legnano*, evoked patriotic sentiment, and music contributed in a significant way to the Italian Revolution of 1848. This tradition of music's role as a means of loyalty maintenance continues, for example, in the present use of music in the military as a means of boosting morale, and the playing and singing of patriotic songs and hymns at important state events.

*Personification* denotes the process by which a country develops a sense of national identity; the ways in which it differentiates itself from another. This typically involves such visible and symbolic emblems as national anthems and flags, and is governed by identity norms that specify the ways in which this is to be accomplished.

Music constitutes an important means whereby a sense of national identity is developed. States have embraced national anthems written during wars and revolutions enshrining times of fervent action (for example, *La Marseillaise*) or penned during periods of comparative peace as contemplative songs (for example, *God Save The King [Queen]*).[12] Music has also come to symbolize the political aspirations of a people. Governments of small countries who have felt their indigenous musics to be under attack from external influences (for example, Sweden, Canada, Tanzania, Trinidad, and Jamaica), have intervened with policies designed to protect and promote the interests of their distinctive musical heritage.[13]

*Socialization* refers to the way by which the individuals within a country come to share a collective belief system and to act as responsible citizens in that country. It implies some blending or melding of individual belief systems in arriving at the collectivity, whether envisaged as the will of the people as a whole or of those in positions of power. As such, it is governed by ideological norms that dictate the procedures and means by which this is to be achieved.

Music has played an important socializing role since antiquity. Plato saw music (and, more broadly, the arts) as a central element in education within his *Republic*.[14] Moreover, the idea that "music should be 'thought of as an instrument of civic education' "[15] is certainly not a new one, as the internationally pervasive socializing role of folk songs demonstrates. The Chinese, for example, have a long history of ideological and political purpose in music exemplified, more recently, in the not entirely successful efforts to promote strict musical guidelines during the cultural revolution.[16] Similar efforts by other twentieth-century totalitarian states to control music according to their ideological aesthetics have had mixed success partly because musicians have long regarded their art as transcending national boundaries.[17]

The concept of a close tie between music and ideological change has been advanced by several writers. Conrad Donakowski, for example, shows how "the idea and practice of music in the romantic era were integral to the awakening of a more complete and democratic view of human nature and society."[18] He argues that musical impulse was translated into revolutionary rhetoric and programs of progressive education by means of similar evangelistic techniques to those used in Judaism and Christianity. Also, Jacques Attali[19] elaborates a theory of music as prophetic of political and economic order and change, and shows that the musical expression of the eighteenth century prefigured the political thought of the nineteenth century and, in turn, foreshadowed the political reality of the twentieth century.

A belief in the importance of the arts in education has led states to consider carefully the nature of music education in their schools and propose programs to promote their objectives. In the United States, for example, the American school music movement was at the vanguard of the common school movement during the mid-nineteenth century, the rationale being that music would help produce better citizens, promote the interests of a democratic state, and inculcate habits of order and discipline along with a greater reverence for God and a concern for one's fellows.[20] Similarly, the Hungarian adoption of a unified program of musical education devised by Zoltán Kodály in the 1940s was designed to protect and promote the heritage of Hungarian folk song that faced possible extinction without a program of mass education initiated by the government. [21]

The rise of internationally pervasive popular musics, particularly since World War II, has complicated this picture because such musics have at times criticized the state or rejected the traditional values and aesthetics underlying, not only Western art music, but other classical traditions and indigenous musics as well. Moreover, the growing internationalism in music during the twentieth century has necessitated socialization not only in the musics of a particular state, but in those of other nations—a fact that has further broadened the scope of socialization in and through music in state schools.

*Information exchange* is the process by which knowledge is disseminated either within the state or internationally. It is governed by communication norms that specify what is to be communicated by whom, to whom, in what form and under what circumstances, including both overt communication and espionage.

Music has historically formed an important avenue for international communication. Indeed, as John Dewey observes, "works of art are the only media of complete and unhindered communication between man [or woman] and man [or woman] that can occur in a world full of gulfs and walls that limit community of experience."[22] Not only have composers expressed political views on international events, as for example, in Beethoven's support of the ideals of the French Revolution and, later, of Napoleon,[23] but there are numerous examples of internationalism in musical themes themselves.[24] This is illustrated by a fascination with the East apparent in Mozart's opera *Die Entfürung aus dem Serail*, and the borrowing of themes from the music of other countries evident in Brahms's *Hungarian Dances* and Bizet's opera *Carmen*. Migration (either forced or voluntary) has resulted in acculturation, or a melding of various aspects of cultures—the indigenous and the new—illustrated in the development of jazz and the spreading of musics associated with religious minorities such as the Mennonites.[25] Internationalism in music education is also evident in the work of Carl Orff who derived inspiration in the development of the Instrumentarium, or distinctive instrumental ensemble that forms the basis for his *Schulwerk*, from the Indonesian gamelan and various African xylophones.[26]

Music has also provided a vehicle for propaganda and a cover for espionage. Not only did the Stuart kings find a "most persuasive vehicle for political propaganda in the elaborations of the court masque," but it was not unknown for musicians to combine their art with espionage abroad. Christopher Hogwood cites several examples:[27] Richard Coeur-de-Lion is reputed to have been discovered in captivity in the castle of Durenstein in Austria as a result of the efforts of the trouvère Blondel "who wandered Europe singing outside every prison and castle, until finally his song was answered by Richard." Pelham Humfrey, one of the most talented boys in the Chapel Royal, was sent to France by Charles II ostensibly to absorb the style and technique of Lully's "*violons vingt-quatre*," and on his return received an inordinately large payment of 200 pounds from secret service funds, although, according to Samuel Pepys, he was "not improved by his travels." John Dowland, musician-composer, was also paid from the secret service funds of James I when he returned from employment in the court of Denmark, and it was reported of Count St. Germaine "who made so much noise at that time, not only with his fiddle, but his mysterious conduct and equivocal character" that he had "now retired from the world."

Not only was music regarded as a propaganda weapon by rulers such as Emperor Maximilian I, whose Hofkapelle became almost unrivalled in Europe,[28] but musicians also devised song texts and opera plots to reflect political concerns or to offer political commentaries. Some of Jacquet of Mantua's motets, notably, "Cantemus Domino," "Jam nova perpetuo," "Quis Incredibili," and the state motet "Hesperiae ultimate invicto regi," underscored various aspects of his employer's political activities.[29] Also, Cornwell Rogers suggests that music, particularly massed choral music, was so well thought of as a propaganda weapon during the French Revolution that patriotic music and singers were exported to assist the revolution in neighboring countries.[30] Later, the Italian opera houses became symbolic battlegrounds during the *risorgimento*.[31]

International relations in respect of music have intensified in the twentieth century partly due to the vastly more important international communication in, about, and through music, notably the impact of phonograph records on cultural communication. In recent decades, the international marketing of records has made possible an unprecedented sharing of musics and musical knowledge, especially of that popular music marketed by the music industry mainly through the multinational companies. As a result of technological changes over the past several decades, it has been possible to use music as a propaganda agent in a manner unprecedented in the past.[32] These new technologies have also created such international problems as copyright ownership and record piracy, problems which international law and agreements have thus far not been entirely successful in addressing.[33]

*Cooperation* denotes the idea of individuals and groups within states, or of nations, working with each other, and rests on mutuality norms that are based on the mutual and complementary interests shared by those within a country or internationally. Mutuality norms control the procedures by which this is to be done and the limits to which it may extend.

Music has historically provided an important means of promoting political goodwill and peace between nations. Small or weak states have sought good relations with their larger neighbors or conquerers by means of musical flattery, as the portrayal of Francis I of Austria as a "godlike lawgiver from whom all Italy's blessings flowed" in an allegory presented at La Scala, Milan, illustrates.[34] Cooperation between, and exchange of musicians, however, has only been possible where political and diplomatic links were already in place, exemplified in the exchange visits by members of the Imperial and Gonzaga courts and those between various Italian city-states ruled by the Este, Gonzaga and Medici dynasties in the sixteenth century.[35]

In more recent times, the Council for Cultural Cooperation, established January 1, 1962, as one of the specialized committees assisting the Committee of Ministers in the Council of Europe, announced one of its objectives: "To preserve and develop Europe's cultural heritage, having regard to its diversity and to the specific contribution of each country, and to promote access to and appreciation of it."[36] This followed the Paris Convention signed by 15 member governments of the Council of Europe, in which each contracted to "take appropriate measures to safeguard and to encourage the development of its national contribution to the common cultural heritage of Europe;" to "encourage the study by its own nationals of the languages, history and civilisation of the other Contracting Parties and to "consult with one another within the framework of the Council of Europe with a view to concerted action in promoting cultural activities of European interest." Indeed, the Council for Cultural Cooperation has seen itself as "the first example of an international organization responsible for defining and implementing a program based on multilateral cooperation in the cultural field at the level of a major 'region.' ''[37] Its efforts in the field of music are documented in a series of studies published under its auspices[38] and its announced aim is to "democratise" music; to encompass and stimulate mass popular musical cultures rather than to solely promote the interests of classical European musical traditions.[39]

Several examples of internationally organized cooperation in music may be cited. The Berne Copyright Convention of 1886 enunciated the basic principle that "the creator of a work of music or a text is entitled to some kind of remuneration when the work is performed in any country that has ratified the convention. Other copyright conventions—the Copyright Convention (1952), Rome Convention (1961) and Phonogram Convention under the Geneva Convention (1971)—have subsequently aimed at the international protection of the rights of performers, phonogram companies, and broadcasting and television organizations. Various organizations have also promoted international cooperation through music. These include: UNESCO—through such bodies as the World Intellectual Property Organization (WIPO); the International Music Council (IMC)—which has consultative status with UNESCO—through its various affiliated organizations, the International Federation of Musicians (IFM), International Society for Music Education (ISME), and the International Federation of Producers of Phonograms and Videograms (IFPI), to name a few.[40] Moreover, goodwill visits by musicians have been made possible through international agreements for cultural exchange, such as U.S. bilateral agreements with the USSR and the People's Republic of China.

*Competition* refers to the process whereby individuals within a country or countries strive with others to acquire and control scarce and valued resources and is manifested politically, economically, and in other ways. It is governed by resource allocation norms that control the manner in which these goods and services are to be disbursed.

Music has long been a part of the system of economic exchange. Once musicians organized into guilds and entered into professional service, their art also became a business, one that expanded rapidly, especially in the nineteenth century as a result of technological change and mass marketing techniques. The mass printing of cheap music, the rise of the public concert, the promotion of musical virtuosi, and the growth of amateur involvement in musical performance during the later eighteenth and nineteenth centuries subsequently burgeoned into an internationalism in music in the later twentieth century in the wake of mounting technological change and international marketing. Popular music, in particular, came to be viewed as the "music industry" in which the profit motive assumed vital importance. Indeed, as Aaron Copland observes, "Music is no longer merely an international language, it is an international commodity."[41]

The impact of technological change and mass communication, especially over the past two decades, has been internationally pervasive. Phonograph record production, for example, is concentrated in the hands of a relatively few multinational companies funded principally by U.S. interests, all part of bigger media and hardware production concerns, and linked together through a network of holding companies and license deals. Moreover, the United States has dominated internationally by virtue of the size of the U.S. market. Such is the international marketing by multinationals that they not only operate in many countries but now refer to "mega-sellers," of sound recordings that sell billions of copies internationally. Further, the growing internationalism in music has generated tensions between those countries who have signed international agreements and treaties that monitor and regulate the "products" of the music industry and those who have not, between those who comply and those who do not.[42]

Small countries find their indigenous cultures under external pressure from the multinationals.[43] The tendency for folk musics to become spectacles removed from their natural social contexts and brought within the economic exchange system, stylistically altered and standardized for the purposes of sound reproduction, and held in low regard or even forgotten by some of the people, has led governments to take action, to sponsor indigenous musics and to help facilitate private enterprise in a bid to compete with the multinationals.

Interpretations of the impact of Western music on indigenous musics differ. Roger Wallis and Krister Malm suggest that the current international music scene generally seems to represent a trend to an overarching transculturalism, where an internationally pervasive Western popular music culture both contributes to, and is influenced by, musics of other countries. They see this as having either of two effects in the future: the "attainment of a global music culture available to almost everybody"; or "the emergence of a multitude of types of music arising out of new living conditions and new technologies, at the same time as traditional music is adapted to new environments. . . ."[44] Bruno Nettl paints a picture of diversity, of the survival of traditional world musics and their adaptation to the Western world. He argues that "the coming of Western music, rather than bringing about the homogenization of world music, has actually helped to make the twentieth century a period of great musical diversity." Here, he makes an important distinction between "modernization," or "the incidental movement of a system or its components in the direction of Western music and musical life, without, however, requiring major changes in those aspects of non-Western tradition that are central and essential," and "westernization," or "the substitution of central features of Western music for their non-western analogues, often with the sacrifice of essential facets of the tradition."[45] He suggests a trend toward modernization rather than Westernization and concludes:

If there is a general conclusion to be drawn from the ways in which the world's societies have responded to the coming of Western music, it is that each has tried, sometimes at great cost, to retain some significant degree of musical identity; and that each has found ways to symbolize, in its music, the positive, negative, and ambiguous aspects of its relationship to European-derived lifeways and values.[46]

## A THEORETICAL FRAMEWORK

I turn now to the suggestion of a theoretical framework in which the interface of music and international relations may be analyzed. Two assumptions are outlined. Together, they provide a basis for future action. The first is that while music is a universal phenomenon in the experience of humankind, musical meaning is not universal. While anthropologists and ethnomusicologists, for example, John Blacking,[47] have posited the notion of the universality of musical phenomena—that musical experience is common to all known societies from the simplest to the most complex—musical meaning is not universal in that it is not shared by all societies. There is a sense in which an individual from one culture may not fully enter into the musical experience of another in the same way as one who has been born and lived in that culture.

In an attempt to explain the phenomena of musical experience and the nature of musical meaning, some philosophers, for example, Susanne Langer,[48] have conceived of the musical event in terms of individual experience and paid insufficient attention to the social conditioning that is necessary in order for a person to interpret music. Others have seen the meaning of musical experience in sociological terms. Graham Vulliamy and John Shepherd,[49] for example, have viewed it in a Marxist context of ideological class struggle and argue (after Peter Berger and Thomas Luckman)[50] that the psychological construction of reality is itself socially construed in the sense that the social environment shapes the self-image to a large degree. Similarly, Edward Tiryakian[51] posits the notion of an assumptive frame of reference (AFR), the individual interpreting the actions of others (and his or her own) in the light of a unique perspective that is socially informed. Jacques Attali,[52] for example, sees music in politico-economic terms as the agent whereby power may be exercised. Once music entered into exchange, he argues, it lost its extra-musical contextual, mythical and mystical value and this led to its devaluation as it was exercised in the context of political power. On the other hand, some psychologists, notably, Robert Borger and A.E.M. Seaborne[53] suggest that heredity and genes may play a more important role in explaining causation in human behavior than had previously been thought by environmentalists, implying that a solely social explanation of human behavior—and by extension, of musical meaning—may be somewhat simplistic.

These different conceptions of musical meaning are reconciled when one recognizes that the psychological and social experience of music are in tension.[54] To focus attention on the individual experience and individually interpreted meaning of music does not negate the compelling importance of the social reality, of meaning that must be understood in terms of the structures and functions of music in society, and vice versa. Such a wider view takes account of those aspects of music that seem to lend themselves to intuitive apprehension and those that are more influenced by, or apprehended in, social and cultural terms.

Various philosophers of music including musicians, for example, Ferruccio Busoni and Charles Ives,[55] have described what they variously saw as a tension between what on the one hand may be represented as the substance, the inner spiritual quality of music, and the manner, the outer sensuous form or appearance as it were, of music. As Ives wrote, this inner substance seems to give some music a timeless quality, an appearance of moving in keeping with the flow of society so that it appears ever with us, in contrast to that music which "dates" or is seemingly left behind the societal flow because it relies upon outward appearance or form. Moreover, Friedrich Schiller[56] posits the idea of artists as both *in time*, in that they are children of their time, and *for all time* in that their work is intended to have lasting value. The view of music as constituting a dialectic of tension between substance and manner implies a similar dialectic in musical meaning, where meaning is apprehended both as an inner psychological experience and one that is principally informed by an understanding of its style and outward social manifestation.

Similarly, one might also conceive of a dialectic between the form of music and its function; between form, or that musical meaning to be found within the music itself in an understanding of its structure, or what Langer describes as its "significant form,"[57] and its function, that is, the purposes it fulfills within the social group and its extra-musical meaning.

Given that these polarities intersect—substance and manner, and form and function—it seems that substance and form are more individually apprehended and amenable to psychological analysis while manner and function are construed in more social terms and thereby suited to sociological analysis. Allowing that psychological interpretation is informed, in some degree, by social experience and vice versa, this allows a richer image of the nature of musical experience. While it may be true that a social explanation is couched at a higher level of generality than is a psychological explanation and is therefore more inclusive, it cannot replace the latter. A combination of approaches allows the true complexity of the picture to emerge.

I have elsewhere viewed the problem of the universality of music and the multiplicity of musics and musical meanings that these imply within the context of "spheres of validity," a concept borrowed from K. Peter Etzkorn (following Georg Simmel)[58] to denote sociomusical groups, each sharing a common view of the meaning of music where persons outside a particular sphere of validity do not share the same meanings as those within it. Moreover, spheres of validity are dynamic entities that are constantly in a state of "becoming." Given the assumption of a dialectic between the individual and social experience of music, this notion of a sphere of validity may be broadened to encompass tensions between individual and social interpretations of music, between substance and manner, and form and function of music.

Spheres of validity in music form, maintain themselves and decay in a variety of ways during the course of their life cycles, influenced by a variety of social institutions including the family, church, government, music profession and commerce, among others. The seven processes, identified above, illustrative of the role played by music in international relations provide evidence of only several of these influences, notably, those of government, commerce, and technological change, and thereby constitute an as yet incomplete picture.

The idea of music as a universal phenomenon without universal meaning has important implications for international relations. Spheres of validity may transcend political boundaries, for example, Western art music may be shared by individuals and groups in European states or beyond. They may be more or less contiguous with state borders to the extent that these circumscribe a particular culture within a unitary society. Or a plethora of overlapping or distinctly separate spheres of validity with a corresponding variety of musics may coexist within a given state, manifested in a variety of musical subcultures as is the case in Canada, the United States and Belgium, among others. In countries that have been colonized by Western Europeans, for example, Jamaica, a variety of musical meanings are apparent in the contrasts between Western art and folk music, and indigenous musics, some of which are influenced by the West. Evidence of musical imperialism is seen in the lower status accorded indigenous music in favor of the music of the old British Empire. In such "small countries," aspiration for political and economic independence causes them to promote the interests of their indigenous musics and to assert the validity of their own particular musical heritage.

The second assumption is that the Gaia Hypothesis[59] offers a view of planet earth as an interrelated dynamic system of organisms of different levels of complexity in delicate balance. Whatever affects one part of the ecosystem affects other parts. This hypothesis applies not only literally to human stewardship of the earth's environment but figuratively in the world of social affairs and international relations as well. It offers an alternative vision to that prescribed in a technological society[60] and suggests spontaneity and intuition as complements to deliberate rational behavior, and the possibility, indeed the necessity, of reflection on the validity of ends rather than the preoccupation with a quest for efficient means that become ends in themselves. It opens up debate, promotes new ideas and fresh images that threaten or even contradict those that undergird the rule of technology, and, in so doing, it places technology in a proper perspective and enhances the dignity of humanity within society.[61]

The variety of world musics is a precious heritage worthy of protecting and nurturing. As dwellers on planet earth, international goodwill and understanding are also purposes that are important to all human beings. To this end, various potentially conflicting social processes must be kept in balance: international competition with cooperation; hedonistic tendencies of nations toward personification and image preservation with the need for information exchange among them; and a state's concern for loyalty maintenance with the sense of a person's wider responsibility to the entire earth achieved through the process of socialization.

Music provides an important means whereby such a balance may be achieved. It offers evidence of competition and cooperation; personification and image preservation, and information exchange; and loyalty maintenance to a state and socialization of a sort that promotes internationalism in music. While its role may tend both toward or away from international understanding, the Gaia Hypothesis suggests that it be used in the context of international cooperation. Certainly, the socialization process constitutes a way this may be done. Within a state's educational system, music provides a means whereby students may be made aware not only of their own musical heritage, but of those of other countries as well.[62] States may also promote the exchange of musicians providing a continuing lifelong education for their citizens. Two examples of these processes at work may be seen in the continued development of the International Society for Music Education in promoting the interests of internationalism in music, and a widening interest by music researchers in ethnomusicology—the study of world musics—as a branch of serious study.

But music offer more. In a world oriented toward technology and materialism it enriches the life of the mind and the human spirit through an appreciation of the beautiful. Friedrich Schiller and Herbert Read follow Plato in his radical argument that the arts, among them music, are so fundamental to the educational process as to constitute education *through* the arts.[63] Others point to music's contribution to the imagination, indeed, as Aaron Copland[64] notes, music cannot be appreciated without the imagination. Not only does it enhance personal well-being, but if envisaged within the context of the Gaia Hypothesis, music can contribute to harmony in international understanding and relations.

## NOTES

1. Henry Zentner, *Prelude to Administrative Theory* (Calgary: Strayer, 1973), ch. 7.

2. See Christopher Hogwood, *Music at Court* (London: Victor Gollancz, 1980); Henry Raynor, *A Social History of Music from the Middle Ages to Beethoven* (New York: Taplinger, 1978) and *Music and Society Since 1815* (New York: Schocken, 1976).

3. Iain Fenlon, *Music and Patronage in Sixteenth-Century Mantua*, 1 (Cambridge: Cambridge University Press, 1980), p. 84.

4. See Henry Cart de La Fontaine, ed., *The King's Musicke: A Transcript of Records Relating to Music and Musicians (1460–1700)* (London: Novello, 1909); Edward F. Rimbault, *The Old Cheque-Book, or Book of Remembrance of the Chapel Royal, from 1561 to 1744* with intro. by Elwyn A. Wienandt (1872; reprint, New York: Da Capo, 1966); Hogwood, *Music at Court*, pp. 29, 30, 36.

5. Hogwood, *Music at Court*, p. 9.

6. Samuel 18:7 *Revised Standard Version*.

7. Fenlon, *Music and Patronage*, pp. 83, 116.

8. See Alan Yorke-Long, *Music at Court: Four Eighteenth Century Studies* (London: Weidenfeld and Nicholson, 1954), pp. 43–70.

9. See Hogwood, *Music at Court*, pp. 20–24.

10. See Conrad L. Donakowski, *A Muse for the Masses: Ritual and Music in an Age of Democratic Revolution, 1770–1870* (Chicago: University of Chicago Press, 1977), pp. 50–51.

11. See Arnold Perris, *Music as Propaganda: Art to Persuade, Art to Control* (Westport, CT: Greenwood, 1985), ch. 2.

12. For a survey of national anthems see Paul Nettl, *National Anthems*, 2nd. enlarged edition, trans. Alexander Gode (New York: Frederick Ungar, 1967).

13. See Roger Wallis and Krister Malm, *Big Sounds from Small Peoples: The Music Industry in Small Countries* (New York: Pendragon, 1984), chs. 3, 7.

14. For Plato's theory of education through art see his *Republic*, 3. 401–402; *Laws*, 2. 653–656, 7. 796–816.

15. Donakowski, *A Muse for the Masses*, p. 250

16. See Arnold Perris, "Music as Propaganda: Art at the Command of Doctrine in the People's Republic of China," *Ethnomusicology* 27, no. 1 (1983): 1–28.

17. Some musicians in Nazi Germany, for example, cooperated with the Germanization process in music and others did not. Hans Werner Henze, *Music and Politics: Collected Writings, 1953–81*, trans. Peter Labanyi (London: Faber and Faber, 1982), p. 30, mentions Karl Amadeus Hartmann who refused to allow his

compositions to be published or performed by the Nazis. Norman Lebrecht, *Discord: Conflict and the Making of Music* (New York: Universe, 1983), ch. 7, notes examples of musicians who fled into exile during the period leading up to, and during World War II.

18. Donakowski, *A Muse for the Masses*, Preface.

19. Jacques Attali, *Noise: The Political Economy of Music*, trans. Brian Massumi (Minneapolis: University of Minnesota Press, 1985), p. 4.

20. See Estelle R. Jorgensen, "William Channing Woodbridge's Lecture, 'On Vocal Music as a Branch of Common Education' Revisited," *Studies in Music* (University of Western Australia), no. 18 (1984): 1–32.

21. See *The Selected Writings of Zoltán Kodály*, Ferenc Bónis, Zenemukiadó Vállalat, eds., trans. Lili Halapy and Fred Macnicol (London: Boosey and Hawkes, 1974), pp. 24–33, 119–126, 160–162.

22. John Dewey, *Art as Experience* (1934; reprint, New York: Paragon, 1979), p. 105.

23. See Maynard Solomon, *Beethoven* (London, Toronto, Sydney, New York: Granada, 1980); J. H. Elliot, "The French Revolution: Beethoven and Berlioz," in Arthur Jabobs, ed., *Choral Music* (Harmondsworth [Middlesex], England: Penguin, 1963), pp. 201–216; Fan Stylian Noli, *Beethoven, and the French Revolution* (New York: International Universities Press, 1947).

24. See K. Peter Etzkorn, ed., *Music and Society: The Later Writings of Paul Honigsheim* (New York: Wiley, 1973), pp. 165–169, for a discussion of internationalism in music.

25. See Helen Martens, "The Music of Some Religious Minorities in Canada," *Ethnomusicology* 16, no. 3 (1972): 360–371.

26. See Carl Orff, *The Schulwerk*, vol. 3 of *Carl Orff/Documentation. His Life and Works*, trans. Margaret Murray (New York: Schott, 1978).

27. See Hogwood, *Music at Court*, pp. 9, 12, 16, 41–43.

28. See ibid, pp. 25–28.

29. See Fenlon, *Music and Patronage*, pp. 76–77.

30. See Cornwell B. Rogers, *The Spirit of Revolution in 1789: A Study of Public Opinion as Revealed in Political Songs and Other Political Literature at the Beginning of the French Revolution* (Princeton: Princeton University Press, 1949), pp. 25–26.

31. See Donakowski, *A Muse for the Masses*, ch. 10, especially pp. 242–243; Walter H. Rubsamen, "Music and Politics in the 'Risorgimento'," *Italian Quarterly* 5 (1961): 100–120; R. J. B. Bosworth, "Verdi and the Risorgimento," *Italian Quarterly* 14 (1971): 3–16 (suggesting some equivocation in Verdi's political views).

32. Kenneth Shore, "The Crossroads of Business and Music: A Study of the Music Industry in the United States and Internationally," diss., Stanford University, 1983 (Dissertation Abstracts International, 44/05A, p. 1233) notes that the multinationals have been able to shape public taste "not so much by a direct predetermined control by record companies over the music product, but rather by the exclusion of alternatives."

33. See Wallis and Malm, *Big Sounds from Small Peoples*, ch. 6; Helmut Steinmetz, "Copyright, Neighbouring Rights, and Piracy in Austria," in Kurt Blaukopf, ed., *The Phonogram in Cultural Communication* (Wien, New York: Springer-Verlag, 1982), pp. 141–150.

34. Donakowski, *A Muse for the Masses*, p. 242.

35. See Fenlon, *Music and Patronage*, chs. 3, 4.

36. Council of Europe. *An Experiment in Multilateral Cultural Cooperation in Europe: The Council for Cultural Cooperation*, 1972, p. 6.

37. Ibid, quoting articles 1, 2, and 3 of the Paris Convention (1954).

38. See Council of Europe. Council for Cultural Cooperation. *Music Industries and Creativity*. Cultural Policy Studies, ser. 4., 1983; *Technological Development and Cultural Policy*. Cultural Policy Studies, ser. 5., 1984.

39. See *An Experiment in Multilateral Cultural Cooperation in Europe*, pp. 20–22.

40. See Wallis and Malm, *Big Sounds from Small Peoples*, ch. 2.

41. Aaron Copland, *Music and Imagination* (Cambridge, MA: Harvard University Press, 1952), p. 18.

42. See Wallis and Malm, *Big Sounds from Small Peoples*, ch. 4. Ongoing problems are reported in the press, notably *Variety* and *Music Trades*, passim.

43. Ibid, p. 11. Also see pp. 12–15, and ch. 7, for a description of the specific actions governments have taken.

44. See ibid, pp. 297–302, for a discussion of the distinctions between transculturalism, cultural exchange, cultural dominance and cultural imperialism and pp. 324–325, for a sketch of future possible developments.

45. Bruno Nettl, *The Western Impact on World Music: Change, Adaptation and Survival* (New York: Schirmer, 1985), pp. xiv, 20.

46. Ibid, p. 165.

47. John Blacking, *How Musical Is Man?* (London: Faber and Faber, 1976).

48. Susanne K. Langer, *Philosophy in a New Key*, 3rd. ed. (Cambridge, MA: Harvard University Press, 1957).

49. Graham Vulliamy and John Shepherd, "The Application of a Critical Sociology to Music Education," *British Journal of Music Education* 1 (1984): 247–266; "Sociology and Music Education: A Response to Swanwick," *British Journal of the Sociology of Education* 5, no. 1 (1984): 57–76; "Sociology and Music Education: a Further Response to Swanwick," *British Journal of the Sociology of Education* 6, no. 2 (1985): 225–229.

50. Peter Berger and Thomas Luckmann, *The Social Construction of Reality: A Treatise in the Sociology of Knowledge* (1966; reprint, Garden City, NY: Doubleday, 1967).

51. Edward Tiryakian, "Sociology and Existential Phenomenology," in Maurice Natanson, ed., *Phenomenology and the Social Sciences*, (Evanston,IL: Northwestern University Press, 1973), 1: 199–201.

52. Attali, *Noise*, p. 19, points to three strategic uses of music by power: "to attempt to make people *forget* the general violence," "to make people *believe* in the harmony of the world"; and "to *silence*, by mass producing a deafening, syncretic kind of music, and censoring all other human noises."

53. Robert Borger and A. E. Seaborne, *The Psychology of Learning*, 2d. ed. (Harmondsworth [Middlesex] England: Penguin, 1982).

54. This theme is also discussed by John Shepherd (John Shepherd et al., *Whose Music?: A Sociology of Musical Languages* [London: Latimer, 1977], pp. 55–56), who suggests "an open-ended relationship between music and society."

55. Ferruccio Busoni, "Sketch of a New Esthetic of Music," and "Charles Ives, "Essays Before a Sonata," in *Three Classics in the Aesthetic of Music* (New York: Dover, 1960).

56. Friedrich Schiller, *On the Aesthetic Education of Man in a Series of Letters*, trans. and foreword, Reginald Snell (1954; reprint, New York: Frederick Ungar, 1965), pp. 50–55.

57. Susanne K. Langer, *Feeling and Form* (London: Routledge and Kegan Paul, 1953), p. 32.

58. See Estelle R. Jorgensen, *A Critical Analysis of Selected Aspects of Music Education* (Calgary [Alberta], Canada: Department of Educational Administration, University of Calgary, 1977), ch. 4; K. Peter Etzkorn, ''On the Sphere of Social Validity in African Art; Sociological Reflections on Ethnographic Data,'' in W. L. d'Azevedo, ed., *The Traditional Artist in African Societies* (Bloomington: Indiana University Press, 1973), pp. 343–373.

59. This hypothesis originally suggested to me by Professor Ronald Laura, is outlined in Fritjof Capra, *The Turning Point: Science, Society, and the Rising Culture* (1982; reprint, Toronto, New York, London, Sydney: Bantam, 1983), pp. 284–285. On the goddess, Gaia, see Charlene Spretnak, *Lost Goddesses of Early Greece* (Boston, MA: Beacon, 1981); I am indebted to Mary Reichling for the suggestion of these references. The female imagery here evokes the notion of a different perspective or ''voice'' beyond the masculine in human affairs. See Carol Gilligan, *In a Different Voice: Psychological Theory and Women's Development* (Cambridge, MA: Harvard University Press, 1982). A similar systems view of the world is offered in Verner Bickley and John Philip Puthenparampil, *Cultural Relations in the Global Community: Problems and Prospects* (New Delhi [India]: Shakti Malik, Abhinav Publications, 1981).

60. Jacques Ellul, *The Technological Society*, trans. John Wilkinson (New York: Vintage, 1964).

61. K. Peter Etzkorn, ''Notes in Defense of Mass Communication Technology,'' in Blaukopf, *The Phonogram in Cultural Communication*, p. 103, suggests that mass communications technology has much to offer society, especially in enabling the individualization of musical experience and making it more widely available.

62. Christopher Small, *Music—Society—Education*, 2nd. rev. ed. (London: John Calder, 1980), ch. 9, offers an approach to music education consistent with these ideas.

63. See Reginald Snell's Introduction in Schiller, *On the Aesthetic Education of Man*, p. 17; Herbert Read, *Education Through Art* (London: Faber, 1943), p. 1.

64. See Copland, *Music and Imagination*, p. 7.

# 6
# *Justifying War: A Philosophical Critique*

Jeffery L. Geller

## THE NATURE OF PHILOSOPHICAL TREATMENTS OF WAR

Not only did the Vietnam War raise practical questions concerning the military and political failure of U.S. policy in Southeast Asia, it also raised a number of questions that come under the purview of political ethics. Numerous articles and books have appeared in the aftermath of the war that examine the ethical implications of modern military combat. One particular line of reasoning, because of the deep and enduring influence it exerts on philosophical discourse, is worthy of special consideration. Warren Steinkraus describes this reasoning and evaluates its influence in the following passage:

There are some values greater than life itself, and these great principles must be preserved no matter what the cost. Currently, some thinkers are quite prepared to risk nuclear chaos in order that ideal principles will not be thwarted. This version of the justification for war is heard so frequently that it begins to have the status of one of those holy truths of mankind no sane person would dare challenge. Whether the argument is relevant anymore, if it ever was, is something that needs to be looked into by a cautious philosophical mind. Philosophers by the hundreds have rushed to the colors, in both East and West, with apologias of this sort.[1]

This essay will examine critically the attempt to justify war in terms of a trade-off between the value of human life and the principle of justice.

Though there has been a lively debate concerning the applicability of utilitarian principles to the analysis of war, utilitarians are understandably reluctant to discuss strafing, spraying of napalm, and the use of pellet or needle-spraying anti-personnel weapons against rural villages in the name of maximizing happiness.[2] With respect to the questions of the moral legitimacy of war (*jus ad bellum*), the main representative of utilitarianism is, somewhat surprisingly, the just war tradition. Stanley Hoffman criticizes Michael Walzer's philosophy of war for the compromise Walzer strikes between utilitarianism and absolutism.[3] In fact, the utilitarian strain in Walzer's thought is an integral feature of the just war theory, which contains a clause forbidding wars in which the probable benefit, measured in terms of objectives sought, is not favorably proportional to the degree of destruction necessary to achieve those objectives. A substantial portion of the philosophical discussion which addresses the question of *jus ad bellum* is framed in this same mixture of utilitarian and nonutilitarian precepts. Whereas the principle of proportionality (cited above) exemplifies the utilitarian strain in the just war tradition, the nonutilitarian strain includes considerations about the intrinsic moral character of the cause for which and the intention with which a nation goes to war. This essay will concentrate on the principle of proportionality.

The precepts which constitute the just war doctrine are regarded by authors working within the tradition as permanent and universally applicable. To outsiders, however, the alleged permanence and universality are anything but self-evident. As a consequence, contemporary just war theorists are as concerned with justifying their doctrine as they are with justifying war. Several authors attempt to establish the relevance of just war theory to contemporary political affairs.[4] Anthony Kenny claims that the just war tradition offers the best theoretical framework within which to consider moral issues involving war.[5] Walzer's *Just and Unjust War*, which will be the main focus of this chapter, gives a philosophically sophisticated account of the moral problems surrounding war from within the system of rules provided by the just war framework.[6] As indicated above, the system of rules elaborated and defended by these theorists is conceived as basically stable through major historical changes. Citing Walzer, Gilbert notes that "the ethical criteria for judging goals and conduct of war have objectivity and historical stability across special epochs and major theory changes."[7] The unyielding monolithic structure of these philosophical treatments of war, I will argue, impedes philosophers working within the just war tradition in their pursuit of international peace.

Despite Descartes's best efforts, philosophical argumentation does not take place in a rarified atmosphere free of presuppositions. Much of contemporary philosophical literature concerning war suffers from a deficiency in the sort of criticism that makes us aware of our implicit presuppositions. A few theorists recognize this deficiency and attempt to correct it by investigating our conceptualization of war. Ronald J. Glossop, in *Confronting War,*, devotes one chapter to the conceptual framework in which such problems are discussed.[8] In their article, "Conceptualizing 'War'," Benjamin A. Most and Harvey Starr examine various possible conceptualizations and assess their utility in "peace research."[9] John J.

Weltman, writing in the *International Studies Quarterly*, appeals for us to "examine the underlying intellectual assumptions" of our theories of international politics.[10] He argues persuasively that we ought to investigate the "assumptions and categories that the investigator brings with him into the analysis."[11] According to Weltman, "We must be aware of the extent to which our intellectual predispositions follow from those traditions of thought about social reality in which we are embedded, often without realizing the extent to which our attitudes are so constrained."[12]

Carrying the process of philosophical self-criticism one step further, some writers call for a reorientation of our thinking. According to Iredell Jenkins, "Our initial mistake in dealing with the issues of war and peace is to employ the wrong categories."[13] In "The Epidemiology of Peace and War," Francis A. Beer advocates the adoption of a more scientific perspective in "polemology" or "peace science."[14] John Somerville, in his book, *The Peace Revolution*, states that "paxology" (the study of peace) requires a basic change in our way of thinking.[15] Writing in the *Monist*, Edward Black states that "The terrifying power of modern weapons makes it imperative to rethink . . . the function of war."[16] What makes modern war so problematic, according to these theorists, is as much our failure to develop an adequate basis for discussion as the possibility of reducing the earth to a lifeless cinder.

In response to the imperative to reappraise our thinking about political ethics, this essay will investigate the structure of several contemporary philosophical treatments of war. My first objective will be to analyze the pattern of discourse in which war is justified in terms of the trade-off between human life and justice. My second objective will be to determine whether the conceptual frameworks that underlie this discourse conform to such standards of rationality as openness to counterarguments. Third, I will ascertain whether these frameworks adequately serve the purposes they are intended to serve. Finally, in the event that they fall short, I will try to discover their weaknesses as a first step toward establishing a more adequate conceptual framework.

## A CRITICAL ANALYSIS OF THE JUST WAR MODEL

The last two decades have witnessed a resurgence of interest in a form of argumentation with a long and celebrated history in the philosophy of international affairs. With its origins in the thought of Plato, Aristotle, and Cicero, it found mature expression in the works of Ambrose, Augustine, and Aquinas and was further elaborated by such theorists as Vitoria, Suarez, and Grotius.[17] Several contemporary authors, including Murray, Ramsey, Walzer, Wellbank, Phillips, Johnson, Kenny, and Teichman, place themselves expressly in the intellectual line which descends through Augustine and Aquinas to the present. The general contour of the conceptual framework shared by these philosophers since the time of Aquinas is well known: theoretical positions on the legitimacy of war are placed on a scale ranging from "pacifism" to "realism" with the "just war" theory occupying the middle position. Even before elaborating the details of this conceptual framework, problems begin to arise. One of the lessons we have learned over the last two centuries is that the language we "use" is not an innocent and submissive slave to our desire for truth. We, as language users, are also products of language, constrained by the conventions that govern our discourse.

In the case under consideration, the outcome of the debate is largely prejudged by its structure. As one would expect, Aquinas imported a strong Aristotelian influence into the discussion, an influence with which many of us sympathize, but which is nevertheless open to criticism.[18] Owing to the general structure of Aristotelian ethics, there is a presumption in favor of the moderate middleground between the two extreme positions. The "golden mean" appears to be the obvious rational choice over both excess and deficiency of antiwar sentiment. The just war position has the virtue of accommodating both our deep desire for peace and commitment to what might be termed "human rights." War is rightfully considered evil, but is nevertheless deemed necessary under certain circumstances to combat the evil of violated rights or what Augustine refers to as "unjust peace."[19] Advocates of either "extreme" position are chastised for the moral idealism or dangerous militarism which are presumed to be essential characteristics of the respective ideological orientations. But since conceptual structure influences the nature and outcome of the inquiry, we might suspect that this apparent defect results as much from the structure of the discourse as from the intrinsic qualities of either ideological position. Delving deeper into the just war theory, I will demonstrate that this suspicion is warranted.

Philosophers who have adopted the just war model currently face a dilemma. This century has witnessed several changes that have far-reaching implications for that model. The two reasons for linking war and morality are, first, to discover conditions under which war is justified, and second, to discover conditions under which its harmful effects can be mitigated. The first is normally designated *jus ad bellum*, the second *jus in bello*. Though the two fields of investigation can not be strictly separated, I will concentrate primarily on the former. Just war theorists from Augustine on carefully specify the conditions under which a nation is morally justified in resorting to war. These conditions include the following:

1. The cause must be just.
2. The intention behind the decision to go to war must be just: the sort of intention which most clearly qualifies arises out of the desire to defend one's territory against aggression.

3. There must be a favorable "proportionality," a beneficial balance of good and evil effects of the (potential) war.[20]

Conditions (1) and (2) have fallen on hard times: their utility is so narrowly circumscribed that they are virtually irrelevant. Since the most interesting controversy surrounds the principle of proportionality, I will restrict my remarks to condition (3).

As mentioned above, the proportionality clause introduces an element of utilitarianism into the discourse. Within the framework of the just war model, one is expected to weigh the losses (including those of the enemy) which are likely to occur in battle against the probable gains in furthering one's own cause if one has the good fortune to prevail. The most problematic cases from the moral point of view are those in which massive numbers of more or less innocent people suffer and die on a thoroughly democratized battlefield. Whereas it may be possible to calculate the value of soldiers' lives, in terms or "manpower loss" or "body count," the lives of civilians are difficult to figure. To avoid the difficulty of assigning even an approximate worth to the life of a harmless child and in deference to the virtually universal taboo against murder, condition (3) has as a corollary that the activities of war respect the distinction between military personnel and civilians.

With the advent of mass aerial bombardment and deliberate anti-morale campaigns, which inevitably inflict heavy civilian casualties, modern war is at least, prima facie, in conflict with this corollary of condition (3). Since factory production is an integral part of the war machine, it is impossible to imagine war between technologically advanced nations which does not directly affect the populations of industrialized urban areas. In effect, the boundary between combatant and noncombatant is obliterated in modern warfare. Whereas in the past battles were fought by small minorities of trained warriors, today's battlefield is less exclusive. The Luftwaffe attacks on London and the Allied incendiary bombing of Dresden inflicted as many casualties on frightened children as on trained military personnel.

Paradoxically, though civilians are more directly affected by modern warfare than ever before, military personnel are less involved in the business of war. Many members of the U.S. armed services view themselves primarily as civilians in uniform. In their estimation, they are at no greater risk of falling in battle than dock workers, taxi drivers, or short-order cooks. Most members of the infantry, according to David R. Segal, view themselves as employees working for a company with excellent educational benefits, a company that encourages employees to "be all that [they] can be."[21] Other soldiers join the service not because the military is "a great place to start" but to secure the welfare of their families. Significantly, the U.S. Army currently has more dependents than soldiers. Advertizing slogans such as "We're not a company. . . . We're your country!'' which attempt to offset the prevailing view and to attract patriots to military service have proven only marginally effective.

One should not be misled into believing that the attitudes of education-minded or family-oriented soldiers deviate from the official view of present-day military service in the United States. The Gates Commission, charged with assessing the feasibility of an all-volunteer military, treated the armed services as just another sector of the economy, one which must compete with business and industry for the available labor. This position would be untenable if it weren't for the fact that the distinction between combatants and noncombatants has largely been eroded. Noting this fact, Ramsey maintains that total war *means* that there are no noncombatants. "The concept of non-combatancy has," he alleges, "been jettisoned from our minds."[22] As early as 1935, John Dewey observed that the "gulf that once separated the civilian population from the military has virtually gone."[23]

In light of these considerations, theorists working within the just war framework are forced either to abandon condition (3) or to declare all modern war unjust. Considering the extremely compelling intuition that killing innocents is wrong, and the Aristotelian structure of the discourse, neither of the two appears wholly satisfactory. The prevailing sentiment appears to be in favor of declaring modern war inherently immoral. Within the framework of the debate, however, this position is viewed as ignoring or underestimating the evil of injustice.

Obviously, condition (3) is even more problematic in the context of nations armed with nuclear weaponry. On this issue, Clausewitz's theory is highly instructive. He claimed to have observed two tendencies which, when conjoined, produce a very dangerous scenario. First, war tends to be seen as an extension of politics, that is, as another means in addition to diplomacy, economic sanctions, and similarly moderate measures, of accomplishing political objectives. Second, the logic of war leads naturally to increasing escalation. In Clausewitz's words,

If one side uses force without compunction, undeterred by the bloodshed it involves, while the other side refrains, the first will gain the upper hand. That side will force the other to follow suit: each will drive its opponent toward extremes, and the only limiting factors are the counterpoises inherent in war.[24]

Together, these tendencies indicate that war is both probable, in the event that all other expedients fail, and devastating, considering the destructive potential if war should escalate to the use of thermonuclear weapons. Though it is argued that such weapons have altered our thinking about war, so that either it can no longer be conceived as an extension of politics or so that it must be carefully "limited," the status of this utterance is more a hypothetical imperative than a report of fact. As Weltman correctly observes, "There is no automatic prohibition against war in the contemporary world."[25] He argues persuasively that the utterance in question is not a report that the change of thinking is a fait accompli. Rather, it is a directive that if we want to survive, we must conspire to prove Clausewitz wrong.

The possibility of having a war escalate to global annihilation obviously provides a strong incentive to reject all modern warfare. In the face of a phenomenon so different from traditional war that it might warrant a new name (something like "modernwar") or at least a hyphen ("modern-war"), philosophers are more strongly repelled by war than ever before. Indeed, the purpose of philosophical thinking about war seems to have changed. No longer are philosophers content to search for ethico-epistemic criteria for discriminating good wars from bad. According to Robert Ginsberg, "The heart of the philosophic problem of war is action: what steps ought we to take to stop, control, minimize, prevent, or eliminate war?"[26] But to theorists under the influence of the just war model, such "pacifism" is difficult to maintain with the call to justice beckoning in the background. The structural constraints imposed by their mode of discourse prevent them from seeing the need to oppose war with wholehearted commitment.

## TOWARD THE CONSTRUCTION OF AN ALTERNATIVE CONCEPTUAL FRAMEWORK

One way to resolve the dilemma faced by just war theorists is the following: the idea of resorting to war as a means of settling political disagreements could be relegated to the realm of the unthinkable. This suggestion is best understood by analogy. Consider the claim made by Levi-Strauss that the origin of the incest taboo is unthinkable.[27] In turn, this renders violations of the taboo equally unthinkable. In the realm of social and political thought, Amitai Etzioni maintains that the only alternative to policing society, which will ultimately prove futile in any case, is to make such acts as selling highly carcinogenic agents or dumping toxic substances into water remains unthinkable.[28] Along these lines, once war had become unthinkable, it would be removed from the range of political options. Instead of being viewed reluctantly and hesitantly as a last resort, as it is from within the just war framework, war would vanish beyond the horizon of possible options.

The just war tradition serves at present merely to paralyse thought, to block progress toward a dialogue that addresses the unique challenges of our time. The problem is not that the just war model makes war attractive, but that it makes it unthinkable at a time when such thoughts are too dangerous to be entertained. In the light of recent technological developments, war is more aptly conceived as a pathological phenomenon, as a *breakdown* of thinking. Instead of making war unthinkable, the just war doctrine makes the unthinkability of war unthinkable: it forces theorists in the tradition to consider war as an option. On pragmatic grounds, therefore, the first priority of philosophers concerned with peace is to develop an alternative framework in which more productive discourse is possible.

The thesis that modern war must be reduced to a nonoption is not based on "pacifist" convictions. It is important to recognize the general consensus, which cuts across the three classes posited by the just war theory, concerning the necessity of eliminating war. Indeed, those who welcome the arms race frequently do so in the name of deterrence, that is, in the hope that producing increasingly powerful weapons will make their use increasingly unthinkable. Even realists are pacifists in this sense. A new dimension has been added to the agreement which Ramsey has reported between bellicists (realists) and pacifists.[29] When a program for peace goes by the name, "Mutually Assured Destruction," it is clear that the distinction between the two extreme positions has all but collapsed.[30]

In order to render war unthinkable, however, it is not enough to make minor modifications in the outer layers of our conceptual framework. For just war discourse is itself embedded in a more general system of discourse. Paraphrasing Derrida, there are webs within webs.[31] The emphasis on justice and human rights is based on a particular conception of interpersonal and international relations. According to this conception, persons and, by analogical extension, nations are viewed as individual entities with interests that are regularly in conflict with those of other entities.[32] Within the individualistic framework, where the "self" is the locus of interest, relations among various selfs, or between the self and the "other," are problematic. In fact the normal state of affairs, viewed from within this framework, is one of conflict. Bertrand Russell, whose individualistic orientation is evident in his assessment of war, maintains that human beings, by their very nature, are continually mired in conflict.[33] In this conceptual matrix, the function of ethics is to moderate or regulate conflict among individuals. Furthermore, when ethics is concerned with regulating conflict, talk about rights assumes preeminent importance. Assertions of various rights enter our discourse only when it is necessary to protect these rights against encroachment by other individuals (persons, governments, or nations).

The only solution to the problem of war that occurs to philosophers operating within conflictual ethics is to establish a world government with an international police force.[34] The weakness of this solution, as J. F. Thompson persuasively argues, is that

[the] situation would not be basically altered if there were an international police force to enforce the rules and international courts to punish offenders. Since war is an attempt to impose the law on someone, it is highly resistant to the rule of law.[35]

By analogy, this sort of solution would be as effective as imposing the death penalty to deter suicide bombings. Thompson goes on to suggest that

[if] a world authority wanted to prevent determined belligerents from breaking the rules, it would have to go to war itself, with the risk that it would be forced to use the very methods that it wished to ban.[36]

The logic of war thus makes the best approach available within conflict-based ethics untenable.

It is worth noting that nonegoistic particularist frameworks also lead to an emphasis on justice. Marxism, which is generally believed to offer an alternative to liberal modes of discourse, shares the particularist assumptions that lead to a conflictual model of ethics. The difference between liberalism and Marxism (on this issue) is that the units of interest shift from individual persons to socioeconomic classes. In effect, Marx expands the importance of conflict, making it into the single dynamic principle of historical development. Emphasis on economic and social justice, along with the corresponding assertions of rights, is a natural outgrowth of employing the class conflict model to analyze human history. In turn, the struggle for justice may then be cited to legitimate war. Henryk Skolimowski expresses this point as follows:

Marxist ethics, when viewed from the standpoint of universal human concerns, appears parochial and defensive. Let us be aware that part of the essential ethos of Marxism is class struggle. The mentality of the class-war is a form of war mentality. This is often forgotten. The Marxist model of society is one of continuous warfare.[37]

Another theorist, John Somerville, correctly observes that the principles and doctrines of Marxism concerning the conditions under which war is justified are "close to our principles as a nation."[38] With respect to the problem of war, Marx does not offer an alternative conceptual structure.

Particularism and the conflictual model of ethics may themselves be deconstructed, that is, they may also be shown to follow from assumptions deeply embedded in our discourse. One important source of the particularism characterized above is our tendency to analyze, to divide into component parts, as our principle mode of understanding. This tendency, which stems from Cartesian mechanism and runs through Enlightenment thought, leads to philosophical atomism, the ontological counterpart of political, social, and economic individualism. Though it has been widely criticised, the prejudice in favor of analysis so deeply permeates our thought that it is difficult to detect, let alone uproot. Such early nineteenth century writers as Schiller and Shelley recognized the danger of placing too much emphasis on the process of analysis.[39] To rectify the imbalance, they stressed the importance of imagination, which tends to join what analysis tears asunder. As a joining process, imagination leads naturally to morality, according to both authors.[40] Synthetic imagination, they argue, offers a basis for morality that is antithetical to that offered by analytic reason. One way of construing their thesis is as an attempt to subvert particularism. They present an alternative to the view that there are conflicting interests among individuals, classes, or nations which necessarily give rise to a state of mutual alienation.

To evaluate the highly speculative claims of Schiller and Shelley would lead too far from the concerns of this chapter. There is, however, an alternative to particularist ethics that follows similar lines of thought. Carol Gilligan reports that many women practice a type of morality that is significantly different from the prevailing morality of our time.[41] Instead of positing detachment as a necessary condition for justice, this type of morality emphasizes attachment as a necessary condition for care. It remains to be seen, however, whether this pattern of ethical discourse is appropriate in the domain of international affairs. If, as in the just war conceptual framework, one may draw analogies between the interpersonal and international domains, both the poetic vision of Schiller and Shelley and the feminine ethic reported by Gilligan would produce a state of affairs in which particular national interests are subordinated to global interests. Furthermore, the resort to war, which fits all too nicely into a conceptual scheme organized around individuals in conflict, is easily dislodged from a context of union and attachment. This is an example of the sort of morality to which we may turn in order to establish an alternative conceptual framework for discourse on war. Since the objective of this essay is to critique the prevailing mode of discourse rather than to argue for a particular alternative, it is sufficient to have suggested some prospects for future development.

## THE LIMIT OF PROPORTIONALITY

Finally, I will respond to an objection that is frequently raised against critiques of the just war theory. While detractors argue that war has approximately the same moral status as rape, torture, slavery, or theft,[42] supporters argue that it is in virtue of the just war theory that a rational condemnation of war is possible. According to this objection, the just war framework is anything but obsolete: it is precisely on grounds derived from that framework that modern war is to be avoided at any cost.

Returning to the specific question of proportionality, modern war has become prohibitively expensive. Based solely on condition (3), there is a strong tendency toward nuclear pacifism, for example. Such theorists as Murray, Wellbank, and Johnson claim not only that the principles set down by Augustine and Aquinas are the best available despite their inadequacies—as does Kenny, for example—but that they are as adequate today as they ever were.[43] According to them, it is not the failure of the conceptual system that has allowed people of various nations to brutalize each other with ever-inceasing efficiency, but rather, the failure to apply the system.

The main problem with this defense is that it subtly misrepresents the just war position. It is mistaken to say that the framework inherited from Augustine and Aquinas gives grounds for avoiding modern war at any cost. That is exactly what it doesn't do. As along as the just war framework underlies our discourse, justice and peace will be seen as bipolar co-values which may be exchanged one for the other. This "trade-off" situation is particularly awkward since both are fundamental values. The structure of the discourse thus produces an air of tragedy which one writer, Janusz Kuczynski, sums up as follows: "Our situation is *tragic* in the classical meaning of the word, in the sense of an *insurmountable* conflict of values."[44]

Clearly, just war theorists would not acknowledge that the conflict is insurmountable: the purpose of the conceptual framework they employ is to assist us in resolving the conflict in particular situations. The way the theory is intended to function and the way it actually functions are quite different, however. The crucial point is that in a period of "total war," the theory does not yield a total condemnation of war. Instead, constrained by the condition of proportionality, philosophers ask whether there is some degree of evil that would justify even the most devastating war. On this issue, Roger Ruston contends that "Proportionate reasons become more difficult to find as weapons become more destructive, until they become impossible to find altogether."[45] Unfortunately, as Ruston does not fully appreciate, the structure of the discourse impels theorists confined by it to continue the search for justification well beyond the bounds of reason. Predictably, the only conditions under which total war is considered morally tolerable are those in which the threatened evil is itself regarded as absolute or "total." It is no coincidence that we regard our chief political adversaries as "totalitarian." For only when characterized in terms of total evil can we "morally" subject ourselves and our enemies to the terrifying prospect of modern war. If this analysis of the totalizing tendency in just war thinking seems implausible, one need merely examine texts written by leading theorists. Robert Phillips, in *War and Justice*, raises precisely this issue when he speaks of the "supreme emergency" in which one confronts "absolute evil."[46] Walzer measures the crime of murdering innocent people against the "immeasurable" evil of Fascism.[47] It is in this context that Ruston perceives the need to argue that there is a limit to calculations of relativity."[48] Against the background of just war discourse, there is a tendency in a period of total war to treat opponents as totally vicious. Furthermore, when this type of thinking takes hold, the level of trust on all sides is so seriously diminished that no meaningful dialogue is possible. Yet now, more than ever before, it is imperative that the contending parties find a way to overcome the polarization which might lead to war. Despite the best of intentions, just war theorists are prevented by the structure of their discourse from reducing international tension. Until they dismantle the conceptual structure in which peace is viewed as the price of justice, their contribution to international understanding will be less than they would like.

## NOTES

1. Warren E. Steinkraus, "War and the Philosopher's Duty," in *The Critique of War*, Robert Ginsberg, ed. (Chicago: Henry Regnery Co., 1969), p. 18.

2. Elizabeth Anscombe, "War and Murder" in *War and Morality*, Richard A. Wasserstrom, ed. (Belmont: Wadsworth, 1970), pp. 42–53. Jeffrie G. Murphy, "The Killing of the Innocent," *Monist* 57 (October 1973): 544. Thomas Nagel, "War and Massacre," *Philosophy and Public Affairs* 1 (Winter 1972): 123–144. Richard A. Wasserstrom, "On the Morality of War" in *War and Morality*, Richard Wasserstrom, ed. (Belmont, CA: Wadsworth Publishing Company, 1970), p. 99.

3. Stanley Hoffmann, "States and the Morality of War," *Political Theory* 9 (May 1981): 157–165.

4. James Turner Johnson, *Just War Tradition and the Restraint of War* (Princeton: Princeton University Press, 1981). James Turner Johnson, *Can Modern War Be Just?* (New Haven, CT: Yale University Press, 1984). James Turner Johnson, "Toward Reconstructing the *Jus Ad Bellum*," *Monist* 57 (October 1973): 461–488. John Courtney Murray, *Morality and Modern War* (New York: Council on Religion and International Affairs, 1959). William V. O'Brien, *The Conduct of Just and Limited War* (New York: Praeger Publishers, 1981). Robert L. Phillips, *War and Justice* (Norman: University of Oklahoma Press, 1984). Paul Ramsey, *The Just War* (New York: Charles Scribner's Sons, 1968). Jenny Teichman, *Pacifism and the Just War* (New York: Basil Blackwell, 1987). J. H. Wellbank, "Why We May Still Talk About a Just War," *Journal of Social Philosophy* 8 (May 1977): 4–6.

5. Anthony Kenny, " 'Better Dead Than Red'," in *Objections to Nuclear Defense*, Nigel Blake and Kay Pole, eds. (London: Routledge and Kegan Paul, 1984), pp. 12–27.

6. Michael Walzer, *Just and Unjust Wars* (New York: Basic Books, 1977).

7. Alan Gilbert, "Moral Realism, Individuality and Justice in War" *Political Theory* 14 (Fall 1986): 106.

8. Ronald J. Glossop, *Confronting War* (London: McFarland, 1983), pp. 7–18.

9. Benjamin A. Most and Harvey Starr, "Conceptualizing 'War'," *Journal of Conflict Resolution* 27, no. 1 (March 1983): 137–159.

10. James G. Weltman, "On the Obsolescence of War," *International Studies Quarterly* 18, no. 4 (December 1974): 403.

11. Ibid.

12. Ibid.

13. Iredell Jenkins, "The Conditions of Peace," *Monist* 57 (October 1973): 507–526.

14. Francis A. Beer, "The Epidemiology of Peace and War," *International Studies Quarterly* 23, no. 1 (March 1979): 45–86.

15. John Somerville, *The Peace Revolution* (Westport, CT: Greenwood Press, 1975), passim.

16. Edward Black, "Hegel on War," *Monist* 57 (October 1973): 570–583.

17. Plato, *Republic*, in *The Complete Works of Plato*, B. Jowett, trans. (New York: Random House, 1937), bk. 5: 469–471, 1: 732–735. Plato, *Laws*, in Jowett, trans. 2: 410–411. Aristotle, *Politics*, B. Jowett, trans. in *The Complete Works of Aristotle*, R. McKeon, ed. (New York: Random House, 1941), bk. 1, Chapter 8, 1256b, 232–26, 1137. Cicero, De Republica, C. W. Keyes, trans. in *War and Christian Conscience*, Arthur F. Holmes, ed. (Grand Rapids, MI: Baker, 1975), pp. 24–31. Ambrose, *De Fide Christiana* II, 16 in *Patrologia Latina*, 16: 587–590. Augustine, *The City of God* in *Philosophy in the Middle Ages*, Arthur Hyman and James J. Walsh eds. (Indianapolis, IN: Hackett, 1983), bk. 19: vii, xii, 97,100. Thomas Aquinas, *Summa Theologica*, in *St. Thomas Aquinas: Philosophical Texts*, Thomas Gilby, trans. and ed. (New York: Oxford University Press, 1960), 2a–2ae, xxix, xl. I, p. 348.

18. For a critical discussion of the doctrine of the golden mean, which Aquinas inherits from Aristotle, see F. C. Copleston, *Aquinas* (Harmondsworth [Middlesex], England: Penguin, 1975), pp. 214–219.

19. Augustine, *City of God*, pp. 97, 100.

20. This is not intended to be an exhaustive list. From Augustine's time to the present, theorists have also maintained, for example, that a war must be declared by a legitimate authority in order to be considered just.

21. David R. Segal, *The All Volunteer Force: A Study of Ideology in the Military* (1977), passim.

22. Ramsey, *The Just War*, p. 156.

23. John Dewey, *Liberalism and Social Action* (New York: Capricorn Books, 1963), quoted in *The Philosophy of the Common Man: Essays in Honor of John Dewey*, Sidney Ratner, ed. (New York: Greenwood Press, 1968), pp. 134–135.

24. Karl von Clausewitz *War, Politics and Power* (Chicago, IL: Henry Regency Company, 1962). Clausewitz, *On War*, J. J. Graham, trans. (London: Routledge and Kegan Paul, 1966), pp. 75–76.

25. Weltman, "Obsolescence," p. 413.

26. Robert Ginsberg, "War and the Philospher's Duty," in *The Critique of War*, Robert Ginsberg, ed. (Chicago, IL: Henry Regnery Company, 1969), p. vvi.

27. Claude Levi-Strauss, *Elementary Structures of Kinship*, Rodney Needham, ed. (Boston: Beacon Press, 1969), p. 1.

28. Rushworth M. Kidder, "Amitai Etzioni," *The Christian Science Monitor* (April 3, 1967), pp. 16–17.

29. Ramsey, *The Just War*, p. 155.

30. Of course, there remain fanatics for whom the crusade against perceived injustice takes precedence over over the preservation of life. See, for example, William Earle, "In Defense of War," *Monist* 57 (October 1973): 551–565.

31. Jacques Derrida, "Plato's Pharmacy," in *Dissemination*, Barbara Johnson, trans. (Chicago: University of Chicago Press, 1981), pp. 63–63.

32. Immanuel Kant, *Perpetual Peace*, Ted Humphrey, trans. (Indianapolis, IN: Hackett, 1983), p. 115.

33. Bertrand Russell, *New Hopes for a Changing World* (New York: Simon and Schuster, 1951), p. 13. According to Russell, "It is the nature of man to be in conflict with something." Compare Russell, *Has Man a Future?* (New York: Simon and Schuster, 1962).

34. George Modelski and Patrick M. Morgan, "Understanding Global War" *Journal of Conflict Resolution* 29, no. 3 (September, 1985): 391ff.

35. J. F. Thompson, "The Logic of War," *International Journal of Moral and Social Studies* I (Springs 1986): 38.

36. Ibid.

37. Henryk Skolimowski, "Philosophy and Values in the Model for Peace" *Dialectics and Humanism* 3 (1985): 63.

38. John Somerville, "Marxism and War," in *The Critique of War*, Robert Ginsberg, ed. (Chicago, IL: Henry Regnery Company, 1969), p. 141.

39. Percy Bysshe Shelley, "A Defense of Poetry," in *The Complete Works of Percy Bysshe Shelley*, Roger Ingpen and Walter Peck, ed. (New York: Gordian Press, 1965), pp. 109–142. Friedrich Schiller, *On the Aesthetic Education of Man*, Reginald Snell, trans. (New York: Frederick Ungar Publishing Company, 1980), passim.

40. Ibid.

41. Carol Gilligan, *In a Different Voice* (Cambridge: Harvard University Press, 1982), passim.

42. See, for example, John L. McKenzie, *The Civilization of Christianity* (Chicago, IL: The Thomas More Press, 1986), p. 125. Compare A. C. Genova, "Can War Be Rationally Justified?" in Ginsberg, ed. pp. 198–224.

43. See Johnson, *Just War Tradition*; Kenny, "Better Dead"; Murray, *Morality*; and Wellbank, "Talk About Just War."

44. Janusz Kuczynksi, "The Meaning of History and Creative Peace" *Dialectics and Humanism* 11 (Autumn 1984): 497.

45. Roger Ruston, "Nuclear Deterrence and the Use of the Just War Doctrine," in *Objections to Nuclear Defense*, Nigel Blake and Kay Pole, eds. (London: Routledge and Kegan Paul, 1984), p. 59.

46. Phillips, *War and Justice*, p. 69.

47. Walzer, *Just and Unjust War*, p. 253.

48. Ruston, "Nuclear Deterrence," p. 59.

# Part III

---

# Culture and American Foreign Policy

# 7

# *The United States as Ally and Adversary in East Asia: Reflections on Culture and Foreign Policy*

## John P. Lovell

The ambivalence in United States policies toward China that John Fairbank noted in his landmark work,[1] has persisted in U.S. policies more generally throughout East Asia. In recent decades, the United States has pledged its support and has provided military and economic assistance to virtually every noncommunist government in East Asia. Since the 1970s, U.S. technical and military assistance has even been provided to the People's Republic of China. Furthermore, trade with the region has increased to the point that the Pacific Rim now accounts for a larger percentage of U.S. trade than does the region historically accorded primacy in U.S. relations, Europe.

However, the United States's closest trading partners in Asia are also the objects of acrimonious trade rivalry in the late 1980s. Moreover, at one time or another during the twentieth century, the United States has been at war with Filipinos, Japanese, Chinese, Koreans, and Vietnamese.

The vast shifts in U.S. policies, from an eagerness for friendship to a readiness to inflict death and destruction, call to mind Kipling's observations about the meeting of East and West, and thereby lead almost inexorably to questions about cultural influences on policy. Such questions are examined here with exclusive reference to the U.S. experience in East Asia, although obviously generalization will be possible only as analysis moves to cross-national comparisons of policy behavior.

At one level, to say that international relations and foreign policy are culturally conditioned is to belabor the obvious. Human beings are reared in cultural contexts, within which basic values, habits, and beliefs are nurtured. Those who rise to positions of political power in every society are susceptible to the effects of socialization; their behavior and attitudes will have many cultural roots. Moreover, governance itself and the formulation of foreign policy in every nation-state take place within a cultural context. The "civic culture" or "political culture" not only is reflected in procedures and customs that characteristically are followed in transacting political business and making policy decisions, but also in many of the biases and predispositions that condition relations with other nations. In this sense, the images of reality with which the key participants in international relations operate are, at least in part, culturally fabricated.

But perceptual reality may be the product of influences other than culture. Moreover, just as the analysis of attitudes only takes one part way in explaining behavior, so the identification of perceptions is not a comprehensive explanation of policy.

As one attempts to become explicit about the relationship of independent (cultural) and dependent (foreign policy) variables, causality of that relationship appears far from obvious, however enticing cultural interpretations of U.S. policies may be. For example, was the commitment of the Reagan administration to a Strategic Defense Initiative (SDI, or "Star Wars") explicable primarily in terms of U.S. culture, as one recent interpretation would have it?[2] Or are there other variables that might provide a fuller explanation: situational, political-institutional, economic, systemic, the momentum of technology, or even idiosyncratic characteristics of President Reagan's personality that are not mere derivatives of a cultural interpretation?[3] Similarly, did "American culture [lead] us into Vietnam and make us fight the way we did," as one recent treatise on the subject contends?[4] Or, as other accounts maintain, does the explanation lie in distinctive characteristics of the U.S. political process, or in organizational doctrine and inertia, in the mindset not of an entire culture but of policy elites, or in other factors?[5]

The answers one gives to such questions hinge in part on how one conceives of "culture" and in part on the evidence one treats as sufficient proof of the influence of culture on foreign policy.

## THE CONCEPT OF CULTURE
## AS APPLIED TO FOREIGN POLICY

The social science literature provides no uniform guidance in conceptualizing *culture*; on the contrary, what is notable is the diversity of definitions.[6] At the core of most definitions, however, is the notion of culture as a set of customs, mores, beliefs, and values that are "passed on from one generation to the next by learning [i.e. socialization processes]—and not by inheritance."[7]

The important early development of the study of culture in the twentieth century was done by anthropologists, based largely upon observations of relatively simple tribal communities. In such a setting, findings regarding the significance of particular traditional practices, rites of passage, taboos, superstitions, and folklore, could and did provide the basis for reasonably confident generalizations about the cultures being studied. Modern communities are more complex. As explained in ensuing discussion, in a society such as that of the United States in the late twentieth century, intracultural variation tends to be at least as significant as are modal values and beliefs, thereby rendering generalization hazardous.

The sensitivity of social scientists to such variation came only gradually. As with many other areas of social science research (e.g., administrative theory, survey research), impetus for the development of the concept of culture was provided by applied research demands of World War II. The works of Margaret Mead and Geoffrey Gorer are illustrative of important efforts to refine the concept.[8]

In *The American People and Foreign Policy*, published in 1950, Gabriel Almond was somewhat more hesitant than Mead and Gorer had been to generalize broadly about the American "national character." However, treating generalizations by various observers, from Tocqueville to Mead and Gorer, as informed speculation, Almond applied them to the development of several broad hypotheses about fluctuations in popular "moods." Noting that abundant evidence revealed that most U.S. citizens were uninformed about and often disinterested in foreign policy issues, he found it important to distinguish the "general public" from an "attentive public," "policy and opinion elites," and "official policy leadership." Moreover, the polling data that Almond cited made distinctions among respondents according to variables such as socio-economic background, education, and region.[9]

Although the concept of "national character" continued to have currency into the late 1950s and early 1960s, social scientists who used the term tended to do so with numerous caveats. For example, Arvid Brodersen, although generally supportive of the concept in a 1957 commentary, noted that "the fundamental difficulty in coping with highly differentiated cultures has not been overcome in any of the national character studies to date."[10] Emily Nett, in a 1958 article, was more consistently skeptical in her appraisal. Among the numerous shortcomings that she identified in efforts that had been made to apply the concept, were that little attention had been paid to "the interaction between the institutional requirements [of social organization] and the behavior of the elites, and the role that degrees of conformity-deviation in the social structure play as an active ingredient in the dynamics of change."[11]

An approach to dealing with cultural influences on politics while acknowledging differentiation of culture was to focus on "political culture." Cross-national studies launched in the 1960s under the leadership of Gabriel Almond and Sidney Verba provided a particularly important example of such an approach. The political culture concept is of continuing interest and, as modified below, it provides a starting point here for suggesting indicators of the relationship of culture to foreign policy that the present author finds useful.

Almond and Verba define *political culture* as "the particular *distribution* of patterns of orientation toward political objects among members of a nation," using "political objects" to refer to political institutions and structures, the incumbents in political and governmental roles, and political and governmental actions and policies.[12] Uniformity of orientation is not assumed; rather, the patterns are to be identified by empirical investigation.

In order to focus on the portion of the "orientation toward political objects" that is likely to be especially pertinent to explaining foreign policy behavior, it is useful to modify the Almond-Verba conceptualization in two ways: by explicitly identifying salient subcultures, and by noting dimensions of values and beliefs that are likely to be especially germane in shaping a foreign policy orientation.

## AMERICAN CULTURES

Cultural differentiation is particularly striking in a society such as that of the United States, which has had and continues to experience a large influx of immigrants, and which is characterized by a high degree of social and geographic mobility. In such a setting, the processes by which social mores, values, and beliefs are acquired, modified, and transmitted are complex and the results are diverse. Childhood socialization practices typically constitute the core mechanism by which culture is perpetuated in traditional societies. In contrast, in complex modern societies such as that of the United States, socialization experiences beyond childhood take on added importance. With multiple reference groups, individuals may share more values and beliefs with schoolmates or professional colleagues that they do with members of the extended family. (For that matter, the scientist, the artist, the physician, or even the professional soldier may discover that he or she has as much if not more in common with his or her counterpart in other cultures as with some members of his or her own society.)

Thus, one may speak of the importance of *subcultures*. These have been evident in the U.S. experience regionally (e.g., New England, the South, Appalachia); along ethnic, racial, or religious lines; sometimes along generational lines (e.g., in the 1960s) or according to gender (e.g., feminist subculture); and often within groupings corresponding to occupation and the workplace (e.g., the Foreign Service subculture, the Marine Corps subculture).

Professional careers such as the law, medicine, the military, or the Foreign Service are characterized by selective recruitment and an intensive period of indoctrination and training, which typically concludes with a formal rite of passage recognizing the admission of newly qualified members to the professional community. To the extent that subsequent jobs or assignments build upon the early sense of camaraderie, it comes through the experience of relatively similar demands and responsibilities. The sharing of distinctive values and beliefs among members is a familiar pattern.

Beyond the Foreign Service and the military profession, one also finds the emergence of communities of like-minded individuals, such as among White House or National Security Council staff members, where selection provides a basis for mutual esteem, and where the nature of the common experience qualifies as being "special." The "band of brothers" phenomenon among presidential advisors is familiar (and not without its potential hazards in terms of "groupthink," as well as its potential benefits in terms of esprit and motivation to meet high performance standards).[13]

To recognize that a range of subcultures exists is not to argue that it be fully incorporated into every research effort to identify the link between culture and foreign policy. Nor is it to argue that generalized interpretations of the cultural roots of a particular body of foreign policy experience are necessarily invalid or useless. Such interpretations can be valuable, for example, in highlighting recurring biases or misperceptions that exacerbate conflict when cultures collide. John W. Dower's important recent study, *War Without Mercy: Race and Power in the Pacific War*, is of this genre. Similarly, Frances Fitzgerald's Pulitzer Prize–winning 1972 book, *Fire in the Lake*, was valuable particularly for describing in detail facets of Vietnamese life, customs, traditions, and politics that about which U.S. policymakers should have been but were not well informed.[14]

On the other hand, attention by the scholar to variation according to politically salient subcultures is a useful check against overgeneralization about cultural influences. Moreover, analysis of the distinctive outlook and operating style of groups and organizations that are deeply involved in the foreign policy process can provide rewarding insights into the dynamics of policy.

For example, as Andrew Scott discovered in his analysis of the workings of the U.S. State Department, "To discuss the operation of the Department of State without considering the role of the subculture is like trying to explain tidal change without reference to the role of the moon."[15] John Harr, author of an in-depth study of the American career diplomat (Foreign Service officers, or FSOs), has made a similar observation. Repeated efforts to reorganize the State Department have been frustrated, Harr concluded, "because the basic problem is cultural rather than organizational"—that is, a problem of FSO traditions and customary practices rather than one of the departmental structure.[16]

Within the Foreign Service, the small group of "Old China hands" of the 1930s and early 1940s had formed special bonds of camaraderie based on common mastery of a language that few Americans spoke and common experience in a land torn by political upheaval and war.[17] The so-called "fall of China" to Communism in 1949 provided the occasion for a purge of China hands from their positions, on the grounds that FSO reports critical of Chiang Kai-shek and his entourage were evidence of disloyalty or at least poor judgment. James Thomson, Jr., who served in the State Department as an East Asian specialist, found that the "fall of China" continued to have a chilling effect on the outlook of State Department personnel during discussions of the U.S. involvement in Vietnam.[18]

Paul Kattenburg, a Southeast Asian specialist in the State Department in the 1950s and 1960s, has argued persuasively that despite the China legacy, area experts remained in the Foreign Service who might have made a valuable contribution to policy formation regarding Vietnam, had they been heeded. The culture of the Foreign Service, Kattenburg notes, places a premium on sensitivity to the realities of local contexts, leading to the recognition that indigenous problems often are resistant to externally imposed solutions. But the "action-oriented" ethos that characterized foreign policy beginning with the Kennedy administration led key officials to regard the caution of FSOs with disfavor.[19]

The military profession provides another vivid example of a subculture the features of which merit study by the student of foreign policy. Morris Janowitz plumbed the essential features in his landmark "social and political portrait" more than a quarter of a century ago. Among the interesting findings was one of contrasting clusters of policy views and career orientations, alongside shared traditions, customs, and values. Military officers who could be described as "absolutists" had political views quite different from those of "pragmatists," for instance, and those who continued to define their professional role as that of "heroic leader" were not happy when top leadership positions went to those with a "managerial" view of role requirements.[20]

Similarly, Morton Halperin has shown how the "organizational essence" of each armed service is derived from its distinctive traditions, mission, and technology. The shared belief by its members in the "organizational essence" leads them to an orientation toward policy issues that contributes to organizational rivalry and bureaucratic politics.[21]

William Hauser, himself a career military officer who had a combat command in Vietnam, has explored internal frictions such as these as well as others such as "careerism" or "ticket-punching" in a critical examination of the U.S. Army in Vietnam.[22] A more recent study by another Army officer, Andrew Krepinevich, usefully traces the fixation within the Army subculture on what he calls "the Army Concept"—doctrinal assumptions stemming from the World War II experience that fatally hampered the adaptation that was required to the very different warfare in Vietnam.[23]

Based upon participant observation with U.S. soldiers in Vietnam and in the Dominican Republic, sociologist Charles Moskos has demonstrated that there is an "enlisted culture" in the armed services with values and beliefs at variance with those that prevail among commissioned officers. It is a finding that cautions against the initiation of policy commitments that are based largely on a "can-do" orientation of the military officer corps.[24]

More broadly, Richard Barnet has plumbed the "operational code" of those who have responsibilities as "national security managers." Barnet, who served with the State Department, the Arms Control and Disarmament Agency, and (in a consulting role) with the Defense Department, argues that a "hairy-chest syndrome" combines with systems of "absolution" and other subcultural norms to predispose those who manage national security policy to favor military or covert military solutions to foreign policy problems.[25] One can dispute Barnet's findings, as one can the findings of other authors cited here. However, the point at hand is that such studies usefully probe not merely the general cultural context of policy-making and execution, but more precisely the prevailing norms and practices that define the institutional settings in which policy makers operate.

## FOREIGN POLICY–RELEVANT
## DIMENSIONS OF CULTURE

There remains the question, How do the customs, mores, values, and beliefs of culture and subcultures become manifested in foreign policy? Here I would distinguish the analytical task of explaining specific policy decisions and actions from that of explaining broad patterns of policy continuity and change. The more narrow the temporal scope of one's analytical focus, the more one is likely to need to turn to explanatory variables that bear only a peripheral if any relationship to culture and subculture. Conversely, the broader the temporal scope of one's search for patterns of foreign policy, the more relevance cultural and subcultural variables are likely to have, although even in the quest to explain broad policy patterns, culture and subcultures are far from the only variables of probable interest (see Table 7.1).

To put the matter somewhat differently, if one is interested in making a link between culture and foreign policy, this is most likely to be feasible if one examines patterns of policy action and commitment over a period of years. In contrast, if one wishes to determine why, at a particular point in time, decision makers selected option A rather than options B or C, one is likely to have to introduce explanatory variables other than culture.

For example, it seems reasonable to hypothesize that cultural biases contributed both to a Euro-centered focus in U.S. policies after World

**Figure 7.1.**
**Variables in Explaining Foreign Policy**

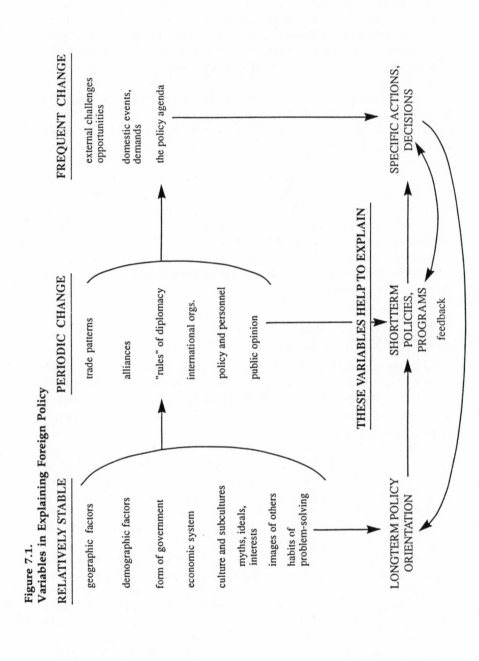

War II and to a recurrent use of military force to advance or protect U.S. interests in regions such as Central America and Asia. On the other hand, the task of explaining specific policy choices, such as President Harry Truman's decision to commit U.S. forces to combat in Korea in June 1950, lends itself to a concern with the kinds of situational, structural, and informational variables that Glenn Paige applied to his thorough analysis of the Korean decision, perhaps supplemented by social-psychological variables of the sort Irving Janis has applied to a variety of policy decisions in his study of "groupthink."[26]

The postulated link between cultural/subcultural variables and foreign policy can be made more evident by highlighting three dimensions of culture that seem particularly fruitful for investigation.[27]

The first of these consists of prevailing beliefs and myths that are associated with a nation's historical experience by its leaders and its people, and the views that they have of the nation's current role and status in world affairs. Wide acceptance by Americans of an image of the United States as a superpower, maintaining a benevolent Pax Americana in world affairs, is a far cry from the prevailing recognition of America's relative weakness that had provided George Washington, Thomas Jefferson, and their contemporaries with a prime rationale for a foreign policy of nonentanglement in the political affairs of other nations. On the other hand, some early myths have lingered in U.S. experience, if adapted to changing circumstances. The image of America as a "City upon a Hill," for instance, which had inspired John Winthrop and the Puritan settlers in the New World, has been evident in varying form in subsequent generations, providing a twentieth century rationale for intervention abroad.[28]

The student of foreign policy might find it possible to gather data not only on widely prevailing images of "who we are" and of the nation's destiny, but also data on the distinctive variants that are found in particular subcultures. For instance, the light that Peter Karsten is able to shed on the "naval mind" (as he terms it) during the era of Alfred Thayer Mahan enriches our understanding of the expansionist impulse of that generation. Karsten shows that although naval officers appeared ready to accept uncritically the proposition, "my country, right or wrong," the same officers expressed a low regard for the "softness" that they observed in the American culture. Moreover, they tended to regard businessmen with contempt, and missionaries (especially those deemed to be pacifists) with scorn, even as they served "as the shield and sword of American economic expansion" and of the advance of Christianity.[29]

A second dimension of culture that merits investigation for its explanatory relevance for foreign policy is that of images that policy elites and public hold of other nations, other world regions, and of other "actors" in world politics, such as international institutions. Such images can contribute to pronounced policy biases. As noted earlier, John

Fairbank has described the fluctuations in U.S. policies toward China in response to shifts among discordant images—exotic images, emphasizing the oddities of Chinese culture from a Western perspective (e.g., men with pigtails); idealized images that provided the rationale for support of the China of Generalissimo and Madame Chiang Kai-shek against the invading Japanese; and disillusioned images of an ungrateful China that turned to Communism.[30]

Similarly, from a study of U.S. newspaper coverage of Korea from the mid-nineteenth century to 1945, supplemented by a review of communications from U.S. diplomats in Asia, John Chay has shown that U.S. policies in those years rested on fuzzy and stereotyped images of Korea and Koreans.[31]

A third important dimension of culture that merits analysis by the student of foreign policy consists of habits and attitudes that become institutionalized regarding problem solving in human relationships. That is, we may hypothesize that foreign policy behavior will reflect cultural modes of problem solving, deep-rooted beliefs and attitudes about compromise and conflict in human affairs, and cultural or subcultural norms that govern the resort to force to resolve disputes. In his review of U.S. diplomacy in the first half of the twentieth century, George Kennan found a recurring tendency among U.S. policy makers toward a "legalistic-moralistic approach to international problems." He explained this in part in terms of the deep impact that the legal profession has had upon U.S. statesmanship, and in part on historical experience, including the legacy of the crusade to bring about the "unconditional surrender" of the enemy in World War II.[32]

Ernest May is one of a number of critics of U.S. policies in Vietnam who has noted the grip that the "lessons" of the 1930s (most notably, the Manchurian crisis and the appeasement of Hitler at Munich) had on U.S. policymakers as they formulated policies toward Vietnam in the 1960s.[33] The May book, and the sequel co-authored with Richard Neustadt,[34] are important not only in pointing to a dimension of culture that is relevant for its influence on foreign policy, but also for the stress on policy learning. Culture is transmitted through learning. But governments "learn" from previous experience not simply through cognitive processes that one associates with individual learning, but also through political processes, as alternative or even contrasting "lessons" that have been absorbed by different observers or participants in the previous experience compete for incorporation into doctrine, organizational procedures, and institutional structures.[35]

## CONCLUSIONS

An important next step in any rigorous effort to trace the influence of culture on foreign policy is the development of operational measures of both independent and dependent variables. This chapter has been designed to chart the path simply by suggesting some refinements of the term "culture" that seem helpful in the light of extant literature on the U.S. policy experience in East Asia. The influence of culture on U.S. foreign policy is discernible primarily in broad patterns of historical experience, rather than in discrete policy decisions and actions. The cultural differentiation of a complex modern society requires attention not merely to the general characteristics of U.S. political culture, but also to values, beliefs, and practices that prevail in policy-relevant subcultures.

Virtually all serious students of U.S. relations with East Asia have been cognizant of the importance of cultural factors to an explanation of the pattern of U.S. foreign policy. The challenge for future research is to improve our analytical ability to distinguish cultural influences on foreign policy from the impact of a myriad of other factors.

## NOTES

The author is grateful to Richard Fredland for perceptive comments on an earlier draft of the essay.

1. John King Fairbank, *The United States and China*, 3d ed. (Cambridge, MA: Harvard University Press, 1971), esp. chaps. 13 and 18.

2. Jeff Smith, "Reagan, Star Wars, and American Culture," *Bulletin of the Atomic Scientists* 43 (Jan./Feb. 1987): 19–25.

3. A convenient compilation of some of the pertinent empirical research findings about the explanatory relevance of these and other variables appears in Patrick J. McGowan and Howard B. Shapiro, *The Comparative Study of Foreign Policy: A Survey of Scientific Findings* (Beverly Hills, CA: Sage, 1973). One of 16 chapters in the book is devoted to "cultural variables." A more recent collection of essays and research reports is provided by Charles F. Hermann, Charles W. Kegley, Jr., and James N. Rosenau, eds. *New Directions in the Study of Foreign Policy* (Boston, MA: Allen & Unwin, 1987). Particularly pertinent to the present discussion is a chapter by Martin W. Sampson III, "Cultural Influences on Foreign Policy", pp. 384–405.

4. Loren Baritz, *Backfire: A History of How American Culture Led Us into Vietnam and Made Us Fight the Way We Did* (New York: Ballantine Books, 1985).

5. See, for example, Leslie Gelb, with Richard Betts, *The Irony of Vietnam: The System Worked* (Washington, DC: Brookings, 1979); Harry Summers, Jr., *On Strategy: The Vietnam War in Context* (Washington, DC: GPO, 1981); Paul M. Kattenburg, *The Vietnam Trauma in American Foreign Policy, 1945–1975* (New Brunswick, NJ: Transaction Books, 1980).

6. A. L. Kroeber and Clyde Kluckhohn have identified and critically reviewed 160 different definitions in English by social scientists from various fields, in "Culture: A Critical Review of Concepts and Definitions," *Papers of the Peabody Museum of American Archeology and Ethnology* 47, no. 1 (1952), quoted by Kluckhohn in "Culture," in *A Dictionary of the Social Sciences* (New York: Free Press, under the auspices of UNESCO, 1964).

7. Elvin Hatch, "Culture," in *The Social Science Encyclopedia*, edited by Adam Kuper and Jessica Kuper (London: Routledge and Kegan Paul, 1985), p. 178.

8. See Margaret Mead, *And Keep Your Powder Dry: An Anthropologist Looks at America*, expanded ed. (New York: Morrow 1965); and Geoffrey Gorer, *The American People: A Study in National Character*, revised ed. (New York: Norton, 1964), p. 15. Mead has explained (p. xi) that her study was written "as a social scientist's contribution to winning the war and establishing a just and lasting peace. It was frankly and completely partisan." The work therefore largely glossed over differences among Americans (although it should be added that there was a tendency for such differences to be submerged in an era that called for unity of effort). The English anthropologist, Gorer, had studied under Mead and Ruth Benedict and had served with them during the war on a U.S. Committee for National Morale. His own work, although published in 1948, still reflected much of the wartime mood of unity. Gorer was somewhat more critical in his assessment than Mead had been. Moreover, he noted (p. 15) the difficulty of making "valid generalizations about nearly a hundred million people scattered over half a continent." However, he concluded that generalization was possible because, in contrast to Europeans who were isolated from one another by local traditions and inbreeding, Americans had shared a historical experience that encouraged a common outlook.

9. Gabriel A. Almond, *The American People and Foreign Policy* (New York: Praeger, 1960).

10. Arvid Brodersen, "National Character: An Old Problem Re-examined," *Diogenes* 20 (Winter 1957): 468–486; reprinted in *International Politics and Foreign Policy*, edited by James N. Rosenau (New York: Free Press, 1961), p. 306.

11. Emily M. Nett. "An Evaluation of the National Character Concept in Sociological Theory," *Social Forces* 26 (1958): 297–303, reprinted in *Human Behavior and International Politics: Contributions from the Social-Psychological Sciences*, edited by J. David Singer (Chicago: Rand McNally, 1965), p. 112. As late as 1961, Alex Inkeles was still holding out hope for developing a body of empirical generalizations about "national character." However, his review of a substantial body of relevant literature faulted much of it for "failure to take account of the differentiation within large national populations." His proposal for remedying this deficiency, which retained a concern for cultural influences on behavior while largely abandoning the concept of "national character," called for the development of "a comparative social psychology of the political process." Alex Inkeles, "National Character and Modern Political Systems," in *Psychological Anthropology: Approaches to Culture and Personality*, edited by Francis L. K. Hsu (Chicago: Dorsey, 1961), pp. 172–208, reprinted in *Politics and Social Life: An Introduction to Political Behavior*, edited by Nelson W. Polsby, Robert A. Dentler, and Paul A. Smith (Boston: Houghton Mifflin, 1963), pp. 175, 189.

12. Gabriel A. Almond and Sidney Verba, *The Civic Culture: Political Attitudes and Democracy in Five Nations* (Boston, MA: Little, Brown, 1965), pp. 13–15. Emphasis added. Concurrent with the emergence in the 1960s of studies of "political culture" were efforts to define and measure "political development," and to identify its relationship to "economic development." The tortuous path pursued in such explorations will not be described here.

13. See Irving L. Janis, *Groupthink: Psychological Studies of Policy Decisions and Fiascoes*, 2d ed. (Boston, MA: Houghton Mifflin, 1982); also Alexander L. George, *Presidential Decisionmaking in Foreign Policy: The Effective Use of Information and Advice* (Boulder, CO: Westview, 1980).

14. John W. Dower, *War Without Mercy: Race and Power in the Pacific War* (New York: Pantheon Books, 1986). Frances Fitzgerald, *Fire in the Lake: The Vietnamese and the Americans in Vietnam* (New York: Vintage Books, 1973).

15. Andrew M Scott, "The Department of State" Formal Organization and Informal Culture," *International Studies Quarterly* 13 (March 1969): 1.

16. John Ensor Harr, *The Professional Diplomat* (Princeton, NJ: Princeton University Press, 1969), p. 96.

17. E. J. Kahn, Jr. *The China Hands: America's Foreign Service Officers and What Befell Them* (New York: Penguin Books, 1976). See also, Paul Gordon Lauren, ed., *The China Hands' Legacy: Ethics and Diplomacy* (Boulder, CO: Westview, 1987). FSOs with other regional specialties, such as the Europeanists, also tended to have their own distinctive outlook. See Martin Weil, *A Pretty Good Club: The Founding Fathers of the U.S. Foreign Service* (New York: Norton, 1978).

18. James C. Thomson, Jr., "How Could Vietnam Happen? An Autopsy," *The Atlantic* (April 1968), pp. 47–53.

19. Paul M. Kattenburg, *The Vietnam Trauma in American Foreign Policy, 1945–1975* (New Brunswick, NJ: Transaction Books, 1980).

20. Morris Janowitz, *The Professional Soldier: A Social and Political Portrait* (New York: Free Press, 1960).

21. Morton H. Halperin, *Bureaucratic Politics and Foreign Policy* (Washington, DC: Brookings, 1974).

22. William L. Hauser, *America's Army in Crisis: A Study in Civil-Military Relations* (Baltimore, MD: Johns Hopkins University Press, 1973).

23. Andrew F. Krepinevich, Jr., *The Army and Vietnam* (Baltimore, MD: Johns Hopkins University Press, 1986).

24. Charles C. Moskos, Jr., *The American Enlisted Man* (New York: Russell Sage, 1970).

25. Richard J. Barnet, *Roots of War: The Men and Institutions Behind U.S. Foreign Policy* (New York: Pelican Books, 1973), esp. chap. 5.

26. Glenn Paige, *The Korean Decision* (New York: The Free Press, 1968). Janis, *Groupthink*, 2d ed.

27. The variables listed here are a somewhat modified version of those discussed in John P. Lovell, *The Challenge of American Foreign Policy: Purpose and Adaptation* (New York: Macmillan, 1985); see especially the discussion of "Orientation to the World Environment: Generalized Assumptions, Images, and Goals," pp. 53–58.

28. Baritz, *Backfire*, chap. 1, finds the "City on the Hill" myth still active in the policy thinking that led America to Vietnam. The subsequent use of the phrase by President Ronald Reagan attests to the durability of the metaphor.

29. Peter Karsten, *The Naval Aristocracy: The Golden Age of Annapolis and the Emergence of Modern American Navalism* (New York: Free Press, 1972), p. 149.

30. Fairbank, *The United States and China*, 3d ed., pp. 289–295.

31. John Chay, "The American Image of Korea to 1945," in *Korea and the United States: A Century of Cooperation*, edited by Youngnok Koo and Dae-Sook Suh (Honolulu: University of Hawaii Press, 1984), pp. 53–76.

32. George F. Kennan, *American Diplomacy, 1900–1950* (New York: Mentor Books, 1952), pp. 82–89.

33. Ernest R. May, *"Lessons" of the Past: The Use and Misuse of History in American Foreign Policy* (New York: Oxford University Press, 1973).

34. Richard E. Neustadt and Ernest R. May, *Thinking in Time: The Uses of History for Decision Makers* (New York: Free Press, 1986).

35. On American "learning" from the Vietnam experience, see Earl C. Ravenal, *Never Again: Learning from America's Foreign Policy Failures* (Philadelphia, PA: Temple University Press, 1978). On organizational learning in the military, see John P. Lovell, "'Lessons' of U.S. Military Involvement: Preliminary Conceptualization," in *Foreign Policy Decision Making: Perception, Cognition, and Artificial Intelligence,* edited by Donald A. Sylvan and Steve Chan (New York: Praeger, 1984), pp. 129–157.

# 8

# *Culture in U.S. Foreign Policy since 1900*

Frank Ninkovich

Although diplomacy functions within cultural and intercultural contexts, historians of diplomacy have traditionally slighted cultural explanations of foreign policy in favor of tried and true concepts of power and interest. Whatever the habits of historians, insightful statesmen have always recognized that diplomacy also requires reckoning with cultural values which, because of their crucial role in shaping perceptions, are more significant than either ideological beliefs or abstract ideals. In one way or another, nearly all the major U.S. statesmen of the twentieth century took cultural factors into account as part of their approach to diplomacy; indeed, culture played a prominent and often decisive role in their decision making. This chapter will suggest—with a very broad brush—some of the ways in which cultural considerations affected their assessments of high policy.

Over the course of the twentieth century, the thinking of U.S. statesmen on the relationship between power and culture—between developments that take place at the levels of social structure and values, respectively—has undergone a dramatic shift. Briefly put, at the turn of the century, cultures were thought to be easily changeable and were viewed from a universal framework while, in contrast, the conception of the United States's hard interests was defined in limited geographic and functional terms. By the 1980s, the relationship had been reversed: Thinking in terms of unique and durable cultures became the rule whereas the functional interests of the United States were defined as having a universal scope. This conceptual change had a lexical counterpart in the gradual disappearance of terms like civilization and world opinion, once rhetorical staples of U.S. diplomacy, from the discourse of U.S. statesmen.

As the United States made its noisy entrance onto the world stage in the late 1890s, a key element of its emerging internationalism was the hope that a world order could be cemented around the common modern values of an industrializing, increasingly liberal-democratic "civilization." No better example of this cultural optimism exists than in Theodore Roosevelt. Roosevelt's policies have traditionally been viewed as a reflection of his macho personality, itself the embodiment of a young America grasping at world power status; indeed, the image of Theodore Roosevelt as a Harvard-educated social Darwinist in drag, whose gaudy intellectual plumage fails hopelessly to conceal the hairy masculinity beneath, is still the dominant view of the man. Roosevelt, however, was no primitive. He was an intellectually brilliant, highly cultured, and cosmopolitan individual with an enviable understanding of world politics who put his considerable knowledge of culture and history to practical use as an integral part of his foreign policy.[1] If Roosevelt's rhetoric is put to the test by seeing how well his diplomacy squared with his rhetoric of civilization, it is clear that culture played a significant role in his foreign policy.

In the Western hemisphere, where his aggressive actions appeared calculated to stake out a U.S. imperial preserve against hungry European interlopers, Roosevelt justified his imperialist policies in terms of a common cultural mission shared by the developed powers. This could easily be construed as so much pious breast beating were it not for his desire to see a great power enforcing a Monroe Doctrine for Asia, much as the United States was doing in the Caribbean. Despite his oft-stated preference that a single power take jurisdiction over Chinese modernization in the interests of civilization at large, the absence of suitable stewards led him to conclude that a balance of power in Asia was the only alternative for the time being.

As for Europe, no conclusive test of his cultural sympathies took place during his presidency. Following his retirement from office, however, he was among the first Americans to advocate a militant anti-German policy in 1914, not because U.S. interests were militarily threatened, but because Germany's ruthless violation of Belgian neutrality had flouted the civilized standards of diplomacy. According to Roosevelt, Britain stood "for humanity, for mankind," whereas Germany, a military despotism occupying what he conceived to be a lower level of cultural development, was civilization's enemy in a war that was "in its essence one between militarism and democracy."[2]

The historical vision of an advancing civilization, which he viewed as the gradual evolution of cultural constraints over the imperatives of brute force, gave Rooseveltian diplomacy a global dimension and provided it with ideological coherence, even to the point of determining when and where he would intervene militarily. Still, even though Roosevelt spoke endlessly about civilization, he talked little of interdependence, and he showed almost no interest in economic matters. The world was still structurally fragmented for Roosevelt, in military and economic terms.

His handpicked successor, William Howard Taft, sought to fill this lacuna by emphasizing the functional characteristics of the modernization process. In the belief that modern diplomacy was economic, Taft was willing to make policy on the assumption of functional interdependence by using financial diplomacy as an instrument of cultural progress. His failed attempt to transform the competitive diplomacy of imperialism in China into a cooperative enterprise makes little political sense unless one is aware of Taft's assumption that common values, and therefore common interests, made possible a noncompetitive China policy. This approach ruled out a diplomacy of sharp elbows in China in which the United States would have been willing to back its interests vis-à-vis Japan militarily.

As Taft's secretary of state, Philander Knox, put it: "The development of commerce and industry and the necessary exchange of commodities have caused nations to see that their interests are similar and interdependent, and that a like policy is often necessary as well for the expansion as for the protection of their interests."[3] Taft's eagerness to sign comprehensive arbitration treaties with the major European powers and his enthusiasm for judicial settlement of international disputes reflected his conviction that there existed a growing community of sentiment among the great powers, a cultural core around which he proposed to wind the legal armature of his treaties. These treaties would rest "upon the practically simultaneous operation of the common mind and the conscience of the world upon common knowledge."[4]

The U.S. policymaker with the greatest faith in the possibilities of cultural change was Woodrow Wilson. Like Taft, Wilson believed that the world was functionally knit together, describing it at various times as a finely tuned machine or a unit that "could not be taken to pieces," but for Wilson these connections had implications that Taft had not contemplated. In addition to being an economic whole, the world was militarily one also, and all the more dangerous for that. For Wilson, World War I, apart from its idealistic possibilities, heralded the end of the formerly self-contained and self-regulating European balance of power. The resulting disappearance of barriers to global war raised the most terrifying possibilities for the future, of which World War I, horrible as it was, provided only a suggestive foretaste.

In world public opinion, Wilson thought he saw the potential for another kind of unity that would resolve the problems growing out of economic and military interdependence. The usual way of interpreting Wilson's faith in public opinion is to equate it with the universal triumph of democracy. While that interpretation is correct as far as it goes, its emphasis on political change diverts attention from the cultural dimension of Wilson's thought, with its emphasis on the role of values that originate outside a political framework. For Wilson, the emergence of world opinion was anterior to politics, for it signified the arrival of that epochal point in history, the creation of "a new international psychology."

Without the firmest possible organic foundation in human sentiment, the League of Nations would be an ineffectual "debating society" for which he had little use.[5]

Wilson the utopian was also a lifelong legal conservative who believed that law must be firmly rooted in tradition and historical continuity, a view that seemed to leave little room for the reconciliation of the world's many clashing cultural viewpoints. But Wilson also believed in human nature, the "common pulse in us all," and in the mutability of culture. Customs, he felt, could be altered by war, and this war, he made clear, was "going to strip human nature naked" and force men "to stand face to face without any sort of disguise, without any sort of attempt to hoodwink one another." Liberalism as a philosophy promotes disruption and change, and Wilson as a good liberal believed he was witnessing rapid cultural change in which the creative destruction of particularist mentalities was unveiling the unobstructed yearnings of human nature.

Because of this almost mystical faith in world opinion, Wilson has often been accused of idealistically wanting to do away with the balance of power, but this is a distorted view of his thinking. He believed, like many contemporary students of geopolitics, that the European balance was historically dead and that any attempt to resurrect it would inevitably break down. If so, the possibilities boiled down to either creating a system of collective security based on world opinion or living in a world in which any local aggression might escalate into a world war. Inasmuch as the first option proved to be unworkable, Wilson's successors were forced to grapple with the latter.

The Wilsonian scheme was breathtaking in its sweep. It encompassed a global view of political, military, and social interaction and presupposed a cultural ecumene among advanced nations in which discussion rather than power would be used to settle international disputes. Yet Wilson was obviously mistaken about the degree of cultural uniformity then possible. In the United States, the Senate was not about to abandon sacred policy traditions. In Europe, the undiminished force of nationalism, hierarchical racial and cultural distinctions that sanctioned inequality among nations, and new ideologies that competed for the allegiance of mankind, especially Bolshevism, demonstrated that the world was nowhere near to attaining the level of comity which Wilson professed to see in human hearts.

In the circumstances, an extreme reaction to Wilson's blend of catastrophism and utopian promise was inevitable. The disillusionment struck hardest among those who had occupied the core of Wilson's apostolic circle, the most notable example being one Herbert Clark Hoover. Hoover had been present at Versailles and enthusiastically preached the Wilsonian gospel upon his return home, but in the aftermath of the League of Nations debacle he retreated to what he thought was a more realistic and manageable reliance on functional interdependence.

The irony of Hoover's intellectual odyssey is that, in terms of experience abroad and firsthand familiarity with a broad variety of cultures, he was the most cosmopolitan president of the twentieth century. Nearly two years of his life had been spent aboard ship, traveling the seven seas from one engineering job to another, time he used to bone up on the history and traditions of the nation in which he would be working. Yet the more time he spent abroad and the more conversant he became with foreign customs, the more passionately American he became, firmly convinced of the unique virtues of his native land. As a result, Hoover was an early traveller down the path of cultural pluralism which most Americans would later take.

Lifted to power by his reputation for humanitarianism, Hoover did not really believe in humanity. His disillusionment with the peacemaking process in Paris, especially with the cultural frictions that seemed to take it over, were palpable in his *Memoirs*. "Destructive forces sat at the peace table," he wrote. "The future of twenty-six jealous European races was there. The genes of a thousand years of inbred hate and fear of every generation were in their blood."[6] In addition, postwar Europe was a breeding ground of ideological hatreds. Having had to deal firsthand with the chaos attending the rise of Bolshevism, Hoover upon his return was determined to prevent the infection from spreading to the United States.

His contribution to updating U.S. values to meet modern social conditions was a slender little volume, *American Individualism*, which, whether he intended it or not, referred more to U.S. cultural uniqueness than to personal character. "America is a distinct social personality," Hoover insisted, "and personality is characterized by a peculiar reaction to problems, a unique way of doing things. The war revealed this individual note."[7] The key to Wilsonian internationalism had been world public opinion, a universal view of cultural interaction that presupposed a convergence of values, but Hoover was now convinced that the United States had "grown far apart from Europe." Like the historian Charles Beard, who in the 1920s asserted the existence of an organically distinct U.S. identity in *The Rise of American Civilization*, Hoover saw the United States and Europe as geographic embodiments of two separate historical processes.[8]

The man whose name would become synonymous with isolationism in the 1930s was also intimately familiar with the facts of twentieth century interdependence. His international business experience had schooled him in the reality of global markets, a world raw materials base, and an international financial system. His wartime experience as food administrator had amply demonstrated, if only for the duration, man's interdependence in foodstuffs. Yet his disillusionment led him to believe that not only could the United States stand apart from a European war, but that his nation could, for all intents and purposes, be self-sufficient economically if need be. Unlike Wilson, he believed that the European balance of power still operated and that the oceans continued to guarantee U.S. security.

There was a universalism of sorts in U.S. policy of the 1920s, but its businessman's preoccupation with economic interdependence lacked the belief in cultural communion that lay at the heart of Wilsonianism. European perceptions of the U.S. approach merely underscored this institutional emphasis. The U.S. model was widely assumed among Europeans to lack spirit, based as it was on a machine ethic and a view of the world as a gigantic, soulless economic mechanism. The utopianism of the 1920s lay in the realm of functional rationality, bred of a confidence that business professionals could apply their expertise in the successful management of global prosperity.

U.S. businessmen and international bankers, with the encouragement of the State Department, contributed mightily to stabilization in Europe and to an impressive restoration of productivity by the end of the decade. In Asia, the diplomats took a more forward role by promoting naval disarmament and an end to the diplomacy of imperialism. But this structural approach to cementing international harmony failed to generate a consensus on underlying values. Japanese and Chinese nationalism continued to grow apace in Asia, whereas in Europe racist and fascist doctrines made inroads. These trends, coupled with the economic contradictions of business internationalism, set the stage for the conflicts of the next decade.

With the coming to power of Franklin D. Roosevelt and his New Deal in 1933, the stage seemed set for a revival of some variant of Wilsonianism. Roosevelt, after all, had run as a vice presidential candidate on the 1920 ticket and campaigned lustily for the League of Nations. During the 1920s, he had criticized the functional approach of business internationalists as a policy conducted "from the dollars and cents point of view."[9] He realized full well, of course, that "our present civilization rests on the international exchange of commodities,"[10] but that approach seemed hardly adequate. Equating purely economic internationalism with selfishness and materialism, both of which he believed to have been behind the arms competition that led to World War I, he advocated instead a new spirit of international relations, a spirit of true service in which "all the world recognizes all the rest of the world as one big family."[11] Stressing cultural form over economic function, he argued that "as in the relations between individuals, so the attitude and spirit are controlling factors in the affairs of nations."[12]

FDR's cosmic view of mankind was implicit in his 90%–10% theory of international relations, an early argument that relied on the Wilsonian assumption that the mass of people the world over were, in their hearts, united in their longing for peace, this in contrast to the small percentage who, misled by irresponsible leaders, were stirring up trouble. "We could get a world accord on peace immediately if the people of the world could speak for themselves," he argued.[13]

Nevertheless, Roosevelt had given notice prior to his election that his approach would not be the same as Wilson's. Given the prevailing interest in state-managed economies, corporatism, planning, and fiscal and monetary experimentation, internationalism even of the functional economic variety was difficult to advocate in a decade of global depression noted for its nationalist tendencies. As for strategic internationalism, until the late 1930s FDR's rhetoric shied away from claiming any connection between the military broils of European and U.S. security.

Ever the practical politician, Roosevelt prudently acknowledged that U.S. participation in the League of Nations was no longer a possibility. Having accepted the reality of the American people's perception of the League as a purely European organism, he set his sights instead on achieving his internationalist goals through informal collaboration with the League or, if necessary, by pursuing international cooperation without it. In commenting on a proposal by Under Secretary of State Sumner Welles for a 1937 international economic conference which for a time would be FDR's preferred solution to the international crisis, Assistant Secretary of State Adolf Berle described this approach as "nothing more than the kind of thing which the League of Nations did except that it is not mortgaged to maintaining the status quo."[14]

Instead of relying on organized world opinion, Roosevelt and his secretary of state, Cordell Hull, preferred to preach, to set an example, and to hope that the League could hold up its end of things. With respect to the Good Neighbor Policy toward Latin America, which was often interpreted as an isolationist policy in which the United States stuck to its hemispheric knitting, Roosevelt always made clear his hope that its example would have global resonance. "Things in the Americas are in every way most hopeful and I hope that there will be at least some moral repercussions in Europe," he said, without making clear how the message could be translated into political reality.

Ultimately, preaching and the power of example failed and, by 1940, the administration was openly admitting that a civilization with presumably similar transcultural values binding it together had failed completely to stem the tide of fascism. Not only did the tenor of FDR's military thinking change, as the strategically holistic premises of the domino theory went into effect, so too did his cultural assumptions. In puzzling out the causes of the German drive for world domination, FDR parted company with Wilson, who had always taken pains to insist that the United States was not fighting the German people. Though his statement at the Casablanca conference early in 1942 indicated that the United States would only hold responsible the Nazi leadership, FDR and his coterie were far more harsh in private.

The problem, they believed, was not simply Hitler, but the Germans and their culture. "Too many people here and in England hold to the view that the German people as a whole are not responsible for what has taken place—that only a few Nazi leaders are responsible. That unfortunately is not based on fact," wrote FDR.[15] Similarly, Secretary of State Hull argued that "this Nazism is down in the German people a thousand miles deep and you have just got to uproot it, and you can't do it by just shooting a few people." If ideology was rooted in culture, Germany was clearly a bad culture, which meant that appeals to common values would be of little avail. FDR opposed a generous policy in the spirit of Grant's treatment of Lee at Appomattox because he felt that "Germany understands only one kind of language."[16] Obviously, that language was power. A similar logic, amplified by racial differences, applied to Japan.

The futile attempt at rallying international public opinion in the 1930s and the failure to rely on timely force in halting expansionism in Europe and Asia led FDR to depart significantly from Wilsonian cultural assumptions in his planning for the postwar world. Despite the great wave of internationalist enthusiasm in the United States surrounding the creation of the United Nations and UNESCO, the view at the top was far different. FDR had to face the reality of cultural gulfs not only with the enemy nations, but also with the Soviet ally. Well aware that culture was more than skin deep and that culture and historical tradition to some extent determined political systems and ideologies, FDR was faced with the difficult problem of cementing a global order without benefit of the cultural and civilizational glue that Wilson had relied upon in his version of public opinion.

As was his tendency in domestic affairs, FDR in his foreign policy resorted to a nonideological pragmatism that departed in two major ways from Wilsonianism. A novel feature of the United Nations, despite its resemblance to the League, was that peacekeeping would rely on power, in particular the power of a grand alliance that continued into the postwar years. Whereas Wilson rejected the Congress of Vienna as a model, FDR accepted it, though with his usual discretion. Rather than rely on world opinion to keep the peace, the Security Council was given that task while the General Assembly was turned into a debating society—precisely what Wilson had wished to avoid.

But what, besides fear of another war, was to keep this alliance in being? Lacking cultural bonds, FDR sought to create psychological ties. In addition to the deterrent value of shared historical memories of the war's destructiveness (as opposed to Wilson's overarching liberal interpretation of history), FDR hoped to substitute the psychology of friendship among leaders for the cultural bonds of community—an approach that Wilson would have found repugnant. Thus he emphasized amicable personal dealings with Churchill and Stalin as a means of generating trust. Getting along with the Soviets was perceived as a nurturing of friendship, while cooperation meant creating a network of postwar institutions that would continue and expand upon the base of functional wartime collaboration. Unfortunately, given Roosevelt's poor health, the change-ability of U.S. politics, and the logjam of geopolitical problems backed up by war's end, this was a very fragile foundation.

Though Roosevelt's world order was culturally particularist, politically it was more universal than Wilson's system—Soviet partnership alone testified to that. Moreover, unlike the post–World War I settlement, which was Eurocentric partly as a result of Wilson's belief that Asian peoples had not yet attained civilized parity with the white powers, FDR was quite willing to incorporate the Chinese into the club, even though he believed them to be culturally retrograde and inscrutable. Since a comprehensive structure had to be created, one that could be based on uniformity of values, FDR did not have to be selective. There would be no millennium under FDR's system, but then again if things went well there would be no disaster of the kind Wilson had envisioned if world opinion were not heeded.[17]

The pessimistic view of cultural change produced by the failure of world opinion was accompanied by a more negative view of human nature. The pursuit of perfectionism through cultural change, after all, was pointless unless there existed common attributes in human nature that could become the bases for a liberal world order. The emergence of a sobered "liberal realism" in the 1940s, epitomized by the writings of Reinhold Niebuhr, was characterized by the growing consciousness of the existence of original sin, which was only another way of saying that human nature was flawed. If so, even accelerated cultural change through liberal processes would not bring the promised utopia. The implication for policy was that henceforth the world would be made safe for pluralism, not for a world of democracies reflecting a global general will. It was, however, a pluralism based on the belief that only liberal capitalist institutions could provide the matrix of tolerance in which multiform beliefs would flourish.

The recognition of the strength of cultural forces in a plural world was evident in virtually every aspect of postwar U.S. policy. The formation of NATO and other supranational institutions in Europe during the 1950s was accompanied by a good deal of hopeful talk about common values, but the process of European integration was entered into precisely in the recognition that those values were missing. The crux of the problem was always how to create a bond of supranational sentiment whose absence lay at the core of European frictions. The approach finally adopted was frankly based on the assumption that the creation of an institutional infrastructure would slowly bring about the sense of common identity that Europeans patently lacked. Dean Acheson's memoirs, *Present at the Creation*, were aptly titled in describing the role of institutional architect undertaken by the United States in the postwar years.

If cultural disunity characterized an alliance that presumably shared the core values of an endangered civilization, the gulf was even more pronounced with one's enemies. The debate over the fundamental causes of U.S.-Soviet antagonism was not phrased in such terms, itself a significant phenomenon, but it nevertheless had cultural implications. The argument raged inconclusively as to whether the Soviet problem was an outgrowth of traditional power factors, in which case Russian history and cultural tradition were the problem, or whether it was instead rooted in ideology, which implied the subjugation of an innately democratic population by a conspiracy within the Kremlin.

Although many credulous Americans, among them some seasoned diplomats, viewed communism as a spiritual malaise that lay at the source of power conflicts, responsible senior statesmen for the most part viewed it as a rhetorical mask for traditional Russian power drives. Ideology depended on Soviet power for its existence even as it justified it, but of itself possessed no intrinsic universal appeal; it was a second-order phenomenon that lived off power. Having no common cultural allegiances, peoples could coalesce only around centers of power with their respective universal ideologies.

The most cogent analysis of the problem was made by State Department Russian expert George Kennan, who deduced Soviet motives from his understanding of Russian national character. Employing a psychological approach to the study of culture, Kennan argued that Soviet behavior was deeply rooted in Russian history, with communist ideology veiling the traditional rule of a small group of men. "Basically this is only the steady advance of uneasy Russian nationalism, a centuries old movement . . . in [the] new guise of international Marxism," he argued.[18] Ideology, because it had been grafted onto deep cultural-historical roots, could not be minimized. But since cultural differences had always been mediated by power politics, and since the basic preoccupation of the Soviet leadership was with power, he believed that the two nations could successfully communicate at that level. It seemed fair to conclude that Soviet intentions could be modified by power and that superpower relations could be successfully managed by traditional diplomacy.

The argument as to whether culture or ideology was more fundamental may have had implications for the conduct of short-term diplomacy, but for the long term it made little difference. Given the unshakable grip of Soviet power, there was next to no hope of rapid, millennial change through the elimination of a few fanatics at key points in the Kremlin. Consequently, Kennan visualized the U.S.-Soviet relationship as

a sort of long-range fencing match in which the weapons are not only the development of military power but the loyalties and convictions of hundreds of millions of people and the control or influence over their forms of political organization. . . . It may be the strength and health of our respective systems which is decisive and which will determine the issue.[19]

As the National Security Council recognized, policy had to be maintained "for a period long enough to encompass a respectable portion of the organic process of growth and change in Soviet political life."[20]

Containment sought a short-term stabilization, but its principal objective was historical: victory in a long-term civilizational struggle for which no time limit was set. Inasmuch as there seemed no way of changing Soviet values or institutions from the outside, the emphasis had to be on long-term secular decay from within in the hope that the USSR's aggressive energies would be sapped by its internal contradictions. Thus the goal was not to remove political obstructions to common values, but by means of politics to buy time for the creation of those values. For Wilson, cultural change induced by the trauma of the Great War had been the means to a millennial political transformation; now, however, cultural transformation had become the long-term goal of political maneuvering. Formerly the solution, culture had become the problem.

The new skepticism with regard to cultural change was reflected in occupation policy toward the defeated enemies. Clumsy attempts to redirect German and Japanese culture after the war, despite some residual liberal enthusiasm in favor of sweeping reform, were quickly abandoned in favor of structural solutions. As one basic document candidly acknowledged: "it has been vividly demonstrated through our experience in Germany and Japan that the psychology and outlook [i.e., culture] of a great people cannot be altered in a short space of time at the mere dictate or precept of a foreign power, even in the wake of total defeat and submission."[21]

The continuing decline of culture as an organizing concept for U.S. policy in the 1950s was visible also in the functional programs of nation building undertaken by the U.S. in the third world. Americans had come to assume that modernization would take place once the underdeveloped nations installed the appropriate infrastructure of institutions. Theorists and policymakers alike were determinists who "saw political development flowing from economic development."[22] This structural approach to development stood in marked contrast to the belief, formerly applied by missionaries and philanthropic foundations, that modernization would come through acculturation, especially through the diffusion of the scientific mentality that was thought to lie at the heart of Western technical and political progress. But now changes at the level of social structure alone were thought to be sufficient to bring about attitudinal transformations. The enthusiasm for modernization, essentially a sociological ideal, was coming to replace the enthusiasm for cultural transformation, which was essentially an historical ideal.

By the mid-1950s, the idea of cultural relativism, whose scholarly heyday was the 1930s but which had by now filtered down to the general population, was beginning to take hold. With the elimination of race as a reasonably acceptable explanation of persisting differences among peoples, many of the obstacles to change once believed to be due to racial factors were now attributed to cultural resistance.

The waning faith in cultural solutions contributed to the triumph of the domino theory, which assumed that, in the absence of world public opinion, global power dynamics would take over. The idea of world opinion still figured in the assessments of domino theorists, but it no longer referred to the common human sentiment underlying culture. Once viewed as a redemptive force, it now referred to a culturally plural environment whose loss would pave the way to a global totalitarian rigidity. In this sense, world public opinion began more and more to resemble traditional definitions of prestige, long a psychological adjunct of power diplomacy. A vestigial universalism remained, however, in the domino theory's assumption that failure to halt aggression would result in wholesale perceptions of weakness throughout the world. In this curious sense, the so-called "psychological domino theory" carried on the belief in a monolithic world opinion by ignoring cultural differences that made for heterogeneous responses. Wilsonians had bumped into the frustrating reality of cultural particularism, but so too in their own way did the cold warriors. Underrated in one case, culture was altogether ignored in the other.

For those who questioned the domino theory's logic of power and viewed culture from a relativist perspective, a pluralist conception of culture could have anti-interventionist implications. The impact of relativism became evident when opponents of the Vietnam War began increasingly to oppose the deepening U.S. involvement on cultural grounds, criticizing the United States's clumsy meddling with what seemed an impenetrable alien culture. For many opponents of the war, winning hearts and minds was neither possible nor desirable in the first place. Whereas President Lyndon B. Johnson had come to believe, as a result of a poignant intellectual odyssey, in the fundamental identity and equality of all human beings, many antiwar activists stressed the impossibility of grafting U.S. values upon other societies. Culture, the conceptual linchpin of early twentieth century U.S. diplomacy, had become a concept stressing the insurmountable mental barriers in the world.

An August 1968 New York *Times* interview with renegade Democrat Eugene McCarthy provides perhaps an extreme and embittered indication of this new attitude:

I [interviewer] asked him [McCarthy] the final question about Vietnam: "How are we going to get out?" He said "Take this down. . . . The time has come for us to say to the Vietnamese, We will take our steel out of the land of thatched huts, we will take our tanks out of the land of the water buffalo, our napalm and flame-throwers out of the land that scarcely knows the use of matches. We will give you back your small and willing women, your rice paddies and your land.'' He smiled. ''That's my platform. It's pretty good, isn't it?''[23]

The chairman of the Senate Committee on Foreign Relations, J. William Fulbright, made much the same point when he argued to the president that the Vietnamese were ''not our kind of people.'' Though Johnson took this as a racial slur, Fulbright only meant to say that the United States was unable to understand the Vietnamese and the entrenched mysteries of their Confucian order.

While for some, culture was seen as too strong, in some circles it continued to be perceived as a weak force vulnerable to rapid change. To the extent that technology was breaching local barriers and creating a homogenized world society, a sentimental portion of U.S. liberalism began to inveigh against the susceptibility of cultures to the serpent of structural change. Much as environmentalists wished to preserve as many animal species as possible, the argument was made that cultures in all their purity ought not to be destroyed by modernization. Increasingly influential was the view, broadcast by influential anthropologists like Clifford Geertz, that humanity was expressed through culture and that a man without culture was not human.[24] With culture assuming a sacredness that it had not before possessed, deracination assumed a sinful aura. Cultures were no longer good or bad, merely different; no longer measured by a common standard of civilization, they were incommensurable. The belief in the desirability of cultural change, formerly a major characteristic of liberalism, had given way to a belief in cloistered values.

Though ostensibly rooted in the egalitarian view that all cultures are created equal, the relativist outlook actually made possible a more rigid stratification of peoples. In its more extreme forms, this notion of humanity envisioned mankind more as a zoological park than a community, one in which cultures were insulated from contact with a dangerous environment. This anthropological rigidity, one that has since come to be rejected by anthropologists themselves,[25] was profoundly antihistorical. Not only did it represent the rejection of the universal historical vision that had animated liberalism at the beginning of the century, but by delegitimizing power intervention and eschewing changes in the realm of values, it ignored the necessity of historical change altogether. The new view of culture, fearful of the total destruction of national essences, operated without benefit of a historical perspective that might realistically have accepted the inevitability of cultural change or, from the standpoint of ideals, might have sought to channel it in a cosmopolitan direction.

But this was liberal thought in a minor key. The dominant and more realistic segment of liberal thought continued to advocate historical change for the transformation of values. Unlike the good old days, however, when the common historical destination was assumed, the effects of that transformation were now far from clear. This was most evident in the changed relationship between the United States and China. With the restoration of relations in 1978, Beijing sought to foster its "Four Modernizations" by picking up the cultural relationship so abruptly curtailed in 1949. As tens of thousands of mainland Chinese students streamed into U.S. universities to absorb the expertise necessary to modernize their country, it seemed that the two nations were finally approaching a long-awaited cultural meeting of the minds.

Yet, from the standpoint of U.S. China experts, there was no questions of Americanizing China. Close cultural contacts were deemed desirable from the geopolitical standpoint of the new Washington-Moscow-Beijing triangle, but the question of common values was completely up in the air. What sort of values were Americans trying to foster? Would modernization in fact bring the two nations closer together? No one seemed to know, everyone taking it on faith that things would work out for the best—that is, if they had a faith. The kind of deep cultural friendship that once was thought to undergird U.S.–Chinese relationships seemed an elusive, perhaps unattainable, goal. With the emergence of a dynamic and sophisticated China scholarship in the United States, East Asia was no longer inscrutable, yet in some ways it was more inaccessible than ever.[26]

Early twentieth century views of culture had been based on the Enlightenment-derived belief that a rational human nature lay beneath the cake of custom, a human nature that would be liberated once superficial cultural differences had been scraped away. As part of the general decline in natural law thinking, the modern view has seen a weakening of belief in the idea of human nature and a corresponding strengthening of the idea of culture. To use a computer analogy, whereas formerly culture was viewed as being akin to random memory, volatile and changeable, post–World War II thought came to see it as a built in "read only" memory, not subject to ready manipulation.

This transformation of the role of culture in U.S. diplomacy was closely related to the rise and decline of U.S. utopianism in the twentieth century. In its main outlines, the shift in the relationship between values and social structure came to resemble the pattern suggested by the French sociologist Émile Durkheim in his classic *The Division of Labor in Society*: As the structural interdependence of the world (organic solidarity) increased, its cultural unity (mechanical solidarity) appeared to evaporate. While being pushed inexorably closer together at one level, mankind seemed to be pulled further apart and increasingly fragmented at another. At the level of cultural perception, the tendency to think in terms of a fragmented mankind was not unique to Americans. As the historian François Furet has noted, the multiplication of national historical sensibilities in an era of increasing interdependence has led to a situation in which "human space has become homogeneous even as time has ceased to be so."[27]

Ironically, then, as Americans became more cosmopolitan and more fully aware of the plurality and tenacity of cultural tradition, their particularist view of culture cut across the grain of what was, in most other respects, a tenaciously universal vision of their nation's foreign policy interests. Equally important, although beyond the purview of this essay, was a related long-term development. Despite the historically intimate and often critical policy connection between conceptions of culture and power, neither the existence of this intellectual gap nor the question of whether and how it might be bridged seemed to concern U.S. statesmen of the 1980s. Only the future would determine whether meaningful concepts of civilization and world opinion, minus the confusions of the past, would be introduced into their understanding of international history and foreign policy.

## NOTES

1. See, for example, Frederick W. Marks, III, *Velvet on Iron: The Diplomacy of Theodore Roosevelt* (Lincoln, NE: University of Nebraska Press, 1979) and Richard H. Collin, *Theodore Roosevelt, Culture, Diplomacy, and Expansion* (Baton Rouge: Louisiana State University Press, 1985).

2. Frank Ninkovich, "Theodore Roosevelt: Civilization as Ideology," *Diplomatic History* 10 (Summer 1986): 221–245.

3. Knox speech to the Pennsylvania Society of New York, December 11, 1909, Box 45, Knox Papers, Library of Congress Manuscript Division.

4. Knox speech, "International Unity," December 11, 1909. Knox Papers.

5. An address to the Italian Parliament, January 3, 1919, *The Papers of Woodrow Wilson* (Princeton, NJ: Princeton University Press, 1966) 53: 598 (hereafter PWW); from the diary of Colonel House, August 30, 1914, PWW, 30: 462; an unpublished prolegomenon to a peace note, November 25, 1916, PWW, 40: 69.

6. Herbert Hoover, *Memoirs: Years of Adventure, 1874–1920* (New York: Macmillan, 1951), p. 437.

7. Herbert Hoover, typescript forword to M. Friedman, *America and the New Era*, in Herbert Hoover Presidential Library, West Branch, IA (hereafter HHPL).

8. Hoover, address before the San Francisco Commercial Club, October 9, 1919, HHPL.

9. FDR to Mrs. J. Malcolm Forbes, August 20, 1928, Box 104, Family, Business, and Personal Papers, Franklin D. Roosevelt Presidential Library (hereafter FDRPL).

10. FDR speech at Buenos Aires, December 1, 1936, in Edgar Nixon, ed., *Franklin D. Roosevelt and Foreign Affairs* (Cambridge, MA: Harvard University Press, 1969) 2: 519.

11. FDR, *Whither Bound*, May 18, 1926, Box 109, Family, Business, Personal, FDRPL.

12. FDR, speech at Syracuse, NY, September 27, 1936, speech file, #251, FDRPL.

13. FDR speech, December 28, 1933, in Nixon, *Franklin D. Roosevelt and Foreign Affairs*, 1: 560.

14. Memo by Adolph Berle, October 13, 1937, in Beatrice Bishop Berle and Travis Beal Jacobs, eds., *Navigating the Rapids 1918-971: From the Papers of Adolf A. Berle* (New York: Harcourt Brace Jovanovich, 1973), p. 140.

15. Quoted in Paul Y. Hammond, "Policy Directives for the Occupation of Germany," in Harold Stein, ed. *American Civil-Military Decisions* (Birmingham: University of Alabama Press, 1963), p. 355.

16. FDR to Hull, April 1, 1944, in Elliott Roosevelt, ed., *FDR: His Personal Letters 1928-1945*, (New York: Duell, Sloan and Pearce, 1950) 2: 1504.

17. The Roosevelt years also saw the adoption by the Department of State of a formal program of cultural relations the fate of which was emblematic of the changes then taking place. While it may seem ironical that the significance of culture in foreign policy declined precisely at the point in time when the U.S. Government began to integrate cultural programs into its foreign policy apparatus, the failure of world opinion, which at one time had been counted on to create a modern world order, clearly required the political management of international relations. The triumph of the enthusiasts for the cultural approach in getting their concerns recognized in policy thus turned out to be an unknowing admission that their larger ambitions had failed. On this point see Frank Ninkovich, *The Diplomacy of Ideas: U.S. Foreign Policy and Cultural Relations, 1938-1950* (New York: Cambridge University Press, 1981).

18. George Kennan, "The Long Telegram," February 22, 1946, in Thomas H. Etzold and John Lewis Gaddis, eds., *Containment: Documents on American Policy and Strategy 1945-1950* (New York: Columbia University Press, 1978), p. 54.

19. Ibid.

20. NSC 20/1, "U.S. Objectives with Respect to Russia," August 18, 1948, ibid., p. 188.

21. NSC 20/1,, "U.S. Objectives with Respect to Russia," August 18, 1948, ibid., p. 192. Lest this be interpreted as a complete rejection of reliance on cultural resources, it should be noted that the success of democracy in those two nations demonstrated the existence of indigenous cultural resources which were capable of supporting democracy.

22. Robert A. Packenham, *Liberal America and the Third World*, (Princeton, NJ: Princeton University Press, 1973), p. 6.

23. *New York Times*, August 4, 1968, Dec. 7. 25:3.

24. See, for example, Clifford Geertz, "The Impact of the Concept of Culture on the Concept of Man," in Geertz, ed., *The Interpretation of Cultures* (New York: Basic Books, 1973), pp. 33-54.

25. Elvin Hatch, *Morality and Culture* (New York: Columbia University Press, 1984).

26. See Frank Ninkovich, "The Trajectory of Cultural Internationalism," in Joyce K. Kallgren and Denis Fred Simon, eds., *Educational Exchanges: Essays on the Sino-American Experience* (Berkeley: University of California Press, 1987), pp. 8-23.

27. François Furet, *In the Workshop of History* (Chicago: University of Chicago Press, 1984), p. 70.

# 9
# *U.S. Foreign Policy as Manifest Theology*

Johan Galtung

## AN ARCHETYPE FOR U.S. FOREIGN POLICY: THE BASIC METAPHOR

President Taft stated in 1912:

We are not going to intervene in Mexico until no other course is possible, but I must protect our people in Mexico as far as possible, and their property, by having the government (in Mexico) understand that there is a God in Israel and he is on duty. Otherwise they will utterly ignore our many great complaints and give no attention to needed protection which they can give.[1]

And Richard Challener, after citing this quotation, then proceeds to say that: "The Lord now donned the uniform of a United States Naval Officer, and his duty was no longer restricted, as in 1911, to American territorial waters".[2] To some the only surprising words in a fairly standard speech from the head of state of a very interventionist country would be "God in Israel." The exact borders of Israel may, indeed, be debated. But the location is generally in the eastern Mediterranean/Middle East/West Asia, not in North America, in the United States, even as a way of referring to the United States of America. And yet this expression, often in the form "God's New Israel" occurs very frequently in U.S. history, from the Mayflower and the founding of the Plymouth Colony (1620) onwards.

The reason is obvious. We are dealing here with one of the most potent metaphors in Occidental history, by Occidental referring to the part of the world inspired by the Kitab, the Old Testament in general, and the first five books (of Moses) the Torah, in particular. The story is basic in Judaism, Christianity, and Islam (in that order). Given that these three together for a long period have constituted the largest religious grouping of humankind, and have heard the story for 3000, 2000, and fourteen hundred years, respectively, we can safely assume that we are dealing with an archetype, so deeply internalized in the culture as to be taken for granted. They are the raw material out of which the social cosmology of a people is made, the assumptions built into deep ideology and deep structure, never to be questioned.[3]

The story is beautiful and powerful. A people in diaspora, a small people, escaping from a domineering, repressive power, in search of a New Beginning. The small people have a Big God, Yahweh, not only the most powerful of them all, but the only one. The leader, Moses, has a "special relationship." A covenant is revealed on Mt. Sinai. Yahweh gives to the Jews in the diaspora a special status as "most favored nation": the Jews are His Chosen People, with a Promised Land, Eretz Israel. As such, they are given a tremendously important role as the guiding light for other, and by implication, lesser peoples.

But they have to keep, in everyday prayer and observations, their side of the covenant, the Ten Commandments known to Christians and other norms more specific to Judaism. In other words, there is a relationship between the special status as most favored nation and the fulfillment of their side of the covenant. Yahweh would be under no obligation to support His Chosen People in their quest for the Promised Land if the chosen people were to stray away from the moral course laid out for them, very clearly, on Mt. Sinai. The smallest people with the biggest god[4] and a clear mission in the world if and only if they keep their side of the pact. In other words, a linkage between moral behavior as defined in a religious context and foreign relations, relations to other peoples. Fulfilling the commandments becomes not only an individual obligation and a condition for personal salvation, but a collective obligation to be fulfilled by everybody for collective survival. Internal religious control becomes a social necessity.

This could lead to a theocratic state, with state and church fused into one, the priesthood seeing to it that the people of the convenant fulfil their part. As a minimum it would lead to a strong relation between state and religion. That relation would, presumably, be stronger the more monopolistic the position of that particular religion, and not only relative to other religions, but to any culture that might serve to inspire alternative archetypes, including ideologies.

For many of the Founding Fathers of the United States this was not a problem, it seems. As elect Puritans[5] for generations, even centuries, essentially reading only one book, the Bible (but both Testaments), competitive metaphors were less available than in more settled and more heterogeneous settings. And the problem seems not to be why they seized upon Israel and the Covenant as a metaphor; the problem would have been to explain why they should not have done so. Human beings reason, and learn, by isomorphism. It would be impossible not to recognize similarities between the archetype and their objective and subjective reality. They were certainly in the diaspora, escaping from the domination and repression, if not of a foreign people making them captives and slaves, at least from the oppression exercised by clergy and nobility, by landowners and merchants in late feudal, early capitalist England. They certainly had come to a land. They were strict in adhering to the commandments. Why should not they also be chosen, if not by Yahweh, then by His "successor," the Christian God? And why should not the land be the Promised Land? And if so, and if they were really chosen (and that would have to be proven), why should they not also be the guiding light for all other peoples, being the people closest to God?

Isomorphism is a strong master over the human mind. Reality is compared to an archetype reinforced in them through daily reading and service. So much fits that only the fool or the nasty nonbeliever would not fill in the missing links (elements, relations). And so they did, even to the point of giving their sons and daughters names from the Old Testament and their cities and towns likewise—New Canaan (Connecticut) being one example—going so far as to conceive of the country they were building as God's New Israel, ultimately inspiring President Taft's speech.

## HOW TO APPROPRIATE ANOTHER PEOPLE'S METAPHOR: SOME POINTS

And yet there were two problems: The Promised Land was not empty. And the metaphor was in Judaism, not in Christianity. How this was handled will certainly remain a matter of dispute; what follows here are some points around which hypotheses might crystallize for historical testing—not to mention for testing in future praxis.

If the basic idea is that God helps the chosen/elect/just, then success does not only mean that they were just in the eyes of God but also that the means used to obtain the success were justified. Weber used this principle to establish a link between puritan Protestantism and capitalism. Two or three substantial victories in a single stroke: mundane success, the proof that one is just and even (s)elect, and that the structure built to solidify and institutionalize the success is justifiable—all coming together.

Why should this mechanism not also work internationally, meaning between the early Americans and the Native Americans? If this were, indeed, the Promised Land, then success in suppressing the Natives— be that through absorption (few), expulsion, inner expulsion in the reservations, death by inflicting on them diseases with which they could not cope (and also through starvation), and direct extermination (many)— would only be one more sign of being on the right track, individually and collectively. By implication, failure is not necessarily a sign that the means were unjustifiable, nor the cause (to pave the way for the chosen

peoples' settlement in the promised land). There is the third and important possibility that failure in this world derives from moral deficits, and,
hence, withdrawal of divine support. Settle those problems first (and they
are essentially at the intra- and interpersonal levels) and the relation to
God will be such as to guarantee success: the primacy of *Binnenpolitik*
and *Binnenmoral* over *Aussenpolitik* and *Aussenmoral* to stick to Weber, as
a nontrivial theological consequence.

So the problem was solved, and to the satisfaction of the overwhelming majority of Americans although the idiom today may be more social
Darwinist (we were stronger) and less theological (which does not mean
that the archetype is not working underneath, in the individual and
collective subconscious). Just as the Old Testament provided a convenient
metaphor for the early Americans in their relation to the indigenous
people, what the Puritans in fact did might have provided a metaphor
for Israeli dealings with the Palestinians. But the position taken here is
that of legitimation, not rationalization. People are enacting a metaphor
because they are, if not compelled, at least strongly persuaded by the
archetype to do so. The choice is limited once the archetype is firmly
established. They not only want but want to want what they do.

The second problem, how to appropriate somebody else's metaphor,
leads to a number of important questions for U.S. historiography.[6] Off-
hand, one might envisage three different solutions. First, to take on more
and more elements of the Jewish metaphor, such as the names mentioned above, claiming that we are, if not the real Jews, at least the real Israel.
The former would have been impossible given the strong elements of anti-
Semitism in the Christian tradition, not necessarily because "they killed
Jesus" (what would have happened to the Christian metaphor of one person, not a whole people guiding through suffering if "they" had not?)
but because they refused to recognize him, dead or alive, as the Messiah.
But the second solution was possible, and particularly so as there was
no Israel except as a myth, a dream, as a metaphor. The geopolitical status
was empty.

The next possibility would be to turn against the Jews as people un-
worthy of that elevated status among peoples, having been bad trustees
of the trust God had in them as evidenced by their geopolitical failure.
Anti-Semitism would be justified as an instrument of God's wrath against
a people who had been given a chance, and a major one, and had failed.

And then there is the third possibility, the one ultimately chosen but
only some time after World War II and particularly after [increased
awareness of] the Holocaust [put an end to overt] anti-Semitism. The third
possibility is through a process that can be referred to as "hyphenation,"
co-opting the Jewish element onto the total American body, not only its
enormous intellectual and cultural and entrepreneurial talent as the de facto
intelligentsia in an essentially working-class-recruited, anti-intellectual

society—the United States. The hyphen in "Judeo-Christian faith" is significant. So is the geopolitical, strategic hyphen in Israel–U.S. And— as a very important symbol at the top of U.S. decision making in an important period, also from the point of view of this metaphor—so was the Kissinger-Nixon linkage: Union at the expense of a front against Islam. Three stages or phases in the history metaphor appropriation, begging the question what the fourth stage will be. A return to the first or the second? Incorporation of Islam? Or—*reflection*?

## SOME CONSEQUENCES OF THE ARCHETYPE FOR U.S. FOREIGN POLICY

Imagine now that what has been said in the preceding pages is not only subscribed to by the majority of the U.S. public in general, U.S. leaders in particular, and U.S. foreign policy elites even more in particular, but has become a part of their way of looking at the world; indeed, this is so deeply internalized that Americans themselves are not even conscious of how their perceptions of the world are steered. The United States simply is a nation closer to God than any other, God's Own Country, paying back with the slogan on U.S. bills: "In God We Trust." This is not a question of being told by the leaders that such is the case, nor a question of looking around in the world, or below or beyond, for evidence. The truth of the statement is *apodictic*, about concrete reality, in no need of further tests, a truly synthetic *a priori*.

For that reason the ten consequences that follow have more the character of being logical satellites with interpretations in the concreteness of the international system as we know it today than isolated syndromes, patterns of thinking (sometimes of action) that can be observed simply by watching U.S. foreign policy behavior. No doubt more can easily be proposed, but I have found these ten to be particularly useful as a basis for predicting U.S. foreign policy behavior.

### The Construction of World Space

Below world space, the world system, is presented in two different forms: as a hierarchy and as a system of concentric circles (see Figure 9.1). There are four parts of the world, suspended between Good and Evil. On top is the United States, surrounded by the Center of the world, the Allies who should satisfy at least two of three characteristics: a free market economy, faith in the Judeo-Christian God, and free elections. Another formula, not so explicit, would define the Center as the "industrially advanced democracies." Ideally a country should satisfy all three characteristics to qualify for Center membership, and in addition be *rich*, although this is almost implied by the other three. Great Britain, Israel,

**Figure 9.1.**
**U.S. Construction of World Space**

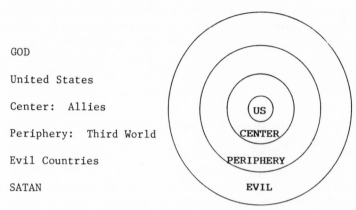

```
GOD

United States

Center:  Allies

Periphery:  Third World

Evil Countries

SATAN
```

and Canada would qualify; and some others like the Federal Republic of Germany, France, and Italy. The list so far is almost identical with the list of participants in the annual economic summits. But there Japan participates instead of Israel, in spite of not being Judeo-Christian, by virtue of being, rather, rich. In principle, Muslim free market economies with democratic election processes might also be eligible. They might even rank higher than Judeo-Christian countries with democratic elections, if the market were less than free—controlled, for instance, by strong public sectors in a mixed, negotiation economy like the social democracies of Northern European countries (perhaps also Israel in some periods). And then there is the third possibility of a free market economy with Judeo-Christian faith but authoritarian rule, a condition frequently found in South America. But there, on the other hand, countries are not rich, so the problem of recognition does not present itself.

The Center can also be defined as the countries which are members of NATO and the European Community, and be extended so as to include all OECD countries. The result would be about the same (except, e.g., for Turkey).

In the next layer is the Periphery, practically speaking identical with the group of Third World countries. They are usually not rich, except for short periods when their commodities can fetch sufficient prices. Of the three possible criteria on which they should match the United States, they at most make two, in general only one.

And outside these countries is the fourth category of Evil countries. The archetypal Evil country would not have a free market economy, nor the Judeo-Christian faith, nor a democratic system. It might, in fact, abjure all three, being explicitly in favor of the complete negation of that formula in advocating a planned economy, "scientific atheism," and the leadership of one single party. Being rich, or at least medium-rich, is not a sufficient condition for a socialist country to cross the fine line into the Periphery, much less approach the Center.

However, whether depicted as a hierarchy or as a system of concentric circles the meaning of the construction cannot be comprehended by a system of, for instance, economic indicators. True, in the jargon of the United Nations the Periphery more or less coincides with the "less developed countries," the Center with the "more developed countries," for a neat ordering of acceptable countries as LDC, MDC, and WDC—for Washington, DC. Nor is alliance formation or membership a good guide; it does not capture the essence of the construction of world space, only the manifestations.

I take the essence to be essentially theological: the suspension of the world between GOD and SATAN. If there is only one God and He is valid for the whole world, what would be more logical than to have only one Satan, with his kind of temptation valid for the whole world as well? Is this not simply the projection of a dichotomous, even Manichaean (or in the Russian version, *bogomil*) perspective on reality, on the world scene? If there is Good, even infinite Good, should there not also be Evil, even infinite Evil? The answer is, of course, that there is no logical implication involved, but some kind of correspondence principle. Those who construct monotheism might also, not by logical but by ana-logic, construct mono-satanism. The world looks orderly that way.

And what would then be more logical than for Satan to clothe himself in world space in *one* evil manifestation, to select *one* actor, just as God has also selected one, the United States? If there is somewhere in the world God's Own Country, why should there not also be Satan's Own Country? Call it the focus of Evil, or the Evil Empire, or whatever; the underlying theology/Satanology is clear.

From that point on one might argue that all that follows is the principle of unity of evil, not the precise nature of evil. In other words, Satan might, over time, change manifestation, but always with a preference for one manifestation at a time. Satan might, for instance, reject communism as his instrument, for instance, because communism becomes too spent, too ineffective to be the instrument of evil it used to be. Satan might find a new instrument, terrorism, full of vigor. There might even be a transition formula with communism supporting terrorism, until the New evil order is crystallized.

Thus, there are possible careers in world space. The sociologically inclined would talk in terms of downward and upward mobility, from Periphery into Evil and from Center into Periphery in one direction, and then the opposite possibility. The theologically inclined would talk in terms of damnation and salvation, fall from grace and return to grace, sin and punishment on the one hand; expiation, atonement, forgiveness on the other. The theological image presupposes that there is in the world somebody who can bestow and withdraw grace. In diplomatic parlance this is known as "diplomatic recognition," or, in economic terms, as "most favored nation status" although both of them are too dichotomous to reflect the quadripartite construction of world space.

Not all recognitions count equally: Recognition by Washington counts more than by anybody else, implicit in the metaphor as being God's representative in the community of nations. In saying so, there is no suggestion of any explicit theological motivation when recognition is extended or withdrawn, only that such acts and the importance accorded to them when emanating from Washington, DC, are compatible with the metaphor and for that reason receive increased legitimacy. Nor is it in any way intended that such feelings surround such acts only in Washington. The mystique of the United States as a nation not like any other is felt all around the world. Behave as if you are anointed and people believe you are—up to a certain point.

As indicated above, this construction of world space is not a Hindu caste system with little or no short-term mobility at all, with mobility only by means of a new incarnation. This is a Judeo-Christian construction with the possibility of making even major, quantitative jumps, like Saul becoming Paul on the road to Damascus. A basic condition, of course, is recognition of the United States as the ultimate recognizer. The operational meaning of being "moderate" as opposed to "dogmatic/fanatic" in the Evil outer circle, beyond civilization, is, if not explicit submissiveness, at least recognition of the United States. Those who already do recognize the United States as the very Center of the system would agree: An active additional recognition by somebody moving from Evil to Periphery, or even from Periphery to Center, legitimizes their own world space construction and their submissiveness. In their eyes, China became a member of the family of nations not through its relation to the UN, but to the United States.

We have indicated above two roads to salvation in the system. One is mentioned in the preceding paragraph: recognition, even submissiveness. The other is mentioned above: to take on the characteristics of the Center in general and the United States in particular, more particularly free market mechanisms, Judeo-Christian faith, and free elections. But it is not enough to live out these institutions ritualistically. The action must spring from an inner conviction, touching the political nerve of the country or at least the leaders. It must be a genuine act of *conversion*, not a temporary, even politically motivated convenience behind the new behavior—Christian conversion, not merely accumulation of merits.

And there is a corresponding conversion for the fall from grace into the cold, the Evil. This can happen as a result of withdrawal of recognition of the United States and/or increase in distance along the three dimensions mentioned. All of these must occur at the same time and accordingly there be no doubt where that country belongs.

It is interesting in this connection to note how the People's Republic of China was able to "graduate" from Evil to Periphery. There was no promise of free elections, and certainly no conversion to Judeo-Christian faith. But there was an indication of an opening toward free market mechanisms, and a very clear recognition of the United States as an actor of world significance that China could ill afford to ignore. Moreover, there was a clear invitation to the United States to help China in achieving economic development, in other words a recognition of U.S. talent in that rather important field. But no Judeo-Christian faith; no free elections.

However, the Chinese also made use of a third way implicit in what has been said above. If you do not become God-like, you can at least reject Satan. China had long experience in hostile rhetoric toward the Soviet Union, and probably also knew very well the political currency value of such rhetoric to U.S. ears. The common enemy theme was played upon. And Washington must in a sense have been bewildered: graduation from Evil no doubt, but up to what level? Into the very Center, as a "ally"? The test for that would be some kind of military reliability and it may well be that feelers in that direction did not yield sufficiently positive results. Also, China was still a "communist country" whatever that meant in the particular Chinese case. In short, the criteria for admission to the Center were not satisfied. On the other hand, China was a little bit too big to fit into the Periphery with its host of miniscule states of various political complexions. The result was probably to treat China the way China treats itself: as nonclassifiable, as China. And the relation remains ambiguous as is to be expected between God's Own Country and the Middle Kingdom.

### The United States Has Not Only a Right but a Duty to Take on Godlike Characteristics

The country closest to God is also God's representative on earth. And the three major characteristics of God are taken to be omniscience, omnipotence, and beneficence. The beneficence is, of course, not to be doubted. To doubt that the United States is essentially endowed with good intentions, even if some of the concrete behavior may look clumsy, gives reason to doubt the doubter, not the United States. Only people or countries themselves located in Evil could harbor such thoughts. Others would accept a little roughness as inevitable when world order is at stake.

However, omniscience and omnipotence do not follow by implication alone. They have to be established, and the world being as it is, with the omnipresence of Satan, that task is in itself formidable, not to mention economically very costly. Sacrifice is called for.

Concretely, this means in practice electronic surveillance all over the world, of course not of those who harbor no evil intentions, but of those who may be suspected to have that of Evil in them. Who fall in which category is decided by the United States alone; there is no court of appeals. Omniscience also implies knowledge of what there is to know, as one God's only representative, in other words having a knowledge monopoly. The concrete manifestation of this syndrome would be the National Security Agency (NSA)—all others not possessing that competence.

And the concrete manifestation of the omnipotence syndrome would be the power to exercise power, in principle of all kinds, all around the world. This calls for a broad instrumentarium of power resources, both in stock and in flow. There must be *cultural* power—for instance, as exercised by the United States Information Agency (USIA)—to propagate norms, values, ideas (Voice of America, Radio Free Europe, Radio Liberty). There must be *economic* power—both from the private sector as corporate capital and from the public sector as assistance (U.S. Aid). There must be *military* power—both of the kind administered by the Pentagon and the undercover variety exercised by the CIA. And there must be *political* power, coordinating these three, and not only in Washington but also in a network of faithful allies around the world who can be trusted to let the stock administered by Washington flow through the channels to some extent subadministered by them when power flow is called for to rectify deteriorating situations.

### The United States' Conflict Behavior
### Is Not Like That of Other Nations

How does a country closest to God make use of the awesome power potential at its disposal? The basic point would be that this is done not like other nations do, in conflict with each other. The United States does not enter as the second party to a conflict. If some country is in conflict with the United States the implication is that that country is wrong, and the task of the United States is to set things straight. The United States enters as a third party, as ultimate conflict manager, not like other countries. But how can the United States be a third party relative to only one country? Very easily: what this means is that the two parties are inside that one country, and the task of the United States is to help the good against the evil forces. But what if that country is only evil, there are no good forces to help? That only shows how evil the country is: it has either eliminated the good forces, or repressed them to the point that they do not even dare to voice their concerns. To be good in the sense of recognizing the United States is not only rational but natural; if that recognition is not forthcoming, something has been thwarted, twisted in an evil direction. And the country deserves to be bombed into the stone ages, or total oblivion, or both.

The rich power instrumentarium provides a tool chest with sufficient variety to be applied judiciously to other countries depending on their ranking in the world order. Different tools for different tasks.

Thus, to the Center countries the United States will probably appear as the "honest broker," reminding them of their duties as Center countries satisfying all criteria. In other words, the cultural power of persuasion would be exercised. In addition, the United States will offer its services as conflict manager, as a third party mediating among equals. And if all of this proves insufficient, some economic power will have to be injected into the "situation," a gentle compensation to one or several of the contestants so as to keep the conflict within bounds, not weakening Center "unity."

Relative to a Periphery country, the instrumentarium broadens via economic power to military power. A conflict between two Periphery countries is like a street brawl, children fighting in a sandbox. The task of the United States is to intervene, grab them by the scruff of the neck, maybe shake them a little to teach them civilized behavior. If they are really intransigent, however, economic power might prove persuasive, like giving them substantial amounts of money each on the condition that they keep peace or at least not engage in overt conflict among themselves, *and* that they recognize the United States as the conflict manager. The task is partly that of a kindergarten teacher, partly the job of the cop among robbers, partly that of the rich uncle, generously inclined, finding open conflict a disgrace for the family, bribing them into more acceptable behavior. Persuasion backed by the combined power of the stick and the carrot.

For Evil countries, however, a totally different approach may be warranted. Real Evil is not only intransigent but also dangerous to all three groups of countries, not only by being physically destructive, but also by being morally contagious. If no persuasion appealing to values helps, if they are not amenable to the gentle power implied by cost-benefit analysis (with some reward for good behavior, and punishment or sanctions for bad), then they may be in for ultimate punishment: destruction, destroying or wasting the "mad dog" as totally beyond redemption. Not relenting, clinging to faith in spite of both temptation and threats, can only serve as proof of one thing: that there is Satan in him. The logic has a long tradition in Christianity in the inquisition and the witch processes, particularly the tautological character of the proof. If he confesses to be evil, then of course he is evil. But if he does not confess in face of such displays of power, then his intransigence can only derive from one source: Satan. In other words, in that case he is also evil; if he were not, the Good voice from above would have moved him.

It should also be noted that such acts by the United States should not be seen as revenge for anything harmful done to the United States or her citizens, at home or abroad. Revenge belongs to ordinary nations, as in a vendetta. Revenge is among equals; punishment is what is exercised from above, from higher levels, administered like in criminal justice for reasons of general prevention, in order to scare others with similar inclinations, or for reasons of individual prevention, in order to prevent that country from persisting in doing evil. The ultimate individual prevention is elimination, a reason why the United States has to possess weapons of extermination.

That, however, only works against evil in small quantities. The big Evil, even the Center of the empire, may be too vast to take on. In that case, the task becomes somewhat more limited: if not elimination, at least containment and readiness to take Evil head on, fighting it out until the bitter end. If Evil can appear anywhere in the world and with any kind of power configuration, then the task of the Good forces is to be able to counter Evil wherever and in any manner whatsoever. If this means readiness to fight two wars, two and a half wars, three and a half wars, five wars, so be it. In this cosmic fight no sacrifice is too high.

One implication of this is that being an Evil country is dangerous not only for the rest of the world but also for that country. Consequently, the United States is entirely justified in preventing a country from becoming Evil even when this country, in a spell of delusion, thinks the United States acts against its own will. Destabilizing a country of that type becomes more than a right of the biggest power on earth; it is a duty. Even a heavy duty, not assumed lightly. But as the ultimate judge of the world order, this task has to be assumed, well knowing that the United States incurs not only negative sentiments but hostility, and becomes very unpopular in certain circles for some periods of time. That is a minor cost when world order is at stake.

### Unconditional Surrender Is the Only Acceptable Outcome in a Fight with Evil All the Time

The necessity for surrender is a very important consequence of the metaphor. To accept less than unconditional surrender would make the United States ordinary, like any other nation engaged in a conflict for less worthy goals than to set the world straight. Ordinary nations might end up with a compromise. But for the United States that would be like the cop making a deal with a robber. Such things happen, but are impermissible, illegitimate. Law and Justice are not to be tampered with but to be respected in their entirety. The task of the cop is to subject the robber to the will of the law, to have him submit willingly or unwillingly, to put him in chains in order to exercise justice.

To do this, it is not only the right but the duty of the United States to possess ultimate weapons, and not in "parity" with any other country, and particularly not with an evil country, not to mention with the Center of Evil, with Satan on earth. To accept parity is to accept moral equality, between right and wrong, not to mention between God and Satan. He who wants God to win over Satan would not only want that but would be struggling, fighting for superiority as opposed to parity. He who goes in for parity, not to mention inferiority, probably does so because deeper down in the crevices and recesses of his mind there is a secret urge for Satan to win, or at least for God to suffer defeat. Why? Not necessarily because of any love for Satan, but because of hatred of God's order. Maybe that person or that country did not quite make it with the United States and wants to take it out on God himself instead of doing what he should do—look into himself, ask why was it that he was not recognized, where he failed, and try to rectify his ways: Anti-Americanism, in short.

What has been said above is not only a formula for the exercise of God's will on earth. It is also a formula with very happy tidings for Evil. *There is a way out*: to submit—but willingly, based on a change of heart—from an inner conviction. All that is needed is to "cry uncle," and from that point on negotiate a new status in the world order. To the repentant sinner upward mobility is possible—if not into the Center at least into the Periphery.

Precisely at this point we encounter the generosity of the United States. With the Evil country down on the ground, spread-eagled, "crying uncle," the United States may decide to proclaim: "thy sins are unto thee forgiven. Stand up, and I shall bestow thee free market mechanisms, Judeo-Christian faith (or at least principles), and administer free elections. And thou shalt not only be permitted into the realm of civilized nations, albeit perhaps at the lower level—as a Periphery nation passing some time in the waiting room of history. Thou shalt also become rich, for out of these three principles working together riches may come, even unto rags—under U.S. guidance." Or, in more theological parlance, "by the grace of the United States." But nobody can reckon with this grace as something that comes automatically. Nobody can cause the United States; the United States is its own cause, like God, according to Luther. The metaphor is not only Christianity, but within, Protestant Christianity.

## There Can Be Nothing Between the United States and God

If the United States is the closest there is to God in the world there is simply no space in-between. More particularly, this means neither any other nation, nor anything supranational. No other nation could rank above the United States culturally by having a superior ideology or culture in general. For what should that be? Which religion could be superior to the Judeo-Christian faith? Which ideology could be superior to liberalism/conservatism with its capitalist manifestations? This combination, with democratic institutions added, has worked throughout the existence of the United States on earth and there is no reason whatsoever to assume that anything superior will show up.

Nor should any nation be economically superior to the United States. The strongest economy in the world should be that of the United States. If another economy looks superior, as the Japanese economy does now, this is a delusion and only due to the working of circumstantial factors (such as imitation of U.S. practices, low salaries to the workers, dumping prices for the goods marketed, theft of industrial secrets to compensate for low level of innovation, sacrifice of living standard by having artificially high saving ratios, getting a free ride militarily by having too low allocations to the military sector, having an artificially weak currency, etc.). Once this factor—to some extent due to the beneficence or negligence of the United States—is removed, the true nature of the relationship will show up, meaning U.S. economic superiority.

The same applies, of course, to military power. Parity is out of the question, superiority is a duty and not only in all possible war theaters, but also in all possible weapons systems. If this is not achievable, then the search will have to be on for the ultimate weapon, a weapon that can seek out and punish, even lay waste, eliminate, exterminate evil wherever it is. Offensive laser beam capacity is inherent in the "star wars" concept, but not in the formula under which it is propagated as Strategic Defense Initiative (SDI), since a strategic offense initiative might throw doubt on the beneficence of the United States, if not on its omniscience and omnipotence rolled into one, in a satellite system capable of both spying and launching a laser attack.

Nor should there be any nation on earth superior to the United States politically. There is an inner circle, the Center. But the ultimate decision is made by the United States alone. Allies may be consulted and should remain grateful if they are—not only after, but even before summit talks with Evil. In the monopoly on summit talks with Evil, monotheism and monosatanism are combined and the greatness of the United States is confirmed in being the only country capable of facing Evil eye-to-eye, maybe even winning over Evil, or at least containing it.

Nor should any supranational principle or institution be on top of the United States. This applies to the United Nations unless that organization can be seen as a medium through which the United States can exercise its beneficial influence over all the world. In other words, as long as the UN is dominated by the United States, it is unobjectionable. The moment this is no longer the case, and not only resolutions but also concrete actions tend to turn against the United States's will, something has to be done about it. The general formula is not "if you can't beat them, join them," but "if you can't beat them, leave them." In concrete cases like

UNESCO, what the United States did was to leave the organization. But there is also the possibility of leaving without leaving, which the United States has practiced for a long time: taking all major decisions out of the UN, creating special fora (one of them being the ultimate summit meeting with the Soviet Union), celebrating uniqueness and separation away from and above the common crowd. If the UN is good, then the United States will be recognized and will be on top as the ultimate good. If the United States is not on top, then the UN can not be good.

The same goes for international law. Truly valid international law would be compatible with the interests of the United States, a nation whose basic morality is not to be doubted. If there is incompatibility, what passes for "international law" cannot be valid. Consequently, the United States is not only entitled not to submit to adjudication, but has a duty not to legitimize adjudication by the illegitimate bodies acting according to invalid "international law" by playing the game as if it were valid. In refusing to ratify or to submit, the United States sends the signal to the world that the world should better take note of and mend its ways, in this case its "laws."

### The United States Is the Ultimate Decision Maker, Not Accountable to Anyone Else

To be accountable to somebody else would mean that there is something between the United States and God, a clear contradiction of the preceding principle. To be accountable is to be ordinary, to be like others, possibly *prima inter pares*, but nevertheless one of them. To listen, to take into account, is not the same as being accountable. For the prime minister of New Zealand, a lay Methodist minister, to demand that the United States should declare the presence or absence of nuclear capabilities in U.S. vessels is to demand that the United States should be accountable even to New Zealand, a country at the borderline between Center and Periphery, possibly even between Center and Evil (a direct downward mobility with no intermediate stay as a Periphery nation, the ultimate fall, is of course possible). This is more than insolence, it borders on sacrilege. The United States and only the United States decides what is inside her ships, and consequently has a policy neither to confirm nor to deny the presence of any nuclear capability. The symmetry between confirmation and denial should be emphasized. These are only two versions of the same basically impossible behavior: to render oneself accountable and thus ordinary.

Nor does the United States have an obligation to engage in behavior, including rhetoric, free of contradictions. Others, accountable to the United States as the rest of the world essentially is, do not have the right to be contradictory. Their task is to behave according to the rules of world order. But at the level of the United States, contradictory behavior, or rather what looks to ordinary nations like contradictory behavior, may be engaged in—such as saying that there will be no negotiation with those who capture hostages, yet doing exactly that; such as saying that there will be no arms transferred to a belligerent nation at considerable odds with the United States, yet doing exactly that. From the vantage point of higher levels of insight possessed by the United States and the particular agencies administering omniscience and omnipotence, such as the National Security Council (NSC), these are marginal contradictions dissolving into a higher unity of purpose at the very Center of the world system, the White House. There is a limit to the capability of ordinary nations in understanding the ways of the United States just as we ordinary human beings are limited in our understanding of the ways of the Lord. The very circumstance that these ways may look contradictory is a necessary if certainly not sufficient criterion of their God-like nature, within certain limits.

### Americanization as a Way of Bestowing God's Order on Others

If the United States is similar to God and the guiding light for other nations, then Americanization, meaning making other nations similar to America, would be the logical way of implementing the world order of which the United States is already emblematic.

In principle there are four ways in which the process of Americanization can take place. It can work on individuals and it can work on countries. The mountain can come to Mohammed in the sense of individuals joining as immigrants or countries joining as the nth state of the United States of America, the USA then being an open set to which others can join, as has happened so far in the slightly more than 200 years of U.S. history. Or Mohammed can go to the mountain, influencing individuals and/or countries, making them adopt the American way of life, even far away from the home of that particular syndrome. Needless to say, none of these four processes excludes the other three. But the first pair certainly implies a more complete process than the second, although it may also be argued that if it is possible to be more Catholic than the pope, then it should also be possible to be more American than America, a pattern found in some client states.

There is a content to Americanization over and above or under and below the three more ideological principles referred to above several times as the magic of the market, faith in the Judeo-Christian God, and holding free elections. There is a way of being and a way of believing and a way of becoming, not only what social scientists would refer to as attitude and behavior. Basic to America as a utopia is the idea of a New Beginning;

of becoming something new by joining. Being born again, in other words. Inside America there are other ways of being born again: by moving West, for instance; by joining a movement, for instance, born-again Christians— a process of quantum jumps where the basic jump may be that of joining America as a utopia.

And this would include certain ways of being, such as faith in competitive individualism, being a good team player, being enthusiastic about one's own organization, always being on the side of the solution rather than of the problem, keeping smiling. The satisfaction of basic needs is, like in all other cultures, surrounded by norms: There are foodstuffs to be eaten; drinks to be consumed; clothes to be worn; housing to be enjoyed; patterns surrounding health, education, work and leisure. And there are those overarching, pervasive symbols like Coca-Cola, McDonald hamburgers, American music, American media, sex and violence, particularly the latter. This new land, this new world—Disney Land, Disney World.

The point about Americanization is not so much the acceptance to the point of enactment and internalization of the whole culture. The point is rather that of not rejecting Americanization. To reject it may be indicative of an Evil inclination; to accept, equally indicative of a good one. The person who rejects some of the symbols of Americanization can, in all fairness, be described as anti-American; if he also rejects some of Washington's policies, then that carries no news, no message: He is only doing what the anti-American person can be expected to do. For that reason, it is perfectly appropriate to try to find out whether the person critical of Washington's policies should not by chance also be critical of such manifestations of the American way of life as those mentioned above. And if he is, there is no reason to bother about his arguments: he is only belaboring, often in complicated ways, his own failure to join the everlasting journey to Utopia. In rejecting the position of the United States as a guiding light for other nations, he is standing on his head, working against the force of gravity, and one might even hypothesize that there could be other symptoms of crimes against nature both in his behavior and deeper down in his inclinations. The step from un-American to anti-American is but a short one, possibly the concepts are even identical if the person has been given a chance to accept Americanization and nevertheless has rejected it.

Possibly what this all boils down to is the implicit definition of America and Americanization as normal in the sense of addressing the human condition better than any alternative; all alternatives, by implication, having elements of the twisted and thwarted, repressed and suppressed, in short, the abnormal about them. Consequently to favor America and Americanization is less an ideological choice, a value attachment then simply a correct reading of the human condition in general and, given the hardships of the twentieth century, the human predicament in particular. This being so, Americanization as a process is doomed to succeed. There may be ups and downs, but the general thrust is unmistakable.

## U.S. Foreign Policy Can Correctly Be Understood as a Choice Between Global Responsibility and Isolation

The United States has a covenant with God; the Center nations and many of the Periphery nations have a covenant with the United States of America. Divine inspiration flows downward along the links defined by the covenants; loyalty/submissiveness flows upwards, from Periphery/Center nations to the United States and from the United States to God. Within the framework defined by this system or world order, the United States is obligated to exercise global responsibility, meaning to do what is needed to organize the world along these lines. Global responsibility has as a condition global presence, if not always in *corpore*, at least through reliable, trustworthy, proven allies, and technologically through the instruments that are the vehicles of omniscience and omnipotence. There can be no such thing as a defensive military doctrine under this heading of "global responsibility": weapons systems have to be maximally far-reaching, long-range, and mobile, in order to live up to the obligations as the very Center of the world order system, establishing trustworthiness, being creditable to friend and foe alike.

And yet there is in the history of the United States an almost equally consistent theme: that of isolationism. Of course, both terms are relative to the technological capacity for transportation/communication at the time, global responsibility being more regional, perhaps even national in the nineteenth century than in the twentieth when, after World War II, it became truly global. So why, given the basic metaphor, should there be room for isolation at all?

There are two obvious answers, and both of them are entirely acceptable within the metaphor, even if global responsibility is even more acceptable.

First, lack of capability. There may be periods during which the United States is short on omniscience, omnipotence, or both. The tools with which to set the world straight may not be at hand, one simple reason being that the money needed to produce those tools has not been made available. There may be insufficient understanding at home of the need to have the capability always present, ready to use. Needless to say, with that inability to submit to the wills of higher forces, those higher forces cannot be expected to provide the United States with the necessary backing either; a covenant is a virtuous circle, but can also become a vicious one when broken by the people of the covenant themselves. After all, allies further down who fail to live up to their obligations cannot be expected to be supported in times of crisis either.

Second, lack of motivation. The United States might withdraw into splendid isolation, feeling rejected by uncooperative, even ungrateful "allies," so-called allies. When something very good is offered and nevertheless is rejected, would not withdrawal be a reasonable course of action? If people do not want what is for their own good, why force them? Would it not be better to wait until they come to their senses, after they have had their spell with Evil and are ready to see the guiding light? At that time, of course, it may also be too late. But the gates through which grace can flow should never be kept completely closed; there should always be a second chance given the gracefulness, the basic beneficence of the United States.

Consequently, a wave-like history of foreign relations, oscillating between global responsibility and isolation is to be expected. The United States discharges its obligations to God and lesser nations. Those who do not understand that this is in their best interest protest and reject the hand that feeds them. It would be less than human if this should not lead to withdrawal; but left to themselves, sooner or later they come on their knees individually or collectively praying for assistance. And a new era of global responsibility is ushered in. And so on, and so forth.

### The Covenant Is Implicit, Not Explicit

Spelled out as it has been done here, highly explicitly, the covenant can be made to look worse than objectionable, indeed, ludicrous. Formulations may be firmly believed in, yet not stand the light of sunshine. Those who are initiated to the covenant know its meaning nonetheless, they are in no need of explicit formulation, nor repetition: a knowing smile, a little gesture, some shoulder shrugging—body language already more than telling to those who are parties to the covenant, looking around to identify other members of the *corpus mysticum*. The talent of the fortieth U.S. president consisted exactly in this: plucking the strings of the covenant, sometimes in vulgar explicitness, but usually indicative and evocative rather than provocative. The noninitiated should not be irritated. Sleeping dogs should continue sleeping lest they wake up, start barking, and reject what is out of their reach anyhow. In-group ritualism is to be preferred.

More particularly, there should be no insistence on Judaism or Christianity as a necessary condition for adherence to the covenant. The covenant is also open to those who accept its mundane manifestations fully even if they are not yet ready for the metaphysical underpinnings and may even reject them. Correspondingly, the rise of Right Wing religious populism is not essential either. As a matter of fact it may even be counterproductive: Many are mobilized under that formula, but there is always the danger that even more are scared away. The United States avows separation of state and church but not separation of state and religion. On the other hand, the territory between church and religion is never well charted; there is organization and there is faith in the organization and the obvious human need for an organization of faith. Hence, the less said, the better. Reagan was elected president on the basis of an implicit religiousness; Robertson was rejected precisely for that reason: his religiousness is too explicit. The foreign policy conclusions drawn may be very similar, but in real life premises may be just as important as conclusions.

Consequently, the whole system, dominated by the United States in general and its centerpiece in particular, are in need of a language in which the U.S. foreign policy as manifest theology can be expressed, but in a completely nontheological manner. The irrational has to be presented as rational in a culture, which, in spite of its profoundly Christian undercurrents, also has a rational form of presentation. One basic thesis of this chapter is that U.S. international relations theory is designed to provide that language wherein all the consequences set forth under their appropriate headings can be arrived at according to the old doctrine of Laplace concerning God: I do not need that hypothesis. All that is needed for an international relations theory is actually a construction of the international system as if there were only two alternatives: hierarchy or anarchy. With anarchy sufficiently decried this option is rejected; what is left is hierarchy. In hierarchy the strongest have to be on top. That reduces the choice to two candidates: the United States and the Soviet Union—and the simple question, which one do you prefer? The rest becomes almost a tautology, the conclusions having been buried in the premises. No third choice is given.

In one sense the practicing believers in mainstream U.S. international relations theory are the secular theologians of the system, presenting marketable justifications of what otherwise might look unjustifiable except to those who are already members of the *corpus mysticum*. One would expect the profession to expand when the United States is in the global responsibility phase of the cycle and to contract when isolationism sets in, social scientists (the rationalizers of the irrational) in this case flocking to intranational relations rather than to the international ones (for instance to sociology).

### Alternative U.S. Foreign Policies Have to Be Compatible with the Covenant

Another basic thesis of this chapter is that the covenant, the basic metaphor, is so deeply ingrained in the U.S. population that the freedom of choice is seriously curtailed. Going back to the preceding point, even if the metaphysical underpinning of the metaphor—that of the United

States is God's New Israel—should not be made explicit nor can the rejection of the metaphysics be made explicit, it is very much like the attitude toward monarchy in a Scandinavian country: it may be difficult to find a majority that explicitly professes to believe in monarchy as an institution, yet even more difficult to find a majority rejecting, explicitly, monarchy.

Consequently one might assume that the United States will continue living in an active partnership with God not only for the rest of this century but for a century more, or two, or three. Take the idea of being a Chosen People away from the American people and the construction— meaning the United States—might well collapse. A lie or not a lie, its removal has deeper implications than unhappiness (according to Ibsen)— some kind of more basic disintegration might follow.

So it may well be that the United States will continue to see itself as the Chosen People, as an embodiment or at least a major instrument of God in the world community. But that also holds an important key to the future. The key is God. Who said that God of the U.S.–God covenant is the God of hard Christianity, a tribal, jealous, revengeful, vindictive, even cruelly aggressive God as reported in the first books of the Old and the last book of the New Testaments? Who said He could not also be the God of soft-line Christianity, compassionate and merciful, with no particular Chosen People or Chosen Peoples—only chosen human beings, including those who claim that they reject Him? In other words, monotheism with no Satan, more like God as portrayed by the antinuclear pastoral letters of the Catholic bishops and the Methodist bishops in the United States, fighting their battles for an alternative U.S. foreign policy.

To change the foreign policy without a change in the underlying metaphor is like pursuing a diet for reducing weight without some change in life-style. There will be a relapse. Yet the change of metaphor need only be minimal, though crucially its aim must be to change the very concept of God. This change does not carry with it any rejection of the idea that the United States is the home of the Chosen People. The United States could continue to be No.1, but thenceforth as the least aggressive, least violent country in the world.

And this has a bearing on the U.S. peace movement. A "nuclear freeze" has no depth—born of the single issue of tradition, but not addressing the underlying metaphor. A single issue compatible with that metaphor can carry the day; an incompatible one is a lame duck. Maybe the theologians understood this better than the peace movement technocrats? And maybe therein lies the key to the future. If theology is the underpinning of aggressive foreign policy, then theology may also be its undoing.

## NOTES

1. Quoted in Richard O. Challener, *Admirals, Generals and American Foreign Policy, 1898–1914* (Princeton, NJ: Princeton University Press, 1973), p. 353.

2. Ibid.

3. For a discussion of social cosmology, see Johan Galtung, Tore Heiestad, and Erik Rudeng, "On the Last 2,500 Years of Western History; And Some Reflections on the Coming 500," in Peter Burke, ed., *The New Cambridge History, Companion Volume* (Cambridge, England: Cambridge University Press, 1979), ch. 12.

4. The quotes could be very numerous indeed. Yehoshafat Harkabi in his "Jewish Ethos and Political Positions in Israel" (The Hebrew University of Jerusalem, 1985), uses these: Numbers 23:9: "a people who live apart and do not consider themselves as one of the nations"; Exodus 34:24: "I will drive out nations before you and enlarge your territory and no one will covet your hand, when you go up three times each year"; Avot 5:23: "Heaven and earth were created only for the sake of Israel." Sigmund Freud, in his *Moses and Monotheism* (New York: Vintage Books, 1967) puts the same relationship this way (p. 143): "Their religion also gave to the Jews a much more grandiose idea of their God or, to express it more soberly, the idea of a more august God. Whoever believed in this God took part in his greatness, so to speak, might feel uplifted himself.— it may be illustrated by the simile of the high confidence a Briton would feel in a foreign land made unsafe by revolt, a confidence in which a subject of some small Continental state would be entirely lacking. The Briton counts on his government to send a warship if a hair of his head is touched, and also on the rebels knowing very well that this is so, while the small state does not even own a warship." The readings made by Freud and Taft of the archetype were very similar, indeed. Leo Baeck, in his beautifully written *The Essence of Judaism* (New York: Schocken Books, 1961), expresses it this way (p. 67): "All Israel is the messenger of the Lord, the "servant of God," who is to guard religion for all lands and from whom the light shall radiate to all nations." Isaiah 42:6f: "I the Lord have called thee in righteousness, and will hold thine hand, and will keep thee, and give thee for a covenant of the people, for a light of the nations; to open the blind eyes, to bring out the prisoners from the prison, and them that sit in darkness in the prison house."

5. See, for instance, Alan Simpson, *Puritanism in Old and New England* (Chicago: The University of Chicago Press, 1955); Robert N. Bellah, *The Broken Covenant, American Civil Religion in Time of Trial* (New York: The Seabury Press, 1975); Sacvan Bercovitch, *The American Jeremiad* (Madison: The University of Wisconsin Press, 1978); Arnold M. Eisen, *The Chosen People in America: A Study in Jewish Religious Ideology* (Bloomington: Indian University Press, 1983); and Conrad Cherry, ed., *God's New Israel: Religious Interpretations of American Destiny* (Englewood Cliffs, NJ: Prentice-Hall, 1971).

6. See National Conference of Catholic Bishops, *The Challenge of Peace: God's Promise and Our Response, 1983* and the United Methodist Council of Bishops, *In Defense of Creation: The Nuclear Crisis and a Just Peace, 1986.*

# 10

## The Use and Abuse of Norms in U.S. Foreign Policy

Kenneth W. Thompson

In the use and abuse of norms, there is always an element of irrationality. Looking back, we celebrate that handful of leaders who were able to follow what history attests was a rational moral and political course. Moreover, even that small group appear to have been more rational in some policies, more irrational in others. Thus, Franklin D. Roosevelt appears rational in the *conduct* of World War II, but not rational in defining the political objectives that the war was to serve. Churchill, in calling on Britain and her allies to turn back Hitler with "blood, sweat and tears," was rational in the norm he proclaimed, but less rational resisting the worldwide tide of anticolonialism.

The intrusion of irrational acts in what leaders and nations may have assumed was moral conduct is not the result of a single cause. One factor is the inevitable tension between any moral imperative and the requirements of successful political action. Noble principles and political success may diverge in practice. This means that the normative theorist must have before him not one but two maps. One map must be that of present day international politics, which portrays the forces at work, the underlying principles and the perennial patterns of international politics. The other map, overlapping at points the first, registers the norms and moral principles of member states and the overall system. The two maps help us to think about the terrain which must be traversed. They link facts and moral reasoning. They help reduce the risk of moving blindly over uncharted terrain but they leave unchanged the possibility of human frailty or mechanical error.

By holding before him the maps of the moral theorist and the political actor, the historian or observer is enabled to look as it were over the shoulder of the statesman. One of the major airlines allows its passengers in certain aircraft to listen to conversations between the pilot and the tower as the latter guides the choices the former must take. The process goes on both in landings and takeoffs. If tragedy strikes, the responsible safety and airline officials seek to recover the aircraft's recorder. Through it, they are able to understand better than the pilot or the air controller did the full nature of the choices communicated and the measures actually taken against a wider background of possible choices at the time. The maps of the pilot and the controller overlap at points but they are not the same. So it is with the statesman and the historian. After the fact, the historian seeks to understand the lessons of history that account for the stateman's successes and failures. History can be a handbook of foreign policy, especially for the political theorist who searches for underlying principles. The historian or philosopher can look beyond the fact of a single event to the consequences. In this, a second element that transcends rationality comes into play.

Intentions, motives, and ideology are factors to take into account in normative evaluation but they are difficult to penetrate and are so in a dual sense. First, who can say what the innermost motive of the statesman may have been? And second, in politics and foreign policy good motives, noble intentions, or a particular ideology are no guarantee of good policies or the desired consequences. Who can speak with confidence in judging as good or bad the intentions of statesmen? In terms of conscience and intentions was Chamberlain bad and Churchill good or Carter bad and Truman good? Any normative judgment that fixes exclusively on good or bad intent or good or bad ideology is likely to ignore social and political circumstances and the constraints under which leaders make their choices.

Beyond the matter of intentions, any too simplistic measurement of the morality of political action that focuses solely on the act itself is likely to flounder in the realm of consequence. From a political standpoint, consequences over time are more measurable and of great importance. Yet consequences also partake of irrationalism and the unpredictable. The Protestant Reformation had as its major objective the opening of the Scriptures to the sovereign choice and interpretation of the individual Christian. In practice, it resulted in the emergence of the unbridled sovereign nation-state. The French Revolution, which was to bring liberty, equality, and fraternity to Europe, brought instead Metternich's era of legitimacy and the status quo. Wars that are fought to turn back the threat of one imperialism almost always are followed by the rise of some new threat. It is difficult to recall many examples of vast catalysmic events that had precisely the consequences contemporary observers prophesied.

Another factor that complicates a straightforward rational approach to norms and foreign policy is the influence of domestic politics. Amidst the continuing debate between those who advocate the primacy of foreign policy and those who insist domestic politics determines all policies including foreign policy, the definition and formulation of norms is held hostage. The important question remains which rules and controls the other. President Franklin D. Roosevelt knew that the national interest required that at some point the United States would have to resist Hitler's march through Europe. To prepare U.S. public opinion to resist Hitler, Roosevelt had to cajole, beguile, and maneuver the national will. Indeed, only the tragedy of Pearl Harbor finally cleared the way for the action FDR knew was required. The norm of defending freedom or of restoring the balance of power in Europe was not resolved in any direct or logical way but instead was settled through the workings of the political process. In the end neither foreign policy nor domestic politics was determinative but a complex and evershifting relationship between the president, the congress and the public.

## THE USE OF NORMS

According to some respected thinkers, the role of norms is to restrain and to guide nations and other international entities in their relationships. Another view of norms is that they serve to register and institutionalize an underlying consensus. A third view is that norms generate and apply standards in action. A fourth approach throws the spotlight on obstacles that resist their being put into effect. A fifth emphasis is on norms as limitations or restraints on conduct that would otherwise be without external constraints.

In law, scholars point to three different types of norms that are aspects of what Roscoe Pound described as a "hierarchy of legal norms." The first are rules which can be interpreted in a narrow and inflexible sense. They admit of no discretion. They are clearly and unequivocally defined within national and metropolitan jurisdictions. Stopping at a red light is a rule and so are filing income tax returns by April 15 and driving on the right side of the street. Whether someone is rich or poor, he or she must file on April 15, or, whether driving a Cadillac or a Volkswagon, stay on the right hand side of the road. Rules are a vital but small part of national or domestic law and an even smaller and less effective form of international law as recognized and ratified by separate nation-states.

Principles in law constitute a jumping-off place for legal reasoning. Principles are not nondiscretionary or automatic. They involve such ideas as contracts not being binding unless supported by a sufficient consideration. Something is given as a quid pro quo for a commitment or promise. This fact enters into leal analysis and judgment.

Standards are vaguely worded norms for desired human conduct. The U.S. Constitution is full of them. They are subject to legislative and judicial interpretation. Because of the broad and general nature of standards, the Supreme Court often arrives at 5–4 decisions. Such standards include due process of law, the equal protection clause, unreasonable restraint of trade, and cruel and unjust punishment. To standards, justice Holmes's statement of the crystal fallacy applies: "The word is not a crystal transparent and unchanged but the skin of a living thought." The words in a standard may vary in time and thought but they are not expandable as an accordion. In some instances words may allow for broad areas of discretion; in other instances they can be more narrow and precise.

The norms in international law and international morality most clearly resemble standards. They reflect a high order of generality. When a judge on the International Court of Justice or a statesman acts, he has a broad and flexible range of choice because the nouns involved are highly general and open to creative determination. In treaties affecting territorial status, for example, the Court must search for meanings of territorial status as in the treaty between the Netherlands, Denmark, and West Germany, negotiated before the continental shelf was even known. Laws and norms cannot be simply stated where creative analysis must play so major a role.

In international relations, norms can restrain and guide nations and other international entities in their relationships, but such restraints are subject to the compulsion of interests and power. Thus, a nation whose leaders before and following World War II had more to say about international law than other nations' spokesmen denied, in 1984, that international norms applied, at least as defined by the International Court of Justice, to U.S. interests in Central America over a two-year period. In invoking the proposition that an international norm may be a lodestar to guide nations, no one should suppose that even the most "law-abiding" nation will seek as its guide the normative judgments of the international community if it concludes, legitimately or not, that its interests are threatened.

It is also true that international norms may institutionalize an underlying consensus of values. However, law cannot go beyond the degree of underlying consensus in effect. In the words of the late Judge Charles de Visscher, a judge on the Court: "Neither politics nor law will ensure equilibrium in the world without the 'moral infrastructure' " or solidarities on which community must rest.[1] De Visscher explains that: "Every society rests at once upon material and upon moral factors. It is the resultant of solidarities active enough to call for an organization of power and sufficiently conscious of a common good to engender the idea of law and the sense of obligation."[2] National divisions such as those separating class from class have yielded to national solidarities. Forces of solidarity and cohesion within a nation result from its resistance to external pressures and internal sentiments of loyalty. The nation has triumphed over subnational forces.

But for international norms, de Visscher concludes: "The international community has no such decisive factor of social cohesion."[3] It can make appeals for sacrifices to a common supranational good as in movements for universal collective security of world government. But such appeals are "hardly accessible to the immense majority of men." Nowhere does the comparison emerge in sharper contrast than in responses where essential interests are at stake. De Visscher sums up the differences in a singularly penetrating statement:

In the State it is the vital interests, the most highly political, that evoke the supreme solidarities. The opposite is the case in the international community. There one observes minor solidarities of an economic or technical order, for example, but the nearer one approaches vital questions, such as the preservation of peace and prevention of war, the less influence the community has on its own members. Solidarities diminish as the perils threatening it grow. The solidarities that then assert themselves turn back to their traditional home, the nation. On the rational plane, men do not deny the existence of supranational values; in the sphere of an action they rarely obey any but national imperatives.[4]

An opposing view of norms, de Visscher notwithstanding, is the view of the interdependence school that solidarities of an "economic and technical order" generate new standards in action. A modest version of this viewpoint is the functional approach of David Mitrany which he described as an approach, not a theory. A veritable flood of successor views have followed Mitrany: neofunctionalism, transnationalism, Nye and Keohane-style interdependence theories and post–Nye and Keohane. While proclaiming the fact of profound worldwide changes in the form and character of the international system, none has refuted the view about solidarities in matters of vital interest about which de Visscher wrote.

Another approach to norms places the emphasis on obstacles to the realization of wider norms. Whereas some normative thinkers have argued that lack of faith in higher goals or failure to support worldwide institutions was the problem, de Visscher maintained: "The central problem of the normative order is henceforth much less the leal validity of the formal process of elaborating international law than the obstacles confronting its extension."[5]

In the 1968 revised edition, de Visscher explained further what he meant:

The ambition to make international law the subject of a rigorously autonomous scientific discipline and the fear of contaminating it by contact with political facts have contributed much to the abuse of abstract reasoning at the cost of the observant spirit. This had dangerously obscured the bearing of power. . . . We cannot strengthen international law (or other norms) by ignoring the realities that determine the operation of power.[6]

The fifth version of norms emphasizes the role of norms as limitations on conduct that might otherwise be unrestrained. "From the Bible to the ethics and constitutional arrangements of modern democracy, the main function of . . . normative systems has been to keep aspirations for power within socially tolerable bounds.[7] Norms and moral rules in international politics are alternately overrated or underestimated but in the protection of human life in peace and in war they limit conduct. Certain acts that might be expedient for statesmen are nontheless not carried out. Norms exercise a restraining influence on the behavior of statesmen and the struggle for power. Such norms are most evident in affirming the sacredness of life, especially in times of peace.

Within a framework of these five concepts of norms, we turn now to some conclusions on the proper place and use of norms. First, a realistic norm is one that recognizes that the highest moral standard for nations may be the convergence of their national interests on some objective or set of objectives that prove mutually beneficial. The Marshall Plan for Europe and the United States is an example of a program based on the mutuality of national interests. Such a standard can guide nations in their relationships. It is at the same time more modest and realistic as a guide than are towering moral principles that lie always beyond reach.

A second perspective on morality and norms concerns their institutionalization. Here Reinhold Niebuhr offered a helpful distinction. Niebuhr found that two ideas compete in attempts at the definition and organization of the good. One is the Aristotlean attempt to define the good as "conformity to a pre-established ontological pattern of being." Many peace plans for the institutionalization of order and justice rest on Aristotleanism. Niebuhr searched for a more flexible and realistic concept and found it in Santayana's phrase: "the harmony of the whole which does not destroy the vitality of the parts." The unique vitality and freedom of the parts and the harmony that results when the coercive force of tyranny does not wholly constrain them provides a flexible normative criteria for this sphere. Power can serve as a counterweight against power in the interests of justice. Santayana's criteria can help statesmen find the point where the general good and the national interest come together, if they do.

Norms in international relations are in the process of becoming. A normative theory has to recognize the existential fact of the differences between ideals and interests. An historical situation cannot produce a normative theory that can tell you how much you should trust the future against the present or the past against the present or future. However, as the international system has moved into the nuclear age, the idea has gained credibility that resort to violence is immoral. The dynamics of the system has generated a new standard and statesmen seek to apply it in action.

A fourth approach to normative theory or the study of politics in terms of ethical desiderata is to recognize the obstacles standing in the pathway of realizing such goals. One obstacle is the alarming tendency of some political scientists to confine themselves to facts as contrasted with values. Ethics and purpose relate to practical matters and the foremost obstacle to international ethical desiderata is the fact that nations are locked into the nation-state system with its primacy of national ethics and purpose. Lacking is a norm or set of norms for evaluating national interest norms above and outside the state system. Students must understand the processes and standards of moral discrimination within the state system, the levels at which normative thinking is necessary and possible, and the hierarchy of values in international society.

Finally, norms do limit and restrain state behavior even when state conduct falls short of the norms proclaimed. In Niebuhr's words, hypocrisy is "the inevitable by-product in the life of any nation which has some loyalty to moral principles, but whose actions do not fully conform to those principles. The price of eliminating those hypocrisies entirely is to sink into a consistent cynicism in which moral principles are not operative at all." Norms are restraints on actions that might otherwise follow only the law of the jungle. Morality, mores, and laws are forms of restraint that limit sheer expediency. Even hypocrisy, which demonstrates the tension between moral claims and actual conduct, illustrates the place norms may occupy in international relations.

## THE ABUSE OF NORMS

If the use of norms includes their serving as guides and restraints for nations, the institutionalizing of consensus, the generating of standards, measuring the effects of obstacles, and delineating the limitations that are constraints on sheer expediency, the abuse of norms involves the turning aside of each of these principles. The abuse involves the disregard of the fundamentals on which proper use of norms must be based. It has been said that every virtue carried to its excess can become a vice.

The first abuse of normative usage in our time is ideological warfare. Men and nations always pretend to have a purer devotion to morality than they actually have. They are not as pure in actions as in the intentions they proclaim. Moral pretension appears in a nation's claim that it has acted not from self-interest or to preserve national security, but in obedience to some higher purpose. For Britain and the United States, the manner in which higher purposes are defended has normally been relatively benign. For the totalitarian powers, ideology as linked with the inevitability of the historical process has been pursued with uncontrolled fervor. In the late twentieth century, ideologies are defined in religious terms and the era of holy wars has returned, as in the struggle between Christians and Shiite Moslems in the Middle East. Democracies that had been considered the best guarantee against the spread of war have shown themselves to be as bellicose as Mirabeau predicted national assemblies would be at the time of the French Revolution. When the norms that are intended to guide and restrain nations become the ruling creeds of crusading ideological movements, restraint and prudence are displaced. Conflict replaces compromise and accommodation in the relations of states.

A second abuse relates to the institutionalizing of consensus on norms among nations. One form of this abuse results from the misunderstanding of the existing consensus and the tendency to equate economic solidarity with the moral infrastructure. A host of theorists, and especially the interdependence theorists, exaggerate, whether consciously or not, the degree of moral and political consensus. In their haste to prove that ancient patterns of international politics no longer obtain, they confuse technical with political relations. The task of building the oral foundations that Judge de Visscher describes is given short shrift in the literature on interdependence.

A different abuse but one which has had important expressions is the organization of self-appointed groups or guardians of normative thinking in quasi-political bodies of theorists and intellectuals. Little noticed is the shift that has taken place from the 1950s to the 1980s. In the 1950s, the important contributions to normative political thought were by individual scholars few if any of whom were associated with social and political movements. Reinhold Niebuhr, Hans J. Morgenthau, Paul Tillich, George F. Kennan, Walter Lippmann, Clinton Rossiter, Daniel Boorstin, and others wrote as individuals and inspired new thinking on political morality and values. In the 1980s, the individual has been swallowed up in social and political movements, especially on the right and left. Leading moralists are found in organized groups of neoconservatives, neoliberals, the Moral Majority, and countless other groups. Spearheading these movements have been disappointed academicians, politically ambitious columnists, and men and women with a passion for the opposite of anonymity. Normative theorizing has taken on a self-conscious political cast, much as in earlier decades supporters and opponents of economic planning, the United Nations, and arms control organized themselves for political action. Whereas moral philosophy has for centuries been considered the province of individual philosophers, it has in the 1980s become to a considerable extent a political action movement. This change and the substituting of tactics for theorizing and dogma for the search for truth has gone largely unnoticed, perhaps because certain columnists function as judge and jury and the influence of the media is all pervasive. Groups generate their own standards, for example, in the equating of morality with crusading anticommunism and oppose those who refuse to join what becomes a church or a cult. The high priests denounce those whose outlooks differ, engage in rhetorical overkill, and fall just short of inquisitions in their judgments of other thinkers. They demand extreme policy measures without ever shouldering the responsibility of bringing such policies to fruition. They are moralists in policymakers' clothing without any thought or intention of doing the policymaker's hard work. Freed of all responsibility for consequences, these moralists then denounce those who try and fail to implement impossible objectives.

In such a climate of opinion, the careful study of obstacles to wider normative perspectives is considered defeatist. Only faithlessness to a single dogmatic normative position is seen as standing in the way of the progress of a "chosen people." There is little point of discussing the resistance that national sovereignty imposes on the realization of some wider moral vision. For crusading nationalism, provided it is *my* nationalism, is considered the ultimate moral principle. Wiser normative thinkers have noted that liberty, while an essential norm and regulative principle in defining political morality, is not sufficient. It falls short of being an absolute political norm. National self-determination, which was an international expression of liberty, became, in fact, an absolute for some post–World War II statesmen. It led to the breakdown of the European economy when it obscured the harmonizing role that had been played by the Austro-Hungarian Empire. In a situation where the statesman must weigh both national self-determination and social and economic order, he cannot cling to only one grand simplifying dogma. For commitment to this perspective, as to the goal, communism may seem to explain everything in a kind of fairyland description of a complex world while actually confusing and distorting the hard realities along the route to a better world.

Finally, an approach to norms that talks only about their role in restraining and limiting conduct is, of course, not the whole story. It is, however, a necessary point of departure and part of that story less likely to lead to a great cataclysmic event. Yet the idea of norms as restraining forces is anathema to true believers. It throws a shadow on what they conceive as a holy mission. Restraint, balance and practical morality run counter to every precept of the more visible moral crusades. The greatest abuse of normative thought is failure to remember with Cromwell to believe by the bowels of Christ you may be wrong.

## NOTES

1. Charles de Visscher, *Theory and Reality in Public International Law*, trans. by P. E. Corbett (Princeton, NJ: Princeton University Press, 1968), p. 94.

2. Ibid., p. 90.

3. Ibid.

4. Ibid., pp. 90–91.

5. Charles de Visscher, *Theory and Reality*, 1st ed., trans. by P. E. Corbett (Princeton, NJ: Princeton University Press, 1957), p. xii.

6. De Visscher, 1968 edition, pp. vii–viii.

7. Hans J. Morgenthau and Kenneth W. Thompson, *Politics Among Nations: The Struggle for Power and Peace*. 6th ed. (New York: Knopf, 1985), pp. 243–244.

# Part IV

---

# World Cultures and International Relations

# 11

# *Gender, Skill, and Power: Africa in Search of Transformation*

## Ali A. Mazrui

As Africa approaches the third millennium of the Christian era, three major transformations are needed and, to some extent, have begun to unfold. First, there is the domestic revolution in relations between the sexes; second, there is the need for a revolution in technology and skill all over the continent; and third, there is the need for transforming Africa's power relations within the global system.

The three revolutions of gender, skill, and power are intimately intertwined. The history of Africa since 1935 is, to a large extent, a preparation for these three revolutions.

A fundamental change in relations between the genders has been occurring partly because of Africa's interaction with other cultures in this period. Islam and Western colonialism came with alternative paradigms of relationships between the sexes. Both the family and African society at large are caught up in these tensions of culture change. It is this question of gender in African society since 1935 that we address first.

### GENDER ROLES IN TRANSITION

Africa since 1935 has witnessed significant changes in the role and status of women in Africa. In many traditional cultures there has been a belief that God made woman the custodian of fire, water and earth. God himself took charge of the fourth element of the universe—the omnipresent air.

Custody of fire entailed responsibility for making energy available. And the greatest source of energy in rural Africa is firewood. The African woman became disproportionately responsible for finding and carrying huge bundles of firewood.

Custody of water involved water as a symbol of both survival and cleanliness. The African woman became responsible for ensuring that this critical substance was available for the family. She has trekked long distances to fetch water.

The custody of earth has been part of a doctrine of dual fertility. Woman ensures the survival of this generation by maintaining a central role in cultivation and preserving the fertility of the soil. Woman ensures the arrival of the next generation by her role as mother and the fertility of the womb. Dual fertility becomes an aspect of the triple custodial role of African womanhood.[1]

What has happened to this doctrine of triple custody in the period since 1935? Margaret Hay demonstrates how the Great Depression and World War II changed the situation as migrant labor and conscription of males took away a bigger and bigger proportion of men from the land. This was compounded by the growth of mining industries like the gold mining at Kowe from 1934 onwards:

The long-term absence of men had an impact on the sexual division of labor, with women and children assuming a greater share of agricultural work than ever before. . . . The thirties represent a transition with regard to the sexual division of labor, and it was clearly the women who bore the burden of the transition in rural areas.[2]

Women in this period, from the 1930s onwards, became more deeply involved as "custodians of earth." In southern Africa the migrations to the mines became even more dramatic. By the 1950s a remarkable bifurcation was taking place in some southern African societies—a division between a male proletariat (industrial working class) and a female peasantry. South Africa's regulations against families joining their husbands on the mines exacerbated this tendency towards gender apartheid and the segregation of the sexes. Many women in the front line states had to fulfill their triple custodial role of fire, water, and earth in greater isolation than ever.

The wars of liberation in southern Africa from the 1960s took their own toll on family stability and traditional sexual division of labor. Some of the fighters did have their wives with them. Indeed, liberation armies like ZANLA and ZIPRA in Zimbabwe, and FRELIMO, in Mozambique, included a few female fighters. But on the whole, the impact of the wars was disruptive of family life and of the traditional sexual division of labor.

After independence there were counterrevolutionary wars among some of the frontline states. The most artificial of the postcolonial wars was that of Mozambique initiated by the so-called Mozambique National Resistance (MNR or RENAMO). The movement was originally created by reactionary white Rhodesians to punish Samora Machel for his support for Robert Mugabe's forces in Zimbabwe. After Zimbabwe's independence, the Mozambique National Resistance became a surrogate army for reactionary whites in the Republic of South Africa—committing a variety of acts of sabotage against the fragile postcolonial economy of Mozambique.

Again, there have been implications for relations between the genders. In addition to the usual disruptive consequences of war for the family, the MNR, by the mid-1980s, had inflicted enough damage on the infrastructure in Mozambique that many migrant workers never got home to their families in between their contracts with the South African mines. The miners often remained on the border between South Africa and Mozambique, waiting for their next opportunity to the mines without ever having found the transportation to get to their families in distant villages of Mozambique.

It is not completely clear how this situation has affected the doctrine of "dual fertility" in relation to the role of the African woman. One possibility is that the extra-long absences of the husbands have reduced fertility rates in some communities in Mozambique. The other scenario is that the pattern of migrant labor in southern Africa generally has initiated a tendency toward de facto polyandry. The woman who is left behind acquires over time a de facto extra husband. The two husbands take their turn over time with the woman. The migrant laborer from the mines has conjugal priority between mining contracts if he does manage to get to the village. He also has prior claim to the new babies unless agreed otherwise.[3]

If the more widespread pattern is that of declining fertility as a result of extra-long absences of husbands, the principle of "dual fertility" has reduced the social functions of the fertility of the womb and increased the woman's involvement in matters pertaining to the fertility of the soil.

On the other hand, if the more significant tendency in mining communities in southern Africa is towards de facto polyandry, a whole new nexus of social relationships may be in the making in southern Africa.[4]

Other changes in Africa during this period which affected relationships between men and women included the impact of new technologies on gender roles. Cultivation with the hoe still left the African woman centrally involved in agriculture. But cultivation with the tractor was often a prescription for male dominance.

Mechanization of agriculture in Africa has tended to marginalize women. Their role as "custodians of earth" is threatened by male prerogatives in new and more advanced technologies. It is true that greater male involvement in agriculture could help reduce the heavy burdens of work undertaken by women on the land. On the other hand, there is no reason why this belief in workload for women should not come through better technology. Tractors were not invented to be driven solely by men.

Another threat to the central role of the African woman in the economy in this period has come from the nature of Western education. It is true that the Westernized African woman is usually more mobile and enjoys more freedom for her own interests than her more traditional sister. But a transition from custodian of fire, water, and earth to keeper of the typewriter is definitely a form of marginalization for African womanhood. Typing is less fundamental to survival than cultivation. Filing is less basic to the human condition than water and energy. The Westernized African woman in the second half of the twentieth century has tended to be more free but less important for African economies than the traditional women in rural areas.

The third threat to the role of the African woman in this period came with the internationalization of African economies. When economic activity in Africa was more localized, women had a decisive role in local markets and as traders. But the colonial and postcolonial tendencies toward enlargement of economic scale have increasingly pushed the woman to the side in international decision making. It is true that Nigerian women especially have refused to be completely marginalized, even in international trade, but on the whole, the Africans who deal with international markets and sit on the Boards of transnational corporations are overwhelmingly men. And at meetings of the Organization of Petroleum Exporting Countries (OPEC)—where Muslims predominate—there are additional inhibitions about having even Nigeria represented by a female delegate.

But what is the future avenue that is likely to change the balance between men and women in public life in Africa? The reasons why women are politically subordinate are not to be sought in economic differentiation. Women in Africa are economically very active; women in Saudi Arabia are economically neutralized. And yet in both types of society women are politically subordinate. And so, economic differences are not the real explanation of political subjection of womanhood.

What is indeed universal is not the economic role of women but their military role. All over Africa (and indeed all over the world) women are militarily marginalized. What will one day change the political balance between men and women is when the military machine becomes bisexual. The Somali army has started recruiting women. The Algerian air force has started recruiting women pilots. Both Muslim societies in Africa are beginning to give a military role to women. But the future needs more than tokenism in gender roles. In this continent of coups we may have to wait for the day when the announcement of a coup in West Africa reads as follows: "Brigadier-General *Janet* Adebiyi has captured power in a military takeover in Lagos."

But technology is not only linked to the relationship between men and women in Africa; it is also linked to the wider configuration of power in the world.

The period since 1935 has witnessed the emergence of a world divided between an increasingly prosperous northern hemisphere and a persistently disadvantaged southern hemisphere. The concept of "the Third World" was, of course, born in this period of history—as the North was split between East and West in *ideological systems* and the world between North and South in both *skill* and *income*. In the global context, Africa, in this period of history, has had to look at itself partly in terms of this North-South divide. The continent's global allies have increasingly become the rest of the Third World.

## TOWARD DUAL SOLIDARITY

Two forms of solidarity are critical for Africa and the Third World if the global system is to change in favor of the disadvantaged.

*Organic solidarity* concerns South-South linkages designed to increase mutual dependence between and among African or Third World countries themselves. *Strategic solidarity* concerns cooperation among Third World countries in their struggle to extract concessions from the industralized northern world. Organic solidarity concerns the aspiration to promote greater integration between Third World economies. Strategic solidarity aspires to decrease the South's dependent integration into northern economies. The focus of organic solidarity is primarily a South-South economic marriage. The focus of strategic solidarity is either a North-South divorce, a new marriage settlement, or a new social contract between North and South. The terms of the North-South bond have to be renegotiated.

We start also from the additional basic observation that economic flows are in any case far deeper between North and South than between South and South. On the whole, southerners do far greater trade with the North than with each other, and have more extensive relations of production with industrialized states than with fellow developing countries. But those economic relations between North and South are distorted by a tradition of dependency involving unequal partnership. The structural links give undue advantage and leverage to the North  and leave the South vulnerable and exploitable.

What then is the way out? How can these two forms of solidarity help to ameliorate the Third World's predicament of dependency and its persistent economic vulnerability?

One of the more neglected areas of cooperation is humanpower and humanpower training. A start has been made in manpower exchange between some Third World countries and in the field of manpower training across Third World boundaries. But the importance of this area has been grossly underestimated.

It is not often realized that the most obstinate line of demarcation between North and South is not income (criteria of wealth) but technology (criteria of skill). The entire international system of stratification has come to be based *not* on ''who *owns* what'' but on ''who *knows* what.'' Libya and Saudi Arabia may have a higher per capita income than some of the members of the European Economic Community, but Libya and Saudi Arabia are well below Western Europe in skills of production and economic organization. Indeed, members of OPEC do not even have adequate skills to control or drill their own oil.

Nowhere is this demonstrated more clearly than in southern Africa and the Middle East. Less than 5 million whites in South Africa have been able to hold to ransom a black population in a region ten times as large as their own. They have held neighboring blacks to ransom both economically and militarily. The main explanation is not simply because South Africa is rich, but because that wealth has been extracted through African labor and *European* expertise. South Africa's neighbors have African labor too. Some of them are also rich in minerals. What the blacks have lacked indigenously is the superior technology of production and the accompanying culture of efficient organization.

In both South Africa and Israel the cultural variable is critical. Had Israel consisted entirely of Middle Eastern Jews, the Arabs would have won every war. Indeed, it would not have been necessary to have more than the 1948 war. After all, Middle Eastern Jews are not very different from their Arab neighbors in culture and skill. In a war against fellow Middle Easterners, the numerical preponderance of the Arabs would have triumphed against Jews long before the numerical advantage was reinforced by Arab petro-wealth.

What has made the Israelis militarily preeminent is not the Jewishness of 80 percent of the total population, but the Europeanness of less than 50 percent of that Jewish sector. It is the European and Western Jews who have provided the technological foundations of Israel's regional hegemony.

If then the ultimate basis of international stratification is indeed skill rather than income, what is Africa to do in order to ameliorate the consequences of its technological underdevelopment?

The more obvious answer is for Africa to obtain the know-how from the northern hemisphere as rapidly as possible. But there are difficulties. Countries of the northern hemisphere are often all too eager to transfer certain forms of technology, especially through transnational corporations, but the South's need for certain technological transfers only helps to deepen relationships of dependency between the two hemispheres.

On the other hand, there are other areas of technology that the North is not at all keen to transfer. Preeminent among the taboos is the transfer of certain branches of nuclear physics and technology. The computer is part of the phenomenon of dependency through technology transfer; the nuclear plant or reactor is a symbol of dependency through technological monopoly by the North. The transnational corporations are often instruments of northern penetration of the South through technological transfer; nuclear power, on the other hand, is a symbol of northern hegemony through technological monopoly.

The dual strategy for Africa and the Third World is both to learn from the North and to share expertise among themselves. Those aspects of technology which are being freely transferred by the North should be "decolonized" and stripped of their dependency implications as fast as possible. Those aspects of technology which are deliberately monopolized by the North should be subjected to southern industrial espionage in a bid to break the monopoly. Pakistani scientists have been on the right track in their reported efforts to subject northern nuclear monopoly to southern industrial spying. If Pakistan becomes Islam's first nuclear power and decides to share the nuclear secrets with a few select fellow Muslims like Egyptians or Libyans, that trend would be in the direction of enhanced technological cooperation among Third World countries.

That is one reason why the brain drain from the South is not an unmitigated disaster. What would be a catastrophe is a complete stoppage of the brain drain. It is vital that the South should counter-penetrate the citadels of technological and economic power. The counter-penetration can take the form of African engineers, teachers and professors, medical doctors and consultants, businessmen and scientists, working in the North. The North needs to be more sensitized to southern needs not only by the speeches of southern statesmen and ambassadors, but also by the influence and leverage of southerners resident in the North.

In any case, there is no law of gravity that says expertise can only flow from the North to the South. There is no gravitational logic that says that European teachers teaching African children is natural—but African teachers teaching European children is not. The structure of scientific stratification in the world should rapidly cease to be a rigid caste system— and allow for social mobility in both directions. Of course, too big a brain drain from the South northwards could deeply hurt the South—but the trouble with the present level of the brain is not that it is too great, but that it is grossly underutilized by the South, itself. Professor Edward S. Ayensu, a Ghanaian research director at the Smithsonian Institution in Washington, DC, has argued that there is a large potential pool of Third World experts, resident in the northern hemisphere, who would be only too glad to serve for a year or two in developing societies, if only their services were solicited. What is more, the northern institutions where they work would, according to Professor Ayensu, be sympathetically inclined toward facilitating such exchanges from time to time if so requested by Third World authorities.[5]

If that were to happen, it would be a case of tapping the brain drain on the basis of a triangular formula. The flow of expertise would be, first, from South to North, then North to South, and then South to South—often involving the same southern experts or their equivalents, sharing their know-how across hemispheres.

This sharing of southern experts by both North and South would be a more realistic formula than the tax on the brain drain which Professor Jagdish Bhagwati of the Massachusetts Institute of Technology has often recommended as a method of compensation by the North toward the South for manpower transfer. Unfortunately, while the North may indeed be willing to share with the South some of its newly acquired southern experts, the South itself has shown more enthusiasm for borrowing "pure" northern experts than for borrowing southern experts residing in the North. The psychological dependency of the South is less likely to be impressed by an Indian or Nigerian expert coming from the United States than by a U.S. expert with far less understanding of the Third World. The American is regarded as "the real thing" in expertise—while the Indian statistician or Nigerian engineer is deemed to be a mere southern "carbon copy."

Fortunately, all is not bleak. There is some movement of expertise between Third World countries. Dr. Boutros-Ghali, Egypt's minister of state for foreign affairs, assured me in an interview in Cairo in 1983 that Egypt had "two million experts" working in other countries, mainly in Africa and the Middle East. South Asia also exports a considerable body of expertise to other parts of the Third World.

Some of the traffic in expertise across Third World frontiers is caused by political instability and economic problems at home. Qualified Ugandans and Ethiopians are scattered in almost all the four corners of the Third World, as well as in the North. So are qualified Ghanaians, southern Africans, Nigerians, and others.

Then there is the inter–Third World traffic of experts caused by the magnetism of petro-wealth. The Gulf states have a particularly impressive variety of human power from different lands. Two Ghanaian scholars visited the University of Petroleum and Minerals in Dhahran in the Kingdom of Saudi Arabia in the summer of 1984. They were impressed by the Ghanaian presence in the research complex of the university. They were also surprised to learn about "24 highly qualified Ghanaian medical officers working in and around this University town of Dhahran."[6]

To summarize, there is a *push factor* in some of the less fortunate Third World countries which forces out many native experts in search of alternative opportunities in other countries. But there is also a *pull factor* in the wealthier Third World societies which magnetically attracts workers and specialists from other lands. Together, the two forces are helping to lay down some of the foundations of organic solidarity within the Third World in the field of know-how.

What is lacking is an adequate linkage between organic and strategic solidarity in this field of evolving Third World expertise. A systematic program which would enable Africa to borrow some of the southern experts now residing in the North could become an important stage in the evolution of a merger between organic and strategic solidarity.

Behind it all is the realization that the ultimate foundations of international stratification are not income differences, military gadgets, or demographic variations. Ultimate power resides neither in the barrel of the gun nor in the barrel of oil—but in the technology which can produce and utilize both efficiently. A New International Economic Order would be void without a New International Technological Order. Africa needs strategies of solidarity to realize both.

## FOUR FORMS OF POWER

But although *the power of skill* is at the moment overwhelmingly in the hands of the North, there are other areas of power that the South possesses but underutilizes.

OPEC is an illustration of *producer power*. From 1973 to 1983 OPEC grossly underutilized its leverage. Instead of using that golden decade to put pressure on the North for fundamental adjustments in the patterns and rules of the world economy, OPEC concentrated almost exclusively on the price game, a game of short-term maximization of returns.

There is a crying need for other "producer cartels," no matter how weak in the short run. Cobalt has more promise as a mineral of leverage than copper, and would involve fewer countries. Experimentation in a cobalt cartel could pay off if Zaire asserted itself a little more decisively as an independent power. After all, Zaire has the credentials of being the Saudi Arabia of cobalt when the market improves in the years ahead.

The Third World has also underutilized its *consumer power*, regionally specific and patchy as it is. The Middle East and African countries like Nigeria are especially important as consumers of Western civil and military hardware, technology, and household products. Occasionally Nigeria or individual Middle East countries flex their muscles and threaten to cancel trade contracts or to refuse to renew them. But such muscles are flexed usually for relatively minor issues—like protesting against the television film *Death of a Princess* or when an Arab or African delegation is snubbed by a Western power. The consumer power of Africa and the Middle East could be used as leverage for more fundamental changes in the exchange patterns between North and South.

The fourth form of power currently underutilized by the South is *debtor power*. President Julius Nyerere of Tanzania, upon being elected chairman of the Organization of African Unity in November 1984, identified development, debt, and drought as the three leading concerns of the current African condition. Of course, African debts are modest as compared with those of Latin America, but Nyerere identified debt as a source of power and not merely as a source of weakness. At the first press conference after his election, Nyerere lamented that the Third World was not utilizing the threat of defaulting more efficiently to induce Western banks to make more fundamental concessions to the indebted.[7]

It is indeed true that if I owe my local bank a few thousand dollars, I am vulnerable—but if I owe the bank millions of dollars, the bank is vulnerable. Tanzania still owes so little that the country is still very vulnerable. But Nyerere virtually declared that if he owed as much as some of the leading African debtor countries owed, he would simply refuse to pay. (Africa's leading debtor nations include Nigeria, Egypt, and Zaire. South of the Sahara, Africa's debt by 1986 was over 90 billion dollars.)

In reality, Tanzania would still be vulnerable unless there was substantial strategic solidarity among both African and Latin American countries. The utilization of debtor power requires considerable consensus among the indebted. The Western banks have evolved a kind of organic solidarity of their own as well as mechanisms of almost continual consultation. The creditors of the North are united—but the debtors of the South are in disarray. Africa and Latin America need to explore the possibility of creating a strategic solidarity of the dispossessed and the indebted—to help induce the Shylocks of the North to make concessions on such issues as rates of interest, schedule of payment, methods of payment, and the conditions for a moratorium or even total debt relief where needed.

Fundamental as all these areas of strategic solidarity are, they are no substitute for organic solidarity in terms of greater trade, investment, and other interactions among Third World countries themselves. Here, the Less Developed Countries (LDCs) are caught up in one of several contradictions. In their relations with the North, the LDCs need to diversify their economies. But in their relations with each other, the LDCs need to specialize in order to increase mutual complementarity. Uganda could revive its cotton industry and sell the fiber to Kenya to process into a textile industry. This specialization would help the two countries develop in the direction of complementary specialization. But the imperatives of Uganda's relations with the world economy as a whole dictate diversification of Uganda's industry rather than specialization. This is an acute dilemma which Third World countries need to resolve as a matter of urgency. They need to find a suitable balance between diversification for North-South relations and specialization in South-South trade.

Related to this is the imperative of finding alternative methods of payment in South-South trade. The principle of using northern currencies for South-South trade has been very stressful. The bogey of "foreign exchange" has bedeviled southern economies. Tanzania, Zambia, and

Zimbabwe have been exploring possibilities of reviving *barter* as a basis of at least some aspect of their economic relations. Nigeria, in the 1980s, has experimented with "counter-trade"—exchanging its oil for manufactured goods. The new detente between Kenya and Tanzania also envisages areas of barter trade between the two countries in the years ahead. And if Uganda's cotton did feed Kenya's textile industry more systematically in the future, it would not be unrealistic for Kenya to pay back Uganda in shirts and processed military uniforms, rather than in hard foreign exchange.

Another area of organic solidarity among Third World countries concerns the issue of sharing energy. There have been years when Kenya has needed to get a third of its electricity from the dam at Jinja in Uganda. Uganda is still a major supplier of power to Kenya.

The Akosombo Dam on the Volta River in Ghana was also designed to be a major regional supplier of electricity in West Africa. Unfortunately the level of water has been so low that far from supplying power to neighbors, Ghana has periodically had to ration power domestically. Ghana has sometimes needed electrical cooperation from the Ivory Coast. Southern African dams like Kariba have had more successful regional roles. They all symbolize a kind of pan-Africanism of energy, organic solidarity through interlocking structures of hydroelectric power.

An integrated European steel complex once served as midwife to the birth of the European Economic Community (EEC). Indeed, the integrated steel industry was envisioned as an insurance against any future fratricidal war in Europe. If European steel production was interlocked, industrial interdependence was at hand—and separate military aggression in the future would therefore be less likely.

In the same spirit, interlocking electrical systems between Third World countries should deepen mutual dependence—and create incentives for cooperation in other areas.

The struggle for a more integrated Africa has encountered many setbacks—from the collapse of the East African Community of Kenya, Uganda, and Tanzania to the substantial drying up of the Akosombo Dam.

An experiment worthy of Africa's attention and study is Southeast Asia. The struggle for a more integrated Southeast Asia is more of a success story—as the Association of Southeast Asian Nations (ASEAN) has emerged as a major economic and diplomatic force in the affairs of the region. The struggle for a more integrated Arab world is a mixed story—ranging from the positive promise of the Gulf Cooperation Council to the negative internecine squabbles of Arab politics. Libya and Egypt are often close to conflict.

In Latin America regional integration is also a mixed record. Central America in the 1980s is tense under the clouds of war. On the other hand, Chile and Argentina—through the mediation of the Vatican—have diffused the sensitive issue of the Bege Channel. Economic cooperation has had its ups and downs throughout the region, but the ideal of greater integration is still a live flame. Africa should watch this distant political laboratory with fascination.

The northern hemisphere, as a whole, is divided between two economic blocs which coincide with the ideological divide. The split is of course between the socialist world of COMECON (Council for Mutual Economic Assistance/CMEA) and the capitalist world of the North Atlantic Treaty Organization (NATO).

Africa, as a Southern region, on the other hand, is still in multiple fragments. It is now in search of the elusive secret of putting the fragments together. It is in search of the secret genius of cohesion. Strategies of solidarity are but means to an end. The goal is distant and difficult—but Africa's reach should exceed its grasp or what's a heaven for?

But should Africa's "reach" extend to participation in the politics of nuclear power? Where does Africa fit into these nuclear calculations? How have cultural and racial inequalities affected Africa in the nuclear age? It is to this theme that we must now turn.

## AFRICA VERSUS THE NUCLEAR AGE

It is symbolic of the basic African condition that the first form of African participation in the nuclear age concerned a raw material. Uranium is of course as indigenous to Africa as "the flame trees of Thika" or the baobab tree of Senegal. Africa in the 1930s and 1940s helped to provide the uranium that launched the Western world into the nuclear orbit.

To change the metaphor, Africa was in attendance at the birth of the nuclear age. It was in part Africa's uranium from Zaire that helped to set in motion the first nuclear reactor in North America. And for better or for worse, Africa's uranium may have gone into those dreadful atomic bombs that were dropped on Hiroshima and Nagasaki in August 1945. But of course Africa had no say in the matter. An African resource had simply been pirated by others—and once again played a major role in a significant shift in Western industrialism.

Not that uranium was all that scarce even in the 1940s. What was significant was that, outside the Soviet Bloc and North America, uranium seemed to be substantially available only in black Africa. As Caryl P. Haskins put it way back in 1946, "[Uranium] stands next to copper in abundance, is more abundant than zinc, and is about four times as plentiful as lead."[8]

Of course, since 1946 other reserves of uranium ore have been discovered in the world, including in different parts of Africa. African uranium has continued to fill many a reactor in the Western world, and to help create many a nuclear bomb.

The second service (after uranium supply) which Africa rendered to the nuclear age was also symbolic. Africa provided the desert for nuclear tests in the early 1960s. In this case Africa's nuclear involvement had shifted slightly from a purely indigenous resource (uranium) to a partially Islamic context (the Sahara). The transition was from providing indigenous nuclear material to furnishing a neo-Islamic laboratory in the desert for a Western bomb. At least two of the legacies of Africa's triple heritage (indigenous, Islamic, and Western legacies) were inadvertently involved—from the mines of Zaire to the sand of Algeria.

The third African point of entry into the nuclear age has been through the Republic of South Africa. For better or worse, South Africa has probably become a nuclear power or is close to it. This provides the third leg of Africa's triple heritage. Indigenous resources (Africa's uranium), a semi-Islamic testing laboratory (the dunes of the Sahara), and an actual Western productive capability (white South Africa's expertise).

A circle of influence developed. The progress of the French nuclear program and its tests in the Sahara probably helped the Israeli nuclear program. This was a period when France was quite close to Israel in terms of economic and technological collaboration. The French helped the Israelis build a nuclear reactor at Dimona and seemed at times to be closer to the Israelis in sharing nuclear secrets than even the Americans were. The evidence is abundant and clear—the French nuclear program in the late 1950s, and 1960s served as a midwife to the Israeli nuclear program. And French tests in the Sahara were part and parcel of France's nuclear infrastructure in that period.

By a curious twist of destiny, the Israeli nuclear program, in turn, came to serve as a midwife to the nuclear efforts of the Republic of South Africa in the 1970s and 1980s. Relations between the two countries cooled a little after the Sharpeville massacre of 1960 and when Israel briefly considered the possibility of extending aid to African liberation movements in southern Africa. But by 1970 there were clear improvements in economic relationships. And after black Africa's almost complete diplomatic break with Israel in 1973, cooperation between Israel and South Africa entered new areas, including the nuclear field. When a nuclear explosion occurred in the South Atlantic in September 1979, the question that arose was whether it was primarily a South African nuclear experiment undertaken with Israeli technical aid, or primarily an Israeli explosive experiment carried out with South Africa's logistical support. A cover-up policy was pursued by both countries, helped in part by their Western allies, especially the Carter administration in the United States. The cyclical nuclear equation was about to be completed. The Sahara has aided France's nuclear program, France had aided Israel's nuclear design, and Israel had in turn aided South Africa's nuclear ambitions. Kwame Nkrumah's fear of a linkage between nuclear tests in the Sahara and racism in South Africa had found astonishing vindication nearly two decades later. It was in April 1960 that Nkrumah addressed an international meeting in Accra in the following terms:

Fellow Africans and friends: there are two threatening swords of Damocles hanging over the continent, and we must remove them. These are nuclear tests in the Sahara by the French Government and the apartheid policy of the Government of the Union of South Africa. It would be a great mistake to imagine that the achievement of political independence by certain areas in Africa will automatically mean the end of the struggle. It is merely the beginning of the struggle.[9]

It has turned out that Nkrumah's thesis of "two swords of Damocles," one nuclear and one racist, was in fact prophetic. The Republic of South Africa is using nuclear power as a potentially stabilizing factor in defense of apartheid. The old nuclear fallout in the Sahara in the 1960s involved a linkage between racism and nuclear weapons that is only just beginning to reveal itself.

But the cultural and technological inequalities between white and black in southern Africa affect other areas of security—conventional areas as well as nuclear domains. The Republic of South Africa has used its technological superiority to bully its black neighbors into submission and into "nonaggression" pacts. The sovereignty of Mozambique, Angola, Botswana, Lesotho, and even independent Zimbabwe has been violated from time to time, sometimes with utter impunity. European technological leadership in the last three centuries of world history has been inherited by people of European extraction operating in Africa—and has been used as a decisive military resource against black Africans. South Africa's neighbors have begun to appreciate what it must feel like to be Israel's neighbor—for both South Africa and Israel have seldom hesitated to use blatant military muscle at the expense of the sovereignty of their neighbors.

Again, cultural and technological inequalities have played a part in these politics of intervention. As we have indicated earlier, Israelis have enjoyed military preeminence for so long not because they are Jews but because a large part of their population is Western and European. We have argued that had the population of Israel consisted overwhelmingly of Middle Eastern Jews, the Arabs would have won every single war they fought with their Jewish neighbor. Numbers would have counted. Middle Eastern Jews in Israel are often more hawkish and eager to fight the Arabs, but the military capability for assuring Israeli victory has come more from their European compatriots. Again culture has played a decisive role in deciding victory and defeat in military equations.

The danger both in the Middle East and southern Africa lies in pushing the weak too far. We have already seen how desperate conditions in the two subregions can easily become fertile ground for different forms of terrorism. For the time being, that terrorism in the two geographical areas has not yet gone nuclear. But if the cultural imbalances between Israeli and Arab, between white and black, continue to deepen the sense of desperation among the disadvantaged, we cannot rule out the possibility of their acquiring those nuclear devices one day from radical friends elsewhere. Powerlessness also corrupts—and absolute powerlessness can corrupt absolutely.

But once again there is one kind of powerlessness the implications of which are particularly distinctive—the powerlessness of women on issues of war and peace. Related to this issue is the whole question of the psychology of *nuclear macho*. It is to these sexual questions that we must now return.

## THE GENDER OF NUCLEAR WAR

In societies that are vastly different from each other, war has so far been preeminently a masculine game. "Our sons are our warriors"—this has been almost universal. Daughters have had different roles as a rule. Even countries like Israel, which involve women substantially in issues of war and peace, have tended to be protective of women in the allocation of combat duties.

If it is indeed true that there is a pronounced *macho* factor in the psychology of going to war, we cannot ignore the macho factor when we are discussing *nuclear* war. Perhaps that is indeed what is distinctive about war in the nuclear age—it has become too important to be left to men. The whole human species is at stake—men, women, and children. And while the human race has managed to survive for perhaps 3 million years in spite of the violent proclivities of the caveman, nuclear power requires the most fundamental of all human revolutions—a truly androgynized system of social and political power.

It is true that the most famous women rulers in the twentieth century have tended to be "iron ladies" with a taste for nuclear credentials— Golda Meir, Indira Gandhi, as well as Margaret Thatcher. These are the Dahomey Amazons of the Nuclear Age. But for as long as most societies remain primarily male dominated, the women who succeed in the power game will tend to be approximations of what men regard as tough and heroic. Africa and the rest of the community could only discover the true impact of women on decisions concerning war and peace when the power system as a whole has acquired true sexual balance, commensurate androgyny.

Are we to assume that women in Africa and elsewhere are generally less violent than men? The answer is "Yes"—though the reasons may be more cultural than biological. Our information is inadequate about the causes, but there is no doubt about the correlation between violence and masculinity. The jails of crimes of violence are a solemn testimony; the wars across history; the concentration camps and their Eichmanns. Of course, the world has also produced brutal women. But while men and women have had an equal share in determining births, men have had an overwhelmingly larger share in determining deaths. Men and women are cocreators of the human race, but men have often been solo destroyers of large chunks of that race. The female of the species is the senior partner in the process of baby making; the male of the species has been the senior partner in the business of corpse making. In the twentieth century alone there has been no female equivalent of Hitler, or Stalin, or Pol Pot, or Idi Amin, or the more brutal architects of *apartheid*.

In reality we cannot be sure that an androgynized power system either in Africa or on the world stage will in fact succeed in moderating the violent inclinations of states. But perhaps nothing short of a gender revolution can stand a chance of containing the nuclear threat to the species. If that does not work either, the future will be grim indeed for the human race as a whole as it faces its own escalating technological capacity for planetary self-destruction.

## TOWARD THE FUTURE

There is one happy prospect that black Africans can contemplate which the Arabs are denied. Black Africans can contemplate the prospect of inheriting the white bomb of the Republic of South Africa. As we have argued elsewhere, before the end of this century the blacks of South Africa will probably succeed in overthrowing the regime of white supremacy. In the wake of the racial war that has to precede the black victory, half the white population would probably have had to leave the Republic. But it seems almost certain that half the white population of South Africa would in the end also still remain behind. Through that other half, South Africa's nuclear capability would be transmitted from white control to black control.

It is therefore a fair question to ask whether the prospect of a nuclearized South Africa today is a blessing or a curse for the rest of Africa. Is it possible that white South Africa's nuclear bomb is a short-term nuisance for black Africa but a long-term advantage? Are South Africa's blacks going to be the legitimate heirs of South Africa's nuclear capability before the end of the century?

There is little doubt that white South Africa's bomb is irrelevant to the survival of apartheid. The main threat to South Africa's racist regime is internal to South Africa—and the regime is unlikely to use nuclear devices in the streets of Soweto. Such a use would, in any case, precipitate a white exodus—at least as serious a crisis for apartheid as the rebellion of blacks.

But while nuclear power is of marginal significance in the fortunes of present-day South Africa, it may be more significant in the post-apartheid era of the Republic. As the new rulers inherit the white nuclear bomb, they will be transformed from the status of being the most humiliated blacks of the twentieth century to the status of becoming the most powerful blacks of the twenty-first century. Black-ruled South Africa will of course remain not only one of the richest countries in the world in terms of mineral resources, but also one of the most industrialized in the southern hemisphere. The nuclear capability will remain part of a wider industrial complex.

But can such "horizontal nuclear proliferation" be a cure to vertical proliferation? Again the underlying hope lies in creating the necessary culture shock for a serious commitment to *universal* nuclear disarmament. In any case, black inheritance of South Africa's bomb will not be horizontal nuclear proliferation in the usual sense. No new *country* will have been added to the membership of the nuclear club—only a new *race*. For the first time the nuclear club will have a black member. At the most, the horizontal proliferation will have been across the racial divide rather than state boundaries. And since northern nuclear powers are more afraid of South African blacks handling the bomb than of South African whites doing so, the new black member of the nuclear club may well precipitate an agonizing reappraisal as to whether the club should exist at all. The racial prejudices and distrust of the white members of the nuclear club may well serve the positive function of disbanding the club—and dismantling the nuclear arsenals in the cellars that had constituted credentials for membership.

But nuclear disarmament is not enough. There is need to reduce the risk of war. After all, once the "genie" of nuclear know-how is already out of the bottle, it can be reutilized if war broke out—and a new nuclear arms race be inaugurated. The ultimate evil is man's proclivity toward war, and not merely the weapons with which he has fought it.

But what kind of fundamental revolution could stabilize the gains in nuclear disarmament and reduce the risk of war? In order to answer that question we need to ask that other question: What has been the most persistent characteristic of war in all societies, across all time, traversing all cultures?

No, the most persistent attribute of war has not been the consistency of motives—for men have fought for reasons that have ranged from greed to glory, from gold to God, from liberty to land, from sex to soccer. The motives have varied but war has continued.

The most recurrent attribute of war has not been its technology either— for we know that the technological range has been from the spear to the intercontinental missile.

Nor has war been a peculiarity of certain climates—for men have fought under the blazing sun as well as in snow drifts.

No, the most persistent attribute of war has not been its motivation, technology, organization, goals, or geographical context. As we have indicated, it has in fact been its *masculinity*.

But with the coming of the nuclear age, war has become too serious to be left to men. The power system of the world does indeed need to be androgynized. The most poignant of all paradoxes amounts to the following imperative: *If man is to survive, woman has to bear arms.*

Africa originally declared woman as custodian of fire, water, and earth. The nuclear age is redefining the scope of the triple custody globally. Africa once entrusted to woman both the *survival* of this generation and the *arrival* of the next generation through the doctrine of dual fertility. The nuclear age is expanding that responsibility into a planetary agenda for collective self-preservation. Africa's three future revolutions of gender, skill, and power will find their supreme fulfillment when African women take the lead in universal nuclear disarmament and effective arms control. War has for so long worn a masculine mask. Peace may one day unveil a feminine face—perhaps black in complexion.

## NOTES

1. I am indebted to the late Okot p'Bitek, the Ugandan anthropologist and poet, for stimulation and information about myths of womanhood in northern Uganda. Okot and I also discussed similarities and differences between African concepts of matter and the ideas of Empedocles, the Greek philosopher of the fifth century BC. Consult also Okot p'Bitek, *African Religions in Western Scholarship* (Nairobi: East African Literature Bureau, 1971).

2. Margaret Jean Hay, "Luo Women and Economic Change During the Colonial Period," in *Women in Africa: Studies in Social and Economic Change*, ed. by Nancy J. Hafkin and Edna G. Bay (Stanford, CA: Stanford University Press, 1976), p. 105.

3. There is no doubt such arrangements occur in Mozambique. What is not clear how widespread de facto polyandry is becoming in Southern Africa.

4. I am indebted to the field research and interviews in Southern Africa which accompanied the BBC/WETA television project "The Africans: A Triple Heritage" (1985–1986).

5. Edward S. Ayensu, lecture on "Natural and Applied Sciences and National Development," delivered at the Silver Jubilee celebration of the Ghana Academy of Arts and Science (Accra), November 22, 1984.

6. The two Ghanaian visitors were Professor Alexander Kwapong, vice-rector of the United National University in Tokyo, and Professor Edward Ayensu of the Smithsonian Institution in the United States. See Ayensu's lecture (mimeo), Ghana Academy of Arts and Sciences, (Accra), November 22, 1984.

7. The Voice of America's African Service broadcast a recording of both Nyerere's speech and Nyerere's press conference. One such broadcast by V.O.A. African Service was on Saturday November 24, 1984, Greenwich Mean Time (GMT).

8. Caryl P. Haskins, "Atomic Energy and American Foreign Policy," *Foreign Affairs* 24, no. 4 (July 1946): 595–596.

9. Kwame Nkrumah, *I Speak of Freedom: A Statement of African Ideology* (London:Heinemann Educational, 1961), p. 213.

# 12
## Asian Culture and International Relations

Michael Haas

### INTERNATIONAL HISTORY OF ASIA AND THE PACIFIC

Although grouped together in recognition of the rise to prominence of Asian countries that front onto the Pacific Ocean, no two regions of the world could be more different in historical experience than continental Asia and the islands of the Pacific. While mighty empires dominated the continent 2500 or more years ago, ambitious migrations of seafaring peoples began to spread from the periphery of Asia to remote archipelagos in the Pacific. The history of Asia is of hierarchically organized state relations interrupted by intrusions of imperialist countries to wrest control of resources and markets, while the Pacific islands coexisted in a somewhat more egalitarian manner until imperial powers arrived.

### CONCEPT OF "ASIAN AND PACIFIC CULTURE"

Despite geographic and historical diversity, the peoples of Asia and the Pacific can nevertheless be said to share a common culture in regard to international relations. If by "culture" we refer to shared beliefs and sentiments that serve to orient leaders of states to their roles as international actors,[1] Asian and Pacific states have similarities that are a function of similar historical circumstances.

The reason for this convergence, as argued herein, is that historical conditions shaped a common interest in peaceful modes of state behavior, interlopers from outside the region further underscored the virtues of peaceful statecraft, and the destiny of countries of Asia and the Pacific has come to depend more and more upon efforts to forge a common identity and a compatible operational code in foreign policy. The purpose of this chapter, accordingly, is to document the existence of indigenous Asian and Pacific cultures, the breakup of these norms, and the resulting dependence on outside forces with the advent of Western imperialism, then to discuss how the "Asian Way" and "Pacific Way" have emerged in recent decades as modes of regional liberation from outside influence by asserting a common identity.

## TRADITIONAL ASIAN AND PACIFIC POLITICAL THOUGHT

Emperors of China regarded their society, organized along the principles of Confucius and Mencius, to be superior; all other states were to pay tribute and make visits to the Middle Kingdom to attest the supremacy of Chinese authority and culture in Asia.[2] Confucian principles stressed the display of superiority through courtesy, virtuous example, and suasion rather than using force to resolve conflicts; a ruler was subject to the principles of nature, too, and failure to observe correct statecraft would cause a ruler to lose power. The ruler is responsible for instructing those in a subordinate status on the rules of proper conduct lest society disintegrate into chaos. Moreover, should a ruler govern unwisely, such that calamities result, inferiors have a right to rebel so as to install a ruler who is more attuned to the principles of proper conduct. As a superior state, China was to approach other states with the aim to "be indulgent to its offenses, pardon its errors and failures, relieve its calamities, reward it for its virtues and laws, and teach it where it is deficient."[3] Although inferior states were to pay tribute, China in fact was to distribute largesse in even greater quantity to those who paid tribute. The tributary system served as a ritual to ensure regular communication with vassal states, lest they become disobedient. War is justified only to punish unrighteousness. Current Chinese aggression at the borders of Vietnam, we are reminded, is to teach Hanoi a "lesson," a practice historically pursued with non-Chinese barbarians unexposed to Confucian principles but even then only in extreme emergencies. Annihilation of another state was considered to be akin to the murder of one individual by another and hence unjustified. Confucianism was a doctrine of universal love and respect for all. The history and practice of rule in China did not live up to Confucian standards, but the norms of Confucianism provided a ready critique of events and trends of Chinese history, thereby serving as China's main cultural tradition.

Kautilya's Hindu theory of international politics stressed a balance-of-power strategy to wage war as needed to avoid conquest and domination by outside forces.[4] The ruler is supposed to look out for all people as children in a family, so the domestic political theory was closer to the teachings of the Buddha than to international realpolitik. The concept of "righteous conquest" gained acceptance as war for glory rather than for profit or power. The victorious ruler should be conciliatory toward the conquered people, wear local dress and follow local customs, reconstruct their economy, gain the support of leaders of the conquered state, and restore law and order. Conquered rulers are urged to be submissive to the conqueror while biding their time to overthrow the new king in order to achieve independence. The chivalry of warfare ensured that no atrocities occurred. But warfare was nearly perpetual, and there was never enough time to develop the fine art of administration that held together the Chinese empires. The ruler was counseled to make alliances (with the enemies of their enemies) and to tie down enemies in battles with these allies. Internal politics, thus, were to be conducted with compassion, external politics with vigilance. Contemporary Indian absorption of Goa and Sikkim, as well as New Delhi's support for Bangladesh's war of independence from Pakistan, are well within the realpolitik tradition of Indian political thought.

Muslim thought, as found in the *Koran* and writings of its interpreters, projects a view of the world divided into two camps—the universal World of Islam and the World of War (that is, a world enjoying Allah's peace and harmony juxtaposed alongside a world in disorder).[5] Moslem rulers in Asia have been active in Islamic international organizations, the first prime minister of Malaysia subsequently serving as the first secretary-general of the intergovernmental International Islamic Organization at Jeddah. The fraternal relationship between Islamic Indonesian and Malaysian leaders since the mid-1960s have been exemplary in this regard. But religious observances have not been carried out as separatist activities, isolating Moslem from non-Moslem countries in Asia. The need to spread Islam to nonbelievers requires Moslem leaders to have cordial relations with non-Moslem leaders as well, so long as the latter do not threaten the advance of Islam.

Since the peoples of the Pacific were sparsely settled on thousands of islands over vast areas and separated by rough seas, they did not develop complex bureaucratic systems of rule. While Melanesian society valued personal skills somewhat more than hereditary bases for leadership, Polynesian society was divided into commoners and various levels of chieftainship. War, used to determine the extent of a chief's domain, was regulated by specific codes of conduct.[6] For example, war was in daytime, with the place and time agreed upon. No war took place during certain times of the year, and a truce could be declared at any time during battle. Once war started, it was pursued with ferocity; the vanquished were slaughtered unless they were successful in pleading to live as slaves of the victorious chiefs. Defeated peoples are often thought to have escaped to new islands to the west.

Though Melanesians were more inclined to fight to defend their societies, what was most impressive to the Westerners who first arrived in Polynesia was the friendliness of the people.[7] For centuries the Pacific islanders treated themselves and others with extraordinary courtesy and kindness at an individual level, a spirit call *aloha* in Hawaii, with similar meanings and spellings in other Pacific languages. Subsistence economies accustomed the people to a sense of community in which everyone felt obligated to assist everyone else to ensure mutual survival and happiness. In both parts of the Pacific the practice of talking out social problems, with all interested parties present, remains the primary method of conflict resolution.

## WESTERN INTRUSION INTO ASIA AND THE PACIFIC

While the Roman Empire ceased to hold the Western world together, Asia had several civilizations more or less at peace. Europeans wanted some of the costly and exotic goods produced in Asia, but trade was perilous. Trading companies wanted exclusive access, and they called upon their governments to establish colonial control over territories adjacent to their outposts in Asia, by military force if necessary. Colonialism in due course carved up the territories of most of Asia and the Pacific.

The political effects of colonial rule on the peoples of Asia and the Pacific were many. In Asia trade and travel were restricted, indigenous industries were destroyed, and colonies began to ship raw materials to the West. In the South Pacific subsistence agriculture was transformed into export-oriented industry, making the peoples economically dependent. The local populations received limited benefits, if any, and lost a sense of control over their own destinies.

During World War II Imperial Japan demonstrated the weakness of Western colonial powers in Asia and the Pacific. Although Japan tried to justify its role through such slogans as "Asian solutions to Asian problems" and "Greater East Asia Co-Prosperity Sphere" as early as the 1920s, Asian countries were not eager to exchange European domination for Japanese direction. As a result, nationalist movements gained considerable popular support during World War II. When Western countries tried to reestablish control in 1945, their legitimacy had already been called into question, and the cost of continued imperialism was perceived as excessive to many politicians in the metropolitan countries. Institutional independence was the inevitable result, some countries attaining their sovereignty sooner and more peacefully than others.

The legacy of colonial rule did not facilitate warm relations among the newly independent countries of Asia. Since the leaders of the new states did not know one another, and their countries had not conducted relations since the precolonical era, artificial borders drawn by the imperial powers guaranteed that there would be conflict in the immediate postcolonial period. As independence was achieved by indigenous elites who had been trained abroad, leaders of the new states had learned Western practices and principles of diplomacy quite well. Traditional Confucian, Hindu, Moslem and other principles of diplomacy were also applied to some extent, but Asia experienced more war in the period from 1945 to 1965 than any other region of the world.[8]

Meanwhile, political independence did not bring economic independence. Corporations with head offices in metropolitan countries remained, and the economies of what were to be called "developing countries" were vertically integrated into a world capitalist system in which Asian and Pacific countries exported raw materials at unfavorable terms of trade. History provided two models for economic development— capitalist prosperity through a long period of economic ups and downs and the Soviet Union's remarkable success in modernizing quickly through state direction of the economy in just 40 years. The victory of the forces of Mao in China by 1949 frightened capitalist countries in Asia. The result was increased bilateral aid, the development of programs of multilateral economic assistance through various United Nations agencies, and an extension of the cold war to Asia. Institutionally, the UN Economic Commission for Asia and the Far East (ECAFE) in Bangkok, known as "the economic parliament of Asia,"[9] began to formulate ambitious plans for economic development. Commonwealth countries formed the Colombo Plan for Economic Development in South and Southeast Asia as a non-UN conduit for aid to the region in 1950. And the Southeast Asia Collective Defense Treaty of 1954 led the following year to the establishment of a secretariat (the Southeast Asia Treaty Organization, or SEATO) to administer programs associated with the treaty. The new states of Asia thus became even more dependent upon Western funds, Western technology, and Western priorities for the region after 1949. Although indigenous countries of Asia were in a majority during deliberations of ECAFE (later renamed ESCAP, for the Economic and Social Commission for Asia and the Pacific) and at the Colombo Plan's Council and Consultative Committee, the focus of discussion was on how much aid the outside powers were willing to supply, so the real aspirations of many countries remained unstated.

## THE "ASIAN WAY"

The nature of the debate and the rhetoric in ECAFE, Western-oriented and -dominated as it was, contrasted with more relaxed diplomacy conducted bilaterally within and between Asian countries, often inspired by the Confucian, Hindu/Buddhist, Muslim, and other indigenous influences. As Asian leaders began to deal directly, they found that many so-called principles of international relations observed in Western political experience could not be applied satisfactorily in an Asian context. The tradition of sharp disputation in the West clashed with the need to save face in the Asian context, for example. A process of unlearning Anglo-European practices was associated with a "rediscovery," selective of course, of more traditional Asian methods for conflict resolution; this learning process proceeded quietly throughout the 1950s. In due course the new style of diplomacy was described as the "Asian Way," though old styles have persisted as well.

No single individual is responsible for codifying or defining the Asian Way. The process of developing the Asian Way was spontaneous and almost simultaneous throughout the capitals of Asia. As Japan and Thailand had never lost their independence, one might presume that they would be in the forefront of the development of the Asian Way. But Japan's attempts to assume the role of Asian superpower, both past and present, isolated them from the more egalitarian elements at the core of the concept. Thanat Khoman, Thai foreign minister during the 1950s, encouraged the development of a uniquely Asian method of diplomacy, but so did many other leaders. U Nyun, who became the executive secretary of ECAFE in 1959, is the one who coined the term Asian Way. His aim was explicitly political—to steer discussion away from the concerns and priorities of the countries outside Asia and toward the aspirations and needs of developing countries inside Asia. U Nyun was careful not to define the Asian Way in specific terms; he was not declaring that there was a kind of anthropologically derived set of principles of Asian diplomacy though this indeed was an unmistakable implication of his repeated references to the Asian Way during ECAFE meetings. His objective, to encourage outside countries to be more attentive to and respectful of statements of Asian delegates, was largely successful at ECAFE. The Asian Way was practiced outside UN organs in the quiet diplomacy of regional cooperation during the 1960s as well. In 1967 principles identified with the Asian Way motivated the foreign ministers of five Southeast Asian countries to form the Association of South East Asian Nations (ASEAN), an institution that embodies the spirit of the Asian Way more fully than U Nyun's ECAFE or the current ESCAP. The Asian Way has thus served to define a new political culture within which Asian diplomacy has been pursued more recently.

To find out the content of the Asian Way, we cannot rely on any single primary source. Actions, speeches, and writings of U Nyun, Thanat Khoman, and others have provided clues, but the sources of the Asian Way appear to be a reconstruction of methods for conflict resolution perceived to be part of the traditional cultures of countries less directly affected by Confucius, Kautilya, and Mohammed. The Asian Way is a synthesis of all of these approaches yet transcends them as well in that it is politically motivated. Insofar as international relations is concerned, it would be inaccurate to say that the Asian Way is the sole cultural standard today, but the Asian Way has made such dramatic inroads into the consciousness of diplomats in Asia in the last three decades that it appears to be the most prominent norm of Asian diplomacy as regards methods for conflict resolution today.

There are two levels and six principles to consider in any effort to understand the Asian Way. The first level consists of general beliefs and orientations toward human and international relations. The second level consists of practices and specific procedures followed in concrete situations. In both senses the Asian Way constitutes an operational code that explains how Asian statesmen ideally prefer to conduct their affairs today at the international level.

First, in regard to general principles, the Asian Way is largely a recognition that there must be "Asian solutions to Asian problems," a slogan popularized by Japan in the 1920s but also a tenet of Thai foreign policy, which has sought to avoid reliance on outside powers. This principle means that Asians prefer to solve their own problems in their own way, rather than inviting Western countries to proffer advice concerning policies with respect to national development and international conflict. The outsider is viewed as having too marginal an interest or understanding of Asian problems to be in a position to make a genuine contribution to Asia, except under limited and temporary circumstances. The principle may be traced in concrete terms to the Lahore Convention, adopted at the annual meeting of ECAFE in 1951. Prior to 1951, Western countries had more votes in ECAFE than Asian countries, and they insisted on controlling the outcome of meetings by overparticipating in debates, calling for votes, and by pressuring Asian countries into adopting particular positions. As a result, ECAFE was unable to act positively on behalf of the best interests of the people of Asia. The Lahore Convention sought to end Western interference of this sort by declaring:

the time has come when clearer recognition should be given to the principle that member countries that belong to the region should make their own decisions in the Commission on their own economic problems. . . . In pursuance of this principle the member countries of the Commission not in the region would be willing, as a general rule, to refrain from using their votes in opposition to economic proposals predominantly concerning the region which had the support of a majority of the countries of the region.[10]

Second, as Thanat Khoman stated, the Asian Way comprises a "spirit of tolerance and partnership" which contrasts sharply with the "concept of domination and subjection" that typified the imperialist powers in their initial dealings with Asian peoples.[11] Given ethnic divisions and national rivalries, international relations should be likened neither to fights, to games, nor to debates, but instead to informal discussions in which each party is accorded equal status. There is no acceptance in Confucian doctrine, for example, of the Western concept of *raison d'etat*, the view that states are not bound by the moral principles applied to individuals. Instead of Westerners' *Gesellschaft*-ish penchant for rational and impersonal calculations preparatory to agreements, it is necessary for Asians to develop personal relationships with one another in order to develop a *Gemeinschaft*-ish mutual trust, whence agreements become possible. According to the Indonesian concept of *mushawarah* (an Arabic-derived word), discussion takes place not as between opposites but as between friends and brothers. Asians feel uncomfortable in situations where the prerogatives of status inhibit the free expression of ideas. This principle of equality of states is manifest in at least three ways. One is the reluctance of Asians to join or form international organizations that are likely to be dominated by a big country, even including Japan. Two, diplomats accept the Buddhist/Confucian principle that bigger countries should exercise restraint in dealing with weaker states, while smaller states should look up to larger states as big brothers. Japan, the richest country in Asia, has often played a role as coequal by declining to exercise a leading or loquacious role in discussions at multicountry conferences. Three, the principle of equality, recognizes that very often it is difficult for an envoy to change positions in the course of an international conference. Countries that hold contrary views, hence, avoid stating differences in a harsh or inflexible manner; all sides at a conference learn to respect one another's view, referring to the experience as an "exchange of views."

Third, the equality principle is related to a third facet of the Asian Way. Power plays, trade-offs, and deals that produce temporary compromises and modi vivendi in Anglo-European bargaining are eschewed by the Asian Way, which operates on the basis of a principle of unanimity. A decision is the outcome of a consensus, a flexible accommodation of opposites that is built up gradually on the basis of what all parties can endorse. The Philipino concept of *pakikisama*, the emphasis on observing correct interpersonal relations, well illustrates the basis for the need for unanimous consensus. This differs from the Western tendency for rigid confrontation of divergent positions followed by a compromise calculated by an implicit mathematical algorithm. In the Asian Way no decision is made unless each party can support the decision in principle. *Mufakat*, to use another Arabic-derived Malay term, refers to the process of building unanimity through discussion rather than majority voting. This principle, rooted as it is in principles of etiquette, is also consistent with the Lahore Convention, which developed in reaction to the stormy sessions in the early years of ECAFE: When Western countries called for votes that compelled Asian countries to take sides on particular issues, some countries voted with Western powers in order to avoid unpleasant castigations from their principal sources of capital aid and technical assistance. Tension between pro-West and neutralist countries, in turn, served to divide Asians. Today, decisions in Asian international organizations are made unanimously without a count of votes. Deliberations are informal in tone, conducted usually in private, with no formal records kept of the proceedings until a public session is held. Malaysia's former prime minister, Tun Abdul Razak once characterized this as "sports-shirt diplomacy" in contrast with the formality of Western "business-suit diplomacy."[12] As a result of the principle of unanimous consensus, conflict that might result in loss of face can be softened, and a joint responsibility for progress emerges from discussions. Decisions are made more on the basis of "give" than "give-and-take," and coercive tactics are avoided in diplomacy. If friction is anticipated at a forthcoming meeting, the meeting is postponed. If a country cannot accept a general view in a diplomatic conference, no decision is made. Thus, in contrast with the Western principle of majority rule, as well as the Quaker principle of having the collective wisdom and judgment of a majority brought to bear in order to shame or ostracize a recalcitrant state or individual, the Asian Way is grounded in the belief that no majority has the right to shame anyone. Everyone is entitled to the dignity of one's own position and need not lose face. It should be pointed out that two times when international organizations pointed a collective finger at an Asian country were at Japan in the early 1930s and China in the early 1950s. In both cases the result was that the countries turned inward and decided to go it alone; the outcome was more intense conflict.

Fourth, there is a recognition that shared objectives, such as the desire for an Asian common market, can be achieved most effectively through small steps rather than merely by drawing up grand blueprints or timetables. Governments and international organizations proceed with caution, in other words, mindful of the famous proverb that a journey of 10,000 *li* begins with the first step. Caution is necessary in order to secure a solid political backing throughout each stage of a project. This Asian incrementalism differs from Western incrementalism, notably of the Fabian variety. The latter sets up an institution and endows it with a mission in a carefully worded constitution or charter. Asian incrementalism, instead, stresses the utility of noninstitutional frameworks for discussion, while operational activities are entrusted to organizations without elaborate constitutional specifications. This practice results from the fact that governments must often try to obtain popular consent without the benefit of strong political parties, pluralistic interest groups, and an informed citizenry. Such conditions require government leaders to engage in a complex process of consultation with organized interests while attempting to anticipate the reactions of those who lack group memberships to represent their views, those who are not accustomed to working through formal structures, and those who only make their views known after specific actions have been taken. Rather than exerting political pressure over proposals in parliaments, Asians prefer to respond to concrete results of decisions. If there are local political centers of authority, national leaders hence must approach them for support, in advance of the launching of a Five-Year Plan. In ECAFE's twenty-fifth year report this principle is stated with considerable cogency:

Priorities of developmental work are determined by the needs of the countries and their willingness to participate. A project will be successful only when there is general understanding of its nature and a conviction of its worth by the countries concerned. As the United Nations has no power of sovereignty, this means working at it, but often also proceeding slowly until a better understanding is developed and national positions and policies are favorable.[13]

This Asian principle of incrementalism recognizes the inherent limitations of any government in a developing country as a catalyst for developmental objectives.

Fifth, matters of implementation, are separated from matters of principle. Asian diplomats obtain a commitment to abstract principles first, such as Malaysia's concept of the neutralization of Southeast Asia, leaving questions regarding the feasibility of putting ideals into practice as matters to be left out of political discussions. Implementation is assigned to administrative subordinates, who are not supposed to throttle the attainment of political objectives. Thus, Asian political leaders intend to keep the primacy of politics above the prerogatives of bureaucracies. Asian leaders will not allow economic difficulties to weaken their political resolve. Secretariats of international organizations in Asia, thus, are modestly staffed and carefully monitored by member governments at annual meetings. The Western preference to make decisions only about matters that can be quickly and optimally translated into action is not part of the Asian Way. Instead of focusing attention on problems related to lack of resources, as would an Anglo-European feasibility study, Asian diplomats prefer to concentrate on objectives and solutions that transcend current limitations.

Sixth and finally, the Asian Way is a Pan-Asian spirit that allows wide latitude for subregional efforts. The Asian Way is not aimed against any state or group of states but instead is based on the concept of *bayanihan*, the Philipino term for a widespread practice of collective self-help at the local level. Within Asia an entire community will provide assistance in projects that benefit individual members, such as moving a family's house by having several dozen persons carry the load on their shoulders over the distance to the new location. This contrasts with the mind-your-own-business individualism and impersonal character of much of Western society. Accordingly, there is a general recognition that international decisions may have to precede national development planning, inasmuch as there should be an end of wasteful economic competition in efforts to sell products at home or abroad. This is the motivation behind the formation of the Association of South-East Asian Nations (ASEAN), and ASEAN's success has in turn inspired the more recent formation of the South Asian Association for Regional Cooperation (SAARC). ASEAN has served as a forum for resolving political conflicts as well as for launching economic projects. SAARC countries perceive that much can be gained by pooling their skills and forming a united front, and more routine resolution to longstanding disputes may result in due course. Regional and subregional economic cooperation will lack credibility so long as political rivalries remain between states, so the Asian Way encourages leaders to accept an international status quo with respect to borders while adapting national development plans to a future international division of labor among the countries of Asia, which must begin at the subregional level before growing. The freezing of the territorial dispute over Sabah should be viewed in this context. Unlike Anglo-European experience, political leaders in Asia operate without much interference from national economic interests and instead must respond to competition from foreign and multinational corporations on a regional and national basis. That many countries are now seeking cooperative strategies is important for our purposes, indicating that economic factors will point to peace.

Each of the above six principles, in sum, reverses an axiom that might be used to describe how Westerners handle public policy matters. The Asian Way emerged as an amalgam of the teachings of Buddha, Confucius, and Mohammed, adapted to modern times. These principles, to be sure, are not alien to Western societies. But the Asian Way is more likely to be a model of performance in Asian public as well as private life, which those in the West endeavor to keep as separate realms.

## THE "PACIFIC WAY"

While Asia was convulsed with conflicts associated with independence from imperialism after World War II, the island states of the South Pacific were considered to be far from both the Cold War and from so-called preconditions for achieving political independence. But decolonization remained the trend, the attainment of which was perceived to be less urgent in the South Pacific. Plans to provide better education, health, and other benefits proceeded in the colonies of Australia, Britain, France, New Zealand, and the United States, but the pace was slow, and demands from the indigenous populations were hardly strident.

Immediately after World War II, efforts at regional cooperation in the South Pacific focused on the needs of outside powers. The South Pacific

Health Service (SPHS) began operation in 1946 to provide medical personnel to Fiji and other countries of the region in part so that tourists from abroad could vacation without fear of contracting devastating tropical diseases. Of course, the primary beneficiaries of SPHS were the peoples of the South Pacific, but their role in decision making was virtually nil. The South Pacific Air Transport Council (SPATC) was set up in 1947 primarily to facilitate civilian air transportation across the Pacific from Australia and New Zealand to North America; the construction and maintenance of airport facilities at Nadi, Fiji, enjoyed high priority. Non-Fijians ran the Nadi airport, though Fijians performed some of the maintenance work. Elements of exploitation were present, though perhaps paternalism was a more accurate description, and independence was thought to be a long way off.

By the mid-1960s many South Pacific islanders had been educated to run their own affairs of state. The bureaucracies of colonial administrations were staffed with a fair share of well trained indigenous civil servants, though expatriates remained very much in control. New Zealand decided to grant Western Samoa full independence in 1962. Fiji followed in 1970, Papua New Guinea in 1975, and most of the remaining colonies raised their own flags in the 1980s. As local officials gradually assumed control of various functions at Nadi airport and health facilities, SPATC and SPHS, two of the earliest regional organizations set up by the colonial powers were phased out (in 1979 and 1969, respectively). With the exception of Vanuatu, France has refused to follow suit.

In the context of the eventual attainment of independence in the South Pacific, Fiji's Ratu Sir Kamisese Mara, longtime prime minister, began to give a series of addresses concerning the Pacific Way in a manner reminiscent of U Nyun's plea for the Asian Way.[14] The arena in which Mara found Western powers particularly insensitive was not a UN organ. Instead, it was the South Pacific Commission (SPC), set up in 1947 before the UN had established regional economic commissions. SPC had undertaken a wide variety of economic, social, and technical projects in the beginning, but countries of the region were not initially represented on the plenary body of the organization. Instead, a Conference of the territorial administrations was to be held triennially to comment on SPC work, more or less after the fact. At the 1965 South Pacific Conference Mara startled fellow indigenous leaders as well as delegates from external powers by proposing that the work programs of SPC should be formulated by countries of the region first, leaving the colonial governments in the role merely of ratifying and funding what had been approved by those destined to benefit from the various projects. In due course, Mara's proposal became reality; the Conference became the plenary organ of SPC, and the organ (known as the Commission), composed solely of colonial governments, was abolished in 1973. In 1970 he launched the term in an address to the UN General Assembly. Then the launching of the South Pacific Forum (SPF), composed initially of independent countries of the region (thus excluding France and its colonies), provided the Pacific Way with a clear institutional home by 1971. At the same time, Australia and New Zealand, who felt a special responsibility for the island states of the South Pacific, were included as equal partners in international cooperation in the region.

Similarities between the Asian Way and the Pacific Way are striking. First of all, they are both politically motivated—aimed at urging indigenous leaders trained outside the region to unlearn Western modes of conflict resolution. Second, the Pacific Way is not an anthropological discovery but rather a reconstruction of practices believed to have existed in the past. Third, the Pacific Way is a call for increased regional cooperation in which the aspirations of countries of the South Pacific are to be at the core, while external powers are to keep their own ambitions for the region very much to themselves. Fourth, the content of the Pacific Way, aptly called "a rather non-specific thing" by New Zealand Prime Minister Wallace Rowling in 1974,[15] has served as a symbol to unite diverse peoples into an awareness of unity and common destiny, though latent rivalry between the island leaders has been articulated in the phrase "Melanesian Way" as a response to the fact that the Pacific Way concept was advanced by Fiji, *Fa'a Pasifika* by Western Samoa. Perhaps more importantly, regional cooperation for the peoples of the South Pacific is an urgent matter; the countries lack basic resources. South Pacific regional cooperation affects the destiny of nearly all persons, so results must be practical and realistic.

We must therefore comment on each of the points of the Asian Way to contrast them, if at all, from the Pacific Way. Since some observers claim that there is a difference between the style of diplomacy followed in Asia and the Pacific Way, our comparison should assist us in identifying important distinctions that will serve to clarify the meaning of both terms.

First, certainly "Pacific solutions to Pacific problems" is at the core of the Pacific Way. We can see this in a number of fascinating instances. For example, each country rotates in responsibility as host for meetings of many regional organizations; but, rather than uniform recordkeeping at the meetings (which would tax the clerical resources of many smaller nations), each host does what it can to provide secretariat functions. A second example, still at the proposal stage, is premised on the fact that the only natural resources of many small island nations are bananas, coconuts, and fish. Aid projects have stressed increased productivity or diversified processing of existing resources, all to no avail in economic terms for a population so small and isolated that even the success of an aid project would make a negligible impact on the prosperity of the country. Accordingly, based on the experience of phosphate-rich Nauru, an idea has arisen that some of the South Pacific ministates should receive a cash contribution, say $10 million, to be deposited in a bank; indeed, Tuvalu now lives on the interest of such deposits. The cost to donor countries is greatly reduced, as all the bookkeeping, airfare, and personnel costs of various projects from now to the next century and beyond are to be saved, and the economic survival of particular countries is assured in an instant. A "Pacific solution" (not an "Asian solution," to be sure) seems reasonable to countries lacking any important natural resources, and Tuvalu is now seeking to establish such a trust fund.

Second, the principles of equality and toleration apply to the Pacific Way as well. "The spirit of the Pacific Way," according to Tekoti Rotan, is "that dialog and discussion in an atmosphere of tolerance and goodwill offers the best prospects for the settlement of . . . differences. . . . "[16] Meetings of South Pacific islanders, so long isolated from one another, are viewed in part as adventures in learning how similar the attitudes and customs of the participants are. The term *brother* is applied widely to reflect social reality more than biology, implying an ideology of mutual help, common origins, and thus common interests; the Hawaiian term *ohana* is often used to refer to the sense of community in which the extended family is broadly defined. Although Australia is the largest donor country in the region, and its delegates can be extremely verbal, the tenor of mutual respect within the dialog of the island nations has caused Canberra to play a constructive "big brother" role, and the island states have ruled out suggestions in some quarters that Australia and New Zealand should be consigned to observer status in such organizations as the Pacific Island Law Officers Meeting (PILOM). Unlike Asia, the peoples of the South Pacific show few signs of hostility toward their former colonial overseers, though there is a common realization that the native population was too often forgotten.

Third, the Asian principle of unanimous compromise," a term coined in 1975 by Cook Islands' prime minister, Sir Albert Henry, who also noted that in the Pacific Way it is expected that "nobody gets left out."[17] Discussion often begins with modest comments by representatives of island nations, who seek outside assistance but feel too humble to make special pleas. Humility and appeals to emotion during discussions among island leaders have cultivated the kind of "give" (rather than Western "give and take") that also characterizes the Asian Way. The South Pacific has been out of the mainstream of twentieth century technology for so long that development assistance can be seen as a form of affirmative action, yet South Pacific leaders show profuse gratitude rather than exhibit a bitter mood of justice denied, which often can be found in Asian regional cooperation. Since warm interpersonal relations are highly valued and must be developed through intimate contact, informality also is a part of any meeting in the South Pacific, where business suits are almost unknown. Indeed, national dress is worn far more often in the South Pacific than in Asia, reminding nonisland countries that the region takes pride in its pre- and postcolonial identity. At the same time, Pacific islanders devote much effort to ceremonial gatherings; this is done in order to indulge the strong impulse to sociability.

Fourth, political will prevails over practical considerations of administrative feasibility in the Pacific as well. The Pacific Forum Line (PFL), for example, was formed in 1977 to provide regular shipping to islands that had been neglected and abandoned; there was a hope of turning a profit but no solid evidence that a subsidy would ever disappear from the time when PFL was approved. Nevertheless, under new management in the mid-1980s, PFL appears destined to break even. The South Pacific Forum has consistently adopted resolutions asking France to stop nuclear weapons tests and to grant independence to its colonies in the region. But it was Australia and New Zealand, not the island states of the South Pacific, which took the nuclear testing issue to the World Court. And after several decades of quiet diplomacy regarding French colonialism, only increased violence in New Caledonia during 1985 prompted South Pacific countries in 1986 to invite the United Nation's Decolonization Committee to put it on the agenda.

Fifth, collective priorities prevail over national self-interest in the South Pacific even more than in Asia. This is because regional cooperation from Western Samoa to Papua New Guinea is not just a means for building solidarity but instead an imperative for economic development. The Pan-Pacific spirit has served to focus attention on common needs and away from internal squabbling. Micronesian states emerging from lengthy U.S. trusteeships have been eager to partake of the spirit by applying for membership in a variety of South Pacific regional organizations. Maori Kiki has stated that joint responsibility and sharing of wealth are Pacific-wide characteristics.[18] No doubt he was thinking of the practice of affluent members of families to share their homes and meals with less affluent family members, a practice that applies as well to the obligations of village leaders toward commoners. Current efforts to provide regular telephone and television service, which might be expected to go to the most populous countries (Fiji and Papua New Guinea), were instead negotiated with Intelsat and other communication satellite corporations on a group basis. The all-or-nothing approach pointed to the volume of business for all island nations and resulted in a comprehensive agreement in 1986 for the region, to be followed up by supplying and servicing ground stations for even Niue, the smallest island nation.

Sixth, to some observers, "Europeans and Asians are regarded as being too serious," as the Pacific Way is considered by Asesela Ravuvu to be "the ad hoc way."[19] The tendency not to plan, to let the future take care of itself, may indeed be in sharp contrast with the Asian Way, which clearly is antithetical to notions of Oriental fatalism. Pacific islanders are seldom fatalistic; they expect everything to work out in time. It is their patience and cheerful regard for the inevitability of amelioration that becomes a kind of self-fulfilling prophecy encouraging outsiders to be even more generous and helpful. The early thrust of the Pacific Energy Programme (PEP), which began in 1983, was on importing biomass and solar technology to increase energy supply; but when the technology broke down, with no one available to be trained to repair or to maintain the equipment, the project may have seemed a boondoggle for foreign manufacturers to dump unwanted machinery in far-off islands. PEP instead realized that the entire project was too ambitious, abandoned the inappropriate technological solution in 1986, and energy conservation is now the focus of its attention. We could call this an instance of capitulation to the impossibility of progress, but a more insightful view would be to say that a practical solution won out.

## CONCLUSION

The Asian Way and the Pacific Way have established themselves as norms of diplomacy in their respective regions of the world. They provide unity toward the outside as well as a sense of cultural affinity despite a past history that has many disjunctions. In Asia, where conflicts have been all too numerous, the Asian Way has provided a basis for conflict management by diverting attention to issues of joint economic development. In the South Pacific, where the key issue is the survival of ministates in a world of overwhelming outside influences, the Pacific Way has pointed toward economic progress by focusing on imperialist neglect as a wrong that needs to be corrected. The principles of relevant solutions to local problems, equal treatment, consensus building through nonconflictual discussion, informal incrementalism, subordination of administration to politics, and collective self-help are means to an end. Their application to Asia and the Pacific varies somewhat, depending on circumstances and traditions, but the essence of Asian culture and Pacific culture is that poor countries seek prosperity and dignity through a diplomatic style from which other parts of the world have much to learn. Indeed, the intended result of both codes of diplomacy is to place outside powers in a somewhat defensive position. The Asian Way and Pacific Way have established a dialog on how former imperialist powers can most effectively provide the peoples of the region with the diplomatic equivalent of reparations for past exploitation.

At the same time, Asia differs from the Pacific in style. Within Asia conflict must be bridged by integrative activities, so the progress of Asian regional cooperations may be described by the functionalist model:[20] depoliticized arenas for international collaboration, once politically sanctioned, have brought about a more peaceful mood, as technocrats from ostensibly hostile countries work together smoothly on behalf of the common goal of economic development. In the calm Pacific it is as if the suggestions of conflict theorist Georg Simmel[21] have been taken to heart: Poor countries have surfaced a certain amount of hitherto latent conflict into their relations with their former colonial rulers in order to achieve a more integrated, harmonious solution.

But any effort to draw sharp distinctions between Asian culture and Pacific culture can only be an exaggeration. Functionalist theory applies to the South Pacific, and conflict theory applies to Asia as well. In practical terms, the unity of the Asian/Pacific region has been recognized in a number of ways. The earlier parenthetical notes that the Economic Commission for Asia and the Far East (ECAFE) became the Economic and Social Commission for Asia and the Pacific (ESCAP) and the Asian Coconut Community (ACC) is now the Asian-Pacific Coconut Community (APCC) should provide a clue. Over time, a dozen or so other Asian regional organizations have expanded to include members from the South Pacific, who have felt reasonably satisfied in these organizations while insisting that such organizations reciprocate the courtesy by adding the word "Pacific" to the title.

The Asian Way and the Pacific Way are not always observed by countries in the two regions. First, the principles are norms of conduct; international politics does not always live up to ideals. Second, some regional countries are unable to deal with each other on the basis of these norms, since they require reciprocity; North and South Korea, for example, are on a semiwar footing with each other. Third, outside powers have not learned enough about the two operational codes, yet remain in Asia and the Pacific as important influences; Australia and New Zealand have had more alternative to learn about the Pacific Way, since they play central roles in most regional organizations of the South Pacific. The Asian Way and Pacific Way were designed in part to facilitate the advancement of indigenous countries, as shields against the influence of outside powers. The objectives of economic development, peace, rolling back vestiges of imperialism, and of simply being oneself in diplomatic undertakings are widely shared in Asia and the Pacific, creating bonds that will continue to endure.

## NOTES

I wish to thank Ron Crocombe and Terence Wesley-Smith for helpful comments on an earlier draft of this chapter.

1. Lucian W. Pye, "Introduction: Political Culture and Political Development," in *Political Culture and Political Development*, eds. Pye and Sidney Verba (Princeton, NJ: Princeton University Press, 1965), p. 8.

2. John K. Fairbank, "Tributary Trade and China's Relations With the West," *Far Eastern Quarterly* 1 (1942): 1.

3. Tso-ch'iu Ming, quoted in M. Frederick Nelson, *Korea and the Old Orders in Eastern Asia* (Baton Rouge: Louisiana State University Press, 1945), p. 16.

4. A. L. Basham, *The Wonder That Was India* (New York: Taplinger, 1967), ch. 4.

5. Majid Khadduri, *War and Peace in the Law of Islam* (Baltimore, MD: Johns Hopkins Press, 1955).

6. Kenneth P. Emory, "Warfare," in *Ancient Hawaiian Civilization* (Tokyo: Tuttle, 1965), ch. 22.; L. L. Langness, "Traditional Political Organization," in *Anthropology in Papua New Guinea*, ed. Ian Hogbin (Melbourne: Melbourne University Press, 1973), pp. 142–173. Micronesia has had little opportunity to have an input into the "Pacific Way," and is not described herein.

7. Anne Chowning, *An Introduction to the Peoples and Cultures of Melanesia* (Menlo Park, CA: Cummings, 1977); Gavan Daws, *Shoal of Time* (New York: Macmillan, 1968), ch. 1; K. R. Howe, *Where the Waves Fall* (Honolulu: University of Hawaii Press, 1984), ch. 13.

8. Melvin Small and J. David Singer, *Resort to Arms* (Beverly Hills, CA: Sage, 1982), p. 80.

9. David Wightman, *Toward Economic Cooperation in Asia* (New Haven, CT: Yale University Press, 1953).

10. Quoted in Michael Haas, "The 'Asian Way' to Peace," *Pacific Community* 4 (1973) :503.

11. Quoted in ibid., p. 503.

12. Ibid., p. 504.

13. Ibid.

14. Ratu Sir Kamisese Mara, *Selected Speeches* (Suva: Government Press, 1977).

15. Quoted in Ronald G. Crocombe, *The Pacific Way* (Suva: Lotu Pasifika Productions, 1976), p. 4.

16. Quoted in ibid., p. 15.

17. Ibid., p. 20.

18. Ibid., p. 24.

19. Ibid.

20. See Michael Haas, "International Integration," in Michael Haas, ed., *International Systems* (San Francisco, CA: Chandler, 1974), ch. 8; David Mitrany, *A Working Peace System* (Chicago: Quadrangle, 1966); James N. Schubert, "Toward a 'Working Peace System' in Asia: Organizational Growth and State

Participation in Asian Regionalism," in Michael Haas, ed., *Basic Documents of Asian Regional Organizations* (Dobbs Ferry, NY: Oceana, 1985), ch. 9.

21. Georg Simmel, *Conflict and the Web of Group-Affiliations* (New York: Free Press, 1955); Louis Coser, *The Functions of Conflict* (New York: Free Press, 1956).

# 13
# Cultural Style and International Policy-making: The Latin American Tradition

## Roland H. Ebel and Raymond Taras

Perhaps in no other part of the world is a region's culture perceived to be so distinctive and identifiable and, at the same time, so influential in the political process as in Latin America. For many observers of international politics, Latin America has become synonymous with *caudillaje* culture that is said to span the length and breadth of the continent; in turn, Central America is closely associated with military rule and the machismo culture it is claimed it spawns. Despite the existence of such widely held stereotypes, few observers have searched for linkage between these regional cultures and international policy-making.

## THE CONCEPT OF POLITICAL CULTURE

The elements of national culture that are relevant to a study of international policy-making are those that serve as inputs into the political system. Put differently, it is the politicized dimension of culture—not its more general anthropological aspects—that is of interest to us. There has been, however, a long-running debate among scholars investigating political culture as to whether the concept should encompass psychological perceptions only, or should also include observed behavior. We recall that, according to a pioneer in this field, Sidney Verba, "The political culture of a society consists of the system of empirical beliefs, expressive symbols, and values which defines the situation in which political action takes place. It provides the subjective orientation to politics."[1] A second classic study, a path-breaking five-nation comparative investigation of civic cultures by Almond and Verba, adopted a similar analytical framework: the authors made clear they employed the concept of culture in only one of its many meanings—that of psychological orientation toward social objects. Perhaps the most ambitious effort to operationalize such a limited understanding of the term was the comparative study of seven Communist states undertaken by Archie Brown and Jack Gray. For them, Communist political culture was viewed "in terms of subjective orientation to history and politics, of fundamental beliefs and values, of foci of identification and loyalty, and of political knowledge and expectation."[2]

In a follow-up study carried out by Brown nearly ten years later, the author seeks to vindicate this position by referring to the newer literature found in cultural anthropology which, too, displays "a strong intellectual tendency to exclude from the scope of culture not only laws and formal institutions (which were sometimes included in the past) but also behavior patterns."[3] Paradoxically, therefore, the operationalization of the concept of political culture—defined as it is by a political scientist such as Brown—places the field of political science only on the analytic periphery of the term and unquestionably gives preeminence to the disciplines of social psychology and cultural anthropology.

While the "subjectivist school" of political culture has proved an attractive alternative to social scientists wishing to carry out empirical research, a number of eminent scholars, such as Samuel Huntington and Jorge Dominguez, have considered manifest political behavior as an inseparable part of political culture. Robert C. Tucker has more explicitly argued that a behavioral approach has the added value of comparing beliefs to actions, thereby distinguishing "ideal cultural patterns" from "real" ones.[4] In the field of Communist studies, where the concept of political culture has most frequently been operationalized, the majority of scholars has opted for the combined subjective and behavioral approach. Thus, in his study of the Soviet Union, Stephen White wrote: "Political culture may be defined as the attitudinal and behavioral matrix within which the political system is located."[5]

In summary, we postulate that a nation's (or a cultural region's) political culture is made up of three components: political values, attitudes, and behavior. Political values are the idealized norms of how a proper political system should be structured and operated. This often produces what Frank Parkin has described as "the concept of a dominant value system."[6] Political attitudes are the reality-based orientations of people toward the political process. This is sometimes called the "modal" political culture. Political behavior is the way individuals and groups apply their political values and attitudes in concrete situations.

This essay will attempt to lay out what the writers conceive to be the basic characteristics of the dominant political value system of Latin America; identify some of its competing value systems; and distinguish between political behavior patterns, on the other. It will then attempt to relate these facets of the Latin American political culture to the Latin American foreign policy style.

## LATIN AMERICAN POLITICAL CULTURE

### The Dominant Value System

Latin America is what Louis Hartz calls a "fragment culture";[7] that is, it is an offshoot of its Iberian mother culture. As such, certain selected characteristics of the late fifteenth and early sixteenth century political culture of Iberia were brought to the New World where they were implanted in virgin soil and subsequently flourished to a greater degree than they did in the mother country. Thus, as a generalization, it might be said that contemporary Latin America is "more Hispanic" than is contemporary Spain. Howard Wiarda has made the point that the major movements that produced modern Western culture—the Reformation, the Industrial Revolution, the Enlightenment, and the democratic revolutions of the eighteenth century—largely bypassed the Iberian world.[8]

What were the specific cultural traits that the Spanish conquerors brought to the New World "fragment" that embedded themselves so completely in the political life of the nations of the region? In brief, they were hierarchy, authoritarianism, patrimonialism, corporativism, political monism, and paradoxically, political rebelliousness and resistance to authority. These cultural traits have taken different forms during different historical periods and under different socioeconomic circumstances. However, in spite of massive social, economic, and political change, they have proved remarkably durable, as the hierarchical and monistic character of the contemporary Sandinista regime attests.

To understand the nature of the political culture so strongly implanted in Latin America, one has to understand the character of the Conquest itself. What Latin Americans have called *La Conquista* was really a continuation of *La Reconquista*, only carried on in overseas areas ranging from Buenos Aires to Manila Bay, and from northern California to Tierra del Fuego. The political and military patterns utilized to effect the reconquest of the Iberian peninsula were simply transported, after the defeat of the last Moorish stronghold of Granada in 1492, to the New World as a means of achieving new conquests.

During the *Reconquista* two contradictory patterns of political organization were utilized by Spain to achieve its objectives: (1) a policy of local self-rule and decentralized military organization on the advancing frontier; and (2) a policy of centralization and monocratic rule in territories firmly under the control of the crown. Thus, two competing cultural strains arose in the Spanish empire concurrently: a culture of political centralization and authoritarianism so ably documented by Claudio Veliz, and a culture of decentralization and resistance to authority.[9] The first was the political culture of Madrid, the second the political culture of the frontier. The first was essentially Thomistic and organicist, stressing the values of order, stability, and hierarchy.[10] The second was essentially localist and stressed the use of various strategems to avoid control from Madrid as much as possible.[11]

The political values of the crown and the central authorities of Madrid were, theoretically at least, based on the political philosophy of St. Thomas Aquinas. Very briefly, for the Spanish Thomist the good society was the well ordered, hierarchical society made up of governmentally sanctioned social constituents each playing its proper function in an organically integrated society. The end of social order was the achievement of the common good (*bien comun*)[12] as defined by the theologians and moral philosophers of the day and legislated and administered by a social and governmental elite. The means of attaining that end were the creation of a hierarchically organized polity that encouraged complementarity rather than competition, and sought order and balance.

To achieve order and balance, a complex system of social and political institutions was envisioned, designed to reflect the traditional Hispanic principles of governance: political monism, organicism, legal idealism and patrimonialism. As the apex of the social and governmental order was the monarch who, with the guidance and assistance of the governing elite which held seats on the various royal councils and advisory bodies, was the chief guardian of the order and common good of the society. As such, he was above the positive law (*ley*), but subject to the higher or natural law (*derecho*) as discovered by the theologians and moral philosophers. Below the peninsular elite and presiding over the affairs of the colonies was a highly structured bureaucracy which, formally at least, had a strong directive and interventionist role in the colonies. Social, economic, religious and political affairs were extensively regulated by centrally and minutely drafted rules and regulations.

Political monism was reinforced by legal idealism which, in contrast to the Germanic tradition which stressed custom and the law of the folk, emphasized the ideal and the universal.

In this tradition, law, of necessity, flows from above. It is to reflect the correct principles of social and political organization as determined by philosophers and theologians. It is the duty of the monarch to determine, on the basis of these principles, the law of the land. The Crown (and later, the state) is the law-giver, not the people.[13]

Organicism was reflected in the recognition and protection of certain powerful corporative groups such as the church, the military, the craft and commercial guilds, the landed estates and the Indian communities. These organizations were charged both with controlling the activities of their members and with defending their interests before the organs of the state. As such they performed both a governing role and a restraining role on the government.

The potential rigidities of organicism and bureaucracy were counterbalanced, to a considerable extent, by patrimonialism under which functionaries of the colonial bureaucracy were considered to be under the monarch's personal authority. Flexibility was achieved by the creation of overlapping jurisdictions, by issuing ordinances that could later be rescinded, and by the exercise of the moderating power.

The Hispanic tradition of political monism, organicism, legal idealism, and patrimonialism has forged the dominant political value system of Latin America. This value system, which Glen Dealy has termed "monistic democracy," stresses order, stability, leadership by elites (whether ideological, economic, or military), fear of competition, abstract planning, and constant attempts—albeit often abortive ones—to create the good society from the top by governmental fiat.

There was also, to use Richard Morse's suggestive terminology, a "Machiavellian" side to the Thomistic vision—a rebellious, localist, lawless side to the Hispanic concept of governance.[14] This resulted from a number of factors emanating both from the nature of Hispanic Thomism and from the nature of the conquest. First of all, Thomism postulated the right of revolution if the government did not act on behalf of the common good. And how was it possible for any group of decision makers located in Madrid always to determine the "common good" of an empire so far-flung and economically and ethnically diverse as the Spanish dominions of the sixteenth and seventeenth centuries when speed of communication was measured in weeks and months?

Local resistance to authority—even rebellion—became the political way of life in much of the empire. Thus, although the Spanish imperial system was formally centralized and bureaucratized, functionally it was highly decentralized and loosely governed. Thus the two contradictory and paradoxical political traditions of Latin America grew up side by side: the authoritarian, bureaucratic and monistic tradition so well described by Claudio Veliz and Glen Dealy; and the decentralized, rebellious, "power contender" tradition described by Charles Anderson.[15]

These two traditions, although varying in form and content in different periods, have vied for dominance throughout the 175 years of Latin American independence. The past 50 years have seen Latin America "fragmented" by competing political monisms—Marxism, developmentalism, Peronism, falangism, and so on—which begin their political life as Machiavellian movements of disorder and rebellion (often in the name of pluralism) only to impose an authoritarian, hierarchically structured monistic system upon their societies when they come to power. Political monism in Latin America, therefore, has both its Machiavellian and Thomistic manifestations.

Standing with the two monistic traditions is a third—pluralistic democracy. Although its roots go back to the democratic revolutions of the eighteenth century, until the last 40 years it functioned primarily as an abstract intellectual ideal and, with a few exceptions, never penetrated deeply into the Latin American political culture. However, since the end of World War II it has increasingly been able to mount a serious challenge to the dominant monistic tradition. The extent to which one can talk about a "democratic culture" taking root in such countries as Venezuela and Colombia, as opposed to simply the emergence of specific and often short-lived democratic regimes in countries like Argentina, Brazil, Peru, or Guatemala, is hard to determine with certainty. However, the democratic tradition of peaceful electoral competition between ideological or programmatic parties, loyal opposition, incremental decision making reflecting bargaining and compromise, peaceful interplay between the governmental and/or societal institutions, and the subjection of the executive to the rule of law remain the weaker, less developed aspects of the Latin American political culture.

In summary, the dominant value system of Latin America has been, and continues to be, what has been called political monism—a constant search for a harmonious, noncompetitive social blueprint that can be imposed from the top. However, any monistic system, because of its resistance to political competition, differences of opinion, and thus to change, tends to be brittle and thus subject to fragmentation, disintegration, and collapse. This gives rise to certain behavioral patterns which in some ways constitute separate political/cultural subtraditions in their own right. The first is a powerful insurrectionary tradition that sees violence as the only way of bringing down an entrenched monistic regime where the electoral alternative is not available. However, the challenging groups usually seek to impose an alternative monistic vision of their own. Latin American political life, thus, has tended to oscillate, as Richard Morse suggests, between periods of Thomism and Machiavellianism.

This has stimulated a second behavioral tendency, namely, an amazing institutional inventiveness in the area as Latin American political elites have sought to control the oscillation. However, most of the institutional creativity has been of a monistic nature, ranging from political territorial monopoly arrangements (Uruguay) to quasi-hegemonic party systems (Mexico, Nicaragua) to power sharing agreements (Colombia). In some cases, institutional experimentation has been used to consolidate democracy: the weak presidential system of Costa Rica, the collegial executive of Uruguay and the National Front Agreement in Colombia after 1972.

The third pattern is the use of the "democratic interlude" to resolve a political impasse. Pluralistic democracy is often accepted by the antagonistic forces of Latin American societies as a kind of middle ground between the excesses of extreme monism (bureaucratic authoritarianism, for example) on the one hand, and insurrectionary chaos on the other. Although compromise, bargaining, delay, and acceptance of the politically possible rather than the ideal is not generally satisfactory to many groups, it is often seen as necessary to reducing violence, obtaining foreign aid, or getting rid of a tyrannical regime. The military also often accepts the democratic opening as a means of retiring from the responsibilities of social and economic management.

The search for a democratic interlude explains why democracy seems to come in "waves" and, after reaching a high point on the political shore, recedes back into the ocean of Latin American history, leaving the people of the land once again the task of deciding which monistic group or movement they will follow. A summary of these national political cultural traditions appears in Table 3.1.

### Individual Political Behavior: Caudillaje Man

Within the dominant political value system of Latin America, it is possible to identify a number of class-based or sectoral constellations of political attitudes and behavioral patterns. However, because since the turn of the century the middle classes have been the most active, if not always the most powerful, political sector in Latin America, our attention will focus on this sector. Middle-class activism derives largely from the tremendous surge in urbanization and the resulting rise of populist movements

**Table 13.1**
**Latin American Political Culture Patterns During the Last Half Century**

| Stable Monisms | Alternating Monisms | Alternating Monisms w/ Democratic Interludes | Democratic Tradition w/ Monistic Interludes | Stable Democracies |
|---|---|---|---|---|
| Mexico | Nicaragua | Argentina | Chile | |
| Paraguay | | Bolivia | Colombia to 1972 | Colombia after 1972 |
| | | Brazil | Costa Rica to 1948 | Costa Rica after 1948 |
| Cuba after 1959 | | Cuba to 1959 | | |
| | | Dominican Republic | | |
| | | El Salvador | | |
| | | Guatemala | | |
| | | Honduras | | |
| | | Panama | | |
| | | Peru | | |
| | | Venezuela to 1957 | | Venezuela after 1957 |

in the region. A number of writers have sought to capture the essential character of the political culture of this sector. Social anthropologist John Gillin, writing in 1960, identified ten "middle segment values" which he believed were barriers to modernization and development: personalism, *machismo*, dignity, familism, hierarchy, patronalism, tangible materialism, transcendental values (*Arielismo*), emotion as the fulfillment of self, and fatalism.[16] Similarly, Glen Dealy, in his model of Catholic or *caudillaje* man" (which, incidentally, he extends to a wider range of Catholic countries, such as Ireland and Poland), uses slightly different terms and comes up with a shorter list of traits, but they largely encompass the same attitudes and behavior patterns identified by Gillin. In Catholic or caudillaje culture the dominant value is power in the same way that in Protestant or capitalistic culture it is wealth.[17]

To achieve power, caudillaje man requires a cohort of associates and supporters. "The common man of caudillaje society knows that power depends upon friendship, that there are certain means of acquiring, holding and losing friendship, and that without it one is lost." What are these means of pursuing power through friendship? They are dignity, generosity, manliness, grandeur, and leisure.[18]

The *caudillo* as a political type emerged, as Richard Morse, William Beezley, Martin Needler, and others have suggested, from the breakdown of the colonial "Thomistic Synthesis."[19] Caudillaje man, as a personality type, has its roots in historic *caudillismo* but is perpetuated by the fact that contemporary political monism is inherently unstable and subject to disintegration, and caudillaje personality traits have particular "survival value" under such conditions. Thus, Latin America's dominant political value system—the search for a monistic syntheses—gives rise by its very nature to the caudillaje personality, particularly among the middle sectors which are the most highly activist politically.

In summary, the caudillaje personality type is a reflection of the Machiavellian face of Hispanic monism. The basic Latin American political value system inherited from Hispanic Thomism remains the norm. However, because during and after the Independence Movement the centrifugal, localist, and nuclear forces became dominant, the once "recessive" Machiavellian traits producing caudillaje man became the dominant operative political behavior pattern—but usually in the name and in search of the bien comun.

It now remains to be asked what features of the Latin American political culture discussed in this section have the greatest bearing on Latin American foreign policy and international behavior.

## POLITICAL CULTURE AND FOREIGN POLICY STYLE

Of the variety of specific traits discussed at the outset of this chapter, which appear to have greatest general relevance to the area's foreign policy and international behavior? We would like to postulate that Latin American international behavior can best be understood culturally as involving a contrapuntal relationship between three broad cultural orientations: international monism, clientalism, and nationalism. There is, in other words, a counterpoint between the "Thomistic" search for a stable world or regional order, and, when that fails, a "Machiavellian" recourse to clientalism. Clientalism, in turn, generates what Milenky has called "reactive nationalism."[20]

As a means of understanding this pattern, three general environmental factors have to be considered. The first is the nature of the international system. In a very fundamental way it presents these nations with an environment, a *modus operandi* at odds with the region's political habits and traditions. That is, the lack of a sovereign decision-making center in the international system places a premium on the "democratic" habits and skills of bargaining, compromise, coalition building, and so on. In this sense, the Latin American nations are forced to operate in a much more free-wheeling, pluralistic environment than they are disposed to by their culture. Because of the need to develop the skills and expertise to operate in such a culturally "alien" environment, the foreign policy establishments of most Latin American countries have been more insulated from national politics (and from the behavioral norms and expectations of the national political culture) and the other ministries of government. Foreign policy in the Latin American states had traditionally had a much greater tendency to have an organizational life of its own regardless of the regime in power. This, however, has been changing somewhat as more left-wing authoritarian governments have come to power. In countries like Cuba and Nicaragua foreign policy is less insulated from political and ideological considerations than it was under such *desarrollista* bureaucratic/authoritarian regimes as Argentina, Brazil, or Uruguay.

A second factor is the historical political instability generated by Latin America's monistic political culture. Political monism is inherently unstable. It seeks to impose a top-down order on society on the basis of a political ideology or set of unimpeachable political objectives under the aegis of a charismatic or self-selected political elite. Unfortunately, every political monism spawns rival monisms anxious to impose their conceptions of the bien comun on the society. And, given the area's Machiavellian tradition, they are more willing to take to the streets or the hills to achieve that objective. As a result, these countries, even the largest and intrinsically most powerful among them, have been among the weaker actors in the international system. Consequently, Latin American diplomatic activity and doctrine has often oscillated between exaggerated assertions of national sovereignty and taking refuge under the protecting wing of a more powerful international actor.

A third and related factor is the problem of dependency generally. It is not the province of this chapter to take up a defense or criticism of dependency theory or to go into its causes or the forms it has taken. But without in any way declaring ourselves to be *dependencistas*, it is clear that a combination of economic underdevelopment, relatively small size, and the nature of East-West political competition has made the Latin American nations more vulnerable to outside pressures and influences and, thus, has tended to drive many of them into the orbit of either the United States or, more rarely, the Soviet Union.

Political instability and economic and technological dependency have served to reinforce in international behavior the pattern of clientalism that is so deeply ingrained in Latin American culture. One writer who addressed this phenomenon with graphic imagery was Norman A. Bailey in his essay of two decades ago, "The United States as Caudillo." Bailey begins by contrasting the "lukewarm to frigid" response to U.S. attempts to curb Cuban subversion on the part of the Latin American nations at the San José and Punta del Este Foreign Ministers' Conferences of 1960 and 1961, and the "unanimous and enthusiastic" backing the U.S. blockade obtained from the Council of the OAS during the Cuban missile crisis. What was equally significant, Bailey stated, was that during the first period "anti-Yankee sentiment seemed on the rise among the populace at large, and almost weekly riots and demonstrations in support of Cuba took place in one city or another of the region"; whereas during the second episode, "with the exception of La Paz, there was not a single important anti-U.S. demonstration or riot in any part of Latin America, whereas in some cities there were sizeable pro-U.S. manifestations."[21]

Bailey explains these contradictions, "none of which should have caused surprise in Washington," by the " 'patron' mentality" which had evolved through the centuries in Latin America.

"Strong" but benevolent leadership is the ideal of the Latin American in the national sphere. He is not, of course, a masochist, and if the government or *caudillo* attacks his liberties or what he considers his private concerns, he will resist. At the same time a "weak" government, no matter how benevolent and well-intentioned, is despised and obstructed, especially if it is not, in the individual's opinion, fulfilling its responsibilities.[22]

This psychology, he argues, is carried over into the international sphere. The Latin American nations want a strong but not overly intrusive *patron* who will protect them from the uncertainties of international life. Great Britain fulfilled that role throughout most of the nineteenth century and the United States assumed it roughly at the time of the Olney Declaration in 1895.

During the last decade of the nineteenth and the early part of the twentieth centuries, however, the United States violated the expected pattern of "patronal behavior" by its intervention in Cuba, Puerto Rico, Panama, Nicaragua, and the Dominican Republic. The Good Neighbor Policy, on the other hand, restored the United States to the position of the "beneficent caudillo."[23]

The proper role of America, as the international caudillo in the Western hemisphere, Bailey argued, was to protect the client from the outside world while granting him a relatively free hand in his own bailiwick. Thus, the strongly held principle of nonintervention in the internal affairs of states is compatible with strong U.S. patrimonial caudillaje leadership in the international sphere.

We might postulate that for Latin America a properly working Inter-American system constitutes the international Thomistic synthesis. In it the United States plays the role of the beneficent caudillo (in Bailey's sense) or, from a traditionalist point of view, the role of the "beneficent monarch." Collective security and economic arrangements like the Rio Treaty, the Alliance for Progress, or the Caribbean Basin Initiative (and the principles and policies they seek to apply) constitute the bien comun at any given time. Within the system, each state—in the "familistic" brotherhood of Spanish-speaking states—has its proper role to play, presided over and tended to by the United States through the bureaucracy of the various multinational organizations. *Obedezco pero no cumplo* (I obey but cannot comply) is the reaction of individual Latin American states to what are perceived as the excessive or ill-conceived demands by the United States. At a slightly higher level of resistance, middle-class "reactive nationalism" (e.g., the Caracas demonstrations against Richard Nixon in 1958) comes into play. Full-fledged Machiavellian behavior is reflected in attempts by governments or movements to either lower the involvement of their nation in the Inter-American Thomistic system (e.g., the Arbenz regime) or attempts to withdraw it from the system altogether (e.g., the Sandinista regime). When the Inter-American system becomes "nucleated" (to use Richard Morse's term), the weaker states seek to protect themselves by drawing ever closer to a protective *caudillo*—whether the United States or the USSR.

Applying this conceptualization (or imagery) historically, it might be postulated that following the breakdown of the Iberian empires, the first international monism created by the Latin Americans was the Liberal Synthesis, which lasted from roughly 1860 to 1930. Presided over by the then dominant international caudillo, Great Britain, which provided its clients capital, markets, and the Pax Britannica, the system was guided by the idealistic (Thomistic) doctrine of comparative advantage and sought to achieve the bien comun through the exportation of primary products and the importation of luxury goods. The conditions that made this system relatively successful were the low levels of mass consumption, politicization, and population growth.

The Liberal Synthesis was undermined during the last decade of the nineteenth century and the first two decades of the twentieth by industrialization, urbanization, and population growth due to advances in disease control, all of which served to politicize the urban middle classes and to create the beginnings of an urban proletariat. In addition, Great Britain had relinquished its caudillo role to the United States. The Liberal Synthesis was finally destroyed (except in Central America and the insular Caribbean where it lingered on into the 1940s and 1950s) by the Great Depression which thoroughly disrupted Latin America's "outward-oriented" economy. The hopes and fears of World War II tended largely to ward off the possible Machiavellian international behavior of the Latin American states resulting from the breakdown of the Liberal Synthesis (except for Argentina which flirted with the Axis powers). After the war, fear of Soviet expansionism coupled with the idealism generated by Allied rhetoric and U.S. economic and political dominance caused the creation of what might be called a "developmentalist synthesis" under U.S. leadership. The United States now fully assumed its role as, potentially at least, the "beneficent caudillo." The guiding idealistic (Thomistic) doctrine was that of political and economic development; and the transfer of capital and technology was seen as the means of creating the international bien comun. International "familism" was also reflected in the movements of regional economic integration.

Once again, however, the developmentalist synthesis was undermined by what Julio Jaguaribe, Guillermo O'Donnell, and others have called the problems of populism: deteriorating terms of trade, inflation, industrial noncompetiveness, and hyperpoliticization.[24] These problems were exacerbated by the emergence of the intrusive multinational corporation which the United States was reluctant to control. The disintegration of the synthesis was further accelerated by the attractiveness of Marxist modes of analysis—the competing Thomism of the day—to university students and intellectuals. At the same time the United States was seen as abusing its caudillo status by intervening in the internal affairs of an "obstreperous" populist government—the Arbenz regime.

The 1970s and 1980s have seen the Inter-American system descend into chaos with the emergence of competing international caudillos (the United States and Soviet Union) on the one hand, and a variety of national caudillaje-type leaders (both democratic and authoritarian) on the other. But still the search for the international patron continues. America's budgetary crisis coupled with its intrusion into Central America inhibits its ability to play the role of the beneficent patron effectively. Lack of economic growth and its military and political intrusiveness similarly impedes the Soviet Union in playing that role. A number of so-called "regional actors" (Venezuela and Mexico principally; at times Peru, Argentina, and Brazil) have sought out a *cacique* (local boss) role, but the decline in oil prices, the world agricultural glut, and the debt crisis have undermined these attempts at leadership.

Thus, currently the Inter-American system is in flux. The new fledgling democratic regimes still primarily seek the protective wings of the American eagle, while beleagured popular revolutionary regimes have sought the protection of the Russian bear. The larger states—Argentina, Brazil, Chile, and Peru, primarily, Mexico to a somewhat lesser extent— are attempting either to go it alone or to play the one caudillo off the other. At the same time the combination of terrorism, narcotics smuggling, il- licit migration and the possible default on debt has served to reduce the capability of the United States to even operate as a caudillo, much less a beneficent one.

To what extent is the above description of Latin America's culturally based international policy and behavior in accord with reality? One useful summary of the international thinking of Latin American political and academic elites has been provided by Edward S. Milenky. Although published a decade ago, his survey paints an interesting picture of elite attitudes since the war. Most of the writers surveyed, first of all, see the international system in a largely hierarchical fashion with the United States as the dominant power vis-à-vis Latin America. Furthermore, most see their nations as the victims of powerful outside forces—typical clientalist attitudes according to John Duncan Powell.[25] Of the 16 writers or research organizations cited on the matter of their countries' "national situation," only two (General Golbery do Couto e Silva and Julio Jaguaribe) saw certain nations, (i.e., Argentina, Brazil, and Mexico) as having the potential for autonomous development. Milenky noted:

All of Latin America's international options as presented by a cross-section of its foreign affairs analysts, lead to the following conclusions. Regionalists and nationalists accept the status of Latin American nations as regional powers at best, as local powers if possible, and minimally as states capable of mastering their internal affairs.

However, reactive nationalism is central to the thinking of all of the writers surveyed:

Latin American students of international affairs would have their nations seek a familiar catalogue of objectives: sovereignty and autonomy; national development and, if possible national power; and a respected position as actors, not objects, in world affairs.[26]

The one finding in the Milenky survey that does not quite fit our description of Latin American cultural behavior in international affairs is the postulate of an "organicist" desire to fit into an Inter-American system dominated by the United States as beneficent caudillo. He concludes that none of the analysts seek a return to the Alliance for Progress or Pan Americanism. Nevertheless he also asserts that a consensus does exist in Latin America on the future of the region.

Generally, Latin Americans see themselves as members of weak, externally penetrated societies in which great powers, multinational corporations, and international economic relationships play important roles. As a result nation-states in the classic sense of impervious units with a political supremacy over a defined territorial sphere do not exist. Latin American governments are seen as mediators between indigenous and nonindigenous actors and forces. These conditions are the product of underdevelopment and the low power position of Latin American nations in the world.[27]

In all discussions of political reality based on political culture, recognition has to be given to the fact that while any cultural pattern is highly persistent, culture is also subject to change. Latin America is currently experiencing a "democratic wave." Whether this development, which reflects a historically latent yet important tradition of the region, will last long enough to materially affect the national culture and the consequent international behavior of the nations of the area, only time will tell. If it does persist, over the long term this should have the effect of changing the historic patron/client relationship between the United States and the Latin American states into one that lays greater stress on cooperation and mutual interaction. Concurrently, the ability of the United States and the USSR to play the *caudillo* role may also be diminishing, a fact that may produce major changes in Latin America's international behavior.

## NOTES

1. Sidney Verba, "Comparative Political Culture," in Lucian W. Pye and Sidney Verba, eds., *Political Culture and Political Development* (Princeton, NJ: Princeton University Press, 1965), p. 513.

2. Archie Brown and Jack Gray, eds., *Political Culture and Political Change in Communist States* (London: Macmillan, 1979), p. 10.

3. Archie Brown, ed., *Political Culture and Communist Studies* (Armonk, NY: M. E. Sharpe, 1985), pp. 154–155.

4. Robert C. Tucker, "Culture, Political Culture, and Communist Society," *Political Science Quarterly* 88 (June 1973): 182.

5. Stephen White, *Political Culture and Soviet Politics* (London: Macmillan, 1979), p. 1.

6. Frank Parkin, *Class Inequality and Political Order* (London: Macgibbon and Kee, 1971), p. 82.

7. Louis Hartz, *The Founding of New Societies* (New York: Harcourt, Brace and World, 1964), pp. 3–10.

8. Howard Wiarda (ed.), *Politics and Social Change in Latin America: The Distinct Tradition* (Amherst, MA: University of Massachusetts Press, 1974), p. 6.

9. Claudio Veliz, *The Centralist Tradition in Latin America* (Princeton, NJ: Princeton University Press, 1980).

10. See Richard Morse, "The Heritage of Latin America," in Hartz, *The Founding of New Societies.*

11. For a summary of centralist and decentralist interpretations of Latin American governance, see Roland H. Ebel and James Henderson, "Patterns of Continuity in Latin American Society: Political and Historical Perspectives," *Annals of the Southeastern Conference of Latin American Studies* 7 (March 1976).

12. See Glen Dealy, "The Tradition of Monistic Democracy in Latin America: in Wiarda, *Politics and Social Change in Latin America,* pp. 80–90.

13. Ebel and Henderson, "Patterns of Continuity in Latin American Society," p. 95.

14. Richard Morse, "Toward a Theory of Spanish American Government," *Journal of the History of Ideas* 15 (1964): 78–82.

15. Charles Anderson, *Politics and Economic Change in Latin America: The Governing of Restless Nations* (Princeton, NJ: Van Nostrand, 1967), chapter 4.

16. John Gillin, "Some Signposts for Policy," in Richard Adams, et al., eds., *Social Change in Latin America Today* (New York: Harper & Row, 1960), pp. 14, 28–47.

17. Glen Caudill Dealy, *The Public Man: An Interpretation of Latin American and Other Catholic Countries* (Amherst MA: The University of Massachusetts Press, 1977), p. 7.

18. Dealy, *The Public Man,* pp. 8, 34.

19. See Roland H. Ebel, "Thomism and Machiavellianism in Central American Political Development." Paper given at the 44th International Congress of Americanists, Manchester, England, September 5–10, 1982. See also, Morse, "Toward a Theory of Spanish American Government," pp. 118–122; and, William H. Beezley, "Caudillismo: An Interpretive Note," *Journal of Inter-American Studies* 11 (1969): 348–349.

20. Edward S. Milenky, "Problems, Perspectives, and Modes of Analysis: Understanding Latin American Approaches to World Affairs," in Ronald G. Hellman and H. Jon Rosenbaum, eds., *Latin America: The Search for a New International Role* (New York: John Wiley & Sons, 1975), p. 100.

21. Norman A. Bailey, "The United States as Caudillo," *Journal of Inter-American Studies* 5 (July 1963): 313–314.

22. Bailey, "The United States as Caudillo," pp. 314–315.

23. Ibid., p. 320.

24. Julio Jaguaribe, *Political Development: A General Theory and a Latin American Case Study* (New York: Harper & Row, 1973), chapter 22; and Guillermo O'Donnell, *The Bureaucratic Authoritarian State* (Berkeley: University of California Press, 1983).

25. John Duncan Powell, "Peasant Society and Clientalist Politics," *American Political Science Review* 64 (June 1970): 411. The international thinking of writers included in Milenky's survey broke down this way: (1) "taking a hierarchical view with the U.S. as dominant actor": Silva Michelena, F. Herrera, H. Godoy, C. Furtado, A. G. Frank, O. Sunkel, F. Cardoso; (2) "Taking a hierarchical view with the U.S. and U.S.S.R. in a bipolar system": J. Jaguaribe, Arujo Castro, J. Peron; (3) "Taking a multipolar view": M. Kaplan, O. Camilion, K. Vasena. Based on Milenky, "Problems, Perspectives, and Modes of Analysis," pp. 101–103.

26. Milenky, "Problems, Perspectives, and Modes of Analysis," pp. 103, 106, 107.

27. Ibid.

# 14
# Islamic Revivalism and Its Impact on the Middle East and the Superpowers

## Hassan Bakr A. Hassan

Today, another ghost wanders through the West. It is not communism, but Islamic fundamentalism. Preemptive procedures have been initiated against expected Islamic terrorist actions in all Western societies. In the United States, the president is well safeguarded by technological devices and, in reaction to last year's explosion at the Capitol, cement barriers surround the federal buildings on the main streets of Washington.

There is no doubt that the decade of the 1970s witnessed a mushrooming of Islamic movements and ideas, and these have been variously described as an Islamic revival or resurgence, Islam on the march, Islamic reassertion, Islamism, the return of Islam, or the Islamic renaissance. Whether part of the majority or a minority, whether under a capitalist or a socialist regime, whether modernizers or traditionalists, Muslims have been moved by this reawakening.

The main proposition in this chapter is that by the late 1970s, Islamic resurgence movements constituted the major ideology and provided numerous events of dissent in Middle Eastern political systems. It is my conviction that Islamic revivalism is not a reaction to modernization per se, but to a certain type of modernization; that is, Westernization, which contradicts and sometimes ignores the national traditions and cultural symbols of Islam.

Some questions in this respect must be asked. What is Islamic revivalism? What impact does it have on Middle Eastern political systems and the superpowers? How did it rise as a historical phenomenon?

Generally speaking, Islamic Revivalism represents multidimensional phenomena that can be better understood in a comparative socio-historical study as a part of social change in the Middle East.

## SETTING THE STAGE

Western modernists, orientalists, and even a great number of Arab scholars and politicians had begun to believe that Islam no longer constituted a binding social force, ethical system, or political power affecting domestic and international dimensions to any significant degree. Contrary to all their projections, Islam seems to be far from fading away or eroding, especially in the last two decades.

The massive demonstrations that led to the victory of the Islamic revolution in Iran and the ascendance of Ayatollahs and mullas have focused Western interest on the Islamic resurgence and on Islamic political thought. Incidents in the aftermath of the revolution, such as the November 1979 seizure of the American Embassy in Teheran and the taking of some 50 hostages, the emergence of an Islamic resistance movement, and the takeover of Mecca's Grand Mosque in the same year against the U.S.-supported Islamic government in Saudi Arabia, have presented the West with a golden opportunity to incite anti-Soviet feelings among Muslims. The dramatic assassination of Egyptian President Anwar Sadat by Islamic fundamentalists has made it more obvious than before that the uprising of fundamentalism in the Middle East is a product of anti-Western civilization in general, and anti-American in particular.

Many Muslim groups have proclaimed that Islam represents a comprehensive way of life and government: Ayatollahs in Iran, Mujahedeen (in Lebanon and Afghanistan), Islamic Tendency Militants (Tunisia), Muslim Brothers (Egypt, Sudan, and elsewhere), Fedayeen (Palestine), Revolutionary Guards (Iran), Islamic Amirs (Egypt), Grey Wolves (Turkey), and Muhammedania (South Asia).

The writings of some unknown (to Western theorists) thinkers, such as El-Banna, Kotb, Al-Mauddudi, Choucri Mustafa, Al-Fasi, Al-Ghazzali, among others, are very prominent influences on Islamic political thought and practice, in the eyes of fundamentalists.

In the Middle East, where most societies live with crisis as the status quo, traditional religious values are still attractive to both the elites and the masses. The media persistently characterize the rulers as: the shadows of God—"Amir el-Mauminin" (Prince of believers) in Morocco and Sudan, Keeper of the Two Sanctuaries in Saudi Arabia, the believer President Sadat of Egypt, King Hussein, son of "Al-Hashim," Mohammed the prophet's family, the "Saver of Islam" in Libya, together with many similar titles. Even the former Shah of Iran, the most modernized and Westernized of monarchs, claimed in his autobiography to have seen religious signs and visions.

Rarely can the student find a clear-cut definition of Islamic revivalism, except for some detailed descriptions of the phenomenon. Islamic fundamentalism is a product of the interaction between the long historical development of Islam and the hegemony of the West since the eighteenth century. It is a reaction against Western colonialism and values. Revivalism as a "term" is seen, in this respect, as a "wave of religious enthusiasm worked up by powerful preachers."[1] However, since Islam is a religion and a state combined, the latter definition is partially irrelevant. Islamic revivalism is employed in this chapter to refer to the increasing political activism and militancy in the name of Islam by government, parties, and groups. Islamic militancy is defined here as "actual violent group behavior committed collectively against the state or other actors in the name of Islam."[2]

## ISLAM AND MIDDLE EAST CULTURE

Islam originated in the Middle East, becoming a world religion for peoples of all kinds, races, and colors. It reflects mainly Arab culture. Even so, Islam spread more rapidly than other religions. Islam, moreover, has been shaping the whole Middle Eastern culture by its own characteristics for 15 centuries.

Only a century after its inception in Mecca (in Saudi Arabia now) in 622 A.D., the new religion dominated an area extending from the Iberian Peninsula in the west to the steppes of central Asia in the east. By the end of the third century (tenth century A.D.), the intellectual life of Islam had reached the peak of its activity, and Islamic civilization itself had become, through the assimilation of the heritages of many previous civilizations, the new focus of intellectual life in the world. The lands which rapidly became consolidated in Islam, containing such so-called "centers of civilization" as Alexandria, Athens, Cyprus, Sicily, Antioch, Edessa, and Nisibis, played active roles in synthesizing the old cultures of previous religions with the teachings and spirit of Islam.

"But neither the presence of centers of learning nor of scholars and translators would be sufficient to explain the remarkable enthusiasm and determination with which the Islamic world set out to make the knowledge of the ancients its own."[3] The reason is that Islam is the religion of the intellect (al'aql) that leads the man to the Divine.

Specifically, Islamic influence was remarkable in the field of the humanities. While most contributions in science, mathematics, music, art and architecture were mainly influenced by Greek, Persian, and Indian precedents, historiography, philology and literature were greatly influenced by the creativity and initiative of Arab Muslims. "While the roots of Muslim literary tradition were also Persian and Greek, the Arabic was the most influential. . . . As for its impact on Europe, Islam was a transmitter of Greek and Roman thought, bringing back to the West what had been lost during the era of barbarian despoilation."[4]

As noted previously, Western civilization was, by and large, positively influenced in almost every aspect of life by Islam. However, by the fourteenth century the two civilizations had gradually grown further apart. "As Europe regained its spiritual independence, and concentrated on itself in an effort to revive its classical past, Islamic civilization was no longer the teacher, but now became an object of study by the intellectual elite."[5]

## WESTERNIZATION VS. ISLAM

There is no contradiction between modernization and Islam, if Islam is the only influence. By modernization, the student means man's increasing control over nature. "Muhammed Abdu" and "Gamal El-Din Al-Afaghani" were simply nineteenth century leaders of religious modernization who were against the control, from Paris, of monarchs of both Egypt and Turkey. The real battle of Islamic fundamentalism is essentially with modernization when it takes the form and spirit of Westernization. Nowadays, the post-détente era has left the Middle East with an overwhelming role for U.S. power, which accelerates Israel's upper hand over the Arab countries in the region, meaning, in the final analysis, a great disillusionment and disappointment.

Even in the years of the 1950s and 1960s which witnessed the rise of Arab nationalism, Pan-Arabism, and socialism, the fundamentalists fought fiercely, but they gave the new values the chance—as they have said lately in Cairo—to fail. Fundamentalism is a two-faced coin. On one side is the internal oppression from the many faces of dictatorship that have sometimes ruled in the name of Islam, Arabism, the divine right of kings, and nationalism, an important cause of the fundamentalist thrust toward the "Third Way." On the other, the unadopted Westernized values that were superficially planted in the name of modernization, industrialization, Westernization, and others, have created much cultural alienation for the traditionalists who have lived the same way for hundreds of years. The latter found themselves in the dilemma of either accepting the new rules of modernization, and hence the Westernization, of the Muslim societies, or of finding another comprehensive alternative way of life and polity. In addition, the failure of the nationalistic and socialist experiences of the 1950s and 1960s has led to dictatorial regimes, a large gap between the haves and the have-nots, and defeat in 1967 by the enemies of Islam: Israel and America.

Moreover, Israel has been seen by many, if not most, Arabs, not only "as non-Muslim, that is, a representative of a tolerated but inferior religion but its victories are seen as those of a western state led by an irreligious western 'elite'."[6] In sum, Islamic revivalists today do not wish to imitate Western schools of thought. Rather, they aim to eradicate the imperialist forces, especially the Zionist implantation of Israel in the very heart of their land, and to destroy all forms of oppression.

## THE ISLAMIC REVIVALISM

If Westernization is the "challenge," in Toynbee's words, Islamic revivalism is the "response." The Islamic revivalist ideology contains its internal principles as well as its systemic criticisms of foreign ideologies, especially those of the West. Frequently in the literature of Islamic revivalism, the terms "West" and "Westernization" are directly associated with the ideas of neocolonialism and anti-Muslim crusades. To answer the questions related to the critical situation in the Islamic world today, the Islamic revivalists have established their own alternatives to almost every crisis: legitimacy, social injustice, and military defeats by the enemies of Islam, imperialism and Zionism. In this part of this chapter, the author will try to clarify the Islamic revivalists' comprehensive solution through three main aspects: philosophy, ideology, and organization.

Historically, Islamic revivalism is a continuous phenomenon. It may be mute sometimes, but it returns to strike again, especially in critical situations in Middle East history. There are three different phases of revivalism. The first is the old revivalism from the eighteenth century to the end of the nineteenth century, the precolonialist era in the Middle East. Wahabism[7] of Arabia and Sanossia of Libya, among others, are some forms from this era. The main goal was to return to Islam as the only way to overcome Muslim weaknesses, and to "purge irreligious habits and manners of Muslims in order to promote Islam. The second phase arose with the ascendance of Westernization in the European colonialists' era in order to defeat the Western style of modernization. During this era, which began at the end of the nineteenth century and continued until the end of the first half of the twentieth century, many Westernized concepts, such as nationalism, Pan-Arabism, and socialism, attracted adherents in the Arab world. The Afghani-Abdu movement, Muslim Brotherhood,[8] Mauddudi, and others, were some of the forms of revivalism in this era. The third phase began with the 1948 occupation of Palestine and the ensuing defeats of the nationalistic system, especially in 1967. The latter "gave rise to a sustained cynicism which in part led to Islamic resurgence."[9] On this point the author agrees with R. Harir Dekmejian that "there is no such a thing as Islamic revival because politicized Islam and its reform-oriented elements have never ceased to exist despite two centuries of modernization and westernization."[10]

There is no unified ideology for revivalists, but rather, many ideologies, goals, and means. The ultimate goal that revivalists want to realize is a democratic government built upon consultation (Shurah),[11] and restoration of the Islamic identity in all aspects of life. There are four main sources of revivalist ideologies: Quran, Hadith (Mohammed's statements), Sunna (traditions), and the rationalist method. To disclose the Islamic alternative to the Muslim masses there are three main principles characterized as the contemporary revivalist ideologies. The first is the Islamic traditional formula of legitimization (Sharia),[12] which contrasts with both the national and Western non-Islamic models. The second, social justice (adalah), is used to solve social, ethnic, communal inequalities and irregularities. The third, Jihad (holy war), is the means for restoring Islamic honor. Islam in this case is considered "the most martial of major world religions."[13]

With respect to organizations and militant movements, Islam provides two main political advantages. First, "Islamic groups have the mosque as a ready-made meeting place and a forum for agitation. Recruitment usually takes place among devoted mosque goers. Second, Islam provides a distinctive language and vocabulary that separate its users from all other political groups."[14] From Indonesia to Morocco, the Islamic world has experienced many organizations that constituted the body of the revivalists: the Muslim Brotherhood, Islamic groups (Egypt), the Party of Islamic Liberation (Jordan and Egypt), the Jamatti-Islami (Pakistan), the Masjumi party (Indonesia), Alal El-Fassi group (Morocco); the Islamic Tendency movement (Tunisia); the Iran Liberation movement, Jomhori Islami (Iran), the Quaddafi Jamahiria (Libya), Mujahedeen (Afghanistan), Al Mahdia, and Al-Ansar (Sudan). The differences among them are due to the socioeconomic origins and the domestic political order. Figure 14.1 represents the diversity of the Islamic revivalist movements. They are polarized around two main issues: democracy (from arbitrary system to a "Shurah" democratic system) and activism of mobilization (from militant fundamentalism to moderate adaptation) to reflect the intensity of conflict and cooperation in each relationship between the revivalist movement and the domestic political system.

## THE REVIVAL'S IMPACT ON THE MIDDLE EAST

From Morocco on the Atlantic Ocean to Indonesia in the Pacific Ocean, and from Senegal to the southern republics of the Soviet Union, an Islamic fundamentalist tide is rising. From the traditional pre-Western Saudi Arabia that was built on fundamentalism to the revolutionary pro-Soviet Syria, from the most modernized Arab country, Egypt, to the traditional tribal emirates of the Gulf, all Arab nations are experiencing the fire of Islam. The resulting chaos has created a crisis situation for the status quo in the Islamic world.

During this course of developments, all Middle Eastern countries are fiercely confronted with unsolved problems because of rapid and uneven social change. Nationalism, socialism, and other modernizing ideologies,

**Figure 14.1.**
**Graphical Presentation of Islamic Revivalist Movements: Mobilization vs. Democracy**

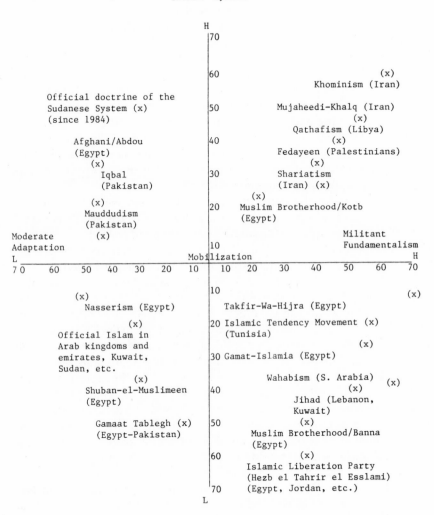

"Shurah" System

```
                                   H
                                  |70


                                  |60                        (x)
                                                     Khominism (Iran)
     Official doctrine of the
     Sudanese System (x)          |50      Mujaheedi-Khalq (Iran)
     (since 1984)                                        (x)
                                           Qathafism (Libya)
          Afghani/Abdou          |40              (x)
          (Egypt)                          Fedayeen (Palestinians)
            (x)                                    (x)
          Iqbal                  |30      Shariatism
          (Pakistan)                       (Iran) (x)

            (x)                       (x)
          Mauddudism             |20   Muslim Brotherhood/Kotb
          (Pakistan)                   (Egypt)
 Moderate   (x)                                      Militant
 Adaptation                      |10                 Fundamentalism
 L _____        _____ H
 7 0  60   50   40   30   20   10 |   10   20   30   40   50   60   70
                             Mobilization

                                 |10
            (x)                                                    (x)
          Nasserism (Egypt)         Takfir-Wa-Hijra (Egypt)

                 (x)             |20 Islamic Tendency Movement (x)
          Official Islam in          (Tunisia)
          Arab kingdoms and                              (x)
          emirates, Kuwait,       |30 Gamat-Islamia (Egypt)
          Sudan, etc.
                 (x)                       Wahabism (S. Arabia)
          Shuban-el-Muslimeen    |40              (x)        (x)
          (Egypt)                               Jihad (Lebanon,
                                                Kuwait)
          Gamaat Tablegh (x)     |50              (x)
          (Egypt-Pakistan)                 Muslim Brotherhood/Banna
                                           (Egypt)
                                 |60              (x)
                                           Islamic Liberation Party
                                           (Hezb el Tahrir el Esslami)
                                 |70       (Egypt, Jordan, etc.)
                                   L
```

Arbitrary System

that have provided legitimacy to most modern Arab political systems, were not able to resolve the urgent problems that confronted them or to offer any promising prospects of doing so. "Instead of concentrating on overcoming underdevelopment, they provided political rhetoric and promised miracles in an age of crisis and increasing poverty."[15]

From this position, the fundamentalists "caught the end of the robe," seeing "Jihad" as the only way to restore the rule of God both internally and externally. Sayed Kotb attacked the Arab nationalists and secular writers in the 1960s: "The westernization of Dar Al-Islam (the abode of Islam) has obliged the secular rulers to separate Islam from the state, as they do in Dar Al-Harb (the abode of war) between the church and Caesar. That must have not happened in Dar-Al-Islam. Islam is both a state and a religion simultaneously."[16] The real Jihad (fighting a holy war) is to universalize the rule of God by defending the Islamic state against an external non-Muslim threat, if not by expanding the realm of Islam at the expense of the non-Muslim realm.

Jihad was one of the main themes of Islamic revivalist movements. Putting the idea into practice has brought unrest to the whole contemporary political system in the Middle East. Some of these systems have done their best to contain the problem. Some were overthrown by Islamic revolutions, and some leaders were murdered or assassinated.

From the beginning of the 1960s to the present, both the ruling elites and the opposition have been affected by the reawakening of Islam. More specifically, there is a clear-cut differentiation between the "official" Islam and the Islam of the "masses" in the Middle East. Islam of the masses means, in general, a means of political change and revolution; on the opposite side, "official" Islam is devoted to justifying the status quo. The conflict between the two forces continues in Middle Eastern political systems. In 1969, official Islam—condemned even by some progressive leaders like Nasser—won a round in its battle with fundamentalism. King Faisal and other moderate leaders could collectively institutionalize the official Islam by holding an Islamic Conference each year. The first "Islamic Conference" was held in Rabat, Morocco. In contrast, the Islam of the masses was just abandoned as "a political ideology in many countries of the Middle East."[17] As a result, Islamic revivalism has become the ideology of political opposition against the existing political orders (the official Islam) in the Middle East. It is important, in this respect, to "underscore that this renewed politicization of the sacred had begun much earlier than the political upheaval in Iran."[18]

As a matter of fact, the turning point came in Egypt in the early 1970s. The recent emergence of Islamic militant movements in Egypt attracts special attention, since Egypt is the center of the Arab-Muslim world. Islamic groups, such as the Party of Islamic Liberation, Muslim Brothers, Jihad, and others, were supported by Sadat, the "believer president."

Sadat intended to weaken the leftist opposition. But, by the end of the 1970s and his visit to Israel, Islamic fundamentalists represented a real danger.[19] The success of the Islamic revolution in Iran and the overthrow of the Shah by the progressive Islamic Alliance, has increased the prospects of Islamic fundamentalists not only in Egypt, but all over the world of Islam.

The postrevolution era has signaled real threats to the sheiks and sultans in the pro-Western Gulf countries. In the name of Islam, Iran has continued to fight Iraq, to support the actions of the Lebanese "Islamic Jihad," and to launch other operations aiming at destabilizing the traditional official Islam in favor of the "Revolutionary Islam." These actions will mainly satisfy the ambitions of Iran's ally Qaddafi of Libya. His record shows "activity in some fifty countries."[20] These actions include support for almost any liberation movement as well as for Muslim autonomist and revivalist movements. In the same area is Tunisia. "Disillusioned with the Western-style values embraced by Bourgiba, students of the University have been turning for political inspiration to Islamic groups."[21] Therefore, the students are not the "children of Bourgiba" as the latter suggested, and the University is not controlled by his socialist party any more. In Syria, the Sunni Muslim Brothers were completely defeated by the heavy blow of the Shiite-Alawite ruling elite. The fundamentalists failed to adapt their ideas to the current issues of the 1970s even when they had the majority of the population on their side. In Sudan, Muslim Brothers gained some advantages under the unpopular regime of Numeri. But now they are suffering greatly under the new regime's reformers and secular elites.

In short, the 1970s proved to be an explosive period in the history of Middle Eastern Muslim politics. As described above, stable governments were shaken and several Muslim rulers were removed from office by coups d'état or assassinations. While such events were not in themselves unusual, the substantial reemergence of Islam's role and function in Middle East politics was surprising. Islamic activists used Islam as the only measure by which to judge established governments as autocratic, politically corrupt, economically unjust, and spiritually and morally illegitimate.

## SOME IMPLICATIONS FOR THE SUPERPOWERS

There is no doubt, in the minds of Revivalists, that both the capitalist and socialist systems are the products of Western civilization and are ruled by enemies of Islam. Like Stalinists following the tenets of their creed, Islamic fundamentalists hold themselves to the old notion of the early days of Islam, and they follow the statements of Muhammed, the Prophet. Accordingly, Muslims are in the House of Peace and Islam (Dar-el-Salam), while on the other side, non-Muslims live in the House of War (Dar-el-Harb). Therefore, the latter ought to be liberated by "Jihad" (fighting the holy war). Later on, this notion would be developed by Revivalists such as Kotb and Mauddudi to cover the Muslims who are now living in the Second State of Ignorance or Quasi-House of War.

In addition to the points outlined previously, two main categories of implications, one horizontal and the other vertical, are of concern to the superpowers. The horizontal category of impacts can be seen in four main streams: world stratification, atheism, destabilization, and terrorism. World stratification was well known even before the era of the 1970s. But the neofundamentalists have manipulated the theory to work as a vehicle for Islamic unity and solidarity in the face of the "world forces of tyranny." OPEC and AOPEC, the World Muslim League and other global Muslim organizations, such as the World Assembly of the Muslim Youth and the World Muslim Congress, have been successful in organizing scattered Muslim groups and unifying them under one Islamic umbrella. This unity, and the increasing political and economic influence of the Organization of Islamic Conferences, are some important factors contributing to the strengthening of international Islamic solidarity.[22] Out of the hands of the "official" Islam, there is another wave of unification among the "Islamic groups," whether Shi'at or Sunni, all over the world, under the leadership of the Iranian Ayats, Qaddafi, or the Wahabists of Saudi Arabia.

With regard to atheism, the Revivalists think that the international forces of atheism (USSR, China, the United States, etc.) have intentionally acted to abandon the application of Islam and oppress the Muslims of the world through their internal ruling puppets. While the first State of Ignorance had prevailed before the emergence of Muhammed's Message, the world is experiencing the second State of Ignorance. Jihad is the only Islamic way, internally and externally, to confront the superpowers of ignorance and bring them down to earth. Consequently, organizations, networks, and institutions have been established throughout the Muslim world to play active roles in strategically disseminating Revivalist ideologies and actions.

In relation to world chaos and internal destabilization, it is clear that in the post-détente era, there has been much ambiguity and confusion in international relations. (The Chinese expressed their anxiety, early on, when Mao described the whole situation as "world political chaos.") The Revivalists depict the whole issue as if there is an agreement among the world forces of tyranny and atheism to suppress the rest of the world, among which are the Islamic countries. In response, the underground Islamic movements sharply turned to anarchic political actions.

In addition to what was outlined above, a wave of terrorism has been launched against the oppressive external powers and the nation-state symbols which were unable to fulfill their own promises to meet basic human needs. Terrorism, as an illegal and irregular means of action, has not only horrified local governments, but has also destabilized the whole world system. Its visible goals are to destroy the prestige of the world "Forces of Ignorance," demonstrate the power of the oppressed Muslims on earth, and reveal the insufficiency and weakness of the ruling puppets (servants of the great-world satans) in the face of imperialism (either European or Soviet), Zionism, and reactionary forces.

The vertical category of impacts mainly refers to each country per se. The United States is in the forefront of enemies. It is the "great Satan," as Khomeini and his followers call it. The United States supports official Islam as a representation of conservatism, regardless of its oppressing means and misuses of wealth (something Khomeini's propaganda calls the "American Islam"). The inseparable connection between Israel and the United States has brought the latter a great deal of antagonism. So, in this region of the world of rich natural resources and anticommunist allies, there is no doubt that U.S. strategic interests are in jeopardy in the arc of crisis. Clearly, the strong support of Qaddafi, Khomeini, Assad, and others for the Black Muslim movement represent the long arm of Islamic Revivalists inside the United States itself.

As for the Soviet Union, contrary to both the Marxist and Revivalist rhetoric, the Soviet Union benefits the most from the current situation, except in rare instances. The long historic record of Soviet support for the PLO, its lack of colonial experience in the Middle East, and its being a close neighbor to the Middle East can decrease the amount of antagonism toward the Soviet Union. On the other side, there are some deep-rooted reasons for antagonism: the invasion of Afghanistan, communism as a world power of atheism, and the oppression of about 60 million Muslims in the Soviet population. These will have a tangible impact on the conflict in the Middle East and will retard to some extent the acceleration of both the national and social liberation uprisings. Moreover, since the Iranian Revolution, the revivalists have made the southern Soviet republics targets for Islamic liberation.

Other regions have been affected by the Islamic ferment. In China, the recent Muslim revolts in Yunan and Xinjian provinces are believed to have been triggered and encouraged by the worldwide resurgence of Islamic Revivalism, and they have been linked to the demand for local political autonomy.

The superpowers accept these antagonisms as the cost of maintaining their hegemony. But the emergence of Islamic Revivalism, which is more likely to be accompanied by the triggering of protracted social conflicts in all Middle East countries, will make the cost prohibitively high in the near future.

## CONCLUSIONS

Jihad (fighting a holy war) is the major ideology of Islam, rather than any other factor, such as modernization or development. After 14 centuries of Islamic civilization, the writings on Jihad are enormous compared to writings on any other issues.

Throughout its history, Islam has played the role of an iron curtain that defended the Middle Eastern cultures and traditions even when they suffered under the most racist and anti Islamic colonial regimes, giving Muslims a sense of superiority, purity, and Ezza (dignity) toward others. Since the beginning of the 1970s, Islamic revivalists have tried to play the same role in the face of the neocolonialist wave of Americanization and Westernization in the Middle East.

Even though the Islamic revivalists claim to have a comprehensive alternative to modernization, they provide neither solutions nor a way to reach them. The main task must be to overcome the severe problems of underdevelopment and protracted social conflict within a serious socioeconomic structural framework. On the positive side, Islamic revivalists have raised expectations for social change and national liberation. On the negative side, they have not been able to create their own "Third Way" of development in adopted modern terms. Moreover, they have no clear-cut constructive structural framework to solve the current problems of contemporary Middle East politics. If they had one, it would be modest and oversimplified. In this respect, the new revivalists are much poorer than their predecessors, the earlier fundamentalists and modernists such as Abdu, Afghani, Mauddudi, Kotb, and Banna. These latter men were prepared for the upcoming changes in the Middle East of their time.

Accordingly, there is nothing inevitable about the future of Islamic revivalism in the Middle East. Either it weakens—the fate of its popular and powerful predecessor, the Muslim Brotherhood—or it survives and flourishes. The decisive issue will be whether the revivalists are able to find and adapt a synthesis between the tradition-rooted religion of Islam and the urgent problems that need structural solutions in the contemporary systems of the Middle East and the Muslim world.

## NOTES

1. John Gage Allee, ed. Webster's *Encyclopedia of Dictionaries* (New York: Oddenheimer, 1978), p. 317.

2. Saad E. Ibrahim, "Anatomy of Egypt's Militant Islamic Groups," *International Journal of Middle East Studies* 12, no. 4 (December 1980):427

3. Sayed Hossein Nasr. "Islamic Conception of Intellectual Life," in *Dictionary of the History of Ideas* (New York: Charles Scribner's Sons, 1973), p. 639.

4. For more details on the Islamic impacts on Western civilization, see Don Peretz, *The Middle East Today* (New York: Praeger, 1986), pp. 39–42.

5. Peretz, *The Middle East Today*, p. 43.

6. William E. Griffith, "The Revival of Islamic Fundamentalism: The Case of Iran," *International Security* 4, no. 1 (Summer 1981):132.

7. Wahabism is a religious political movement first founded in Hijaz, now Saudi Arabia. The movement began in the latter decades of the eighteenth century. Its founder, Mohamed Ibn Abdel Wahab, was a principal fundamentalist of Najd in Central Arabia. Ibn Abdel Wahab and the family of Al-Saud together fought to unite the Arabian Peninsula. Najd, long an independent state and center of the Wahabi Sect, fell under Turkish rule. But in 1913, Ibn Saud, founder of the Saudi Dynasty, overthrew the Turks. He took the Hijaz in 1925 and by 1926 the whole of Arabia was under his control. As such, Saudi Arabia is the culmination of this effort. For more details, see: John S. Habib, *The Ikhwan Movement in the Najd: Its Rise, Development and Decline* (Ann Arbor: University of Michigan Press, 1970).

8. The Muslim Brotherhood Society was founded in Ismailia, Egypt, in 1928. Its declared goal as a nonpolitical organization was to establish the Islamic Society upon Sharia through good will and advice. It gradually grew until it became one of the largest mass movements in Egypt in the 1940s. The "new" Brotherhood movement includes various offshoots from the old one such as the Islamic Liberation party, Al-Takfir Wal-Hijra, and some other militant Islamic groups in Egypt and other variants of the Islamic Brotherhood movement in Syria, Jordan, Sudan, and the Gulf States. While the old one had gone through some accommodative attitude changes toward the ruling regimes, the new variant has been much more militant and radical in the process of revivalist movements. See, for more details, E. E. Azar and C. I. Moon, "Islamic Revivalist Movements," *Journal of East and West Studies* 12, no. 1 (Spring–Summer 1983):79–109.

9. Bassam Tibi, "The Renewed Role of Islam in the Political and Social Development of the Middle East," *The Middle East Journal* 37, no. 1 (Winter 1983):7.

10. R. Harir Dekmejian, "The Anatomy of Islamic Revival," *The Middle East Journal* 35, no. 1 (1980):5.

11. Shura, as the Islamic formation of democracy, fluctuates between a narrow and a broad sense. Historically, Muslims began to create their own ideas of democracy as "Shura" 10 centuries after the Greek democracy. In its narrow sense, Mohamed, the prophet, and the first four caliphs (Rashideen) established such an idea according to the "holy" Quran and the teachings of Muhammed. In its broader sense Shura was adopted by both ancient and modern Islamic political writers to handle all aspects of political life, management, peace, and war, choosing a caliph, all ways of production, and so on, in a "democratic" way (using the Western theory of democracy).

12. Sharia refers to the rules of Allah received and practiced by his messenger Mohamed, the Prophet. It is the Islamic Divine law derived from the Quran and Sunnah and from two supplementary sources, Qiyas (legal analogy or measure) and Ijmao (consensus among Ulama). Interpretations of Sharia differ from one theological school to another. There have been four major legal schools regarding the interpretation of the Sharia: Hanafi, Maliki, Shafii, and Hanbali schools. See Azar and Moon, "Islamic Revivalist Movements," p. 83.

13. Dekmejian, ''The Anatomy of Islamic Revival,'' p. 8.

14. Ali E. H. Dessouki, ed., *Islamic Resurgence in the Arab World* (New York: Praeger, 1984), p. 24.

15. Tibi, ''The Renewed Role of Islam,'' p. 10.

16. Sayed Kotb, *Islam's Battle with Capitalism* (Cairo: Day-El-Sherouk, 1978), p. 57.

17. Tibi, ''The Renewed Role of Islam,'' p. 9

18. Ibid., p. 11

19. For more details on Sadat's connection with Islamic Revivalists, see Gillis Kepel, *Muslim Extremism in Egypt* (Berkeley: University of California Press, 1986), pp. 130–138. Also see one of the most challenging books on Sadat's era: Raymond A. Hinnebusch, *Egyptian Politics Under Sadat* (Boulder, CO: Lynne Reinner Pub., 1988), pp. 35–38. Mohamed Heikal, *The Autumn of Fury* (London: Andre Deutsch, 1983), pp. 103–114.

20. D. Pipes, ''This World Is Political: The Islamic Revival of the Seventies,'' in *At the Issue in the World Arena*, ed. S. L. Spiegel (New York: St. Martin's Press, 1981), p. 99.

21. *The Washington Post*, June 2, 1985.

22. Azar, ''Islamic Revivalist Movements,'' p. 108.

# Part V

---

# Issues in Culture and International Relations

# 15
# Communication and International Relations

## Hamid Mowlana

The expanding means of communication and the concomitant informa-tion explosion have brought us into a new era in which knowledge of international and intercultural communication is a prerequisite for un-derstanding interactions among peoples and nations. Since World War II, and especially over the last two decades, increasingly, political, economic, military, and cultural relations in the world have come to de-pend on the transnational flow of information.

This major stream of international communication, which has been greatly facilitated and enhanced by new communication technologies, has been employed as a major means by which powerful national and inter-national systems radiate out and attempt to extend themselves globally. These expanding economic, political, and cultural systems do not, of course, operate in a vacuum; they are protected by powerful military shields which also operate on a global basis and are equally dependent on information technologies. Thus, the study of international communica-tion has become a focus for debate on such issues as global conflict and cooperation, cultural autonomy, national sovereignty, and international development. Indeed, communication in international relations has now become one of the central policy areas nationally and internationally.

The last 40 years also have seen such phenomenon as wars of libera-tion, anti-imperialism, and revolution in many parts of the world, and diverse nationalities and cultural systems in quest for self-determination and a new world order as militarily weak nations confront the major powers, using information and the modern communication technologies available to them, have moved from territorial conquest to establishing, restoring, or maintaining governments that are politically reliable and com-patible with their strategic, military, and economic interests. With the ar-ticulation of new norms and institutions in a number of Third World coun-tries and a sudden decline in distance favoring the rapid mobilization of power in different parts of the world, alongside intense concern with information and persuasion, international communication has occupied a significant rank among the major issues and has become one of the key areas of power in world politics. In short, the battlefield of international politics has shifted from the geographical and the physical, to the ideological, communication, and cultural levels.

## FOUR ASSUMPTIONS ON COMMUNICATION AND INTERNATIONAL RELATIONS

In general, four basic assumptions or approaches have characterized the activities of scholars, governments, media practitioners, and individual citizens in the field of international communication over the last half of the century. The idealistic-humanistic approach characterizes international communication as a means of bringing nations and peoples together, and as a power to assist international organizations in the exercise of their services to the world community. As such, it strives toward increasing understanding among nations and peoples and toward the attainment of world peace. The process of communication here is seen in its most idealistic form.

A second approach, sometimes called political proselytization, sees international communication as propaganda, ideological confrontation, advertising, and the creation of myths and cliches. These are usually one-way communications, and they all require central organizing authorities of some kind. They are thus imbued with a certain authoritarian, totalitarian character that makes it possible to manipulate human beings. This approach to international communication has dominated relations between and among states for the last several years. Research to this end is not concerned with idealistic objectives that promote cross-cultural understanding and the "ethics" of international communication, but rather the task is seen in terms of strengthening one's political position and power of persuasion.

A third, increasingly visible approach is to view information in the international context as economic power. Here, its operation is more subtle, the message more subliminal. Overtly respectable international development projects, business ventures, marketing, trade, and technology transfer have characterized this approach and have usually resulted in the domination of weaker, peripheral nations. "Modernization" of less developed countries has in fact resulted in their conversion to Western ways and has made them more amenable to control by Western power centers. Since this process, sometimes referred to as "Westoxification," may make its converts want to behave in ways different from their natural ways, it could result in a certain schizophrenic paralysis of creative power.

The fourth approach to international communication is to view information as political power. Here, information, in the form of news and data, is treated as a neutral, value-free commodity. A study of international mass media, the wire services, the production of literature, and cinema and television programs, reveals a concentration of means in a few countries. When information is conveyed from one country to another, the cultural content of the source is conveyed, and that may not always be in the best interests of the recipient. This imbalance of means is one of the principal foundations behind the call led by Third World nations for a "new and *balanced* flow of information" rather than simply a "free flow" as supported by the West.

## FACTORS CONTRIBUTING TO THE GROWTH OF INTERNATIONAL COMMUNICATION

Research and writing on international communication have subsequently experienced astonishing growth since World War II and especially during the last two decades. Among the factors responsible for the increased study and research on communication and international relations are:

1. The development of modern information and communication technologies, and their use and impact on the nature, volume, and content of information and communication.

2. The increased awareness of nation-states, institutions, groups, and individuals of the importance of the flow of information and the existing imbalances, and their consequences and impact on the national and international decision-making processes (day-to-day and long-term), as well as on the individual and private lives of people around the world.

3. The increasing number of international and transnational actors in almost all aspects of the international flow of information with political, social, and economic ramifications, particularly in respect to such areas as trade, marketing, education, and culture.

4. The growing interest in comparative cross-cultural as well as public opinion and image studies, accompanied by the sharpening of our research and investigatory tools and improved means of collecting, sorting, retrieving, and sharing data.

5. And more specifically, the debate generated and articulated over the New International Economic Order and the New World Communication/Information Order in the 1970s, particularly the UNESCO declarations and activities on information flow and communication policies, and the ensuing discussions over the relationship between the economic and communication aspects of the world's resources.

As the supply of information is increasing at an extraordinary rate, both internationally and domestically, information and equal access to it are seen as vehicles for reducing dependency in economic, political, and cultural relations. In a broad sense, the study of the international flow of information is another approach to the study of international relations. Consequently, it should include not only the flow of information and messages through technological channels and the conventional media, but it must take into account the totality and the diversity of both channels and messages transferring information across national boundaries. This could include the study of messages flowing through channels that are oriented toward human movements and scientific and artistic pursuits as well.

Therefore, a more realistic and comprehensive analysis of the international flow of information should include the examination of a variety of economic, political, and cultural activities that in major part include the following technological and human interactions in international relations: Satellite and planetary resources—including transborder data flow, computers, and related technologies; newspapers, magazines, books, technical and scientific journals, and news agencies; radio and television and direct broadcast satellite; film, recording and video; marketing, advertising, and public opinion polls; mail, telephone, telegraph, telex, and related telecommunications channels; tourism, travel, and migration, including religious and other personal contacts; diplomatic, military, and political channels; international organizations and conferences; educational, artistic, and cultural exchanges (persons and exhibits, etc.), including conferences and sports.

## INTERNATIONAL COMMUNICATION AS A FIELD OF STUDY

The general field of communication studies is beset by several problems. One is the abundant popularity of "communication" as an organizing concept, which leads to a reckless use of communication terminology, and a proliferation of communication theories. Another is the diversity of the communication field, both in its technological and human dimensions, with research and theorizing going on in many different academic disciplines and subdisciplines. "Information," too, as a technical term has belonged to a wide range of disciplines: computer science, systems analysis and cybernetics, journalism and mass communication, political science, sociology, economics, anthropology, and psychology. These specialties and others have looked at international flow of information from divergent angles.

Here, I shall define international communications as a field of inquiry and research that consists of the flow and transfer of values, attitudes, opinion, and information through individuals, groups, governments, and technologies and their impact, as well as the study of the structure of institutions responsible for promoting and inhibiting such messages among and between nations and cultures. This definition of international communication, therefore, combines both national and international dimensions as it studies the movement of messages across national boundaries between and among two or more national and cultural systems. It entails an analysis of the channels and institutions of communication, but more important, it involves examination of the mutually shared meanings that make communication possible. Therefore, the examination of international communication should include both the content, volume, and direction of information and messages as well as the economic, political, cultural, legal, and technological factors responsible for its initiation and diffusion.[1]

As a body of knowledge, communication in international relations or the growing field of international communication offers an alternative to political, economic, and legalistic explanations of our global order. It can also offer an integrative framework, as it is argued here, in which different levels of analysis and perspectives are included within a common body of knowledge.

However, the efforts in studying international communication have been far from systematic. The diversity of sectors (public, private, and academic) interested in communication, and the myriad of reasons and purposes motivating study have precluded meaningful coordination. This same barrier to coordination, however, is a powerful justification for combining efforts to produce a maximum amount of quality data. One of the barriers to cooperation has been the polarity of the two dimensions of international communication—human and technological—which has, in part, precluded coordination of research between them. The modern and technologically based aspects of communication have received predominant attention at the expense of the human dimension. In short, technological variables, at times, have dominated research efforts where cultural and social variables, which should be considered concurrently, have been neglected. Human and social utilities have not been given as much attention as the technological and economic utilities, nor have they been integrated to show a more realistic picture of the international flow of information.

## PERSPECTIVES ON COMMUNICATION AND INTERNATIONAL RELATIONS

International communication in general and information flow in particular, like other branches of social science, largely acquire their legitimacy and consistency from the perspectives and methods of inquiry used by those who study the subject. Over the last several decades the approaches to the conduct of inquiry in this field have become comparatively more diverse, multidimensional, and indeed, varied. Following are the major perspectives covering the broad area of the international flow of information. It should be noted that the perspectives identified here are by no means mutually exclusive, but may overlap in the attempt to be exhaustive.

## International Relations and Systems Perspective

A number of information flow studies are designed to test some aspect of international relations theories and phenomena. Within this catagory we may find the studies dealing with theories of imperialism, integration, conflict and cooperation, and the general hypotheses aiming at image and perception among and between nations.

Historically, the impact of propaganda during World War I and the development of new techniques in persuasive communication dominated the earlier studies of international political communication. As propaganda and psychological warfare played an important role again in World War II, the study of international political communication became a well established field of inquiry in many universities and institutions around the world. In the post–World War II period, research in this area was greatly influenced by the continuation of the Cold War. The ideological struggle between the United States and the Soviet Union produced yet another round of research.[2] This "war of ideas" was influenced later by several factors, among them, the development of sophisticated atomic weaponry, the rise of the new nation-state and the nonaligned movement in the Third World, and the increase of international economic and commercial flow and the resulting exploration of culture. The major focus was now directed toward a "global elite," and the growing number of technocratic intelligentsia, increasing numbers of whom are linked by many common factors transcending national, cultural, or regional differences.

The major strategy of international political communication in the early decades of this century was the blatant use of propaganda. In the years following World War I and continuing to the end of World War II, a new communication strategy was developed. Encouraged by the potential applications of future propaganda, governments enlisted the cooperation of communication and political scientists. The goal was not to develop analytical frameworks. Strategic warfare was now aimed at destroying a country's infrastructural basis as well as the morale of the population for carrying on the war.[3] The more recent strategy, dating back about three decades and continuing until the present, is a structural and sociological strategy. Its purpose is multidimensional—political, economic, and cultural. Now, the process has been well noticed and commented upon by philosophers, sociologists, and scientists alike. For example, Jacques Ellul has listed several categories of propaganda: political and sociological, agitation and integration, vertical and horizontal, rational and irrational.[4] On all of these levels, propaganda is a condition in which the existing political, economic, and sociological factors allow an ideology to penetrate individuals or masses. It produces a progressive adaptation to a certain order of things, a certain concept of human relations, which subliminally molds individuals and makes them conform to society.

In the United States a generation ago, Harold Lasswell advocated the study of the international flow of information in determining the climate of international action.[5] Since part of the manipulative strategy of politics calls for mood control by the use of both communication and noncommunication, Lasswell focused his interests on analysis of the content of elite-to-elite and elite-to-nonelite media of communication in determining the distribution of common moods as well as the distribution of deviations.

During the last two decades, communication models and terminologies have been used in the study of integration at the international level by such scholars as Karl Deutsch,[6] Richard Merritt,[7] and Bruce Russett.[8] International relations as a communication process has been discussed by Charles McClelland,[9] Davis Bobrow,[10] Chadwick F. Alger,[11] Hamid Mowlana,[12] and others. Communication models and information flow data have been used by Johan Galtung and his associates in the study of imperialism and world systems.[13] As a result, there has been a shift toward a much more extensive and careful use of communication and information data in international political research.

One of the approaches to communication and international relations in the early 1970s that was spreading throughout a major cross section of scholars studying foreign policy and international systems was commonly called "events-interaction analysis." Using communication models and terminologies, and employing mass media and content analysis as their sources and methods, respectively, the purpose was to interpret the "interactions" of nations (or actors) as reflected by the analysis of "events" data. The flexibility of interaction analysis led such scholars as Charles McClelland, Edward Azar, R. J. Rummel, and others to its use in various areas of research involving the study of international conflict, foreign policy behavior, international crisis, links between domestic and international behavior, or simply the monitoring of interactions between any set of "actors."[14] An evaluation of events data movement, the culmination of three years of research and review on this subject, has been elaborated by Robert Burrowes, Gary D. Hoggard, Russell J. Leng, Hamid Mowlana, Warren R. Phillips, Alvin Richman, and Sophia Peterson.[15]

Also, during the 1960s and 1970s, new theoretical interests stimulated researchers to use data about communication, mass media, public opinion, and attitude change in the study of international images. There have been attempts to borrow paradigms—mainly those of mediated stimulus, cognitive balance, and cybernetics—from psychology and related fields. Some have gone still further by introducing ideas concerning the role of information in psychiatry and biology and its relation to international relations. Significant amounts of writing have been done in the area of communication and foreign policy during the last three decades, and the conception of how public opinion and national and international images are formed and held has been significantly changed by such scholars as Herbert Kelman,[16] Kenneth Boulding,[17] Gabriel Almond,[18] Ralph White,[19] and Ithiel de Sola Pool.[20]

More recently, and in the so-called "post-structural" perspective, the questions of communication, language, and ideology and their relations to world order have been discussed by a number of writers in communication, international relations, and related fields.[21]

In general, there seem to be three kinds of communication theory underpinning international relations research: mathematical, sociopsychological, and linguistic. Mathematical theory appears to be a growing field in the United States, the low level mathematical theories coming from empirical and theoretical research done on military strategy and nationalism. For example, I. Richardson,[22] Anatol Rappaport,[23] and Thomas Schelling[24] have been as concerned with developing theories of conflict strategy as Karl Deutsch[25] and David Easton[26] have been with politics and international relations. The sociopsychological tradition has had a tremendous influence on politics and mass media research, and the linguistic tradition has led to such areas as symbol analysis and content analysis.

## Communication and Development Perspective

The communication and development approach undertakes the study of communication and international relations from the perspective of developmental policies and theories—national and international—examining both a nation's internal and external communication systems and its political, economic, social, and cultural development in a national, regional, and international context. During the last three decades, a number of scholars following the trend of international communication research have posited communication squarely within the processes of development. In order to delineate the patterns of international communication research, one must investigate the various models of development which they are seeking to legitimatize. These models of national and international development in which communication models and terminologies as well as communication policies have been incorporated include: (1) modernization by Daniel Lerner,[27] nationalism by Karl Deutsch,[28] and political development by L. Pye and his associates[29] (2) economic development and technological diffusion by D. MacLelland[30] and E. Rogers[31] (3) imperialism, dependency, and underdevelopment by

Dallas W. Smythe,[32] and Luis Ramiro Beltran and his associates[33] (4) revolution, liberation, and human development by such authors as Franz Fanon,[34] Paulo Freire,[35] Ali Shari'ati[36] and Reza Muttahari.[37]

In the 1960s with increasing exposure of both Western and Eastern superpowers and their desires for influence and dominance in international relations, disenfranchised groups within the north and the developing nations in the south criticized the two dominant paradigms of development: the liberal-capitalist and the Marxist-socialist. At a political economic level of material criticism, theories of underdevelopment, based on polemics such as center-periphery, dominant-dependent, and the political economy of information emerged.

At a sociocultural level of idealist criticism, the school of critical research and various scholars from the developing world took on increasing importance. Relations of dominance and dependency were placed within a psychic and cultural context, demanding that individuals and groups liberate themselves in communicative discourse, and the realm of ideas and knowledge.[38]

This category also includes studies on the balance and imbalance of information flow, the direction and pattern of flow, and at times relates it to such factors as ideology, ethnocentricity, commercialism, or proximity. Here the emphasis has been to study the content, volume, and frequencies of communication in general and the message in particular. This has been a growing perspective since the 1960s.

### Institutional and Commercial Perspective

A large segment of international communication literature examines international actors and the impact of political and persuasive messages on the behavior of individuals and nations. The institutional and commercial perspective includes propaganda and policy studies for a variety of purposes such as conflict management, domination, and commercial promotion, as well as stereotyping or image manipulation and control. Additionally, research regarding the effectiveness of the role of actors and institutions—governmental and nongovernmental—and its importance and impact on the international flow of information are included in this perspective. The major emphasis is on content analysis, audience analysis, readership survey, and public opinion poll.

This perspective, which flourished during the 1940s and the 1950s, continues to influence many flow studies at present. For example, one of the early books on the institutional basis of international political communication by W. Phillip Davison attempted to search "for ways in which the United States can use public communication more effectively to advance its foreign policies." Its chapter titles included such topics as: the impact of communication on the individual; communication and organization;

communication in communist states; the political role of communication in democracy; the use of communication to advance policy; foreign information and cultural activities of the United States; the roles of the U.S. government in international communication.[39]

During the Cold War period of the 1950s and 1960s this perspective of international political communication took on bipolar characteristics in which a number of works on the "war of ideas in contemporary international relations" were published both in the United States and the Soviet Union. Thus, Soviet writer Georgi Arbatov, whose work on this subject is mainly linked "with the world division into two sociopolitical systems" along the line of Marxist-Leninist theory, sees the "war of ideas in contemporary international relations" as "a feature characterizing precisely our epoch," which he says "has no precedent in history because the international relations in the transitional periods (i.e., in the period of transition from one socioeconomic formation to another) of the past had always developed under conditions in which worldwide social systems comparable with those in existence today did not and could not take shape."[40]

On the commercial side, the expansion of trade and transnational corporations, especially in the sphere of communication technologies and cultural industry, was mainly responsible for the growing research on international public opinion, audience analysis, market survey, and a variety of international communication projects. Indeed, by the 1970s, and in the process of diffusion and adaptation of modern satellite and computer technologies—the so-called informatics and telematics—the transnational corporation had become one of the most well organized contributing elements to communication in international relations.

### Political Economy and Socio-Structural Perspective

The political economy and socio-structural perspective approaches the study of international communication from the aspect of national and international communication structures, as well as the political economy and the sociocultural dimensions of information. Such research would be concerned with the elements of and factors influencing the process of international flow, including gatekeepers and gate producers, as well as examining the technological and human dimensions and formal and informal institutional structures of both production and distribution aspects of the process of international information flow. This has been a growing line of inquiry since the 1970s.

There are diversities of view within this broad perspective: those who mainly emphasize the political economy of information and those who add the sociocultural dimension to this perspective. Examples of these views can be seen in the works of Herbert I. Schiller, Armand Matterlart, Hamid Mowlana, and Cees Hamelink.

According to Hamelink, the international flow of communication is the main carrier of transnational cultural synchronization. The transnational corporations (TNCs), who are agents of the "metropolitan" economy, are introducing revolution in commercial thinking that the world should be seen as one economic unit. Hamelink prefers the term "cultural synchronization" to "cultural imperialism." In his view, cultural imperialism is the most frequent, but not exclusive, form in which cultural synchronization takes place. Hamelink elaborates that, "the process of cultural synchronization implies that a particular type of cultural development in the metropolitan country is persuasively communicated to the receiving countries. The whole process of local social inventiveness and cultural creativity is thrown into confusion or is definitely destroyed. Unique dimensions in the spectrum of human values, which have evolved over centuries, rapidly disappear."[41] One of his suggestions is his plea for international "disassociation," a term borrowed from Dieter Senghass, and defined as "conscious choice against the delusory offer of integration in an international order which appears to respond to all the interests of the developing countries, but which in fact represents almost exclusively the interests of the powerful."[42]

Using an integrative model of international information flows, Mowlana's projection of the terrain of international communication is inclusive: Its boundaries extend to all aspects of communication both human and technological, both politico-economic and sociocultural. A central thesis is that the inclusion of human factors in the exchange of international information makes current structures of international communication different from what has gone before.[43]

Examining the transnational system in which nation-states exist now, Mattelart outlines a model of development that he thinks is being imposed on the Third World. The road to progress in this model, according to Mattelart, passes through integration into the transnational system. This integration is possible through various forms of subordination of the local bourgeoisie to the transnational system. Mattelart insists that to understand development, one must try to understand the local bourgeoisie. The major goal for the New World Information and Communication Order, according to Mattelart, should be to "reequilibriate an international flow of information marked by an unequal exchange."[44]

Schiller maintains that cultural imperialism develops in a world system "within which there is a single market, and their terms and characters of production are determined in the core of that market and radiate outward."[45] National states, thus, work and impinge on the "pure" workings of the world system. The cultural communication sector of the world system necessarily develops in accordance with and facilitates the aims and objectives of the general system. A large one-directional flow of information from core to periphery represents the reality of power.

Schiller maintains that the crisis afflicting the world at present is twofold: it is ecological—that is, it is a result of massive wastage of resources, compounded by skyrocketing military expenditure which results in resource despoliation and depletion; and it is also social—that is, the disorders induced by the economic, political, and military policies designed to maintain imperial power, result in social crisis. It is Schiller's contention that information and technologies have been seized upon as the means to alleviate and overcome the world crisis, and at the same time, it confers greater authority to information controllers and powerful users. But Schiller, as others in that broad perspective, warns that technological solutions devoid of social accountability will be terribly costly to human lives.[46]

### Technical and Legal Perspective

The technical and legal approach is a combination of the very new and the very old in that these aspects, which have been concerns of scholars for decades, are rapidly revolutionizing the international information system. Studies in this area include the technology as well as the techniques of international information gathering and processing; national and international regulations and standards of information industries as well as of flow, and the resulting issues; and the technical aspects of transferring data, information, and messages across national boundaries or from point to point.[47] Studies in this perspective are expected to increase in the coming years as a result of the rapid development of satellites and computers, the growing power and importance of transnational organizations, and the greater attention of regional and international organizations to the complex problems of technology, information, and services.

Considering it is now clear that the development of modern communication technology and the continuous stream of information flow have increased consciousness of national sovereignty and have made proliferation of states and transnational actors possible, this has generated important functional demands on the international system well beyond its capacity with the existing machinery. This raises important questions about the viability of the prevailing model and order of international information systems to cope with the rapidly changing environments of international relations in general, and international communication in particular.

### NOTES

1. For a comprehensive analysis of the subject see Hamid Mowlana, *Global Information and World Communication: New Frontiers in International Relations* (White Plains, NY: Longman, 1986).

2. Hamid Mowlana, "Trends in Research on International Communication in the United States," *Gazette* 19, no. 2 (1973):79–90.

3. Harold D. Lasswell, *Propaganda Technique in the World War* (New York: Alfred A. Knopf, 1927).

4. Jacques Ellul, *Propaganda* (New York: Vintage Books/Random House, 1973).

5. Harold D. Lasswell, *World Politics and Personal Insecurity* (New York: World Publishing, 1935).

6. Karl W. Deutsch, *Nationalism and Social Communication* (Cambridge, MA: MIT Press, 1953).

7. Richard Merritt, ed., *Communication in International Politics* (Urbana: University of Illinois Press, 1972).

8. Bruce Russett, et al., *World Handbook of Political and Social Indicators* (New Haven, CT: Yale University Press, 1964).

9. Charles A. McClelland, *Theory and the International System* (New York: Macmillan, 1966).

10. Davis B. Bobrow, "Transfer of Meaning Across National Boundaries," in Richard L. Merritt, ed., *Communication in International Politics* (Chicago: University of Illinois Press, 1972).

11. Chadwick F. Alger, "Personal Contact in Intergovernmental Organizations," in Herbert C. Kelman, ed., *International Behavior* (New York: Holt, Rinehart and Winston, 1965).

12. Hamid Mowlana, *Global Information and World Communication* (New York: Longman, 1986).

13. Johan Galtung, "A Structural Theory of Imperialism," *Journal of Peace Research* 8 (1971):81–118.

14. Edward E. Azar, "Analysis of International Events," *Peace Research Review*, Vol. 4; Charles A. McClelland, "Some Effects on Theory from the International Event Analysis Movement," *Sage Professional Papers in International Studies* 1:15–43; Rudolph J. Rummel, "Dimensions of Conflict Behaviour Within and Among Nations," *General Systems Yearbook* 8 (1963):1–50.

15. "Events Data Analysis: An Annotated Bibliography," American Political Science Association, Annual Meeting, Los Angeles, CA, 1972.

16. Herbert Kelman, ed., *International Behavior: A Social-Psychological Analysis* (New York: Holt, Rinehart, and Winston, 1965).

17. Kenneth Boulding, *The Image* (Ann Arbor: The University of Michigan Press, 1971); *The World as a Total System* (Beverly Hills, CA: Sage, 1965).

18. Gabriel Almond, *The American People and Foreign Policy* (New York: Macmillan, 1961).

19. Ralph White, *Nobody Wanted War* (New York: Doubleday Anchor Books, 1970); White, ed., *Psychology and Prevention of Nuclear War* (New York: Free Press, 1986).

20. Ithiel de Sola Pool, "Effects of Cross National Contact on National and International Images," in H. Kelman, ed., *International Behavior* (New York: Holt, Rinehart, and Winston, 1965).

21. See, for example, Edward Said, *Orientalism* (New York: Vintage Books, 1978); Hamid Mowlana, "The Role of the Media in the U.S.–Iranian Conflict," in Andrew Arno and Wimal Dissanayake, eds., *The News Media in National and International Conflict* (Boulder and London: Westview Press, 1984); and Mowlana, "Communication, Change, and Post-Developmentalism: A Conceptual Framework for

Theory and Policy," paper prepared for the Seminar on Communication and Change, University of Hawaii and the East-West Center, Honolulu, July 20–August 1, 1987; Michael Shapiro, "The Constitution of the Central American Other: The Case of Guatemala," paper presented at the Annual Griffith Lecture entitled "New Trends in International Relations Theory: A Post-Structuralist Perspective," The School of International Service, The American University, Washington, DC, April 14, 1987; and R. B. J. Walker, ed., *Culture, Ideology, and World Order* (Boulder and London: Westview Press, 1984).

22. I. Richardson, *Arms and Insecurity* (Chicago: University of Chicago Press, 1960).

23. Anatol Rappaport, *Fights, Games, and Debates* (Ann Arbor: University of Michigan Press, 1960).

24. Thomas Schelling, *The Strategy of Conflict* (New York: Macmillan, 1963).

25. Karl Deutsch, *Nationalism and Social Communication* (Cambridge, MA: MIT Press, 1953).

26. David Easton, *A Framework for Political Analysis* (Englewood Cliffs, NJ: Prentice-Hall, 1965).

27. Daniel Lerner, *The Passing of Traditional Society* (Glencoe, IL: The Free Press, 1958).

28. Karl Deutsch, *Nationalism and Social Communication*.

29. Lucien Pye, ed., *Communication and Political Development* (Princeton, NJ: Princeton University Press, 1963).

30. David C. McClelland, *The Achieving Society* (Princeton, NJ: Van Nostrand Co., 1961).

31. Evert Rogers and F. Floyd Shoemaker, *Communication of Innovations: A Cross-Cultural Approach* (New York: The Free Press, 1971).

32. Dallas W. Smythe, *Dependency Road: Communications, Capitalism, Consciousness, and Canada* (Norwood, NJ: Ablex Publishing Corp., 1981).

33. Luis Ramiro Beltran S. and Elizabeth Fox de Cardona, "Latin America and the United States: Flaws in the Free Flow of Information," in K. Nordenstreng and H. Schiller, eds., *National Sovereignty and International Communication* (Norwood, NJ: Ablex, 1979).

34. Franz Fanon, *The Wretched of the Earth* (Harmondsworth, Middlsex: Penguin, 1967).

35. Paulo Freire, *The Pedagogy of the Oppressed* (New York: The Seabury Press, 1970).

36. Ali Shari'ati, *Marxism and Other Western Fallacies* (Berkeley, CA: Mizan Press, 1980).

37. Reza Muttahari, *Fundamentals of Islamic Thought: God, Man, and the Universe* (Berkeley, CA: Mizan Press, 1984).

38. Hamid Mowlana and Laurie J. Wilson, *Communication and Development: A Global Assessment* (Paris, UNESCO, 1985).

39. W. Phillip Davidson, *International Political Communication* (New York: Praeger, 1965).

40. Georgi Arbatov, *The War of Ideas in Contemporary International Relations* (Moscow: Progress Publishers, 1973).

41. Cees Hamelink, *Cultural Autonomy in Global Communication: Planning National Information Policy* (New York: Longman, 1983), p. 5.

42. Ibid., p. 4.

43. Mowlana, *Global Information and World Communication* (White Plains, NY: Longman, 1986).

44. Armand Mattelart, *Transnationals and the Third World* (South Hadley, MA: Bergin and Garvey, 1983), p. 130.

45. Herbert Schiller, *Communication and Cultural Domination* (White Plains, NY: International Arts and Sciences Press, 1976).

46. Herbert Schiller, *Information and the Crisis Economy* (Norwood, NJ: Ablex, 1984).

47. Anne Branscomb, ed., *Toward a Law of Global Communication Network* (White Plains, NY: Longman, 1986).

# 16
## *Swords into Plowshares: Some Thoughts as to What Went Wrong*

Rick Herrick

The relationship between religion and foreign policy, like most human relationships, is complex and shrouded in ambiguity. On the one hand, we have recently witnessed Jaime Cardinal Sin stand up against political tyranny in the Philippines and actively work to keep the revolution non-violent. A similar role is being played by Bishop Desmond Tutu in South Africa. Within the United States various church groups such as the National Council of Churches, U.S. Catholic Bishops, and other progressive Protestant and Jewish groups have, in the name of religion, condemned the arms race, opposed current U.S. policy in Central America, and led the movement to divest corporate economic assets in South Africa.

On the other hand, the Christian right in the United States and the Reagan administration have used religion to legitimize a policy of fighting global communism. This policy has frequently been characterized in biblical terms as a struggle between lightness and darkness, good and evil, in which U.S. goals and aims are rather self-righteously thought to be more godly than Soviet ones.[1] The real problem here is that this policy assumes that the United States has a special covenant relationship with God which denies God's transcendence and freedom. In a similar way, the state of Israel uses religion to justify its policy of occupying Arab lands that have been settled by Palestinian Arabs for centuries.

Then there is the Khomeini phenomenon. Here religion and nationalism combine to produce a movement that seeks to make the world over in the image of Islam. Military force is used to achieve God's purposes. Sacred martyrdom is held up as the true test of an individual's faith. Terrorism is used against fellow Muslims to cleanse Islam of "satanic" influences and to punish other religious groups and individuals that stand in the way of Khomeini's Islamic revolution.

Religion has also been used to justify violence in separatist movements such as in Northern Ireland and the Hindu/Sikh conflict in India. Until very recently the Dutch Reformed Church in South Africa legitimized apartheid in theological terms. Finally, important Catholic lay and religious leaders in South and Central America have sanctioned the use of violence as a last resort in promoting revolutionary social change in Latin America (Liberation Theology).

It seems clear that the use of religion to justify conflict, particularly when violence is involved, violates the teachings of the world's major religious traditions.

. . . [A]nd they shall beat their swords into plowshares, and their spears into pruning hooks; nation shall not lift up sword against nation, neither shall they learn war any more.

Isaiah 2:4

You have heard it said, ''Love your friends, hate your enemies.'' But now I tell you'' love your enemies and pray for those who persecute you. . . .

Matthew 5:43

Weapons are instruments of fear; they are not a wise man's tools. . . . Peace and quiet are dear to his heart, and victory no cause for rejoicing. If you delight in victory, then you delight in killing; if you delight in killing, you cannot fulfill yourself.

Lao Tsu, *Tao Te Ching*, Thirty-One

Never in the world can hatred be stilled by hatred; it will be stilled only by non-hatred—this is the law eternal.

Buddha

What social relations should you hold with men whose hearts are filled with rancour—who hate both men and men of God? Surely you cannot offer love and friendship to such as seek to destroy your faith and you. Seek protection for you and yours from God and not from God's sworn enemies. But deal kindly and justly with all: it may be that those who hate you now may love you: for God can order all things.

Koran

Nonviolence is the greatest force at the disposal of mankind. It is mightier than the mightiest weapon of destruction devised by the ingenuity of man. It is a power which can be wielded equally by all—children, young men and women or grown up people—provided they have a living faith in the God of love and have equal love for all mankind. My life is dedicated to the service of India through the religion of nonviolence which I believe to be the root of Hinduism.

Mahatma Gandhi *All Men Are Equal*

If the above sample of religious teachings is representative, a question naturally arises as to what went wrong. Why have religious people from all the world's great religious traditions fallen short in regard to living up to these teachings? This chapter offers a few thoughts in answer to this question.

## THE MEANING OF A TRANSCENDENT GOD

The three great monotheistic religions of Judiasm, Islam, and Christianity all begin with the idea of a transcendent God. To say that God is transcendent means that God is not a thing among other things, but, as the theologian Rudolph Otto posits, totally other—beyond human definition and control. In Old Testament terms, God's face is always hidden, the divine essence a deep mystery. God is fully sovereign and free, and essentially different from His/Her creation. Because of this situation, God communicates with people indirectly and with great subtlety. Thus, it is not surprising that there are so many approaches toward understanding religious experience.

The concept of a transcendent God is one that most religious people accept but fail to take seriously or to understand fully. In an effort to understand the will and purposes of God, people often confuse their own needs and wishes with those of the divine. The result is that this God who is fully transcendent and free is often manipulated to serve human purposes. This has led to unfortunate foreign policy consequences from states whose people represent all three of the great monotheistic religions.

Beginning with Islam, one discovers that there are two necessary requirements for the faith. The first is to believe in one God whose essence is transcendent, a deep, impenetrable mystery. The second is to accept Muhammad as God's prophet. Muhammad is believed to be the mouthpiece of a preexistent scripture which was revealed to him in installments over the years and written down in a book called the Koran. Although Islam claims to be linked to all religions, the Koran perfects religion. It is the ultimate revelation, God's final revelation—an amazing statement for a religion that begins with the concept of a God who is fully transcendent and free.

This claim that the Koran is God's final revelation has had important foreign policy consequences throughout history. It was Muhammad's view that Islam could not be Islam unless it controlled political power. The goals to dominate and to exert power over territory have been turned into a religious mission in many Islamic states. The ideas of conquering for the faith and the corollary thought that those who fall in battle are declared immortal have provided for much religious passion which has been used by some Islamic states to further their nationalistic goals.[2] Such consequences have, at least in part, been the result of a religious people who have not understood or been willing to accept the implications of worshipping a transcendent God.

Much the same is true regarding the Old Testament claim that God gave to the Jewish people the land of Israel. Ask a Palestinian Arab, who worships the same God, what he or she thinks of this rather arrogant claim. To acquire a firmer grasp of the historical questions in the dispute, one need only read the Old Testament books of Joshua and Judges and substitute the word Palestinian each time the words Canaanite and Philistine appear. Not only does such an exercise enable one to see more clearly the equal validity of Palestinian claims to the land, but it also raises the question as to whether a God of love would allow such disasters to befall an innocent people.

It is also possible to ask the question of whether God ever speaks so clearly.

I will establish my Covenant between myself and you [Abraham], and your descendents after you, generation after generation, a Covenant in perpetuity, to be your God and the God of your descendents after you. I will give to you and to your descendents after you the land you are living in, the whole land of Canaan, to own in perpetuity, and I will be your God.

Genesis 17:7–8

If so, there would probably be far less confusion on a wide range of political issues that currently confuse and challenge many people.[3] The real problem with such straight talk is that it violates human freedom, it changes a person into a robot, which denies us our greatest gift from God, the right to be decision makers.

The state of Israel claims all the land of Canaan, Palestine, for religious reasons (a gift from God), and this claim is deeply imbedded in the identity of most Jews living both in Israel and in other countries.[4] The problem is that this situation has made it virtually impossible for Israel to deal with Middle East issues through a political process of negotiation and compromise. The situation is further aggravated by Jewish and some Christian groups in the United States which accept Israel's claim on theological grounds. The influence of these groups on U.S. policy has often prevented the United States from playing a truly balanced role in the region.

Finally, it is necessary to examine the Christian claim that Jesus Christ is the exclusive son of God in the same light. Such a claim seems to violate the freedom and transcendence of God. It also has little or no authentic historical validity.

When one examines the history of the New Testament period, what is known concretely about Jesus is that he lived and died on a cross.[5] One could also add that after his death a major religion developed in his name, quite an accomplishment (one might even say a miracle) considering the fact that he was advancing a religion that was both very strange and difficult to his contemporaries. According to the biblical picture, Jesus appeared on the world scene at about the age of 30, with nothing known of his earlier life. The discussion regarding his nature in the Synoptic Gospels (Mark, Matthew, and Luke) shows much confusion among the disciples as to who he was, which seems to be at least partly responsible for his decision to seek the cross (to open their eyes). It is important to note that the first of these gospel accounts was written long after the events (at least 35 years) with the benefit of no written records or documents. The gospel accounts differ among each other and with the writings of Paul on key questions of the Christian faith.[6] All of the New Testament materials were written after the death of Jesus by individuals who were convinced that Jesus was the Christ, the Messiah, the son of God. Thus, what we have in the New Testament is not a history but statements of faith written by people who differed among themselves on key questions on the nature of Jesus.

It is also informative to look at the writings of the early church fathers.[7] One theme that is frequently alluded to is the struggle within the early church that existed among various groups concerning the nature of Jesus. This struggle ended around 200 A.D. after the church had become established and the leadership was able to purge all ''unorthodox'' views. Of the more than 50 texts from the Christian era, most were burned. Fortunately, some of these texts were buried and have recently been found. It is interesting to note that some of the ones found criticize the virgin birth and physical resurrection as naive.

The purpose of the above analysis is not to discredit the Christian faith. I count myself as one of the members of this great tradition. It also does not disprove the claim that Jesus is the exclusive son of God. God is transcendent which means that all things are possible with God. However, the above discussion, if essentially correct, does suggest that a greater spirit of humility and tolerance toward other religious traditions is needed among many Christian groups.

When I picture Jesus, it is clear to me that he was an extraordinary person and religious leader. Like the disciples, I am also confused regarding his nature because it seems so different from my own. If incarnation (the idea that the power of God can take over and control human flesh) is a real possibility in history, then I think it far safer to take the Hindu position that Jesus was one of several such incarnations. The idea that a free and a transcendent God would choose one group and culture for special revelatory treatment violates the sense of God as love which I experience in my heart. The counterargument that Christ is available to all people does not ring true when I think of an Indian child in a rural village who is nurtured and loved by Hindu parents.

The point of all this is that the exclusive Christian claim, the ''I'm number one with God'' syndrome which seems to be an important factor among religious groups of varying traditions, has had significant foreign policy consequences that have certainly violated the teachings of Jesus in the Sermon on the Mount. The Crusades, from the end of the eleventh to the end of the thirteenth centuries, were aggressive foreign wars fought in the name of a person who taught nonviolence and love toward enemies. Moving closer to home, the destruction of a beautiful religion and culture, the stealing of millions of acres of land, and the killing of thousands of individuals, were done by white Christian settlers against a people who had lived on this land in peace for centuries prior to the coming of English colonists. Finally, the moral energy of an exclusivistic faith has often prompted certain Christian groups in the United States to wage a war (both cold and hot) against "godless" communism in all of its myriad forms, in which ends and means were confused, ruthless right-wing dictators supported, and guerrillas armed and equipped who have done little but make the lives of thousands of innocent people living in rural areas miserable.

## EXTERNAL VS. INTERNAL RELIGION

The discussion above seeks to make the point that religion has frequently failed to influence foreign policy in line with the great teachings of peace, universal brotherhood, and global understanding, because the faithful prefer to twist religion to suit their own ends rather than accept the consequences of what it means to worship a transcendent God. Why does this happen? The answer to this question is found in the distinction between external and internal religious practice. The argument developed below suggests that internal religious practice works to transform the individual believer in the direction of greater peace, love, and understanding both within himself and toward his neighbor. Such an individual, as a result, is more willing to accept the consequences of relating to a transcendent God and more likely to apply his or her religion in a way that leads to greater harmony among nations. A similar situation is not true for a religion based on external religious practice that leaves the believer untouched in the area of moral development. Religion and foreign policy in this case are not related for the believer in any meaningful sense.

Beginning first with external religious practice, it is important to note that it is not associated with any one religious tradition but relates rather to certain ideas and methods regarding worship. The key element of faith is what one believes, not what one's heart is set on.[8] External religious practice is a religion of beliefs and creeds which are authoritatively proclaimed and accepted by the believer with little dissent. It is a religion that is often preached with the problem being not so much the content of the message but the fact that the message and the way it is received do nothing to help the believer grow inside. It is, in addition, frequently a religion of spoken prayer in which a God outside is asked to meet specific needs of the believer or the community of faith. It is a type of religious practice that does not penetrate to the heart of the believer.

It is also a religion that feeds the needs and the demands of the individual ego rather than seeking to control or transform them.[9] Robert

Bellah and his colleagues have pointed out in their recent book, *Habits of the Heart*, that most Americans go to church for individual support. In this case, religion performs the role of therapy in which the specific church helps to make the believer feel better about his or her self and thus more able to survive and even thrive in the "rat race" during the rest of the week. It is a religion that accepts the dominant culture of self-centered individualism and does nothing to transform it.[10]

Finally, religion centered upon external practice is concerned primarily with personal salvation rather than ethics. Again, the goal is to feed ego need rather than to transform it. The shouting of the ego not to die is placated with a misunderstood theology of grace.[11] In such a theology the individual is seen as bad (a sinner); however, God willingly intervenes to destroy the evil within so long as the believer accepts certain creeds or formulas of the church. Salvation is never seen as a matter of individual achievement, and thus the believer is left free to go about his or her life relatively unencumbered by ethical demand. As a matter of fact, life in the Kingdom is pictured as a future event, and thus ethical teachings like those found in the Sermon on the Mount are not deemed relevant to this life.

The above analysis is made primarily with the Christian faith in mind; however, a strong case can also be made that similar ideas and practices exist for Confucianism[12] and Islam.[13] There are two problems with a religion dominated by external practice. The first is that static belief systems cannot contain religious truth.[14] The second is that a religion that feeds ego needs rather than seeking to transform them violates the teachings of all great religious traditions. In many ways this is why such religious practice is so popular and widespread because it allows the individual to seek personal salvation along with material success and other ego pursuits. In regard to foreign policy, the practitioners of such religion frequently demand a policy of military strength and the aggressive pursuit of national security interests in order to protect a life of pleasure and privilege.

Moving next to internal religious practice, it is appropriate to begin with Eastern religious traditions because of the well-known association between them and internal religious practice. Although the teachings of Buddhism, Zen Buddhism, Taoism, and Hinduism[15] are rich and varied, there are certain ideas that they share in common and that form a core that describes what is meant by internal religious practice. Each begins with the assumption that there is within every person a finer quality of life that is obscured by the desires and demands of the individual ego. This finer quality of human nature is variously defined as the God within or the real self.

The purpose of internal religious practice is to penetrate beneath the demanding ego which enables the individual to become one with God or his or her higher nature (real self). This goal is achieved through the disciplined use of meditation which concentrates and quiets the mind in such a way that the individual becomes aware of his or her higher nature. What is important is the disciplined practice of the way, not a system of beliefs, dogmas, or creeds. It is the general assumption of Eastern religious thinking that humans are essentially good but full of illusions about the nature of their real self. The purpose of religion is to gently help the individual find his or her best self, which leads to a transforming experience and to the ability to act in new ways.

What may surprise some people is that many of the ideas discussed above pertaining to internal religious practice are also found in the Christian faith. The central idea here is that the Kingdom of God is located within the heart of the individual believer. The Kingdom within is seen as one's best self, a principle of order, wisdom, goodness, and love that resides deep within a person and yet has an outside source. One finds the Kingdom within through meditative practices of quieting the mind and through contemplative prayer.[16] This spirit of quietness makes it possible for God to be self-defined for the believer, and thus the individual relates directly to God rather than indirectly through a system of belief. The goal of such faith is not personal salvation, but unity with God in a relationship of love and obedience.

These ideas are found scattered throughout the gospel writings in places such as the parables about the Kingdom. They are also implied by the teachings in the Sermon on the Mount. One New Testament scholar has argued that an analysis of the grammatical structure of the original Aramaic clearly indicates that Jesus expected his followers to practice such behavior.[17] All the difficult Christian teachings on loving enemies, refraining from judgment, the call to be gentle and a peacemaker, the teachings on adultery, and so on, were spoken in a way to indicate that such behavior was attainable now. There is nothing in that sermon to suggest that such loving action could only be realized in some future kingdom. The teachings imply that each individual is capable of making the changes on his or her own once a proper relationship with God is established.

Perhaps the clearest expression of these ideas is in the gospel of John.[18] The central theme of John's gospel is that eternal life (understood more in a qualitative than a quantitative sense) is now. The Kingdom is to be established in the heart of the individual believer. It is achieved not by the destruction of evil but by establishing a relationship with God based on mutual love and obedience. Humans are not pictured as sinful in essence but as oriented toward darkness. Jesus is seen as the model for living in a relationship with God, a relationship based on mutual love and obedience. The cross represents the highest expression of this love and obedience rather than a symbol for the destruction of evil (sin). When the individual establishes such a relationship with God, he or she becomes oriented toward the light rather than toward the darkness. The love experienced within the divine/human relationship transforms a person and enables that person to respond and to act in a Sermon-on-the-Mount manner.

Internal religious practice leads not to increased feelings of inner warmth and well-being but to different thoughts and actions, to a new perspective on living. As Jesus often taught, it was by their fruits that one would know them. One of the best examples of bountiful religious fruit from the Eastern tradition is the country of Tibet.[19] Tibet is a land in which the whole country was once ruled by the search for inwardness. The key idea of Tibetan Buddhism is compassion for all living things. The entire society, from the highest lamas (teachers) to the lowest peasant, was organized according to this principle. The Dalai Lama (the highest religious and political leader) is seen as an incarnation of this force of compassion as are many spiritually advanced people. The remarkable thing is that the introduction of Buddhism to Tibet transformed a warlike and aggressive Kingdom with much political intrigue and strife into a peaceful state ruled by religion. This system lasted from its establishment in the early seventeenth century until the Chinese invasion in 1959. During that period the country maintained only a token military force to patrol the border with China and no police force whatsoever. Crime virtually ceased to exist. According to the brother of the current Dalai Lama, the success of the system was the result of internal religious practice, not because the people of Tibet were special or in any way saints.[20]

An example of bountiful religious fruit from the Christian tradition is the Society of Friends, or Quakers.[21] The Quakers are a small group of Christians for whom the direct experience of God's love is the central element of their religious life. This experience is believed to be available to all people provided they are willing to sit quietly and patiently. The Kingdom of God is believed to exist within every person, and religious growth (ethics) takes place as the individual becomes more open to the inner light of the Kingdom. These ideas place the Quakers squarely within the tradition of internal religious practice.

The Quakers are probably best known for their stand for nonviolence, a position that is not seen as a tactic but rather as a way to achieve peace within the individual self. War is seen as an absolute evil, and most Quakers have refused to participate in military activities of any kind. It is perhaps less well-known that Quaker settlers maintained excellent relations with Indian communities during the colonial period. They looked on Indians as children of God, not as savages, and it was their general practice to pay a fair price for Indian land. They were also the first abolitionists; however, before becoming leaders in the movement, they saw to it that all the members of their church had freed their own slaves. Compliance was virtually unanimous. Quakers were also the first women's liberationists, again, beginning in their own homes and church. They were also well-known for leading the movements to reform prisons and mental institutions. For Quakers, the experience of God's love always comes first, but it is important that this experience lead to good works. The above history of such works indicates a remarkable record of group compliance to the teachings of the gospel.[22]

The examples of Tibet and the Quakers discussed above indicate the potential of internal religious practice to transform individuals in the direction of a Sermon-on-the-Mount approach to living. When one relates and acts from the perspective of the Kingdom or one's higher self, three important consequences follow that relate to foreign policy. First, one sees wholes, not separate or segmented entities. Thus, for example, religion and foreign policy are seen to be intimately related. The person ceases to divorce religion from other aspects of life. Ends and means become important as do the ethical teachings that can be applied to foreign policy situations. Second, the demands of the ego are either controlled or transformed which means that the pursuit of material pleasure is far less important. This makes the individual less likely to support a foreign policy that is defined exclusively in terms of national self-interest and which aggressively seeks to maintain and to enhance the material well-being of its citizens. Finally, internal religious practice helps one to see more clearly the viewpoint of others (all people have God within) which greatly reduces the energy required to engage in aggressive acts of violence. In short, internal religious practice helps the individual to act in ways that push the world in the direction of greater peace, harmony, and understanding.

## CONCLUSION

The great religious teachers achieved a special unity with God by way of a religion of internal practice. Their teachings reflect the quality of this relationship, and in the area of foreign policy challenge the faithful to resist self-will and to work toward the achievement of world peace and social justice. The examples of Tibet and the Quakers indicate that it can work.

Why, then, hasn't it worked? When one surveys the world scene, it is evident that there are significant numbers of religious people in every nation. Yet we live in a world torn by war and plagued by high levels of social injustice. A spirit of destructive competitiveness pervades the international community which has led to the militarization of the globe. Organized religion has been able to influence this situation only at the margins.

What has gone so terribly wrong? Perhaps the answer is bad theology— too much emphasis on free grace and too little on spiritual transformation. Or, in a similar vein, maybe the churches, at least in the United

States, are at fault for their failure to challenge the prevailing culture of self-centered individualism.

Although there is probably some truth in the two suggestions above, the answer, unfortunately, is not so simple. The real problem seems to be in the nature of internal religious practice. The transformation that occurs as the individual becomes progressively more open to the Spirit of God requires a lifetime of disciplined, hard work. The process not only involves a long journey, but the progress that results is not easily measurable or readily apparent to the faithful practitioner. The net result is that some people do not believe that the process works, others are discouraged from beginning the quest, and still others never proceed very far along the way.

What, then, has happened to religious experience? The voice of the human ego is so loud, and in Western societies the prevailing culture of pleasure and competitive individualism all work to impede the search for the Kingdom of God within. Yet, despite these problems, religious experience seems to be a relevant factor in the lives of many religious people. What seems to take place is that the ego is from time to time surprised or placated in a way that enables a person's higher nature to experience a fleeting glimpse of the divine Spirit. Such experiences provide a foundation of support for an individual's theology. They make the structure of a person's belief system credible, but the experiences are not intense or frequent enough to encourage the recipient of the experience to undertake the lifelong work of internal religious practice.

The result is that most people see and respond to the outside world through the lenses of individual ego and not through the perspective of God's Kingdom. They understand the implications of the great religious teachings, and they would like to live according to them, but they can't. In this situation, the safest and most prudent course is to separate religion and politics and to await and hope for a different kind of Kingdom, one that will exist beyond history and will be organized in such a way that peace and justice can finally reign.

## NOTES

1. A good example of such a practice is Ronald Reagan's speech to the National Association of Evangelicals on March 8, 1983. A complete text of this speech can be found in Strobe Talbott's book, *The Russians and Reagan* (New York: Vintage Books, 1984), pp. 105–118.

2. For a full discussion of these problems in contemporary Islamic societies, see Robin Wright, *Sacred Rage: The Crusade of Modern Islam* (Fresno, CA: Linden Publishing Co.).

3. This question reminds me of Abraham Lincoln's dilemma regarding the problem of slavery. He prayed earnestly for divine guidance on the matter. He was

clearly troubled that God gave clear answers to spokesmen on both sides of the issue but not to him who was responsible for deciding the vexing matter. How could God be for and against the same thing at the same time, he wondered? He could only conclude that God was transcendent, that His will could not be directly determined, that God governed the world in ways that men could not know or influence.

4. I once heard a lecture given by a prominent Jewish theologian regarding the nature of God. One point he made was that he was more comfortable thinking of God in Tillichian terms as the ground of being than as a transcendent person. After the lecture, I asked him whether a ground of being God can give land. He admitted the problem, but never conceded on Israel's right to occupy the land. This is what I mean by being imbedded in Jewish identity.

5. See Rudolf Bultmann, *Jesus Christ and Mythology* (New York: Charles Scribner's Sons, 1958).

6. See Elaine H. Pagels, *The Gnostic Gospels* (New York: Random House, 1979). It is important to note that most New Testament scholars with the exception of some fundamentalists hold this view. I am indebted to Dr. Walter Eisenbeis, professor of religion at Denison University, for pointing this out and for many additional helpful comments on this paper.

7. The following argument is found in most histories of Christian thought. For a further discussion of these questions, see Adolf von Harnack, *History of Dogma*, Vol. 1 and 2 (New York: Dover Publications, 1961) and Arthur C. McGiffert, *A History of Christian Thought*, Vol. 1 (New York: C. Scribner's Sons, 1932).

8. This idea was pointed out to me by James W. Fowler in his book *Stages of Faith*. Fowler is using Tillich's well-known standard of faith as that which concerns one ultimately. The main point is that when an individual is ultimately concerned with satisfying ego needs his or her faith is largely defined in terms of belief systems. In addition, see Paul Tillich, *Dynamics of Faith* (New York: Harper & Row, 1957).

9. See Jacob Needleman, *The New Religions* (Crossroad, NY: Crossroad Publishing Co., 1984).

10. See Robert N. Bellah, *Habits of the Heart* (Berkeley: University of California Press, 1985).

11. A Christian theology of grace is most commonly associated in my mind with the writings of Paul. The ideas within this paragraph came from Karl Barth's *The Epistle to the Romans*, the section in Rudolf Bultmann's *Theology of the New Testament*, that deals with the ideas of Paul, Ernst Kasemann's book, *Perspectives on Paul*, and my own reflections on these matters.

12. Although Confucius was a man known for great personal piety and reverence, his ethical teachings degenerated into a system of rigid rules and social conventions. This rather oppressive system in which the individual was weighed down with rules reminds one of the religion of the Pharisees.

13. Islam is a religion where God wills, judges, commands, and humans obey. There is no idea that the individual should get to know God. In the Shia version, it is also a religion of works in which the individual is seen as having an account with God. If at death the believer has a large credit balance, that person ascends to heaven. If not, things are not so good. The only exception to the above is the

Sufi movement which concerns itself with inner religious experience and belongs with the discussion of internal religious practice below.

14. This idea was pointed out to me by James W. Fowler in his book *Stages of Faith*. See specifically his discussion of conventional faith which is the form of religion practiced by most Americans.

15. A reader interested in a good introduction to Eastern religious thinking should consult Jacob Needleman's *The New Religions*.

16. An excellent discussion of these techniques from a Christian perspective is found in George A. Maloney's *Prayer of the Heart*.

17. See Hans Windisch, *The Meaning of the Sermon on the Mount* (Philadelphia, PA: Westminister Press, 1951) and Hans Dieter Betz, *Essays on the Sermon on the Mount* (Philadelphia, PA: Fortress Press, 1985).

18. The ideas within this paragraph came from C. H. Dodd's *The Interpretation of the Fourth Gospel*, the section in Bultmann's *Theology of the New Testament* that deals with John, and William Barclay's two volumes entitled *The Gospel of John*.

19. For a detailed discussion of the relation between religion and politics in Tibet see Franz Michael's book, *Rule by Incarnation*. A related book, entitled *Tibet*, is written by Figme Norbu and Colin Turnbull. Although less scholarly, this book provides the reader with a beautiful sense of the unique compassion which is Tibet.

20. Figme Thubten Norbu and Colin M. Turnbull, *Tibet* (New York: Simon and Schuster, 1968).

21. For a detailed discussion of Quaker religious ideas and practices see D. Elton Trueblood, *The People Called Quakers* (New York: Harper and Row, 1966). An excellent historical evaluation of Quaker commitment to what might be called the social gospel is found in Margaret Hope Bacon's *The Quiet Rebels* (Philadelphia, PA: New Society Publishers, 1985).

22. Personal note: It may be important to note here that I am not a Quaker nor do I consider myself one who has progressed a long way down the path of internal religious practice.

## SELECTED BIBLIOGRAPHY

Anderson, Walt. *Open Secrets: A Western Guide to Tibetan Buddhism*. New York: Viking Press, 1979.

Bacon, Margaret Hope. *The Quiet Rebels*. Philadelphia: New Society Publishers, 1985.

Barclay, William. *The Gospel of John*. Vols. 1 and 2. Philadelphia, PA: Westminister Press, 1956.

de Bary, William, ed. *Sources of Chinese Tradition*. Vol. 1. New York: Columbia University Press, 1960.

———. *Sources of Indian Tradition*. Vol. 1. New York: Columbia University Press, 1958.

Barth, Karl. *The Epistle to the Romans*. London: Oxford University Press, 1933.

Bellah, Robert N., et al. *Habits of the Heart*. Berkeley: University of California Press, 1985.

Betz, Hans Dieter. *Essays on the Sermon on the Mount*. Philadelphia, PA: Fortress

Press, 1985.

Blofield, John. *Taoism: The Road to Immortality*. Boston, MA: Shambhala Publications, Inc., 1978.

Brown, Robert McAfee. *Religion and Violence*. Philadelphia, PA: Westminister Press, 1973.

_____ . *Theology in a New Key: Responding to Liberation Themes*. Philadelphia, PA: Westminister Press, 1978.

Bultmann, Rudolph. *Jesus Christ and Mythology*. New York: Charles Scribner's Sons, 1958.

_____ . *Theology of the New Testament*. New York: Charles Scribner's Sons, 1951.

Corlett, William, and John Moore. *The Buddha Way*. London: Hamish Hamilton Ltd., 1979.

Cragg, Kenneth. *The House of Islam*. Encino, California: Dickenson Publishing Co., 1975.

Dodd, C. H. *The Interpretation of the Fourth Gospel*. Cambridge, England: Cambridge University Press, 1963.

Eastman, Charles Alexander. *The Soul of the Indian*. Lincoln: University of Nebraska Press, 1911.

Enslin, Morton Scott. *Christian Beginnings*. Parts 1 and 2. New York: Harper & Row, 1938.

al Farugi, Ismail R. *Islam*. Allen, Texas: Argus Communications, 1979.

Fowler, James W. *Stages of Faith*. San Francisco, CA: Harper & Row, 1981.

Harnack, Adolf von. *History of Dogma*. Vols. 1 and 2. New York: Dover Publications, 1961.

Hultkrantz, Ake. *Belief and Worship in Native North America*. Syracuse, NY: Syracuse University Press, 1981.

Kasemann, Ernst. *Perspectives on Paul*. Philadelphia, PA: Fortress Press, 1969.

Maloney, George A. *Prayer of the Heart*. Notre Dame, IN: Ave Maria Press, 1981.

McGiffert, Arthur Cushman. *A History of Christian Thought*. Vol. 1. New York: C. Scribner's Sons, 1932.

McNaughton, William, ed. *The Confucian Vision*. Ann Arbor: University of Michigan Press, 1974.

Michael, Franz. *Rule by Incarnation*. Boulder, CO: Westview Press, 1982.

Momen, Moojan. *An Introduction to Shi'i Islam*. New Haven, CT: Yale University Press, 1985.

Morgan, K. W., ed. *The Religion of the Hindus*. New York: Ronald Press, 1953.

Needleman, Jacob. *Lost Christianity*. New York: Harper & Row, 1985.

_____ . *The New Religions*. Crossroad, NY: Crossroad Publishing Co., 1984.

Norbu, Figme Thubten, and Colin M. Turnbull. *Tibet*. New York: Simon and Schuster, 1968.

Pagels, Elaine H. *The Gnostic Gospels*. New York: Random House, 1979.

Renou, Louis. *Hinduism*. New York: G. Braziller Co., 1961.

Sangharakshita, Bhikshu. *A Survey of Buddhism*. Boulder, CO: Shambhala Publications, 1980.

Talbott, Strobe. *The Russians and Reagan*. New York: Vintage Books, 1984.

Tillich, Paul. *Dynamics of Faith*. New York: Harper & Row, 1957.

Trueblood, D. Elton. *The People Called Quakers*. New York: Harper & Row, 1966.

Windisch, Hans. *The Meaning of the Sermon on the Mount*. Philadelphia, PA: Westminister Press, 1951.

Wright, Robin. *Sacred Rage: The Crusade of Modern Islam*. Fresno, CA: Linden Publishing Co., 1985.

# 17
## Ideology and International Relations: Self-Reliance in China and North Korea

## Han-Sik Park

Substantively, an ideology may be a philosophical system of values, but its vital function has always been in providing political legitimacy for the ruling regime and elite. In this sense, an ideology could be seen as an instrumental means designed to help the regime in attaining its goals. Thus, the content of an ideology is likely to change as the primary goal of the regime changes.

In this chapter, I will discuss the nature of ideological responses to changing national goals as the political system itself undergoes transition through various developmental stages. Additionally, I will examine the function of ideology with specific reference to its implications for determining foreign policy orientations.

### NATIONAL GOALS, FOREIGN POLICY OBJECTIVES, AND IDEOLOGY

Without necessarily adhering to Talcott Parsons' theory of "functional requisites," one can minimally accept the notion that any social system must function so as to attain or accomplish certain goals in order to sustain its existence. Obviously, defining specific goals of political systems with any degree of objectivity is beyond the aspiration of the social scientist. Yet by defining them at a level of greater generality one can achieve a considerable consensus. Gabriel Almond and others persuasively propose a structural functionalist approach, with a particular set of functions which are the common goals that any political system must perform. Although the institutional approaches and procedures for achieving system goals such as political communication, interest articulation, rule making, and adjudication may vary depending on system characteristics, the goals themselves could be said to be common to many political systems.[1] Structural functionalism as a theory, however, does not indicate which of the functions are more urgent or important than the rest. That is, there is no hierarchical ranking of the functional imperatives. The absence of a hierarchy makes the analysis of the dynamics of goal attainment difficult.

In an effort to explain the process of political development, I have proposed a stage theory of social change in which a set of system goals is specified at various developmental stages. The goals include regime formation, political integration, resource expansion, and conflict management. These goals or functions are found in any system at any given point in time but their relative importance or urgency is believed to be different depending on the stage of system development. The changing relative importance of the goals may well explain policy orientations and foreign policy objectives for a particular system. According to the proposed stage theory, the above four goals are hierarchically structured such that regime formation is the very foundation of any political system, followed by political integration, resource expansion, and conflict management.[2]

The process of regime formation involves establishing a government, promulgating a ruling mechanism, and providing necessary means for physical survival of the masses. In this initial stage, government efforts will be centered on agriculture and defense since these are the areas primarily responsible for the conditions necessary for physical survival of the people and the provision of basic needs. The regime will gain popular support as long as it is capable of generating the agricultural goods and security services necessary for the people to maintain their lives. Abstract political ideologies cannot provide policy guidelines in such a situation, although nationalist rhetoric may be prominent in the process of the emergence of a sovereign state. Political ideology as an institution designed to provide legitimacy to the new regime is not expected to function as a vital guide for policy until the process of power solidification is initially completed. When political stability is restored and people's basic needs are reasonably provided, however, the regime may employ an official ideology to legitimize its policies and broaden its power base. This process usually involves political socialization (indoctrination) of the masses as well as extensive political purges, with the ultimate goal of political integration. It is in this process of political integration that the regime seeks ideological legitimacy. Thus, both domestic and foreign policies as well as government actions are to be consistent with the belief systems of the ideology. If the ideology requires policies that could be counterproductive for economic growth, the regime will not hesitate in absorbing any economic setbacks. It is not until the regime elevates its policy goals to the level of resource expansion that economic policies will become pragmatic and growth oriented.

As the regime changes its policy priorities from political integration to resource expansion or economic development, policy options and strategies will be geared to the promotion of material interest. However, pragmatic approaches toward economic expansion could be affected by the belief systems evolved during the political integration period, possibly to the extent that needed policies could be seriously inhibited.

In this chapter, I shall examine the ideology of ''self-reliance'' as it has evolved in China and North Korea. I choose to examine this doctrine for three reasons. First, the idea of self-reliance was exceptionally effective for the purposes of power consolidation and political integration in both of these countries. Second, as witnessed in post-Mao China as well as North Korea today, this very doctrine can be counterproductive to the goals of economic growth and resource expansion once the political system shifts its policy orientation. Third, the idea of self-reliance seems to have become the basis for a new nationalism not only in the non-aligned Third World nations but in the industrial countries that have shown protectionist orientations in the new international economic order.

## SELF-RELIANCE AS IDEOLOGY: CHINA AND NORTH KOREA

Although Mao's political ideology is claimed to be a version of Marxism-Leninism, the essence of its belief system may lie in the doctrine of ''self-reliance'' as a manifestation of developmental nationalism. The ideas of political self-determination, economic self-sufficiency, and military self-defense were closely associated with Chairman Mao, and all major policies were designed to implement these ideas.

When the communist regime was established in 1949, the government was in no position to implement the official ideology of Maoist socialism, as the leadership's primary task was to rehabilitate the production capacity of agriculture, thereby ensuring the physical survival of the masses. The initial period of 1949–1952 was indeed a period of stabilization and recuperation from revolutionary dislocations and the destruction of productive capacities. Even in the ostentatious period of the First Five Year Plan of 1953–1957, socialist ideas took a back seat in favor of pragmatic plans for reconstruction and expansion of productivity. However, with the launching of the Great Leap Forward (GLF) in 1958, a massive restructuring of the social and economic system in accordance with Maoist ideology was attempted. In this process, it was not the economic output or any other pragmatic consideration but rather ideological principles that guided the reform policies. After a period of setbacks in the first half of the 1960s that followed the failure of the GLF, the Chinese communists launched a renewed and more vigorous campaign with the purpose of instilling into the mass consciousness an ideology that would advance the grand goal of political integration. This ''Cultural Revolution'' injected such a massive dose of ideology into this country with one-fourth of the world's population that the system was eventually paralyzed. The ideology of Chairman Mao was so instilled that even the current leadership must accommodate it.

In North Korea, the presence of a political ideology has been as continuous as has the leadership itself. At about the same time that China launched the GLF campaign, North Korea proclaimed a similar campaign in 1958 with the slogan "Let us dash forward at the speed of *Chollima*."[3] This campaign, commonly known as the Chollima Movement, thus began as an ideological effort to achieve political integration. Unlike China, where the reformists experienced serious setbacks, the North Korean version of a "leaping forward" movement has not been seriously interrupted. The smaller and more homogeneous population, the presence of enemies across the border in the South, and the continuity of leadership, have been instrumental in the effective indoctrination of the masses with the ideological doctrine of *Juche* (self-reliance).[4] In fact, the North Korean ideology has been more than a philosophical system of ideas; it has been a practical guide for domestic and foreign policies.

As a basic principle of both Chinese and North Korean ideologies, the notion of self-reliance has been deeply integrated into policies affecting their foreign relations. In what way, then, has this notion been incorporated into policy considerations? We believe there are three areas in which self-reliance has become a vital policy guideline: political sovereignty, economic self-sufficiency, and military self-defense. We will next examine each of these manifestations of self-reliance in greater detail.

### Political Sovereignty

Countries that have experienced national humiliation as a result of foreign intervention tend to support the principle of self-determination. Many of them have sought to maintain a position of neutrality in an era of superpower politics by joining the nonaligned bloc. Both China and North Korea have been actively involved in the nonaligned movement, although in reality they have been making concerted efforts to broaden the socialist base in the Third World by assisting revolutionary regimes and insurgency movements.

During the Cultural Revolution, China's diplomatic relations with other countries were strained by ideological considerations, especially anti-imperialism. China has consistently criticized foreign military intervention in the Third World countries. In the 1950s and 1960s, Mao attacked the stationing of U.S. troops in Southeast Asia and SEATO and U.S. military presence in Thailand and the Philippines. When Pakistani prime minister, Husain Shahid Suhrawardy justified U.S. presence in the region by saying that the "Americans are not enemies of China but only afraid of China's designs in Asia," Mao's reply was, "If because the United States is afraid of us, they must control the Philippines, Thailand, and Japan, then we can say that because we are afraid of the United States, we must control Mexico, Nicaragua and even Pakistan."[5] In fact,

China's position on foreign intervention in Third World countries has been consistent even after the Cultural Revolution as demonstrated by Beijing's denouncement of the Soviet invasion of Afghanistan in 1980.[6] China made it clear that it opposes all forms of foreign domination, either by socialist hegemonism or capitalist imperialism. Even with the normalization of diplomatic relations with the United States, Beijing has not revised its policy of opposing the continued presence of U.S. troops in South Korea.

North Korea's political ties with other nations have been even more closely guided by the doctrine of Juche. Unlike many Third World countries that are utilizing all possible means for economic expansion, North Korea has placed ideological considerations above economic and pragmatic national interest. In most of the nonaligned and socialist countries in the Third World, Pyongyang has established and sponsors institutions for the study of Juche, and large quantities of publications on the ideology are published in different languages for worldwide distribution. For a nation plagued with serious economic problems, especially the repayment of foreign debt, spending rather liberally on an ideologically oriented propaganda project is certainly economically inefficient, yet Pyongyang believes it to be politically worthwhile, as it promotes national sovereignty and political legitimacy.

Despite the celebrated pronouncement of China's "Great Leap Outward" and all the pragmatic policies in the post-Mao era, the principle of self-reliance is seldom debated. In memory of the tenth anniversary of the death of Mao Zedong, *Beijing Review* reminded its readers of the importance of self-reliance, advocated originally by Mao and further promoted by Zhou Enlai:

China must be independent. . . . Chinese affairs must be decided by the Chinese people themselves, and no further interference, not even the slightest, will be tolerated from any imperialist country. (Mao) With respect to foreign relations, we have a basic stand: we uphold China's national independence and the principle of . . . self-reliance. . . . (Zhou)[7]

The communist Chinese ideology from its very inception was founded on the principle of self-reliance. In fact, the Chinese communists saw additional difficulties and complications in becoming self-reliant even for a country normally considered independent, since in their view imperialistic powers have available many and various subtle methods that may be used against a country, such as "organizing military blocs, establishing military bases, and plundering [a country's] wealth by means of various forms of economic exploitation."[8] The Chinese contend that "the path taken by the Chinese people in defeating imperialism and lackeys and in founding the People's Republic of China is the path that should be taken by the peoples of various colonial and semi-colonial countries in their fight for national independence and people's democracy."[9]

China's adherence to self-reliance is clearly reflected in its foreign policies, especially in the early years of the Republic. In defending Chinese involvement in the Korean War, Premier Zhou Enlai said in November 1951 that the Chinese intervention in Korea had not only safeguarded China itself, but had been "an encouragement to all peoples in colonial and semi-colonial regions."[10] It was the desire to cultivate the ideology of self-reliance in other nations that led Zhou Enlai in 1955 to initiate contacts with the newly independent nations of Africa at the nonaligned conferences at New Dehli and Bandung. China expanded its diplomatic activities to Africa in the 1960s as it believed that "the center of the struggle against colonialism is in Africa."[11]

Similarly, the doctrine of self-reliance has been reflected in the foreign policies of North Korea. Pyongyang is widely known as an exporter of military assistance to many Third World countries, and has dispatched military advisers and trainers to a number of countries that are allegedly fighting imperialist aggression (e.g., Nicaragua, Angola, Syria, and Iran). Such policies cannot be comprehended as solely economic and pragmatic considerations of its national interests, but as efforts to support and cultivate the ideology of self-sufficiency in other less developed countries.

In short, both China and North Korea have persistently pursued the ideology of self-reliance not only domestically but as a major facet of their international relations as well. It is not the ideology of Marxism-Leninism but the doctrine of self-determination that has guided their policy choices.

### Economic Self-Sufficiency

According to Mao Zedong and Kim Il Sung, an essential foundation for political independence is for a nation to be economically self-sufficient. In their efforts to promote economic self-sufficiency, the two countries have adopted similar strategies, although post-Mao China has shown some flexibility in economic policies. Policy objectives intended to promote self-sufficiency have included balanced (between agriculture and industry) economic growth, avoidance of trade deficits, promotion of indigenous science and technology, conservation of raw material and fuel bases, and, most of all, the infusion of "right spirit" into the mass belief system. These are not practical ideas for the acceleration of economic growth in underdeveloped countries. As evidenced in Japan, South Korea, Taiwan, and Singapore, a more efficient strategy for economic expansion is through export-oriented policies that often lead to economic dependence on the international system.

The economic policies of China and North Korea have been geared to the construction of a balanced economy, although the heavy industrial sector is given greater emphasis because this sector is directly linked to military self-reliance. Mao Zedong's much-publicized notion of "standing on two legs" implies balanced development between agriculture and industry, as well as between the countryside and the city. In an effort to prevent blind migration to the cities (a chronic problem in developing countries), China has consistently employed measures designed not only to retain rural populations, but also to attract urban white-collar workers to rural areas by creating opportunities for education and medical and social services in the countryside. As is reflected in the "four modernizations" of agriculture, industry, defense (military), and science and technology, Chinese policies of the post-Mao post–Cultural Revolution era are still geared towards balanced development.

North Korea's economic policies have also incorporated the ideal of self-sufficiency. However, where China's economic policies have undergone alterations and refinements, North Korea's have been the model of consistency. As an official publication states, North Korea believes that "An independent national economy means the economy that stands on its own feet without depending on others, the economy which serves one's people and develops relying on resources of one's own country by the efforts of its own people."[12] The same publication also asserts the need for economic diversification instead of concentrating on leading sectors for export: "If the economy is to be immune from the worldwide economic upheavals it must be developed in a diversified and comprehensive way so as to meet one's needs by home production."[13] Further, North Korean ideology maintains that a country cannot be independent from foreign domination without the ability to feed its own people. The regime seems to have achieved a reasonable degree of agricultural self-sufficiency in spite of the fact that the northern half of the Korean peninsula has always been ill-suited for agriculture.

In order to avoid economic dependence, both China and North Korea have made concerted efforts at avoiding large trade deficits. At a time when Third World countries commonly experienced trade deficits, China generally has maintained trade surpluses until 1978, when it began allowing foreign investment and imports of the technology necessary for industrialization.[14] Still, the magnitude of its trade deficits has been kept at a minimum through trade policies designed to avoid intertwining China in foreign commodity markets. One such policy is the restriction on payment for import in foreign exchange. With the exception of imports that are deemed vital to China's development or security, foreign companies are required to purchase Chinese goods for export with credit that they receive for their export to the Chinese market. Through this practice, foreign exploration of the Chinese market is limited by the ability of foreign investors and exporters to place the Chinese goods they receive in exchange. In this way, the government controls trade flow and keeps deficits under control.

In the case of North Korea, the overriding goals of cultivating a personality cult for Kim Il Sung and establishing hereditary power succession by his son made the regime unable to compromise its ideological rigidity, let alone develop pragmatic economic policies. Unlike China where trade with noncommunist countries has recently reached nearly 10 times that of communist countries, North Korea's foreign trade has been mostly with communist systems.[15] Nevertheless, the case of North Korea cannot be an exception to the general trend that when a regime has sufficiently achieved power stability and political integration, it will show interest in economic expansion and prosperity. Pyongyang has shown a more open and conciliatory attitude toward the West and capitalist countries since the early 1970s. This has been encouraged by the precedent of the Chinese, but perhaps more importantly, it may be due to lingering Sino-Soviet tensions, since Pyongyang cannot tilt to one side at the expense of the other. Following the Ping-Pong diplomacy between China and the United States and the ensuing visit of President Nixon to Peking in 1972, North Korea displayed a noticeable change in its attitude toward the international community. In contrast to its habitual condemnation of the United Nations, North Korea became a member of the World Health Organization in May 1973 and sent an observer mission to the United Nations in the same year. Since then, Pyongyang's orientation has been moving in the direction of a "slightly" open-door policy. A series of actions that appear to reveal movement away from the traditional closed-door policy began in 1980 with the acceptance of $8.85 million in technical assistance from the United Nations' Development Program. Since Prime Minister Kang Song-san's announcement to the Supreme People's Assembly in January 1984 that Pyongyang would welcome trade with capitalist countries, North Korea has been exploring avenues for trade with Japan and European countries. Additionally, Pyongyang introduced a joint venture law for the purpose of introducing foreign capital and technology to North Korea.[16] Despite these efforts, however, North Korea has been unable to expand trade with capitalist countries in any significant way, nor has it succeeded in attracting foreign investment. Since the adoption of the joint venture law, only a few Koreans living in Japan who had been loyal to Pyongyang have increased their economic activity with that country. The North Korean lack of success with an open-door policy seems to suggest that the principle of self-reliance might inhibit such a pragmatic strategy.

With regard to technological self-reliance and the utilization of indigenous raw materials and fuel resources, the two countries have shown contrasting policies. While China, with its vast reserves of raw materials and crude oil, is generally self-reliant, North Korea has been continuously dependent on foreign resources, most notably oil from China and heavy industrial goods (including weapons) from the Soviet Union. More than one-third of North Korea's total foreign debt (approximately $3.5 billion) is with its two neighboring communist countries. As a country with minimal trade activity and an annual total trade volume of 1 to 2 billion dollars, North Korea is unable to solve the lingering problem of trade imbalance.

Since the death of Mao and the purge of the "Gang of Four," China has revived its efforts at promoting scientific and technological development by sending large numbers of students and scientists abroad. In the United States alone, some 20,000 Chinese students are reportedly studying at various institutions of higher education. This situation contrasts sharply with that of North Korea, where very few students and scientists are studying abroad.

The present policy changes in China, however, should not be viewed as an indication of the end to socialism or the beginning of capitalism. One need only be reminded of the demotion of Hu Yaobang in 1986, following a series of student demonstrations and civil disturbances demanding further liberalization and democratization. Although the open-door policy itself is seemingly intact, there are recent signs of renewed emphasis on self-reliance as evidenced by the adoption of a resolution on the "Guiding Principles for Building a Socialist Society with an Advanced Culture and Ideology" at the Sixth Plenary Session of the Twelfth Central Committee of the Chinese Communist Party on September 28, 1986. The resolution harshly criticizes the recent social and economic consequences of the open-door policy and private incentives. It further confirms that: "We [China] resolutely reject the capitalist ideological and social systems that defend oppression and exploitation, and we reject all the ugly and decadent aspects of capitalism."[17] In this respect, the Chinese leadership seems to be desiring the economic payoffs of an open-door policy without the accompanying risks of external influences on the Chinese culture.

North Korea represents an extreme case where the "spiritual health" of the masses is regarded as the necessary condition for socialist revolution. In fact, Juche itself may be seen as an ideology based on spiritual determinism. This determinism has even been linked to economic development. The North Korean leadership has been stubbornly insistent on the necessity of spiritual preparedness in overcoming the hardships and difficulties of building a self-reliant economy. "Since economic construction . . . is a revolutionary struggle, without the spirit of self-reliance one cannot undertake the arduous and complex tasks facing the construction of an independent national economy."[18]

To the extent that North Korea insists on spiritual conditioning and/or ideological preparedness, pragmatic and open-door policies are bound to be restricted. While there are few signs of a relaxation in the ideological rigidity that characterizes its domestic politics, North Korea's foreign policy has shown some flexibility in accommodating the growing need for resource expansion.

### Military Self-Defense

The concept of defense or military self-sufficiency has been incorporated into a variety of policy measures in China and North Korea. According to North Korea's Juche, "the implementation of self-reliance in national defense is a military guarantee for the political independence and economic self-sufficiency."[19] Thus, military self-sufficiency is considered a necessary condition for other areas, and that, without peace guaranteed by a strong military, economic and political self-reliance cannot be functionally feasible. Both China and North Korea have strongly promoted their military industries, but of no less importance, each has militarized its society. It seems that their conception of national defense is not limited to the weapons and combat capabilities of the military.

### The Military Industry

It is ideally desirable for any country to be able to produce its own weapons for self-defense. Yet this requires economic resources and sophisticated technology that most Third World countries lack. Thus, the two countries have been forced to concentrate disproportionately large amounts of available resources on their military sectors. This phenomenon is more dramatically evidenced in North Korea's military spending over the years.

According to the World Bank, Chinese military expenditures from 1961 to 1983 were 31 and 48 percent of the total government expenditures. Although official sources from China show substantially less, it is clear that the heavy burden of military spending was detrimental to other sectors of the economy, especially during the Cultural Revolution.[20] North Korea has maintained a defense budget of one-third of its total national budget.

The development of a military industry requires concurrent development in the heavy industrial sector. In the GLF programs of the late 1950s and ever since, China has emphasized heavy industry, although in order to appease the overwhelmingly agrarian population, political slogans have seldom neglected agricultural development. The withdrawal of Soviet nuclear weapons technicians and blueprints in 1960, followed by mounting tensions between Beijing and Moscow, prompted the Chinese to concentrate more on national defense, culminating in the successful testing of an atomic bomb in 1964.

The North Korean military industry has been amazingly strong in view of its overall economic stagnation. This is evidenced in the fact that since the mid-1960s, North Korea has been sending weapons and military advisors to a number of Third World countries. According to U.S. and South Korean sources, some 30 countries imported weapons from North Korea in the 1966–1982 period, and in the same period more than 40 countries, mostly in Africa and Latin America, received military assistance in the form of advisors and experts.[21] For a country with a GNP per capita of $700–800, such a military establishment might not have been possible without the ideological rationale for building a self-reliant national defense at the expense of other sectors of the economy. Such a defense establishment is possible only if the people are ideologically prepared to cooperate with government policies that may not be immediately beneficial to their economic well-being. To this end, the politicization of the masses seems to be vital, and both China and North Korea have indulged heavily in ideological education.

## Militarization of the Masses and Guerrilla Warfare

According to the doctrine of self-reliance, the defense of a technologically and economically underdeveloped country requires more than a strong army. It takes a spirited army and ideologically devoted masses to transform the entire nation into a bulwark against foreign attack. In this regard, preparing the civilian population for combat and transforming them into a militia are important strategies for national defense. The practice of extensive ideological and political training in the military curricula has been commonplace in both Mao's China and North Korea. Both have striven to build politically reliable troops for the purposes of guerrilla or nonconventional warfare.

Mao succeeded in developing the concept of a "peoples war" with a "people's liberation army," in part, because both ideas elevated political commitment over military hardware as the key to victory. On this basis, the ability to match the technological sophistication of the enemy was downplayed, and therefore the need to buy foreign weapons technology and weapons systems was minimized in the mass belief system. North Korea has been even more explicit about politicization of the military as a means of self-defense:

For implementing the principle of self-reliant defense, it is important to give full play to the politico-ideological superiority of the people's armed forces. The decisive factor for victory in war does not consist of weapons or techniques, but in the high political and ideological principles of the popular masses who are aware of the justice of their causes.[22]

In this way, the Pyongyang regime has constantly emphasized the necessity of arming the masses as a matter of political strategy. By instilling in the mass belief system the notion that a people's militia is an indispensable factor in national defense, North Korea has provided military training to the entire people:

Modern warfare is three-dimensional. . . . In fact, no demarcation line can be drawn between front and rear. Hence, in order to repel imperialist aggression successfully, all the people should be ready to fight with arms in hand, and the whole country be turned into a strong fortress.[23]

At all levels of education, the government provides programs designed to militarize the students. Combat training combined with political in-doctrination constitutes a central element of the school curriculum. The philosophy of the slogan "learn from the army," which was so pervasive in the Chinese society during the Cultural Revolution, is still the case in North Korea.

The idea of a people's militia can be very appealing to a country pursu-ing national security without the benefit of conventional military capabilities, since it encourages local self-defense and also increases mass participation. In this way, citizen militias enhance national defense by making it virtually impossible to control a country through occupation of its capital city alone. North Korea has taken this philosophy one step further by participating in the military programs of other Third World countries through its "exports" of advisors and experts on people's militia tactics.

In short, the doctrine of self-reliance has affected the economic and military strategies that influence foreign policy orientations and outcomes. The cases of China and North Korea are demonstrative examples, but they are not the only systems that have incorporated the doctrine into their policy guidelines. In fact, many nonaligned countries have been at-tracted to the doctrine, although most of them have been unable to im-plement it to their satisfaction. We believe the ideology of self-reliance will be a factor in world politics as long as it is an integral part of emergent nationalism around the world. The recent tendency of industrial and post-industrial countries toward foreign policies of self-reliance is quite intrigu-ing. The growing call for economic protectionism against the newly industrializing countries might be seen as a manifestation of nationalist sentiment against foreign dependence.

## CONCLUSION

We have examined the effect of political ideology in determining foreign policies in the context of the doctrine of self-reliance in China and North Korea. We have shown that the role of ideology is more central in some situations than others. Generally, when a regime is in the process of power consolidation and political integration, foreign policy, as an extension of domestic political dynamics, is guided primarily by ideological considera-tions as evidenced in China under the leadership of Mao Zedong, and in North Korea more recently. However, when the regime's policy priority shifts to resource expansion and economy growth, the vitality of political ideology as a determinant of foreign policy will be diminished.

One might also note that as the locus of world politics shifts from the East-West ideological confrontation to a North-South interdependence, where economic interest rather than ideological adherence is a more important consideration, political ideology is expected to lose its significance in global politics. Therefore, to the extent that the Cold War era has come to an end, conventional ideologies are indeed at a waning point.

However, the ideologies of the Cold War era represented different weltanschauungs of the polarized world order, namely capitalistic democracy and socialist communism. These ideologies may have become increasingly less relevant in international politics, but this does not mean that nations will be free from ideological constraint of any kind. In fact, the new economic world order with its increasing functional interactions between nation-states has provoked Third World nations to renew their nationalist efforts against foreign domination, especially in the economic and defense sectors. These countries, many of whom have joined the nonaligned bloc, are attracted to the idea of self-reliance. This very idea may have formed a new basis of ideology apart from the ideological foundations of the Cold War world order. Interestingly, this phenomenon may not be limited to the small Third World nations. This new basis is likely to be reinforced as the industrial nations and the newly industrializing countries find themselves in a relationship of mutual animosity resulting from growing trade frictions.

## NOTES

1. Gabriel A. Almond and G. Bingham Powell, *Comparative Politics: A Development Approach* (Boston, MA: Little Brown, 1966).

2. Han S. Park, *Human Needs and Political Development: A Dissent to Utopian Solutions* (Cambridge, MA: Schenkman, 1984).

3. Wal-yong Kim, "New Demand in Revolutionary Development and the Chollima Work Team Movement," *Kulloja* March 31, 1967

4. Han Shik Park, "North Korea's *Juche*: Its Premises, Promises, and Problems," *Korea and World Affairs* 6, no. 4 (Winter 1982).

5. Golam W. Choudbury, *China in World Affairs* (Boulder, CO: Westview Press, 1982), pp. 236–237.

6. Ibid.

7. Quotes from *Beijing Review*, September 8, 1986. China has been consistent in condemning the Soviet invasion of Afghanistan. For a recent expression of Beijing's disapproval of the case, see *Beijing Review*, February 29–March 6, 1988.

8. *Peking Review*, November 5, 1965.

9. Li Shanoqu's speech at the Trade Union Conference held in Beijing in November 1949, cited in Arthur Stein, ed., *The International Position of Communist China* (New York: American Institute of Pacific Affairs, 1958), p. 11.

10. *New China News Agency*, November 6, 1951.

11. Van Ness, *Revolution and Chinese Foreign Policy: Peking's Support for Wars of National Liberation* (Berkeley: University of California Press, 1971), p. 139.

12. Chang Ha Kim, *The Immortal Juche Idea* (Pyongyang, FLPHA, 1984), p. 315.

13. Ibid., p. 139.

14. Refer to Table 5 of Han S. Park and Kyung A. Park, "Self-Reliance and National Security in the PRC and North Korea," in Edward Azar and Chang-in Moon, eds., *National Security in the Third World: The Management of Internal and External Threats* (College Park, MD, 1988), pp. 121, 123, 125, 128–129, 130–131.

15. Ibid., Tables 5 and 8.

16. Gregory F. T. Winn, "*Sohak*: North Korea's Joint Venture with Western Europe," in Jae Kyu Park, et al., eds., *The Foreign Relations of North Korea* (Seoul: Kyungnam University Press, 1987), p. 301.

17. *Beijing Review*, October 6,1986.

18. Chang Ha Kim, *The Immortal Juche Idea*, p. 317.

19. Ibid., p. 324.

20. *World Military Expenditure* (Washington, DC: U.S. Arms Control and Disarmament Agency, 1971 and 1985).

21. Jong Chun Paik, "Bukhan ui Kunsa Ryuk," in Jae Kyu Park, ed., *Bukhan ui Dae Wae Jung Chek* (Seoul: Kyungnam University Press, 1987).

22. Chang Ha Kim, *The Immortal Juche Idea*, p. 328.

23. Ibid., p. 327.

# 18
## Culture, Modernism, Postmodernism: A Challange to International Relations

Richard A. Falk

### THE CULTURAL FACTOR

As a discipline, international relations has generally neglected culture as relevant or appropriate to its concerns. The most influential forms of inquiry have analyzed interactions among states that rest upon power and wealth. The prevailing realist interpretations of international relations, even as softened by neorealist emendations, are preoccupied with issues of conflict and capabilities treated as matters of "security" or "political economy" on the basis of the primacy of sovereign state actors. Ideology is conceded to be a factor, but normally treated only as bearing on the motivation of political leaders at the state or bloc level, and as connected with their capacity to mobilize resources and to sustain morale and legitimacy in the face of defeat. Leadership, like ideology, is considered mainly in its role as a dimension of political strength that bears upon the power dynamics of relations among states. From Thucydides to Kissinger, the core inquiry of international relations theory examines how major political actors pursue their interests and ambitions given the absence of government, community, morality, or law at the international level. As a consequence, the history of international relations is dominated by wars and peace settlements.

Cultural variations and influences can be assimilated by such a realist understanding of international relations, but only in a restricted way. Different cultural legacies can be regarded as relevant to the internal and external effectiveness of a political actor, or as shaping the style of government and leadership. The ascendency of the West has often been explained in cultural terms associated with the liberation of reason from the grip of superstition and religion, a process traced back to ancient Athens. This process took several centuries to bear its full fruit. It was during the Renaissance that reason as the engine of societal innovation, principally by way of science and technology, generated a dynamic of accelerated development in the leading West European countries. That is, culture underpins differences in civilizational capabilities, especially if these capabilities are measured by the materialist criteria of progress associated with modernism. Yet, intangible criteria of fulfillment connected with social solidarity and a sense of personal well-being may be diminished by the very forms of efficiency required to produce material progress.[1]

Those who emphasize the cultural basis of political action often tend to regard the appropriate unit of analysis to be civilization rather than state.[2] As a consequence, cultural identity is more decisively associated with a nonterritorial notion like "the West" than with any particular territorial actor, although a continental country with an experience of its own, such as the United States, will have a strong, distinct version of Western civilization. To this extent, we can better understand why international relations with its interest in conflict among states will find it not useful to study cultural factors that seem to point toward the interplay of civilization. However, since civilizations, as such, rarely engage in warfare, their life story seems connected more with art and religion than with politics. It is a primary goal of this chapter to challenge such a conceptual tradition of foreclosure.

The framework of modernism associated with the rise of the West is the main intellectual background against which thought about international relations developed. As I have argued elsewhere, the transition from feudalism to modernism in the eleventh through the seventeenth century was expressed within the West by a shift in emphasis by jurists from natural law to legal positivism, that is, from a system of overarching principles and standards resting on revelation and authority to a system dependent upon the direct (treaty-making) or indirect (custom-making) expression of consent by territorial states, which became the exclusive category of the political actor entitled to full membership in international society.[3] In fact, despite the generalizing tendencies of international relations specialists, it seems evident that the early phases of statist diplomacy were an expression of European regional development. The globalist rhetoric was misleading in many respects, including its tendency to disguise patterns of interstate hegemony, especially as between Europe and the rest of the world.

Lurking within this Western cultural legacy, as nurtured and evolved over the centuries by dominant religious institutions and traditions, were several dangerous ideas that continue to exert powerful influences upon political consciousness. There was, above all, in this legacy a deeply embedded sense of "chosen people" as privileged vehicles of progress entitled to exert dominance by some underlying appointment that is then turned back to an original covenant between Yahweh and the Jewish people. However this biblical myth is interpreted, it provides a basis for both a cult of superiority and a mandate to impose one's cultural forms upon all those that resist, whether they are within territorial space (inquisitions) or without (holy wars). This symbolism based on the ravaging character of the evil other can be secularized. The evil that is to be eradicated has become godless communism or heartless capitalism in the opposed materialist calculus of values. The early emphases of religious heresy have given way, at least on a literal basis. Similarly the good may be the blessings of "democracy" or of "socialism," or the alternative ideas of "the market," and "property" versus state planning and socialism. Or, as has happened more recently, both ideologies can converge on a shared commitment to "modernization."

There is another side to this Western cultural heritage that is also embedded in its origins—a disposition to question and challenge authority. Going back to the Jewish prophets and Socrates, we notice in the West a tradition of thought that assigns a subversive role to individual conscience reason, and to moral passion as well. This sense of individual autonomy as a precious attribute of collective human experience has inspired the politics of the West at each principal stage of its evolution. It is evident in the rise of the common law of England as a restraint upon royal authority, in the central claims of constitutional order contained in the French and American Revolutions, especially as expressed through notions of the "inalienable rights" of citizens, and more recently, through the affirmation of welfare rights and, generally, by the gradual establishment of an elaborate framework of international human rights during the last several decades. The extension of criminal liability to German and Japanese leaders after World War II represented an official acknowledgment that the state cannot shield an individual from his responsibility to uphold international law. This experience was generalized in the form of the Nuremberg Principles, which bound all leaders to uphold international law on matters of war and peace. Subsequently, as a result of the interpretation given the Nuremberg Principles by many activists, a claim was posited to validate citizen resistance in the face of crimes of state, a process that has come to be known as the Nuremberg Obligation or a Nuremberg Action.[4]

In this century, the Western/modernist cultural frame has been split into two main historical streams since the Bolshevik Revolution of 1918. The civil war raging within the West on issues of class rule and property rights has accepted as common ground the central idea that the progress of human society depends upon the more and more efficient mobilization of productive forces. Marxism/Leninism carried the capitalist line of materialism a step further by centralizing authority within the socialist state, but attitudes toward growth and nature were indistinguishable. Both ideologies sought rapid and maximum economic growth and both ignored the externalities of industrialization. Both ideologies generated "realists" when it came to international relations, whether the language was that of capabilities analysis and balance of power or that of the correlation of forces. And both accepted the state as the fundamental political actor in international relations for the foreseeable future. In this sense, capitalism (or liberalism) and socialism (or Marxism) present the non-Western world with the two main faces of modernism as developed by Western civilization.[5]

This selective overview of the Western cultural legacy helps focus an initial set of generalizations about international relations as an account of the behavior of territorial sovereign states. First of all, there exists a suppressed tension between individual integrity and collective goals that becomes evident as soon as cultural factors are introduced. This tension works dialectically, and may help explain both the resilience and creativity of the West as a cultural space. The character of this tension arises from the societal interplay between expansionist drives that are implicit in cults of superiority and the critical backlash against unrighteous behavior that arises out of a cultural commitment to conscience and reason, and by these means, to affirm the place of the individual. In this regard, the Western role has been a contradictory one in relation to non-Western societies, both hegemonic and anti-hegemonic, transmitting as a result of its dominance the very ideas that can be reinterpreted to provide the normative foundation for resistance by those victimized. One small instance: children in North Vietnam were made to memorize the Declaration of Independence of 1776 despite the U.S. intervention because it was one of the inspirational sources of Ho Chi Minh's struggle against colonial rule.

Secondly, the West itself is not necessarily entrapped indefinitely within the modernist frame, as its underlying cultural experience antedoted the rise of the state system and seems capable of adapting to poststatal images of world order. At the same time, such a possibility must overcome the momentum of modernism, which is mainly responsible for directly various ecological and geopolitical threats to the viability of *any* form of planetary existence. Apologists for modernism, embattled now to offset the pressure of its limitations, are engaged in a massive exercise of deception and pacification, seeking utopian solutions ("Strategic Defense Initiatives") or relying on a heroic confidence that rationality within the modernist framework remains both necessary and sufficient, despite the assault of nuclearism, interdependence, and ecological decay.[6]

Thirdly, the non-Western forces of resistance have mounted a formidable challenge to Western hegemony on a political plane, but less so on an economic plane. The anticolonial struggle has involved an extraordinary movement in history that was made possible by the potency of various movements of nationalist resistance. Almost everywhere this process has achieved formal independence and a status entitling participation as a full-fledged member of international society (symbolized by access to the United Nations). Almost nowhere has this process of resistance been able to wrest control from the West on matters of economic policy— multinational corporations and banks, as well as various forms of in- debtedness, accountability to international financial institutions, and cur- rency dependence, have sustained an overall pattern of Western economic hegemony. There are, of course, partial challenges to this perpetuation of external control, arising from socialist forms of nationalism and from several prominent instances of successful appropriations of Western technique and practice (Japan, newly industrialized countries—the so- called NICs). That is, there are degrees of economic independence, but the more successful examples, whether capitalist or socialist, seem depen- dent on a cultural adoption of modernism, that is, the Western cultural stance toward reason, science, and technology. This adoption is explicit in the case of capitalist countries, and in later developments, several socialist countries, most notably post-Mao China (with its "four moder- nizations") affirm their modernism more than their socialism.

A different sort of challenge to Western hegemony has been mounted by the Islamic Revolution, and other forms of fundamentalism in the Islamic world. Again, the definition of what is Western is in issue, as Islam arises out of the Judeo-Christian experience, and contains and extends monotheistic claims of assured truth and divine mandate to a particular anointed fraction of humanity. Yet the Islamic world has never adopted the modernist path with any great success; the recent experiences of disaster in the Shah's Iran and Sadat's Egypt suggest how treacherous is an unabashed turning West for cultural inspiration. In this respect, the fundamentalist and traditionalist backlash, by its intensity and reliance upon indigenous culture as a shield against modernist penetration, is a more thoroughgoing repudiation of the colonial experience than ex- perienced by secular politics, even of a radical character. Insisting on tradi- tional dress, disallowing Western music, and some delinking from the world economy carry the drive to self-determination quite far, but not necessarily in a sustainable fashion, or in a manner that is popular or beneficial for the people. To stand apart from modernism often means to be cut off from capital, technology, and markets, and this has meant an inability to address the reality of mass misery. An unabashed recourse to traditionalism can lead to gross abuses of human rights and to the denial of any democratic prospect.

What seems evident is that a strong cultural identity can play a vital role in securing the full independence of non-Western countries in the postcolonial period, but not necessarily in a beneficial fashion, at least as measured by widely shared international standards of human rights and democracy. Similarly, effective restraints upon repressive elements of tradition can create a cultural vacuum that opens up a country to easy penetration, including the crude reimposition of Western "rule." The response of "culture" to the weight of international relations is vividly illustrated by the various phases of Iran's history since World War II.

To elaborate upon the perspective here as to the relevance of culture to the future of international relations, the subsequent sections of this chapter explore modernism as a cultural vehicle for the hegemonic project of the West and then consider two interrelated forms of possible alternative development: first, a postmodern Western sequel, and second, a series of antimodern enclaves of resistance.[7]

## THE RESILIENCE OF MODERNISM

Regarding the civilization unit as more critical to the contours of cultural identity than the sovereign state causes some confusion for the interpretation of international relations (i.e., relations among sovereign states). Yet the confusion is unavoidable. States can act as vehicles for the spread of culture outside the civilizational unit, and are undoubtedly the most important actors in many non-Western civilizations. In the case of Western civilization, its own internal dynamic led to the formation of strong territorial states as the principal political actor. Beyond this, the state became the guardian of an emergent industrial capitalism that contributed to the overseas drive to obtain and protect markets, resources, and investment outlets. This drive was, also, a moving force behind the colonial experience, leading the West to provide an anchor for the first phase of a global political order initially managed from Europe. Postcolonial arrangements have shattered the political dimensions, and, arguably, its ideational dimensions as well.

This Western hegemony is now based on predominance in relation to capital and technology, as well as upon the dissemination of information and aspirational imagery. The multinational corporation, transnational bank, and the transnational news agency are each manifestations of this global order that is based on Western culture, and seem likely to persist. Non-Western countries have shaped their own plans and ambitions by reference to a Western image of already realized modernization, which includes an expanded middle class and a variety of consumer goods. The meaning of life is overwhelmingly associated with material satisfactions and notions of collective gain derived from economic growth as an overall indicator of "progress." Technology makes this modernist worldview plausible, apparently providing ever-new possibilities to extract more from nature for less.

Further, the cultural artifacts of the West have been widely interpreted around the world as literal embodiments of modernism, especially of the United States, which provided the earliest and most spectacular success story, are often spontaneously adopted by local people to hasten the advent of a future with which they identify. The spread of jeans and rock music, of fast food chains and discos, of Holiday Inns and Hilton Hotels, illustrate the missionary penetration of non-Western countries of globally packaged Western orientation. In such a normative atmosphere, those states in the Third World that build rapidly expanding middle-class markets and industrial sectors, are looked upon as "successful," and those that are unable to do so are viewed as "failures." From the perspective of modernist culture, it is less important to assess ecological and demographic pressures, protection of human rights and democracy, and signs of happiness and social integration. Here, the Trilateral countries of North America, Europe, and Japan provide some negative imagery. The United States is the most modernist country, but also, arguably, the one responsible for the greatest density of social distress (crime, suicide, divorce), militarism, and ecological decay.

Yet the darker sides of modernism do not mean that the cultural energy underlying this vision of the future is as yet a spent force. Within modernism are a variety of "checks" designed to avoid its excesses from producing catastrophe. Technology can be deployed on behalf of environmental protection, peace and justice, even human rights. The efforts to halt reliance on chlorofluorocarbons (CFCs) is illustrative—governments seek to respond by imposing restraints that are essentially dependent on voluntary compliance and some of the most flagrant commercial uses are being phased out by voluntary cutbacks beyond what is mandated by treaty because in this setting benign substitutes that are commercially viable have been developed. Materialism can also be softened by religious revival, artistic activity, and societal initiatives. Whether these checks are by themselves sufficient to reverse destructive trends seems doubtful at this stage of history.

In the 1970s the publication of such studies as *The Limits to Growth* and *Blueprint for Survival* represented strident warnings about the sustainability of modernist reliance on growth for progress.[8] These studies argued that there were limits on population density, arable land, capacity to absorb pollution, resource stocks, and that available data showed that these limits were being approached at an accelerating and alarming rate. Apologists for modernism emerged to reassure the West and the world that pessimistic assessments were overgrown and premature, that growth could go on indefinitely, especially if self-evident prudent regulatory steps were taken. Also, it was contended, automatic market adjustments by way of costs would turn behavior in a desirable direction long before the onset of catastrophe. Indeed, the alleged prophets of doom had overplayed their hands on a literal level. The world system was more resilient than they had anticipated, but more threatened than reassuring voices believed.

The 1980s have seen, in turn, a discrediting of the open-ended apologists. A new wave of concerns, often reinforced by authoritative scientific studies, on "nuclear winter," ozone depletion, greenhouse effect, acid rain, ocean pollution, desertification, deforestation, water shortages, demographic pressures, have reintroduced the notion of sustainability of modernist life forms into the political sensibility. There is a less alarmist concern about the ecological future of the human species in the 1980s, but there also appears to be a current sense of resignation, that the process of disintegration has gone too far and that the green social forces needed to build a sustainable future are not serious contenders for power.[9] Unlike the first wave of ecological concern in the 1970s, there is neither dissent, nor as yet, any serious prescription for adjustment. The mainstream political leaders have apparently reached tacit agreements to ignore this crisis agenda of planetary management, and to concentrate their rivalry on matters of local environmental issues, and concentrate on the best tactics for addressing the traditional agenda of national security and economic policy issues.

Here, then, is the central relevance of culture to the main world order challenge facing human society—industrializing, growth-oriented, technology-based modernism has shaped the world economy, mainly in a market-directed fashion. This orientation also has championed the formation of strong territorial states as a means of reconciling nationalism with aspirations for economic development. Modernism, in this regard, is preoccupied with harnessing productive forces. It is insensitive to limits imposed by nature whether organized around the guiding ideas of Adam Smith or those of Karl Marx.

Can this legacy of modernism be overcome or decisively redirected over the course of the next several decades? The adaptive potential of modernism seems far less than necessary to address the magnitude of the challenges facing organized societies around the world or menacing the system taken as a whole. Is there a postmodern possibility? Prior to offering a response, a brief discussion of society-scale responses to modernism in the Third World, let us look at traditionalist repudiations of modernism and some consideration of the resources of non-Western cultures that provide partial alternative patterns of action to modernism.

## TRADITIONALIST REVIVAL AND THE ROLE OF NON-WESTERN CULTURE

As suggested, the Iranian repudiation of modernism was bound up with a rejection of Western culture as brought to Iran in a particularly corrupt and deformed manner by the Shah. The association of the United States's fundamentalism with good, suggested one path by which to escape from Western cultural hegemony, at least temporarily. Only Islam, as revived by a charismatic figure, has seemed strong enough to enable a society to overcome the combined weight of Western political, economic, and cultural weight, and even this deviation from modernism, may turn out to be temporary.

In the post-colonial era of international relations, opening up too quickly to the West can lead to a cultural backlash, especially among Islamic countries. Sadat's move to the West, by way of an accommodation with Israel, through attracting foreign capital and corporations, and by embodying a Western life-style provoked a reaction that included regional alienation, domestic unpopularity, and an unmourned death following a political assassination carried out by fundamentalists.

Whether traditionalism is a viable alternative to Western hegemony even in the Islamic world is by no means established. It is a strong force, especially in the hands of an efficient and ruthless ruler. Yet, by itself, it provides no basis for development, for meeting basic human needs, for providing human rights and democracy. Its emphasis can be negative, a descent into a form of pre- or antimodern darkness.

Possibly, in a subsequent stage, an integration of Western technique and indigenous cultural worldviews can produce a viable basis of action in the world. Arguably, such an integration has occurred to an impressive degree, yet in a variety of forms, in several Asian countries—where modernism has built upon rather than displaced Confucian, and even Buddhist, traditions. From the perspectives of international relations, this kind of integration may contribute a new emphasis on the mediation of conflict. China has exhibited, for instance, such creativity in recent years, possibly most fully in working out a model for the future of Hong Kong that allows the dynamic of decolonization to proceed without rupturing the internal structure of this model of Oriental prosperity premised on liberalism and market economics. To an uncertain and controversial extent, China has relied on its traditional cultural emphasis on harmony, rational leadership, moderation, and unity to work toward a demographic policy that brings resources and population into a manageable balance. In contrast, the more individualistic and communal bias of Hindu culture denies India such an option. Culture matters in establishing limits and options in state/society relations, and these relations are of utmost relevance to participation in regional and global politics. The war system thrives on internal discontent, governmental incapacity. Culture can be either a valuable resource or a formidable obstacle in relation to conflict-resolving and conflict-transforming solutions; this variance is not fixed, but contextual. That is, if the priority is a large-scale common, practical solution, then Confucian cultural forms, especially as evolved in Chinese thought and action, are well-adapted. Yet if the priority is democratic practice and individual, then Confucianism is ill adapted and Hinduism well adapted. Although such a generalization is grossly oversimplified, it does hold up to a superficial extent. With the brief, confirming exception of the Emergency, India has sustained democracy and human rights since independence, but has had almost no success with respect to its attempt to provide centralized, state-initiated solutions for population pressure, poverty, or communal strife. China has had remarkable success in providing unified leadership, especially of a sort that called for moderation and harmony, but almost no positive results from its democratization campaigns. The stability of Marxist-Leninist governance in several Asian countries can also be partially attributed to their Confucian background, and incidentally, the most turbulent experience in recent Asian history arose from the Maoist excesses of the Cultural Revolution which included a harsh repudiation of Confucian, that is, traditional cultural identities.

In sum, international relations reflects the character of leading sovereign states, which in turn incorporate variants of a small number of world civilizational traditions. These states in the postcolonial period cannot operate successfully unless they nourish their cultural roots. These roots influence the choice of governing and developmental options. Each cultural tradition has a wide range of alternatives that are authentic expressions. Islam can support more democratic, developmental paths, and the potency of the fundamentalist path may be a temporary overreaction to a failure by more moderate forms of Islam to prevent destructive varieties of cultural penetration by the West. Confucian China and Hindu India, while penetrated and corrupted at the periphery of their societal existences by the West, retained the integrity of their core experiences.

What seems evident is that an appropriate cultural ground for a strong sense of identity is indispensable for constructive participation in international relations. The converse is also convincing. A repudiation of cultural identity disrupts civil society, and produces turbulent results that generate violence and discontent at home and abroad. Although this discussion has concerned non-Western societies, it pertains with almost equal force to the more backward parts of the West itself as the postwar experience of Poland so painfully exemplifies—the imposition by virtue of foreign military occupation of a Marxist-oriented modernism disrupted Poland's societal belief system, which was centered upon traditionalist Catholic experience. Of course, noncultural factors contributed to a collective mood of resistance, including the Soviet imperial encroachment and the bureaucratic ineptitude of the Polish Communist party officialdom.

## THE POSTMODERN POSSIBILITY

There are reasons to question reliance on postmodernism as a term. Everything from fashion to deconstructive literary criticism has been dubbed "postmodern." In many of these settings postmodern is conceived, above all, as a sequel and reaction to something earlier that was called "modern." Here, too, there is a modernist conception of a state-centric, industrializing world system that is being challenged by a set of emergent alternatives. These possibilities remain too preliminary to name in some definitive manner. To designate these possibilities as postmodern there is implied a potentially coherent reaction and sequel to the modern, but unformed as yet.

At present, it is mainly the consequence of the globalization of Western cultural influences, including its commitment to modernization, that has produced a world order crisis of multiple dimensions: nuclearism, industrialism, materialism, consumerism. Whether the issue is ozone depletion, greenhouse effect, oceanic or atmospheric pollution, ionized radiation, the main causative agents have been evolved and their use concentrated in Western countries, especially the United States. True, this Western pattern of development has been enthusiastically adopted by most of the non-Western world in the postcolonial period. Available methods of interstate cooperation to mitigate the detrimental effects of modernism, whether through treaty standards or institutional arrangement characteristically lack serious coercive mechanisms, and rarely challenge entrenched economic interests. Reliance is placed on moral suasion and voluntary patterns of compliance if a form of regulation can be agreed upon; without the willing participation and consent of the offending state(s), there is virtually no capability to protect the global public interest.

The ascendency of modernism cannot be overcome without underlying shifts in values, beliefs, and guiding myths, that is, without cultural change. Initiatives within oppositional sectors of civil society have prefigured a series of alternative cultural orientations that tend to be nonviolent in their approach to conflict; eco-alert in relation to resources, environmental quality, and developmental tactics; and austere or spiritual in their approach to human fulfillment. These initiatives take a variety of forms that can be partially enumerated:

- *green politics* with its emphasis on environment, peace, democracy, human rights;
- *feminism* with its emphasis on changing the forms and structures of power at all levels of social organization, as well as its insistence on altering the distinction between private and public space;
- *indigenous peoples movements* with their emphasis on a holistic worldview in which sustaining nature provides the ethical foundation for productive life;
- *environmental transnationalism* with its emphasis on protecting endangered species (whales), animal rights, natural heritage (Antarctica, rain forests) in defiance of modernist and statist encroachments; the outlook, priorities, and tactics of Greenpeace are exemplary;
- *communities of resistance* with their emphasis on nonviolent and religiously grounded adherence to standards and norms that take precedence over the authority of the state; the activities of Christian based communities are exemplary

whether the cause involves the redistribution of wealth for the sake of the poor or antimilitarism and antinuclearism for the sake of world peace;

- *transnational populism* with its emphasis on the rights of peoples to challenge the encroachments of modernism without regard to territorial identities, acknowledging that everyone has a state-transcending right to oppose nuclearism or activities that threaten planetary well-being.

These initiatives are difficult to assess. In each category there is considerable variance, and often there are sharp tensions over whether to emphasize short-term reform or longer-term visionary objectives. Do they provide any serious challenge to the most threatening manifestations of modernism? Can they alter the climate of governance sufficiently to shift priorities and behavioral patterns without requiring a revolutionary process? Are these initiatives building toward a new transnational politics that will remake international relations? Are these initiatives best regarded as a series of explorations that are testing the room for maneuver within modernism?

Of course, the future of international relations will be shaped by many other factors as well. The resilience of modernism is evident in such settings as regional integration, regulation of the seas, patterns of consultation relative to financial markets, arms control negotiations, and the activities of international institutions. It is impossible to tell at this stage whether this resilience, together with the cumulative effects of the postmodern challenge, will provide the existing corps leaders with a format for policy that can sustain conditions for life and well-being on the planet over the course of the next several decades.

## NOTES

1. A strong argument along these lines is contained in Stanley Diamond, *In Search of the Primitive* (New Brunswick, NJ: Transaction, 1974).

2. Arnold J. Toynbee, *A Study of History*, 2 Vols. (New York: Oxford, 1934), Vol. 1.

3. See Richard A. Falk, "The Grotian Quest" and "A New Paradigm for International Legal Studies," in Falk, Friedrich Kratochwil, and Saul H. Mendlovitz, eds., *International Law: A Contemporary Perspective* (Boulder, CO: Westview, 1985), pp. 36–42, 651–702.

4. For background relating to the assertion of Nuremberg claims in domestic courts see Francis Anthony Boyle, *Defending Civil Resistance Under International Law* (Dobbs Ferry, NY: Transaction, 1987).

5. Of course, there are many variations of expression on these two main "faces" of modernism, but the commitment to a materialist conception of individual and collective fulfillment provides the consistent element of identity.

6. On the specific concerns of nuclearism, the most revealing treatment is probably that of Joseph Nye *Nuclear Ethics* (New York: Free Press, 1983); on the broader

themes of reassurance about modernism see the influential book, Herman Kahn and Anthony J. Wiener, *The Year 2000: A Framework for Speculation on the Next Thirty-Three Years* (New York: Macmillan, 1967); compare also Zbigniew Brzezinski, *Between Two Ages: America's Role in the Technetronic Age* (New York: Viking, 1970).

7. These are not the only paths to the future. Cultural pluralism, non-Western forms of post modernism, and relapses into various types of anarchy are also possible.

8. Compare Donella Meadows and others, *The Limits to Growth* (New York: Universe Books, 1972); Edward T. Goldsmith and others, *Blueprint for Survival* (Boston, MA: Houghton Mifflin, 1972); my own analysis in this period is contained in *This Endangered Planet* (New York: Random House, 1972); see also Robert L. Heilbroner, *An Inquiry into the Human Prospect* (New York: Norton, 1974).

9. For a fictionalized interpretation to this effect see Günter Grass, *The Rat*, trans. Ralph Manheim (New York: Knopf, 1987).

# Bibliography

Alexandroff, Alan, Richard Rosencrance, and Arthur Stein. "History, Quantitative Analysis, and the Balance of Power." *Journal of Conflict Resolution* 21 (1977): 35–56.

Almond, Gabriel A. and Sidney Verba, eds. *The Civil Culture Revisited*. Boston: Little, Brown, and Company, 1980.

Anderson, Charles W. *Politics and Economic Change in Latin America: The Governing of Restless Nations*. Princeton, NJ: D. Van Nostrand Company, Inc., 1967.

Azar, Edward E., and Chung-in Moon. "Islamic Revivalist Movements; Patterns, Causes, and Prospects." *Journal of East and West Studies* 13. (Spring–Summer 1983): 79–109.

Betz, Hans Dieter. *Essays on the Sermon on the Mount*. Philadelphia: Fortress Press, 1985.

Cohen, Ronald. "Warfare and State Formation: Wars Make States and States Make Wars." In *Warfare, Culture and Environment*, pp. 329–358. Edited by R. Brian Ferguson. Orlando, FL: Academic Press, 1984.

———. "War and the War-Proneness in Pre- and Post-industrial States." In *Peace and War; Cross-Cultural Perspectives*, pp. 253–268. Lecron Foster and Robert A. Rubinstein, eds. New Brunswick, NJ: Transaction Books, 1986.

Dallek, Robert. *The American Style of Foreign Policy: Cultural Politics and Foreign Affairs*. New York: Knopf, 1983.

Davidson, W. Phillips. *International Political Communication*. New York: Praeger, 1965.

Dealy, Glen. *The Public Man: An Interpretation of Latin American and Other Catholic Countries*. Amherst: The University of Massachusetts Press, 1977.

Dessouki, Ali E. H., ed. *Islamic Resurgence in the Arab World*. New York: Praeger, 1982.

Deutsch, Karl W. *Nationalism and Social Communication*. Cambridge: Massachusetts Institute of Technology Press, 1953.

Donakowski, Conrad. *A Muse for the Masses: Ritual and Music in an Age of Democratic Revolution, 1770–1870*. Chicago: University of Chicago Press, 1977.

Etzkorn, K. Peter, ed. *Music and Society: The Later Writings of Paul Honigsheim*. New York: Wiley, 1973.

Fairbank, John K. "Tributary Trade in China's Relations with the West." *Far Eastern Quarterly* I (1942).

Falk, Richard and Samuel S. Kim, eds. *The War System: An Interdisciplinary Approach*. Boulder, CO: Westview Press, 1980.

Fenlon, Iain. *Music and Patronage in Sixteenth-Century Mantua*, vol. 1. Cambridge, MA: Cambridge University Press, 1980.

Ferguson, Mary LeCron and Robert A. Rubinstein, eds. *Peace and War; Cross-Cultural Perspectives*. New Brunswick, NJ: Transaction Books, 1986.

Fried, Morton; Marvin Harris; and Robert F. Murphy, eds. *War: The Anthropology of Armed Conflict and Aggression*. Garden City, NY: Natural History Press, 1967.

Gandhi, Mahatma. *All Man are Equal*, Krishna Kripalni, ed. New York: Continuum Press, 1982.

Geertz, Clifford. *The Interpretation of Cultures*. New York: Basic Books, 1973.

George Alexander L. and Richard Smoker. *Deterrence in American Foreign Policy: Theory and Practice*. New York: Columbia University Press, 1974.

Giannone, Richard. *Vonnegut: A Preface to His Novels*. Port Washington, NY: Kennikat, 1977.

Givens, R. Dale and Martin Nettleship, eds. *Discussion on War and Human Aggression*. The Hague: Mouton, 1976.

Glossop, Ronald, J. *Confronting War*. London: McFarland, 1983.

Griffith, W. E. "The Revival of Islamic Fundamentalism: The Case of Iran." *International Security* 4 (Summer 1981): 132–138.

Gudykunst, Bill, ed. *Intercultural Communication Theory: Current Perspectives*. Beverly Hills, CA: Sage Publications, 1983.

Haas, Michael. "The 'Asian Way' to Peace." *Pacific Community* IV (1973).

———., ed. *International Systems*. San Francisco, CA: Chandler, 1974.

Hafkin, Nancy J. and Edna G. Bay, eds. *Women in Africa: Studies in Social and Economic Change*. Stanford, CA: Stanford University Press, 1976.

Harnack, Adolf von. *History of Dogma*, Vols. 1 and 2. New York: Dover Publications, 1961.

Harris, Louis K., and Victor Alba. *The Political Culture and Behavior of Latin America*. Kent, OH: Kent State University Press, 1974.

Hatch, Elvin. *Morality and Culture*. New York: Columbia University Press, 1984.

Hellman, Ronald G. and H. Jon Rosenbaum, eds. *Latin America: The Search for a New International Role*. New York: John Wiley and Sons, 1975.

Henze, Hans Werner. *Music and Politics: Collected Writings, 1953–81*. Translated by Peter Labanyi. London: Faber and Faber, 1982.

Hogwood, Christopher. *Music at Court*. London: Victor Gollancz, 1980.

Holsti, Ole R. "Historians, Social Scientists, and Crisis Management; Alternative Views." *Journal of Conflict Resolution* 24(1980): 665–682.

Homberger, Eric. "United States." *The Second World War In Fiction*. London: Macmillan, 1984.

Howe, K. R. *Where the Waves Fall*. Honolulu: University of Hawaii Press. 1984.

Hsu, Francis L. K. *Americans and Chinese: Reflections on Two Cultures and Their Peoples*. Garden City, NY: Doubleday, 1970; American Museum Science Books ed., 1972.

Hunt, Michael H. *Ideology and U.S. Foreign Policy*. New Haven, CT: Yale University Press, 1987.

Ibrahim, Saad E. "Anatomy of Egypt's Militant Islamic Groups." *International Journal of Middle East Studies* 12 (December 1980): 423–453.

Jansen, G. H. *Militant Islam*. New York: Harper & Row, 1979.

Johnson, James Turner. *Can Modern War Be Just?* New Haven, CT: Yale University Press, 1984.

_____ . *Just War Tradition and the Restraint of War*. Princeton, NJ: Princeton University Press, 1981.

Jones, Peter G. *War and the Novelist: Appraising the American War Novel*. Columbia: University of Missouri, 1976.

Kasemann, Ernst. *Perspectives on Paul*. Philadelphia, PA: Fortress Press, 1969.

Kelman, Herbert C., ed. *International Behavior*. New York: Holt, Rinehart, and Winston, 1965.

Kepel, Gillis. *Muslim Extremism in Egypt. The Prophet and the Pharaoh*. Berkeley: University of California Press, 1986.

Khadduri, Majid. *War and Peace in the Law of Islam*. Baltimore, MD: Johns Hopkins Press, 1955.

Lasch, Christopher. *The Culture of Narcissism: American Life in an Age of Diminishing Expectations*. New York: W. W Norton, 1978.

Lasswell, Harold. *Power and Personality*. New York: W. W. Norton, 1948; Viking Press, 1962.

Lauren, Paul Gordon. "Diplomacy: History, Theory, and Policy." In *Diplomacy; New Approaches in History, Theory, and Policy*, pp. 3–18. Edited by P. G. Lauren. New York: Free Press, 1979.

Lincoln, Jenny K., and Elizabeth G. Ferris, eds. *The Dynamics of Latin American Foreign Policies*. Boulder, CO: Westview Press, 1984.

Merelman, Richard M. *Making Something of Ourselves: On Culture and Politics in the United States*. Berkeley: University of California Press, 1984.

McGiffert, Arthur Cushman. *A History of Christian Thought*. Vol. 1. New York: C. Scribner's Sons, 1932.

Mowlana, Hamid. *Global Information and World Communication: New Frontiers in International Relations*. White Plains, NY: Longman, 1986.

Munoz, Heraldo, and Joseph S. Tulchin, eds. *Latin American Nations in World Politics*. Boulder, CO: Westview Press, 1984.

Murray, John Courtney. *Morality and Modern War*. New York: Council on Religion and International Affairs, 1959.

Nettl, Paul. *National Anthems*. 2nd enlarged ed. Translated by Alexander Gode. New York: Frederick Ungar, 1967.

Ninkovich, Frank. "The Trajectory of Cultural Internationalism." In *Educational Exchanges: Essays on the Sino-American Experience*. Joyce K. Kallgren and Dennis Fred Simon, eds. Berkeley: University of California Press, 1987.

O'Brien, William V. *The Conduct of Just and Limited War*. New York: Praeger Publishers, 1981.

Ogburn, William F. *On Culture and Social Change*. Chicago: University of Chicago Press, 1964.

Otterbein, Keith. "The Anthropology of War." In *Handbook of Social and Cultural Anthropology*. pp. 923–958. John Honigmann, ed. Chicago: Rand McNally College Publishing, 1973.

————. *The Evolution of War; A Cross-Cultural Study*, 2nd ed. New Haven, CT: HRAF Press, 1985.

Phillips, Robert L. *War and Justice*. Norman: University of Oklahoma Press, 1984.

Ramsey, Paul. *The Just War*. New York: Charles Scribner's Sons, 1968.

Schroder, Paul W. "Quantitative Studies in the Balance of Power." *Journal of Conflict Resolution* 21(1977): 3–22.

Small, Christopher. *Music—Society—Education*. 2nd rev. ed. London: John Calder, 1980.

Small, Melvin. "The Quantification of Diplomatic History." In *Diplomacy; New Approaches in History, Theory, and Policy*, pp. 69–96. Edited by P. G. Lauren. New York: Free Press, 1979.

Talbott, Strobe. *The Russians and Reagan*. New York: Vintage Books, 1984.

Tibi, Bassam. "The Renewed Role of Islam in the Political Social Development of the Middle East." *The Middle East Journal* 37 (Winter 1983): 3–13.

Thomson, James C. Jr.; Peter W. Stanley; and John Curtis Perry. *Sentimental Imperialists: The American Experience in East Asia*. New York: Harper & Row, 1981; Harper Colophon, 1982.

Veliz, Claudio. *The Centralist Tradition of Latin America*. Princeton: Princeton University Press, 1979.

Walcutt, Charles Child. *American Literary Naturalism, A Divided Stream*. Westport, CT: Greenwood, 1956.

Waldhorn, Arthur. *A Reader's Guide to Ernest Hemingway*. New York: Farrar, Straus and Giroux, 1972.

Walker, R. B. J., ed. *Culture, Ideology, and World Order*. Boulder, CO: Westview Press, 1984.

Wallis, Roger, and Krister Malm. *Big Sounds from Small Peoples: The Music Industry in Small Countries*. New York: Pendragon Press, 1984.

Walzer, Michael. *Just and Unjust Wars*. New York: Basic Books, 1977.

White, Ralph, ed. *Psychology and Presentation of Nuclear War*. New York: Free Press, 1986.

Wiarda, Howard J., ed. *Politics and Social Change in Latin America: The Distinct Tradition*. 2nd ed. Amherst: The University of Massachusetts Press, 1982.

# *Index*

# About the Editor and Contributors

JONGSUK CHAY is Professor of History at Pembroke State University. He received his undergraduate and graduate education at The University of Michigan. He is the editor or coeditor of *Problems and Prospects of American-East Asian Relations* (1987), *U.S.-Korean Relations, 1882–1982* (1982), and *The Buffer States in World Politics* (1987) and the autor of *A Symmetrical Diplomacy: Korean-American Relations to 1910* (1990) and a number of scholarly articles and chapters on American-East Asian Relations, American foreign policy, and international relations. His current research focuses on Korean-American relations in the post-World War II era.

ROLAND H. EBEL teaches Political Science at Tulane University where he specializes in Latin American politics. A Michigan State University Ph.D., he has taught at Wheaton College, Oakland University and Western Michigan University. The editor of three books, his articles have been published in Colombia, Argentina, El Salvador, Guatemala and Costa Rica as well as in the United States. He is also the author of *Political Modernization in Three Guatemalan Indian Communities*. Dr. Ebel has just completed a study (with Raymond Taras) of the impact of political culture on Latin American international behavior and is also working on studies of the regimes of presidents Miguel Ydigoras Fuentes and Vinicio Cerezo Arevalo of Guatemala.

RICHARD A. FALK is Albert G. Milbank Professor of International Law and Practice at Princeton University. His most recent books are *Revitalizing International Law* (1989) and *Revolutionaries and Functionaries: The Dual Face of Terrorism* (1988).

JOHAN GALTUNG is at present Professor of Peace Studies, University of Hawaii, Manoa; and Professor of Social Sciences at the Universität

Witten-Herdecke in Germany. Born in Norway in 1930 he founded the International Peace Research Institute in Oslo in 1959 and the Journal of Peace Research in 1964, and is regarded as one of the founders of modern peace studies. He is the author of forty books, among them *Essays in Peace Research*, Vols. I-VI (Copenhagen, Oslo, 1974–88) and more than one thousand articles on peace and development problems and social science theory and methodology. Dr. Galtung's current interests are in the field of civilization theory and the bearing of civilizational codes on peace and development.

JEFFERY L. GELLER is a Professor of Philosophy at Pembroke State University. A Duke University Ph.D., he also did graduate work at Oxford University and at the Frieie Universität Berlin. He received a Fulbright Fellowship to lecture at the National University of Singapore in 1989–1990. His publications include journal articles on subjects ranging from Wittgenstein and Freud to political philosophy.

MICHAEL HAAS, Professor of Political Science, University of Hawaii at Manoa, is the author of *Approaches to the Study of Political Science, International Conflict, International Organization, International Systems,* and three recent books by Praeger—*Korean Reunification: Alternative Pathways* (1989), *The Pacific Way: Regional Cooperation in the South Pacific* (1989), and *The Asian Way to Peace: A Story of Regional Cooperation* (1989). He makes frequent trips to Southeast Asia and was a member of the US-Indochina Reconciliation Team in August 1988. He earned his Ph.D. from Stanford University.

HASSAN BAKR A. HASSAN is an Assistant Professor of Political Science, Faculty of Commerce, University of Assiut, Egypt. He holds a B.S. and M.S. from Cairo University, M.A. and Ph.D. degrees from University of Maryland. Dr. Hassan taught at the Egyptian Military Academy and the Ministry of Education in Egypt before holding his current position. He has worked as a research assistant at the Center for Strategic and Political Studies and at the Institute of Arab Studies in Cairo, Egypt. He is the co-author of three books and the author of more than thirty journal articles on negotiations, protracted social conflicts, East-West relations, Middle East politics, Islamic revivalism, conflict management and conflict resolution.

RICK HERRICK is former Associate Professor of Political Science at Pembroke State University and is currently a visiting professor of the Interdisciplinary Studies at Appalachian State University. He is the founder/publisher of *Quality Life* and the author of numerous articles in scholarly journals and other magazines on international relations and other human affairs.

ESTELLE JORGENSEN is Professor of Music at the School of Music, Indiana University, Bloomington, where she teaches courses in the historical, philosophical, and curricular foundations of music education, sociology of music, and college music teaching. Professor Jorgensen has a B.A. (Hans.) Dip. Ed. from the University of Newcastle, N.S.W., Aushatia, M.M. in music education from Andrew University, Michigan, and PH.D. in educational administration from the University of Calgary, Canada. Prior to taking her position at Indiana University, she was on the Faculty of Music, McGill University, Montreal, where she also chaired the School music department (1977–1982). Professor Jorgensen has authored numerous articles in music education and is presently preparing a monograph on the socialization process in music.

THOMAS J. LEACH is Professor and Chair of the Communicative Arts Department at Pembroke State University. He has a B.S. from the U.S. Naval Academy and M.A. and Ph.D. degrees from the University of North Carolina, Chapel Hill. He is the author of articles on Carl Jung, Herman Hesse, James Joyce, and Gary Snyder. He is a Contributing Editor for *Quality Living*. His primary research interests are myth and consciousness.

JOHN P. LOVELL is Professor of Political Science, Indiana University, is Director of the new multidisciplinary Indiana Center on Global Change and World Peace. He received his M.A. and Ph.D. degrees from the University of Wisconsin. His books include *The Challenge of American Foreign Policy: Purpose and Adaptation* (1985), *Neither Athens Nor Sparta? The American Service Academies in Transition* (1979), and three other authored or edited works. He is the author of numerous articles and chapters on civil-military relations in the United States and in East Asia, on national security, and on organizational culture and learning. His current research focuses on American alliance commitments and on organizational culture and policy learning.

ALI A. MAZRUI received his graduate education at Oxford University and is currently Professor of Political Science at The University of Michigan and Andrew D. White Professor-at-Large at Cornell University. He is also the director of the Center for Afro-American and African Studies, The University of Michigan. He has numerous publications on African studies, peace studies, and international relations.

HAMID MOWLANA is Professor of International Relations and Director of the International Communication Program at the School of International Service, The American University, Washington, D.C. He received his Ph.D. from Northwestern University and has been a visiting professor in England, Argentina, Japan, Egypt, Nigeria and Iran. He has written widely on international relations and international communication and is the author of numerous publications, among them *Global Information and World Communication: New Frontiers in International Relations* (1986). He is vice president of the International Association for Mass Communication Research, and the past president of its International Communication Section.

FRANK NINKOVICH is Professor of History at St. John's University in New York City. He became interested in the cultural aspects of foreign policy while studying at the University of Chicago under Akira Iriye, where in 1978 he graduated with a Ph.D. in U.S. diplomatic history. His publications include two books, *The Diplomacy of Ideas: U.S. Foreign Policy and Cultural Relations 1938–1950* (1981) and *Germany and the United States: The Transformation of the German Question Since 1945* (1987), as well as numerous journal articles. He is now at work on a history that will trace the relationship of conceptions of civilization and power in American diplomacy since 1900.

HAN-SIK PARK is a Professor of Political Science at the University of Georgia. He received a Ph.D. in Political Science from the University of Minnesota. He was a Visiting Professor at the Graduate Institute of Peace Studies, Kyung Hee University (1989) and Seoul National University (1987) in Korea. He has taught and published in a wide range of areas such as human rights policies, comparative politics, and East Asian political systems. He is the author or co-author of numerous books, journal articles, and book chapters including *Human Needs* and *Political Development* (1984) and *Political Development in China and North Korea* (1989).

RAYMOND TARAS is Associate Professor of Political Science, Tulane University. He is the author of *Ideology in a Socialist State* (Cambridge University Press, 1984), *Poland: Socialist State, Rebellious Nation* (Westview Press, 1986), coauthor of *Le debat linquistique au Quebec* (Presses de l'Universite de Montreal, 1987), and editor of *Leadership Change in Communist States* (Unwin Hyman, 1989). His present research focuses on political culture and foreign policy in the circum-Caribbean.

KENNETH W. THOMPSON is Director of the White Burkett Miller Center of Public Affairs at the University of Virginia and J. Wilson Newman Professor of Governance in the University's Department of Government and Foreign Affairs. He is the author of 20 books and co-author or editor of 200 books including *Morality and Foreign Policy; Masters of International Thought; Churchill's World View; Toynbee's Philosophy of History and Politics;*

*Theory and Practice in International Relations;* Political Realism and the Crisis of World Politics; and *Ethics, Functionalism and Power.* He was formerly Vice President of the Rockefeller Foundation.

R.B.J. WALKER is Associate Professor of Political Science at the University of Victoria, British Columbia. A graduate of the University of Wales with a Ph.D. from Queen's University, Ontario, he has held academic positions at Princeton University, the Australian National University and the University of British Columbia. Professor Walker is the author of *One World, Many Worlds,* and is editor or co-editor of five other books including *Culture, Ideology and World Order* (1984) and *Contending Sovereignties* (1990).

JAMES M. WALLACE is Associate Professor of Anthropology at North Carolina State University, and Chair of the N.C. State University Japan Studies Group. His Ph.D. is from Indiana University and he also holds an M.A. from Indiana University in Latin American Studies. His primary interests include international development, technology transfer and international communications.